T0330441

Two Crises, Different Outcomes

A volume in the series

Cornell Studies in Political Economy
Edited by Peter J. Katzenstein

A list of titles in this series is available at www.cornellpress.cornell.edu.

Two Crises,
Different Outcomes

East Asia and Global Finance

Edited by T. J. Pempel and
Keiichi Tsunekawa

Cornell University Press
Ithaca and London

First published 2015 by Cornell University Press
First printing, Cornell Paperbacks, 2015

Printed in the United States of America

Library of Congress Cataloging-in-Publication Data

  Two crises, different outcomes : East Asia and global finance / edited by T.J. Pempel and Keiichi Tsunekawa.
    pages cm. — (Cornell studies in political economy)
  Includes bibliographical references and index.
  ISBN 978-0-8014-5340-3 (cloth : alk. paper)
  ISBN 978-0-8014-7971-7 (pbk. : alk. paper)
  1. Financial crises—Asia—Congresses. 2. Global Financial Crisis, 2008–2009—Congresses. 3. Asia—Economic conditions—1945–Congresses. 4. Asia—Economic conditions—21st century—Congresses. I. Pempel, T. J., 1942– editor. II. Tsunekawa, Keiichi, 1948– editor. III. Basri, M. Chatib. Tale of two crises. Container of (work):
    HB3808.T96   2015
    330.95'0429—dc23   2014022390

Cloth printing   10 9 8 7 6 5 4 3 2 1
Paperback printing   10 9 8 7 6 5 4 3 2 1

Contents

Illustrations

Figures

Tables

Preface

The East Asian countries surprised the world by an astonishingly quick recovery from the devastating economic crisis that hit the region in 1997–98. They repeated a similarly rapid rebound from the Global Financial Crisis of 2008–9 and have continued to increase their share of world production in the years since. Such achievements raise questions about the sources of such resilience and strength as well as about the long-term economic prospects of the region. To explore these questions, the Japan International Cooperation Agency Research Institute (JICA-RI) in 2010 launched a research project on the political economy of the East Asian countries. Keiichi Tsunekawa served as director of the institute at the time. JICA, the most important agency for official development assistance of Japan, wanted to learn lessons from the project that it could utilize in its future cooperation projects with the middle-income countries in East Asia and in its development operations in lower-income countries in Asia, Africa, and Latin America.

During the course of the project, we held two conferences at the institute, the first in September 2010 and the second in February 2012. In addition to the chapters in this volume, papers were presented by Whasun Jho, Min Gyo Koo, Ikuo Kume, Jean-Claude Maswana, Thitinan Pongsudhirak, and Lihui Tian. We thank the JICA-RI for the full financial support of the project. Then deputy director Hiroshi Kato, who is now director of JICA-RI and vice president of JICA, and the managerial staff of the institute, provided us with considerable help in logistics. Fiona Shen-Bayh at the University of California, Berkeley, gave valuable help in preparing the final manuscript. We also benefited from useful comments from participants at the conferences. Finally, we want to express our deepest thanks to Peter J. Katzenstein and an anonymous reviewer who read the manuscript and provided helpful comments and critiques, as well as to Roger Haydon at Cornell University Press for his support and encouragement of the project.

Contributors

Muhammad Chatib Basri is minister of finance of the Republic of Indonesia and professor of economics at the University of Indonesia.

Yun-han Chu is distinguished research fellow of the Institute of Political Science at Academia Sinica.

Richard Doner is the Goodrich C. White Professor of Political Science at Emory University.

Barry Naughton is Sokwanlok Chair of Chinese International Affairs at the University of California, San Diego.

Yasunobu Okabe is senior research fellow at the Japan International Cooperation Agency Research Institute.

T. J. Pempel is Jack M. Forcey Professor of Political Science in the Department of Political Science at the University of California, Berkeley.

Thomas B. Pepinsky is associate professor in the Government Department at Cornell University.

Keiichi Tsunekawa is senior professor at the National Graduate Institute for Policy Studies, Tokyo.

Introduction

Crises, Corrections, and Challenges
T. J. Pempel and Keiichi Tsunekawa

To paraphrase Tolstoy, noncrisis financial situations are happily alike but every financial crisis creates unhappiness in its own way. The differences among crises are particularly salient when one compares the economic devastation that swept across Asia in 1997–98 with the havoc wreaked throughout the United States, Western Europe, and much of the rest of the world in 2008–9. Both crises emerged from the intersection of the explosive growth and acceleration of cross-border financial flows and the political manifestations of that gargantuan financial power. Although both meltdowns were similar in their sweeping devastation to numerous national economies, they differed in that each was triggered by distinct economic factors, each exploded across a different trajectory, and the devastation generated by each varied according to the unique vulnerabilities and strengths of individual political economies.

For East Asia, the two crises were transmitted through distinct channels—hot money, currency misalignments, and a liquidity crisis in 1997–98; trade contraction but far less damage to finance and the core economies in 2008–9. The nature of East Asian vulnerabilities in the two crises was thus quite different. As a consequence the impacts of the two crises across East Asia took demonstrably different forms—a regional financial crisis of short duration in 1997–98, but a trade-driven shock followed by a rather smart East Asian snapback from the notionally global disruptions in 2008–9.

The Asian Financial Crisis (AFC) had few negative impacts on Europe and the United States; if anything it provided instead an opportunity for quick profits by many of their investors. By contrast, the Global Financial Crisis (GFC) staggered both the United States and much of Europe, threatening a global financial freeze-up that was avoided only through massive government intervention using taxpayer money. And the GFC ultimately ushered in an extended period of slow growth, extensive unemployment, fiscal imbalances, and in Europe a currency crisis that for several years challenged the very viability of the euro. As of early 2014, that tableau of miseries remained largely unabated.

Focusing on the differences between these two crises runs afoul of the broad conclusion advanced by Reinhart and Rogoff (2009) in their ironically titled book, *This Time Is Different*. In their book, Reinhart and Rogoff analyze eight centuries of what the authors label "financial folly," underscoring what they highlight as a set of disastrously similar economic conditions that recur with astonishingly consistent levels of frequency, duration, and ferocity. Historically, the authors contend, each time such familiar economic storm clouds have gathered, powerful voices of optimism have outshouted the scattered Cassandras, insisting that past rules have changed, a new economic paradigm is operative, and contemporary worries are misplaced since "this time is different." Only after the same devastating collapses have ushered in their familiar litany of economic afflictions are the worriers proved right (once again). Reinhard and Rogoff's economic data are compelling in highlighting the macroeconomic similarities tying together a wide swath of crises and underscoring the relative ease with which collective greed repeatedly spawns mass delusion.

What their analysis ignores, however, and what this book addresses, are the divergent *political* conditions that gave rise to particular crises as well as the *political* changes that individual crises may catalyze. Focusing exclusively on the macroeconomic similarities among crises, while valuable, is analogous to studying a sequence of disastrous house fires by analyzing the commonalities in combustible materials, winds, and heat without addressing the divergent implications of one having been started by lightning, another by a smoker in bed, faulty wiring in a third, and an arsonist in the fourth.

The GFC of 2008–9 involved a transatlantic meltdown of capital markets that ravaged the financial infrastructures and subsequently staggered the real economies of the United States and most of Western Europe. In striking contrast, national economies in East Asia, despite being initially jolted by the financial storm due to drop-offs in global trade, weathered the crisis far better. As late as 2014, the U.S. economy continued to wobble under the effects of sluggish macroeconomic growth, higher levels of unemployment and underemployment, substantial government debt, stringent fiscal austerity, and the failure or nationalization of many high-profile and previously profitable private financial institutions. Owing to the interconnectedness of global finance, the availability of cheap credit, and an eventual pan-Atlantic housing bubble, most Western Europe countries encountered similar problems. The bursting of those bubbles unleashed a rippling debt crisis that for several European countries became a sovereign debt crisis. Virtually all countries in the Eurozone, along with the United Kingdom, were thus roiled by a wave of economic problems plus deeper than usual domestic political tensions as debate emerged about which national policy directions could best alleviate the economic pain. Eight of seventeen EU countries saw changes in government. In striking contrast, within two to three years after the GFC struck, most East Asian economies were basking in positive fiscal balances, substantial GDP growth rates, rising global exports, only modest unemployment, generally stable political conditions, and positive projections about the economic future of the region as a whole.

The buoyancy that most of East Asia's economies demonstrated so soon after the GFC (Japan being a notable exception) stands in striking contrast with the region's devastation after the AFC of 1997–98. Japan's economic bubble had burst in early 1990 leading to its (first) "lost decade" and an ongoing political effort to regain its economic footing. And then as the "Asian contagion" cascaded across the region, several of East Asia's hitherto "miracle economies" found themselves weighed down by collapsing currencies, bank failures, massive nonperforming loans, parabolic escalations in unemployment, and plummeting growth rates. Public confidence in government deteriorated as well, and several countries including Indonesia and Thailand underwent extensive political transformations triggered by the crisis. Second-order political repercussions were felt elsewhere. In China prior reliance on state-owned enterprises gave way to increased private ownership; in Malaysia advocates of neoliberalism were subjected to a vicious political crackdown; and in South Korea the AFC afforded a new president the opportunity to force a sweeping reorganization of the nation's powerful industrial groups (*chaebol*).

Equally significant, the apparent flip-flop from a miracle region to one in dire straits left many political leaders and analysts in the West triumphant in their conviction that the previous decade or more of dizzying East Asian growth had been little more than a castle built on sand, finally dashed because of the region's collective defiance of what were presumed to be the "universal principles" of economics underpinning the more structurally sustainable economic muscle of North America and Europe (see Noble and Ravenhill 2000; Pempel 1999a; Sheng 2009, passim but especially chapter 3). What a difference a decade makes.

This book examines these two crises in an effort to address two overarching questions: (1) Why did the countries of East Asia fare so differently in these two crises? and (2) Does East Asia's successful weathering of the GFC, particularly when viewed in comparison with the listless economic recoveries and apparent lack of political direction within the United States and Europe, suggest that East Asia is poised for a "second Asian miracle" analogous to that touted by the World Bank in 1993.? If East Asia does perform well economically, even if short of another miracle, how well poised would the region be in the broader context of global economic growth?

The "East Asian Miracle"

To understand the two crises and their effects on East Asia, it is necessary to start with East Asia's phenomenal economic growth prior to the 1997–98 crisis. The collective economic growth rates enjoyed across much of East Asia during the 1980s and early 1990s constituted one of the global economy's more stunning success stories. Japanese growth rates were double those of the OECD countries for nearly thirty years, from the late 1950s until the early 1990s. Japan as the first chapter in the East Asian growth story was quickly followed by exceptional GDP growth rates in Korea, Taiwan, Singapore, and Hong Kong, and later by similarly exhilarating liftoffs in Thailand, Malaysia, and Indonesia, along with those of the notionally communist regimes in China and Vietnam.

No single analysis gave more prominent testimony to this East Asian miracle than the 1993 study by the World Bank. Lauding the successes across what the authors labeled "developing East Asia," the World Bank emphasized East Asia's positively reinforcing cycle of economic development based on high rates of investment and saving, efficient use of resources, moderate inflation, low income inequality, educated workforces, rapid export growth, adoption of new technologies, and political stability, to highlight only the most prominent features.

The report's conclusions reflected the intellectual tensions between the neoliberal economists from the International Monetary Fund (IMF), who explained that the region's collective growth rested on fulfillments of the traditional neoclassical economic agenda, and those who emphasized the centrality of governmental policies, institutional strengths, and selective market interventions as integral to East Asia's success. Not insignificantly, the latter group was roundly applauded by the government of Japan, the key funder of the study.

The finished product was, not surprisingly, unwittingly schizophrenic about the relative balance between the roles played by "getting the prices right" versus "getting the prices wrong." The former concept was advocated by neoliberal economists who operationalized the study, while the latter idea, espoused by theorists of catch-up industrialization, relied on nonmarket compatible policies (see Johnson 1982; Pempel 1978; Woo-Cumings 1999).

The East Asian transformation invariably rested on both, as the analysis in chapter 1 of this book details. It grew out of a positive synergy between government interventionist policies that often defied the prescriptions of neoliberal economics, plus the selective exploitation and embrace of global market forces. Virtually all governments overseeing national economic successes across East Asia rejected the purest neoclassical economic prescriptions in favor of selective protectionist barriers and periodic and targeted government interventions. At the same time, unlike the governments in many other less-developed countries during the same period, those in miracle East Asia sought neither to insulate their domestic industries completely from global forces nor to engage in the levels of micromanagement or the creation of single national champions that could generate high profits for a select few firms at the expense of macroeconomic growth for the country as a whole. Rather, they took advantage of expanding global markets to move their countries from import-substitution to export-led growth, demonstrating that defiance of free market orthodoxy in the short term could be economically beneficial in the long term.

However, as the AFC demonstrated with a vengeance, such developmental strategies were far from invulnerable. Only four years after the World Bank's publication lauding the miracle, many of the applauded East Asian economies were roiled by the AFC. Furthermore, the economic vigor of the Japanese economy had already come into serious question as it lumbered through stubbornly slow recovery after the bursting of its 1985–90 bubble economy. When the AFC struck, Japan was both economically and politically hobbled in the assistance it could credibly offer to its neighbors. The fragility of East Asia's miracle became apparent as previously successful national development strategies ran headlong into the overwhelming counterforces of global finance.

Nevertheless, as post-AFC developments showed and as East Asia's collective performance suggested in the aftermath of the GFC of 2008–9, the countries of the region demonstrated high degrees of underlying strength. Snapback recoveries by the most negatively affected countries after the AFC, and similar recoveries since 2010, suggest that East Asia's early economic successes were more than a historical fluke. In contrast the economic resilience of the United States and much of Western Europe looked far more problematic.

Collective Perspectives

In addressing the two key questions in this book—Why such different impacts on East Asia from the two crises? Is Asia now poised for long-term economic success, a second miracle perhaps?—the contributors to this volume bring a common perspective. To date, analyses of the two crises have been dominated by economists with their disciplinary predisposition to search for causes in the mixture of exchange rates, currency pegs, financial regulations, international financial architecture, long-term versus short-term borrowing, derivatives contracts, and the like. All of us accept the importance of such factors, but we address the issues surrounding the AFC and GFC from our combination of considerable experience in the study of specific East Asian countries and a common intellectual anchoring in the general approaches of political economy. We are convinced that a richer and more insightful understanding of the causes and reactions to both crises can best be achieved by greater sensitivity to the interplay between politics and economics in specific countries, as well as by the interaction of domestic and international forces more generally.

It is our collective view that neither "markets" nor "states" in their most reified incarnations can adequately explain the causes, consequences, and adjustments to these crises; rather, it is their interactions that are critical. Similarly, we are skeptical of any reification of allegedly domestic versus international forces. International relations theories offer insightful and parsimonious explanations for complex phenomena. At the same time, such parsimony too frequently skirts the significance of domestic political conflicts and structures, rendering them peripheral to the key questions we seek to answer about the two crises. Yet exclusively domestic explanations are no more satisfactory in their failure to recognize the interconnected nature of the crises as their impacts spilled quickly over national borders.

As others have noted (see Cumings 1984; Haggard 1986; Pempel 1999b), East Asia's original economic success occurred in the context of a specific set of international circumstances, marked by global bipolarity in which the United States and the Soviet Union competed for allies among developing countries using economic assistance and favorable market openings as frequent inducements.

Unquestionably the exogenous forces of global finance played a vital role in the AFC. The crisis was triggered largely by short-term "hot money" moving into and out of the thriving East Asian economies. When IMF packages were requested (however reluctantly) by Indonesia, Thailand, and South Korea, their strict terms reflected external global financial muscle swamping domestic preferences. Yet equally important, although Malaysia faced a roughly comparable economic situation to these other three countries, it rejected an IMF bailout, largely as the result of domestic political factors, in favor of freezing convertibility of the national currency, the ringgit, and prohibiting offshore banks from trading in its domestic currency. Similarly, political efforts by the financial and governmental leaders of Taiwan have long tilted toward economic policies that frequently defy "economic logic" but prove to be far more prudent than those of many of its neighbors. Such prudence is driven by ongoing political anxieties about the island's diplomatic isolation and the consequent fears about the vulnerability of Taiwan's de facto sovereignty should its domestic economy falter even slightly.

In the wake of the AFC, governments often took quite different measures to adjust to the newly felt global pressures. South Korea, for example, was far more welcoming of foreign investment in that country's banking system than were Taiwan or China. China was quicker and more thorough in attempting to reduce the power of state-owned enterprises (SOEs) than was Vietnam.

Furthermore, as the chapters in this book show, although many national governments confined their post-AFC changes largely to tactical adjustments of their financial policies and institutions, others such as Thailand sought to overhaul the national trade regime, while still others such as China engaged in massive programs of physical infrastructure development. Further, political adjustments were not uncommon. Thus both Indonesia and Thailand were hit by major changes in the very nature of their domestic political regimes, and in Korea the new Kim Dae-jung government that took office at the height of the crisis used the country's economic dislocations to seek substantial partisan advantage through challenges to the chaebol. China, despite emerging relatively unscathed from the AFC, made substantial changes in preexisting economic strategies and the organization of state-owned enterprises (SOEs) largely out of fear that prior policies would ultimately result in negative domestic political repercussions.

From the same perspective, in the 2008–9 crisis most of the exporting nations of East Asia faced massive slowdowns as global demand for their exports plummeted. Indeed, in October 2008 South Korea was on the verge of another capital flight crisis, which was avoided only because of a quick injection of U.S. capital. But East Asia's larger economies were able to contribute to the global bailout orchestrated largely by the G-20, taking coordinated political actions to stimulate their national economies through classical Keynesian budgetary measures. And without a doubt the East Asian countries were helped by the fact that the major economies across Europe, North America, and East Asia collectively rejected domestic protectionist measures such as those introduced on a global scale during the global depression of 1929–32. Domestic political action mitigated deteriorating external economic conditions.

As such examples demonstrate, the two crises and reactions to them involve an intersection between politics and economics that cannot be adequately understood by privileging either discipline over the other. Similarly, external or global forces, particularly the force of global capital and new global financial instruments, are undoubtedly at the heart of the two crises, yet these global economic forces are invariably refracted through different domestic structures, which can frequently mitigate their impacts. Thus our analyses seek to take suitable account of both domestic and international factors, as well as political and economic interactions, as they bear on our two central questions.

A second major perspective that underpins our analysis is the importance of sensitivity to East Asia as a region, fuzzy and inexact as the term *region* may be (see Breslin et al. 2002; Katzenstein 2005; Pempel 2005). Following the end of the Cold War and the demise of superpower bipolarity with its preponderant influence over so much of global politics, interactions among geographically proximate nation-states, including activities in East Asia, have grown in importance as more proximate interactions among neighboring countries demonstrate their growing independence from such macroglobal trends (see Buzan and Weaver 2003; Lake and Morgan 1997; Solingen 1998). Often these regional actions have been cooperative, particularly as they have led to closer economic interactions. In the security arena, in a few regions (though not in East Asia) cooperation has been sufficiently extensive to allow one to speak meaningfully of regional security communities; in both economics and security, however, regional interactions, whether positive or negative, have gained an increased salience in national agendas that was often impossible in the shadow of superpower competition.

Thus, notwithstanding the fact that the AFC eventually resonated beyond East Asia, affecting countries such as Brazil and Russia, the crisis exerted its deepest effects in East Asia and many of these were regional in nature. Indeed as the chapters in this book will show, it was not only countries that were devastated economically that adjusted in its aftermath; other countries in the region, such as China, Vietnam, and Taiwan—countries that largely escaped the worst economic effects, nonetheless adjusted previous policies to enhance their resilience against future vulnerabilities.

Equally important, if 1997–98 showed the contagious links among Asian economies, regional cooperation was forthcoming in its aftermath. The central concern was to enhance regional resilience against any repeat of the region's demonstrated vulnerability during the crisis. Economically, this was played out through deeper production networks, greater foreign direct investment, monetary cooperation, and formal bilateral and minilateral trade pacts (see Katzenstein and Shiraishi 1997 and 2006; Pempel 1999a). Furthermore, despite many national differences in postcrisis adjustments, governments across the region also followed similar paths to enhance existing intra-Asian investment, trade, and monetary cooperation. Such regionwide actions helped to buffer the region against potential future financial shocks and helped minimize the Asian fallout from the GFC.

Finally, it was East Asia as a region, rather than just a collection of separate countries, that emerged from the crisis economically stronger and with a renewed conviction among its leaders that core elements of their prior developmental strategies had proved largely successful and should remain in place. In analyzing these two crises and the ways in which they played out so differently for East Asia on the one hand and the United States and much of Europe on the other, we believe that the interacting concepts of "economic vulnerability" and "economic resilience" are helpful.

Economic vulnerability can be defined as the likelihood that a country's economic development process is hindered by unforeseen, and usually exogenous, events (Guillaumont 2008 and 2009; Cariolle 2010). But as we will see, "economic vulnerability" in the abstract can be the result of highly particular weak spots that will differ from country to country. National economies, and indeed the global economy, are like ecosystems; various components are highly interdependent so that breakdown in one component may well endanger the system as a whole. Large segments of any national, or indeed the global, economy can appear perfectly sound even as quite specific portions of that economy reveal themselves under crises to be the chinks in the suit of armor or the one weak link in the interconnected economic chain that creates systemic ruin. In the phrasing of Zolli and Healy, a complex economic system may therefore be both "robust but fragile" (2012, 25–60).

The concept of "resilience" is widely applied across a range of studies, including architecture, natural disasters, ecosystems, internal organizational patterns, post-traumatic stress, and antiterrorism policies. In virtually all of these cases the central question is: What causes one system to break and another to rebound? As Zolli and Healy ask, "In an age of constant disruption, how do we build in better shock absorbers?" (2012, 3). The core of resilience is the ability either to "withstand external shock" or to "return to normal" after some traumatic event. Briguglio and his colleagues thus define "economic resilience" as "the ability to absorb, cope with or come back from an external economic shock" (2008, 4). They go on to elaborate several macroeconomic conditions that contribute to such resilience, eventually ranking individual countries accordingly. Similarly analysts studying the economic resilience of U.S. metropolitan regions identify key traits that contribute to regional economic resilience (Institute of Governmental Studies 2013): yet the notions of vulnerability and resilience remain more intuitive than theoretically sophisticated.

Despite being underdeveloped in the sphere of political economy, these notions are intuitively helpful in understanding important variations in the performances of different political economies and regions during these two crises. Countries in East Asia demonstrated particular areas of economic vulnerability during the AFC, most notably their vulnerability to rapid inflows of short-term foreign capital. Yet they also showed high levels of resilience in their underlying economic structures by the rapidity of their recoveries. In the GFC, by way of contrast, East Asia was vulnerable to a temporary global trade shutdown but highly resilient to the underlying financial vulnerabilities evident in the United States and so many European countries. And the importance of financial linkages and capital markets within the national economies of the United States and Europe has continued to underscore the vulnerability of their entire economic systems to financial collapse and their lack of more comprehensive national and regional economic resilience in bouncing back.

Five Focal Points

The book addresses two central questions: Why East Asian performances were different during the two financial crises and to what extent East Asia is now poised for sustained economic success? In dealing with these overarching questions, the authors analyze what we feel are five key factors critical to answering them. A starting point is the belief that both the AFC and the GFC took place as the result of a damaging collision between national developmental strategies and the forces of global finance. To address this intersection, we begin by highlighting the essential common elements within the discrete patterns of East Asia's economic growth prior to the onset of the AFC in 1997. How were so many countries in the region able to achieve such substantial jumps in their GDP and per capita incomes for so many years, in the process of catching up with and passing so many other parts of the world? Equally important from a political perspective, how did they achieve such dynamic economies while maintaining relative political stability at home? We make the argument generally, and individual chapters bolster this contention in greater detail for specific countries from Japan to Taiwan to Indonesia, that two factors were particular vital: high levels of capital investment given over to enhanced production on the one hand and close government-business relations on the other. These two features combined to allow individual countries to catch up quickly to more economically and technologically sophisticated countries, to close many of the gaps between where they began economically and where they hoped eventually to be and in the process to incorporate an impressive variety of politically critical socio-economic sectors.

Equally important, however, is a second concern, namely the AFC itself. Certain inherent components integral to East Asian growth prior to the AFC, particularly the high levels of investment and the close ties between business and government just noted, left these same countries vulnerable to what proved to be the pulverizing consequences of fast-moving global capital in 1997–98. Continued high investment and political stability made many of the countries of East Asia particularly tempting targets for large-scale, but often short-term, investment by Western hedge funds, brokerages, and other investors. Neither the governments nor the financial institutions in these East Asian countries were adequately prepared to check the rapid movement of such highly mobile capital, first rushing in, but then equally quickly rushing for the exits as conditions soured.

In short, the pattern of East Asian growth and stability, positive as it was for a time, simultaneously left many countries in the region highly vulnerable to the particular nature of the crisis that ensued. In this sense, the AFC was the consequence of factors well beyond simple failures linked to "crony capitalism" or "moral hazard," two of the most frequently cited reasons for the crisis (see Bosworth 1998; Radelet and Sachs 1998). Such features, to the extent they did exist in certain countries, did not emerge overnight in 1997 and hence provide little independent insight concerning the onset of the regional meltdown. More fundamentally, we argue, it was the interactions between the peculiarities of the domestic political economies of the most severely affected countries and the power of fast-moving global capital wielding highly sophistical financial instruments that provided the combination of tinder and flame that was central to the eventual financial wildfire that ensued.

A third analytic thread critical to understanding the different experiences of East Asia during the two crises centers on the prophylactic actions taken by numerous countries in East Asia aimed at enhancing their economic resilience against any future recurrence of the 1997–98 debacle. At both the national and regional levels, as will be detailed throughout the book, governments took political and economic steps to strengthen resilience against any future financial shocks.

Suffice to say at this point that although the region fared poorly in the AFC, most of the countries used the crisis to institutionalize valuable policy lessons about their vulnerabilities to global capital forces, and most responded with a series of internal adjustments designed to retain the key elements of successful developmentalism that had been put in place and that had initially been so beneficial to their national economic growth and political stability while also making important adjustments at the margins, the result of which was a much higher regional resilience when the GFC struck.

Virtually all countries in the region, for example, moved to enhance their financial regulatory mechanisms and to ensure greater financial prudence; most bolstered their foreign reserve holdings—often to levels that economists argued was economically unnecessary. In addition, governments in the region deepened their monetary cooperation through formal currency swap arrangements that are currently embodied in the Chiang Mai Initiative Multilateralization (CMIM) among other things. Furthermore intraregional trade was boosted with enhanced regional production networks in addition to multiple bilateral and minilateral free trade agreements (see chapters by Basri, Pepinksy, and Okabe in this book; Aggarwal and Koo 2008; Grimes 2006; Pempel 2005, 2006, and 2008). Important for understanding East Asia's better performance in the wake of the GFC is that few of the measures taken followed the dictates of neoliberal economics or moved to install the opportunistic banking systems that prevailed in the United States and United Kingdom. Instead, most governments and financial regulators sought to plug the holes and counter the vulnerabilities that had been made apparent during the AFC while retaining core components of their precrisis developmental strategies.

A fourth point follows logically and runs throughout this volume, namely the GFC. In chapter 1, Pempel contends that both the AFC and the GFC resulted from the baneful interactions between national models of political economy and the power of global financial capital. During the AFC, however, the locus of capital's power was exogenous to the region most deeply damaged; in the GFC, by contrast, the power of global finance was endogenously integral to the political economies of the United States and to a somewhat lesser extent a half-dozen European countries, and it was these countries that were most dramatically affected by the eventual capital freeze-up and its aftermath.

Pempel further emphasizes the importance of financial deregulation to America's political economy during the 1990s and 2000s as well as the focus of financial institutions on maximization of short-term yield and the embrace of sophisticated financial engineering. Also important were the moves toward an economic development model that depended on high levels of public and private sector debt and highly risky financial maneuvers by huge and politically powerful financial institutions in the search for maximum short-term profits. This American model shared important traits with key European financial institutions in Britain, Germany, Ireland, and Iceland. With particular gusto in the United States, the combination triggered a massive housing bubble, dubious financial instruments, and eventually a global financial freeze-up that, owing to the extensive interdependence of global capital markets, tsunamied quickly across the Atlantic. European financial institutions in the United Kingdom, Germany, Ireland, and Iceland were marked by numerous failures and government bailouts. And, subsequently, a much wider swath of economic damage was done by the bursting of housing bubbles in France, the United Kingdom, Italy, Spain, and Ireland, among others, and an ensuring credit crunch that enveloped the entire seventeen-nation Eurozone. National debt downgrades followed as did several years of sustained financial assistance packages with severe austerity demands led by the European Central Bank. The result was a near meltdown of global capital markets, and the sharp braking of economic growth in Europe and the United States. Government bailouts of financial institutions amounted to 24 percent of 2008 GDP in Germany, 25 percent in the UK, and 26 percent in the United States (Stolz and Wedow 2010, 20–21).

In striking contrast, the East Asian economies were far less enmeshed in such high-risk facets of global finance; moreover, in the wake of the AFC many had built sturdy firewalls against the worst excesses of global capital flows and particularly the most pernicious financial instruments. Thus the ensuring global meltdown merely jolted the region rather than crushing it once again. In this crisis, East Asia proved far more resilient than the United States and much of Western Europe.

However, we should not underestimate potentially devastating risks faced by most East Asian economies when the GFC hit the world. Although financial resilience was improved in most East Asian countries and layers of insulation buffered the region's links to the global financial markets, continued dependence on exports remained collectively as deep as ever, exposing a particular area of East Asian economic vulnerability. Consequently, the sudden contraction of the North American and European markets sent powerful aftershocks across East Asia. In fact, exports from East Asia were jolted by the global slowdown and the contribution of the trade balance to GDP growth rate turned negative in 2008–9 in China, Japan, the Philippines, Singapore, Vietnam, and Malaysia (author's calculations from World Bank data). Meanwhile, unemployment jumped by between 0.5 percent and 2.5 percentage points across most of the region (Ahn 2010, 59–62). But the G-20's global commitment to fiscal stimulation and the avoidance of extensive protectionist measures by most major economies throughout the world allowed global trade to resume rather quickly. This in turn allowed East Asia's exports to recover soon after, recatalyzing regional growth.

Thanks to the long-term growth of East Asian economies following the successful post-AFC adjustment and the resultant positive fiscal pictures, when the whirlwind of the GFC struck, most East Asian governments showed far greater systematic resilience, having both the capacity and incentives to implement expansionist fiscal and financial policies. As a result, growth rates of the East Asian countries during the 2008–9 GFC did not go down nearly as much as they had during the 1997–98 AFC. Indonesia, Korea, Malaysia, and Thailand, which had been most seriously hit by the AFC, did far better during the GFC (see table I.1).

Thus the East Asian countries again realized another V-shaped recovery by 2010–11, just as they had after the AFC. In Indonesia, Japan, Malaysia, Philippines, Singapore, and Taiwan, the annual growth rate in 2010–12 even exceeded the post-AFC period (1999–2007). It was just slightly lower in the other four countries (see table I.1). Indeed, by the beginning of 2012 the global situation was such that Ahn (2012), with no small sense of irony, could ask if Asia could save the sinking world economy. It is from that potential irony that we also consider a fifth point: because most economies of East Asia returned to stable and sustained growth by 2010 in contrast to the far more lengthy struggles throughout most of Europe and the United States, this book addresses the question of whether the post-GFC economic resilience in East Asia might presage a second economic miracle, or less dramatically, a return to sustained regional growth that could become an engine of global economic leadership and serve as a model for politically stable development? Or conversely, do most countries in the region continue to face serious domestic and regional vulnerabilities that would make any such predictions unjustifiably optimistic? Individual chapters, particularly those by Basri, Pepinksy, Doner, Naughton, and Chu, address this question for specific countries and for the region as a whole, while the concluding chapter attempts to mobilize the evidence from specific countries and from the current global economic picture to address it at a more general level.

The following chapters provide very positive evidence to support a measure of optimism about East Asia's short- to medium-term economic future. Indonesia for example, as Basri and Pepinsky show in their respective chapters, seems politically, economically, and demographically situated for sustained and solid development for a decade or more. South Korea's economy has performed extremely well since the AFC and is a comfortable member of the OECD emerging as a potent rival in certain key export markets to once indomitable Japan. Both Okabe and Tsunekawa see South Korea's growth prospects as remaining largely positive and certainly its democratic politics,

TABLE I.1
GDP growth rate, 1990–2013

	1990	1991	1992	1993	1994	1995	1996	1997	1998	1999	2000	2001	2002	2003	2004	2005	2006	2007	2008	2009	2010	2011	2012	2013
China	3.8	9.2	14.2	14.0	13.1	10.9	10.0	9.3	7.8	7.6	8.4	8.3	9.1	10.0	10.1	11.3	12.7	14.2	9.6	9.2	10.4	9.3	7.7	7.6
India	5.5	1.1	5.5	4.8	6.7	7.6	7.6	4.1	6.2	7.4	4.0	5.2	3.8	8.4	7.9	9.3	9.3	9.8	3.9	8.5	10.5	6.3	3.2	3.8
Indonesia	7.2	7.0	6.5	8.0	7.5	8.2	7.8	4.7	-13.1	0.8	4.2	3.6	4.5	4.8	5.0	5.7	5.5	6.3	6.0	4.6	6.2	6.5	6.2	5.3
Japan	5.6	3.3	0.8	0.2	0.9	1.9	2.6	1.6	-2.0	-0.2	2.3	0.4	0.3	1.7	2.4	1.3	1.7	2.2	-1.0	-5.5	4.7	-0.6	2.0	2.0
Korea	9.3	9.7	5.8	6.3	8.8	8.9	7.2	5.8	-5.7	10.7	8.8	4.0	7.2	2.8	4.6	4.0	5.2	5.1	2.3	0.3	6.3	3.7	2.0	2.8
Malaysia	9.0	9.5	8.9	9.9	9.2	9.8	10.0	7.3	-7.4	6.1	8.7	0.5	5.4	5.8	6.8	5.0	5.6	6.3	4.8	-1.5	7.4	5.1	5.6	4.7
Philippines	3.0	-0.6	0.3	2.1	4.4	4.7	5.8	5.2	-0.6	3.1	4.4	2.9	3.6	5.0	6.7	4.8	5.2	6.6	4.2	1.1	7.6	3.6	6.8	6.8
Singapore	10.1	6.5	7.0	11.5	10.6	7.3	7.6	8.5	-2.2	6.2	9.0	-1.2	4.2	4.6	9.2	7.4	8.6	9.0	1.7	-0.8	14.8	5.2	1.3	3.5
Taiwan	6.9	7.9	7.6	6.7	7.6	6.4	5.5	5.5	3.5	6.0	5.8	-1.7	5.3	3.7	6.2	4.7	5.4	6.0	0.7	-1.8	10.8	4.1	1.3	2.2
Thailand	11.6	8.1	8.1	8.3	9.0	9.2	5.9	-1.4	-10.5	4.4	4.8	2.2	5.3	7.1	6.3	4.6	5.1	5.0	2.5	-2.3	7.8	0.1	6.5	3.1
Vietnam	5.0	5.8	8.7	8.1	8.8	9.5	9.3	8.2	5.8	4.8	6.8	6.9	7.1	7.3	7.8	7.5	7.0	7.1	5.7	5.4	6.4	6.2	5.2	5.3
United States	1.9	-0.1	3.6	2.7	4.0	2.7	3.8	4.5	4.5	4.8	4.1	0.9	1.8	2.8	3.8	3.4	2.7	1.8	-0.3	-2.8	2.5	1.8	2.8	1.6
Euro area	n.a.	n.a.	1.4	-0.8	2.5	2.9	1.5	2.6	2.8	2.9	3.8	2.0	0.9	0.7	2.2	1.7	3.3	3.0	0.4	-4.4	2.0	1.5	-0.6	-0.4

Source: IMF 2013.

while often tempestuous, provides a stable political backdrop to sustain its economic competitiveness. Growth in China, though it has cooled considerably, continues to be a major engine for global and intra-Asian growth. Other countries in the region, such as Taiwan, Singapore, and Malaysia, among others, are also positioned to do well.

At the same time, despite many positive shards of evidence, any unbridled optimism that a beautiful mosaic of sustained and solid growth will emerge in East Asia must still confront many hurdles. These are by no means small. China faces major political and economic problems in the short to medium term, including the challenge of upgrading its economy from its current labor-intensive dependence, the huge debt problem of many local governments, aging society pressures, widespread pollution, extensive elite corruption, massive gaps in regional development, and waves of locally based popular protests. Any or all of these could trigger widespread political unrest and/or economic slowdown, as many China watchers, including Naughton in his chapter, argue. Continued high growth rates and political stability under CCP rule are by no means ensured (see Shambaugh 2013; Shirk 2007).

Tsunekawa's analysis lays out the reasons why a return to even moderate growth is problematic for Japan absent major political changes. Though the South Korean economy has been doing well lately, its vulnerabilities in both the AFC and the GFC make clear how ephemeral such progress can be. A hostile North Korean regime on its border does not help relieve economic jitters. Similar political jitters resonate throughout Taiwan. And to the extent that South Korea's and Taiwan's successes and problems often mirror those of its democratic neighbor, Japan, there is no guarantee that either of these two can continue to innovate at the cutting edges of technology.

Doner, meanwhile, underscores the ways in which Vietnam, Thailand, and Malaysia remain highly vulnerable to what he calls "the middle income trap," that is, the difficulties of moving beyond labor intensive manufacturing. Thailand is hindered further by ongoing political tensions pitting the privileges of the long-ruling elite against pro-Thaksin, rurally based forces. Can such countries make the technical, educational, and corporate advances that will move their economies beyond their current reliance on cheap labor and component production, thus advancing their production profiles in ways that will give their corporations the capacity to innovate and create technological breakthroughs capable of enhancing their long-term global competitiveness? Similarly Pepinsky notes that island Southeast Asia has a great many problems that might impede future progress, although the problems are rarely the ones identified by laissez-faire economists. Finally, Okabe's analysis of South Korea and Thailand show how difficult it is for any country to break away from path-dependent trajectories in pursuit of nominally ideal, but politically and institutionally problematic, new directions, while Basri's attention to the power of luck in Indonesia's recovery is a helpful reminder that the role of *Fortuna* did not die with Machiavelli.

While the authors in this book are thus impressed by the positive per-formances of the East Asian economies in the aftermath of the AFC and GFC, and their levels of political stability in contrast to the lack of both in the United States and much of Western Europe, all remain chastened by the example of the World Bank in its analysis of the first East Asian Miracle. As mentioned above, barely four years had passed after their rosy predictions before the AFC hit the region. Equally the triumphalism that accompanied Japan's bubble economy from 1985 to 1990 looked increasingly hollow dur-ing the subsequent twenty years of economic sluggishness. Nor should one forget the crash that followed America's "dot com" euphoria. Whatever cau-tious optimism this book may convey is presented with these experiences also in the forefront of our minds as counterweights to the dangers of excessively upbeat predictive hubris.

Two Crises, Two Outcomes

T. J. Pempel

In March 2008, Bear Stearns, a major U.S. global investment bank and securities brokerage, teetered on the verge of bankruptcy. In a move pressed by the U.S. Federal Reserve, the company was absorbed by other financial institutions at a fraction of the value it had held only a month earlier. The Bear Stearns collapse proved to be the first toppling domino in the cascading financial chaos that was to follow. On September 15 of that year, Lehman Brothers, a global financial services firm facing $60 billion in bad investments and unable to secure U.S. government assistance, declared what was then the largest bankruptcy in American history. Because of the tightly interwoven nature of global capital markets, the Lehman failure threatened to freeze all capital movements in a matter of hours, with the near certainty of capital losses vastly larger than the devastating Asian financial crisis of eleven years earlier.

Within one month of the Lehman collapse, numerous high-profile and previously lucrative banks across the United States and Europe had collapsed or were partially nationalized, including the entire private banking system of Iceland. Approximately $27 trillion was almost instantly erased from global stock markets. Some 85 percent of global banks' tier-one capital would have disappeared under mark-to-market accounting principles. If real estate losses were added in, roughly 100 percent of global capital had vanished (Sheng 2009, 376). To head off the impending disaster, the U.S. government committed itself to more than $2.25 trillion in bailouts and liquidity injections, a figure equal to about 16 percent of U.S. GDP while European Central banks pumped in €1.3 trillion through a variety of financial transfusions (Schwartz 2009, xiv). Stunning as the shock was to what Alan Greenspan labeled "virtually every economics and policy-maker of note" (2013, 89), anticipatory vibrations had been given off by the numerous companies that disappeared following the collapse of the "dot com" bubble in 1999–2001; the collapse of

Enron in 2001; in the July 2007 troubles of Deutsche Industriebank (IKB); or in the February 2008 takeover by the British government of the financially troubled Northern Rock Bank; along with the predictions of a number of economists (for other examples, see *Fortune*, August 2008). And of course, in hindsight some might have interpreted the Asian Financial Crisis (AFC) as yet another augury of what would subsequently unfold in the United States and Western Europe.

In fact the 2008 Global Financial Crisis (GFC) and the AFC shared certain financial similarities, a point underscored by Reinhart and Rogoff (2009) in their emphasis on the commonalities among all such crises: the heady brew of low-cost capital, wild-eyed financial speculation, and unfettered optimism— all masked by the conviction that "this time is different." Yet, despite the devastation wreaked across East Asia in 1997–98, and notwithstanding subsequent ripple effects and financial repercussions in countries such as Brazil and Russia, the negative effects of the AFC were concentrated in several countries within a specific geographical region. Equally important, East Asia's troubles in 1997–98 remained distant from the commanding heights of capitalism— Wall Street and the City of London—except perhaps as an opportunity for those centers to profit at the expense of East Asia's misfortunes.

In contrast, the GFC was more sweeping in its wreckage—geographically, economically, and ideationally. With its epicenter in the heart of global financial markets, the GFC raised the question of whether there were fundamental flaws in the organization and operation of the global financial system as a whole. Among the most chastened was Alan Greenspan, former chairman of the U.S. Federal Reserve Bank, who conceded before the House Committee on Oversight and Government Reform almost immediately after the outbreak of the crisis: "Those of us who have looked to the self-interest of lending institutions to protect shareholders' equity, myself included, are in a state of shocked disbelief" (Andrews 2008).

Despite important differences that we examine below and in the individual chapters of the book, a common axis around which both crises revolved concerns the intersection among alternative national strategies of economic development, the power of global finance, and the enhanced complexity of the products of financial engineering. The two crises reveal very different mixtures of economic vulnerability and economic resilience among the economies of East Asia, the United States, and much of Western Europe. And these mixtures in turn offer insights into the quite different performances of these economies during, and after, the two crises.

Global Financial Deregulation and the Role of Financial Engineering

From the end of World War II until its breakdown in 1971, the Bretton Woods system created a constrained system of global monetary stability anchored by the strength of the U.S. dollar and the political willingness of the United States, by far the world's strongest economy, to convert dollars into gold at a fixed rate and to act as the world's lender of last resort (Cohen 1998; Kindleberger 1985 and 1986; Kirschner 1995). Over time, however, the overwhelming economic strength of the United States that had undergirded the American embrace of Bretton Woods was eroded by the rising expenses of the Great Society, the war in Vietnam, and the enhanced export competitiveness of Japan and much of Western Europe. These exports undercut the financial viability of many U.S. manufacturers and threatened the U.S. job market. In a unilateral countermove, Richard Nixon ended the dollar's convertibility, thereby unleashing a period of universal monetary instability punctuated by a series of regional and global efforts to reestablish some measure of the previous era's steadiness and predictability. This included four aborted initiatives in the later 1970s and early 1980s to implement effective controls on financial movements (Helleiner 1994; Simmons 1999). The genie of financial stability, however, was never completely returned to the bottle.

Instead, the United States took the lead in a deregulatory revolution of financial markets that was gradually emulated by the governments and financial systems of numerous other countries, particularly the United Kingdom but also in much of continental Europe and Japan. This deregulatory process was driven by the ideological conviction that it was possible to create what Cerny (1994) once labeled "a self-regulating financial market." The efforts resulted in a "quantum jump in the sensitivity of prices of financial instruments across the world, drawing market actors big and small—and their capital—into the search for paper profits" (Cerny 1994, 319–20).

Such systematic deregulation, as Simon Johnson (2009), formerly of the IMF, points out, catapulted the financial sector into the center of the American economy: "From 1973 to 1985, the financial sector never earned more than 16 percent of domestic corporate profits. In 1986, that figure reached 19 percent. In the 1990s, it oscillated between 21 percent and 30 percent, higher than it had ever been in the postwar period. [In the 2000s] it reached 41 percent. Pay rose just as dramatically. From 1948 to 1982, average compensation in the financial sector ranged between 99 percent and 108 percent of the average for all domestic private industries. From 1983, it shot upward, reaching 181 percent in 2007."

In tandem with the financial sector's soaring structural significance came vastly enhanced political influence. Washington's politicians, responding to the increasing political power—and generous campaign donations—of the financial sector, began shredding existing regulations alleged by the financial sector to be interfering with potentially profit-making financial activities. The cumulative consequence was ever less worry about risk and vulnerability. Most notably, the Glass-Steagall Act, which had long provided a firewall separating different types of financial institutions, following a sequence of erosions for years, was completely repealed in 1999. At least as important in seeding the GFC, in 2000 the U.S. government passed the Commodity

Futures Modernization Act, which effectively deregulated over-the-counter derivatives, including an instrument known as the credit default swap (CDF), which ultimately turned out to be at the heart of the GFC in 2008–9.

Simultaneously, as the costs of international financial transactions plummeted and the speed of such transactions became virtually instantaneous, financial institutions transferred ever more day-to-day investment decisions to math wizards (known as "quants") brandishing Ph.Ds. from fields such as theoretical physics, aerospace engineering, and mathematics. Relying on superfast computers and ever more complex economic models, they created increasingly sophisticated financial products designed to take advantage of millisecond arbitrage opportunities in diverse financial markets around the world. What followed was an explosion of new financial products including interest rate swaps and options, currency swaps, and equity derivatives, along with the second- and third-derivatives of each. Such esoteric instruments increased fivefold in value between 2002 and 2008, to a paper value of $684 trillion, more than ten times the total GDP of the entire world (Wilensky, 2012, 90). And as financial products became more complex, financial institutions were merging and becoming ever larger, with several eventually achieving the status of "too big to fail."

In the process, the American financial sector, and to a lesser extent institutions in countries such as the Netherlands, Germany, France, Iceland, and Ireland, moved toward economic primacy in their respective domestic economies and established themselves as a sector over which governments exerted diminishing levels of regulatory oversight. Global competition spurred deregulatory emulation. As Beth Simmons phrased it: "Technological advances that make international transactions instantaneous and inexpensive in effect raise the cost of trying to seal off the national economy from global capital markets" (1999, 42).

In this climate of dwindling financial regulation, high-speed financial engineering, and ever-tighter linkages among various financial markets, the world's (and especially the United States') most allegedly sophisticated financial institutions and hedge funds took on ever-higher levels of debt (i.e., leverage) in their "search for yield." In the words of Peter Gourevitch: "The capacity to innovate in finance rose to be the supreme goal. Regulation was judged through this prism. Most regulation of finance became suspect as an inhibition on liquidity" (2013, 272). Meanwhile, government policy changes that might have reduced the likelihood of the eventual crisis were either minimized or sidetracked because of the threat they posed to financial sector profits, the underlying belief that markets had become "self-regulatory," and that highly sophisticated investment models would ensure rapid adjustments to such self-regulation (see Streeck 2011). And, as Katzenstein and Nelson make clear (2013a, b), investors and firms became increasingly convinced that the economic world was not pockmarked so much with "uncertainties" for which no one could plan and against which caution was essential, but instead was simply characterized by varying levels of "risk," the statistical probabilities of which were calculable (see Blythe 2013). Such a conviction led financial institutions to borrow ever larger sums of money in order to place ever larger leveraged bets on specific economic outcomes, persuaded that the strategies their computer models had developed would provide sufficient early warning signals to allow rapid adjustments that would prevent overwhelming losses.

In the process, financial markets became ever more deeply enmeshed, as multiple computer-generated models traded with one another across the globe. As Bordo and Landon-Lane observed,

> The recent crisis [shows] the extent to which financial innovation partly in response to the supervision and regulation of the banking systems and financial markets in place in the United States and other advanced countries led to the development of securitization, derivatives and off balance sheet entities designed to evade capital requirements. These innovations were globally linked through financial globalization. This increased global systemic risk. In earlier eras, stock (and bond) markets across countries were linked together during crises but the linkages are much tighter today and occur across virtually all international financial markets. (2010, 44)

So long as high-tech investment strategies proved correct, enormous profits flowed. Yet, as the GFC definitively demonstrated, when computer models failed to offer the anticipated warnings, economic vulnerability proved to be widespread, and the results were disastrous. Katzenstein and Nelson (2013b) underscore the extent to which such risk calculations by individual firms had become separated from systemwide realities in 2007, noting that the Goldman Sachs risk-management team had experienced twenty-five standard deviation moves several days in a row, showing that the company was suffering "a once-in-every-fourteen-universes loss on several consecutive days." Presumably calculable economic risk confronted the inevitability of collective uncertainty and widespread systemic vulnerability. The resulting financial seizure was the culmination of what Susan Strange (1986) over two decades earlier had labeled "casino capitalism."

The situation in the AFC might well have prefigured some of the dangers of this combination of financial deregulation and financial engineering in the United States and its emulators. But the AFC was not about financial deregulation and financial engineering within East Asia. Rather, the crisis resulted when the ever more sophisticated financial instruments and high leverage from exogenous global markets clashed with the national economic strategies being pursued within developing East Asia. To understand the linkage, it is first necessary to highlight two key features behind the collective economic developmental successes of East Asia prior to the crisis.

From Being a Miracle to Needing One

McLeod and Garnaut (1998) used a version of the above heading as the subtitle for their insightful book on the AFC. The phrase captures the contrast between the region's long-running economic success in the run up to the crisis versus its devastation in its aftermath. During the first half of the 1990s and for many years before, a raft of East Asian countries achieved economic growth rates markedly higher than regions such as Latin America, the Middle East, Africa, and South Asia, all of which seemed inextricably mired in an array of unwieldy development problems. In contrast, most East Asian countries began to enjoy a bracing cocktail of political stability, ever-more sophisticated infrastructures, rapid macrolevel growth, expanding global markets for their exports, enhanced employment opportunities for their citizens, a burgeoning middle class, and a horizon that seemed to promise more of the same.

In broad brush terms, the successfully developing East Asian countries were enjoying the benefits of "catch-up economic development," a strategy articulated by Alexander Hamilton for the United States in its early history as well as in the economic theories of Friedrich List and Nicholas Kaldor, along with the analyses of important late-developing countries done by Alexander Gerschenkron (1962). Common denominators included an active role for government pursuing an interconnected set of policies that defied neoclassical economic prescriptions in favor of enhancing their nations' relative positions in the global pecking order. This involved buttressing key industrial sectors through active government intervention, selective reliance on protectionist measures, and systematic market interventions (Chang 1999, 186).

So long as global consumption remained high, governments across developing East Asia were able to buffer such favored sectors and firms from the worst excesses of overcompetition at home. The result was the huge boost in national economic sophistication, increasing shares of world exports, better job prospects for most citizens, and the expansion of East Asia's budding middle class that in turn fostered greater domestic political stability. The result was the political-economic combination that so captivated the world in the late 1980s and early 1990s and that was at the heart of the World Bank's laudatory *East Asian Miracle* study.

This East Asian "miracle" began with Japan's thirty-plus years of GDP growth at levels roughly twice that of the other OECD countries (Johnson 1982; Patrick and Rosovsky 1976; Pempel 1978; Murakami and Patrick 1987–92). Japan's soaring economy and search for global markets eventually incentivized many Japanese companies to undertake substantial investments across the world, but particularly in East Asia (Hatch and Yamamura 1996; Katzenstein and Shiraishi 1997 and 2006). Ultimately, this surge of outgoing Japanese investment, combined with developmental efforts elsewhere across the region, allowed an expanding circle of countries to follow in Japan's rising economic wake (Pempel 1997 and 1999b).

Thus, the newly industrialized economies (NIEs) (South Korea, Taiwan, Hong Kong, and Singapore) and subsequently Malaysia, Indonesia, and Thailand along with nominally communist China and Vietnam all began to enjoy large jumps in productivity, GDP, and exports, along with enhanced political stability. What had begun as a "Japanese miracle" expanded into a regionwide phenomenon (Kojima 2000; Ozawa 2009). Between 1965 and 1990, these high-performing East Asian economies collectively outpaced all other regions of the world by huge margins both in overall growth and in income growth per capita (World Bank 1993, 1–3). Two elements were essential to the success of this late-development catch-up strategy: high levels of investment and close government-business relations.

High Demand for Investment Capital

Successful East Asian economies had a huge appetite for investment capital in their quest for rapid expansion of their domestic levels of production. Analyzing the Japanese developmental pattern during the 1950s and 1960, Murakami (1996) observed that increased investment generated "decreasing average costs" for the country's manufacturers. In this approach, late-industrializers like Japan could benefit from a certain degree of backwardness that allowed them to import the most modern technologies from around the globe and efficiently produce mass consumer goods whose marketability had already been tested in the advanced countries. With technologies easily available through licensing contracts and/or foreign investors and with demand assured by the demonstration effects of rising global consumerism, manufacturing firms across much of East Asian could anticipate that the more they produced, the more they could reduce their marginal costs of production. Herman Schwartz highlighted this Verdoon effect: "The greater the rate of increase of output inside a firm, the greater the increase in productivity. The more a firm produces of any one good, the more experience it gets and the more efficient it becomes at producing not only that good but other, similar goods" (2009, 62).

Critical to the success of this strategy was the ability to sell abroad (unlike simple import-substitution manufacturing practiced in many developing countries). When such strategies work well, firms and countries together become ever more efficient and hence more globally competitive (Chang 1994; Gerschenkron 1962, 166; Haggard 1990; Johnson 1982; Woo-Cumings 1999).

Company goals centered on gaining enhanced market share and long-term expansion of markets, not on booking ever-rising quarterly profits. In this they were helped by the fact that the bulk of the capital for expansion came not from highly volatile equity markets focused on generating short-term dividends for shareholders, but from domestic bank lending, which historically was more patient. Banks supporting such expansion could enjoy stable and regularized profits from "responsible borrowers" who would return interest payments like clockwork (Drucker 1975). One obvious vulnerability was overproduction. In addressing this problem, the government played a key role. According to Murakami, the main function of the Japanese government's industrial policy was to coordinate investment and production among fiercely competing firms through administrative guidance and/or cartel formation; it was, as the government saw it, the only way to reduce the potential waste and danger of "excessive competition" (1996, chapter 8).

The same pattern of economic development based on "decreasing average costs" of production came to operate widely across other East Asian economies prior to the AFC. The key difference between Japan and most others was that Japan's large domestic market played a larger role in absorbing expanding output than in its demographically and economically smaller East Asian neighbors. For such countries, export markets in the United States and Europe took on even greater importance, but since these markets offered a seemingly limitless demand for Asian goods, firms in East Asia continued "decreasing their average costs" of production with apparent impunity.

The high propensity to invest, expand production, and search out markets globally was a common feature for all ten of the East Asian countries covered by this book (China, Indonesia, Japan, Korea, Malaysia, Philippines, Singapore, Taiwan, Thailand, and Vietnam) and overlaps heavily with those covered in the World Bank's study. Gross fixed capital formation as a share of GDP in the 1988–96 period ranged between 21.8 percent (Philippines) and 38.7 percent (Thailand). Even the lowest figure was higher than comparable shares in the United States and EU (based on calculations from World Development Indicators).

Close Government-Business Relations

In addition to "decreasing average costs," a second factor was indispensable to the successful continuation of East Asian growth: assurance of long-term profitability. The large investments needed to sustain "decreasing average costs" carry a high risk of failure due to the combination of long maturation periods plus the probability of fierce corporate competition in the search for added market shares. As a result, investors needed some assurances of reduced market uncertainty and the strong probability of long-term, if not immediate, profitability.

In Japan, as Tsunekawa's chapter discusses in detail, such assurance was provided by the probusiness governments that dominated both the parliament and the cabinets from 1955 until 1993, along with a bevy of complementary political and corporate institutions and policies, all fostering complementary long-term relations among key market players (banks, firms, subcontractors, workers) and between business and government. Virtually all of the other economically thriving East Asian countries shared a similar probusiness political predisposition, including even notionally socialist China and Vietnam. Across the region, national governments and firms, most relatively free from labor and consumerist pressures, and typically devoid of the democratic incentives to promise short term, electorally oriented benefits at the expense of longer-term national goals, collaborated to expand national exports. These in turn boosted national GDP, the end result of which was a collective narrowing of the "catch-up gap" with the more advanced economies.

Although institutions covering subcontractors and workers were less well developed in the East Asian countries aside from Japan, close relations among the government, banks, and firms prevailed broadly throughout the region. Bank-led business groups in Thailand, Korean *chaebol*, *bumiputera* businesses in Malaysia, crony capitalists in Indonesia and the Philippines, state-owned enterprises in China and Vietnam, all in their separate ways, were manifestations of such close relations between the government, finance, and business (Pasuk and Baker 2002; Kang 2002; Pepinsky, Naughton, and Doner in this volume). In Taiwan, government-business networks were nurtured under Kuomintang rule, as Yun-han Chu's chapter spells out, by the government's offsetting the technological and financial weaknesses of small to medium enterprises (SMEs) through various forms of assistance while simultaneously working closely with the financial sector in pursuit of mutually agreed on goals.

Close government-business relations across East Asia helped sustain a regionwide climate that allowed for the pursuit of high economic growth through "decreasing average costs" with far less risk than in polities with less tightly linked ties. The result for much of the 1980s and into the mid-1990s was an upward spiraling economic trajectory for ten or more East Asian countries. It was that remarkable collective performance that led to the World Bank's exploration of the factors behind East Asian "miracle" growth (World Bank 1993).

However, as the Asian Financial Crisis demonstrated with a vengeance, such a strategy was hardly without its vulnerabilities. These economies that had proved so successful in pursuit of the one economic goal they prized most highly, namely catch-up economic growth, showed themselves highly vulnerable to unbuffered infusions of rapidly moving foreign capital. But the policies and structures designed to achieve this growth left them vulnerable to the vicissitudes of rapidly moving global currency. East Asia's economic vulnerabilities became evident when their collective development strategies ran headlong into the tornado of global finance.

East Asian Development Meets Global Finance

East Asia's particular pattern of rapid catch-up development, as noted, necessitated vast amounts of capital investment along with close ties between government and business. During the early phases of their development, these countries relied predominantly on bank lending, rather than stock or capital markets, to meet the almost insatiable demand of individual companies for the ever-higher levels of capitalization required for firm and governmental development efforts (Aoki and Patrick 1995; Johnson 1982; Woo-Cumings 1991). As noted above, East Asian manufacturing firms typically borrowed needed capital from closely aligned domestically headquartered banks, regularly rolling these loans over for long periods of time, in the process fostering stable capital and long-term planning among firms, while simultaneously generating steady interest payments to banks. Governments, meanwhile, used their powers over the national banking systems to direct capital to desired firms and sectors.

Under pressures from global financial powers, including the International Monetary Fund (IMF) and the United States, as well as being driven by fears of losing their global competitive standing, a number of governments such as South Korea, Thailand, and Indonesia began to liberalize their capital accounts in the late 1980s and early 1990s. Typically they also liberalized their equity markets. Importantly, in only a few cases was the rush to liberalize these accounts matched with rigorous regulatory oversight (Stiglitz 2002). Previously tight government regulations constraining the financial systems in largely safe and predictable patterns gave way to a toxic mixture of sporadic government interventions with fewer clear-cut rules, deregulation of corporate paper, heightened incentives for short-term offshore borrowing, and liberalization of capital outflows, all combining to raise the incentives for high-risk behavior by the financial sector (Noble and Ravenhill 2000, 92–95; Hamilton-Hart 2008, 45–46). As a consequence, by the late 1990s a number of East Asian economies were drawing heavily on foreign capital to fuel their rapidly expanding production capacity buildups.

Japanese capital had long flowed to the rest of developing East Asia, largely in the form of long-term foreign direct investment. And from 1986 until 1994, Japanese financial institutions were also heavy investors in short-term bank loans with the outstanding bank credits offered to Asian countries doubling during that period. But these started to decline in 1995 and continued to do so till 2002. In the meanwhile, East Asia's decades-long growth, along with the combination of a high demand for capital and close government-business ties, provided a very tempting investment target for United States and European-based investors, hedge funds, and financial speculators salivating at the prospect of making the kinds of short-term loans or stock purchases that seemed to promise skyrocketing profits from the seemingly unstoppable East Asian miracle (Greenville 2000, 39–40). The result was that the outstanding credits by European banks expanded threefold between 1992 and 1997, surpassing the Japanese total in 1995. Additionally stock purchases by U.S. and European investors climbed rapidly.

This exogenous foreign capital lay at the heart of the troubles that followed. As global interest rates fell in the West but remained high in Asia

(Indonesian borrowing rates were as high as 20 percent), banks and businesses in the countries that were eventually the most deeply affected by the crisis found themselves moving away from their previously exclusive reliance on domestic savings mediated by national financial institutions in favor of often much cheaper borrowing rates from overseas. In many instances money borrowed cheaply from abroad could be loaned out at much higher rates domestically. Foreign private capital consequently moved into East Asia in conspicuously larger amounts. World figures for foreign direct investment show that in 1990, nearly 80 percent of total global FDI went to the developed world while money going into Asia totaled just about 11 percent. That Asian figure rose rapidly to 15.6 percent in 1995 and to 17.2 percent in 1997 (United Nations 1998, 7).

Worth noting is that seven of the ten countries had domestic savings rates higher than their investment rates. The exceptions were Thailand, Korea, and Vietnam. Thus the other seven *could* in principle have financed their domestic investments by relying on domestic savings alone. Yet with growing incentives to use such savings for other investments, such as overseas investments or loans, these countries opted increasingly to rely more heavily on imported capital from abroad. The nature of foreign capital that each country imported varied from one country to another; South Korea welcomed bank loans but not FDI because it feared domination by Japanese firms, while Taiwan eagerly accepted FDI, but not bank loans, as a bastion to reinforce its national security position.

Within East Asia, external capital inflows jumped from an average of 1.4 percent of GDP during 1986–90 to 6.7 percent during 1990–96, with even greater increases immediately prior to the onset of the crisis. For the most negatively affected countries, private net inflows to the five crisis countries (Thailand, Philippines, Indonesia, Malaysia, and South Korea) rose from $40.5 billion in 1994 to $93.0 billion in 1996 (Radelet and Sachs 1998, 2).

Foreign funds constituted the equivalent of about 15 percent of GDP in Thailand and the Philippines, 8 percent for Malaysia, and 5 percent for both Indonesia and South Korea. Furthermore, between 15 and 40 percent of this incoming capital arrived not in support of long-term investment in infrastructural projects, but in far more speculative areas such as property and stocks. As a result, economic growth in the most severely affected economies became ever more dependent on rapidly moving global capital searching for high levels of short-term profitability. As a consequence, the most affected economies proved highly vulnerable to short-term liquidity imbalances and systematic attacks on their currencies, despite the fact that their underlying economies, including long-term budgetary stability, remained solid (Radelet and Sachs 1998). The result was a series of East Asian asset bubbles fueled by new "hot money" flooding in under the conviction that Asian growth would remain unstoppably dynamic and that national governments would backstop any potential losses. As these developing Asian economies succumbed to the temptations of fluid and easily accessible global capital, their developmental strategies confronted what proved to be a combustible mix.

East Asian currencies in the affected countries were generally pegged to the U.S. dollar. And the rush of incoming capital typically involved borrowing short-term in U.S. dollars while lending long-term in local currencies, a formula that proved highly profitable to East Asian borrowers so long as the U.S. dollar was declining in value and Asian exports were booming, as was the case between 1990 and 1995 (Winters 1999, 90). However, when the U.S. dollar began to rise and exports slumped in 1995–96, short-term Asian debts required repayment using ever larger amounts of the local currency. Currencies pegged to the U.S. dollar thus proved highly vulnerable to short-term liquidity imbalances and speculative attacks on their currencies (Radelet and Sachs 1998). Governments across East Asia confronted the choice of ending their U.S. dollar pegs or expending massive reserves in efforts to protect them. As the attacks on local currencies became stronger, the governments saw few options but to devalue. Once currency depreciation started in Thailand, chain reactions followed in other parts of East Asia and the liquidity crisis became regional.

As local currencies dropped, the hot money that had flowed mercurially into Asia was equally quick to move out (Winters 1999). Thus in 1997, five countries saw a net outflow of around $12.1 billion, a remarkable and unexpected swing of capital flows representing around 11 percent of the precrisis U.S. dollar GDP of these countries (Radelet and Sachs 1998, 2).

Financial losses quickly cascaded through the "real economies" of the affected countries. Output losses ranged from perhaps 17.6 percent to nearly 98 percent in the most severely affected countries (Sheng 2009, 98), unemployment rates soared, and some 15–17 million Asians who were not already there fell below their nations' poverty lines (Sheng 2009, 309; MacIntyre et al. 2008, 4–13). Financial packages from the International Monetary Fund were, as has been well cataloged, requested by Thailand, South Korea, and Indonesia. Such bailouts ultimately came with straightjacketing conditions that challenged the developmental models that had been so successfully pursued by these countries (Noble and Ravenhill 2000; Pempel 1999a).

The relative openness to short-term foreign capital inflows distinguished countries that were hit hardest from those that sustained little damage. China, Vietnam, and Taiwan, for example, had strong limits on such inflows in contrast to the most severely hit countries such as Thailand, Indonesia, and Korea. Singapore similarly had a tight regulatory regime in place that buffered the city-state from free-floating speculation. Clearly some governments opted for policies that left their national financial sectors far more vulnerable to rapidly moving capital than those of their neighbors. Indeed, as Pepinsky analyzes in chapter 6, a country like the Philippines, while relatively open in principle, proved far less attractive to foreign investors in search of quick profits.

Though not all of East Asia proved vulnerable to the same fates, the crisis had its regionwide effects. At its height, the AFC triggered declines in the growth rates of all ten East Asian "miracle economies," with the sharpest drops experienced by Thailand, Indonesia, Korea, Japan, and Malaysia. China, Singapore, Vietnam, Taiwan, and the Philippines underwent lighter declines. The hardest hit countries recorded negative growth in their gross fixed capital formation as well. Only substantial currency devaluations and sharply increasing trade surpluses allowed these countries to avoid further deterioration in growth.

The crisis proved less that there was something fundamentally wrong with East Asia's political economies collectively and more that several of East Asian economies had left themselves dangerously vulnerable to the rapacious scythe of global capital (Chang 2000). Within East Asia, consequently, the crisis was broadly interpreted as no more than a short-term liquidity problem that had been exploited by sophisticated Western investors and one that should be dealt with by the tactical eradication of conditions that might leave their economies vulnerable to a repeat of the crisis. The focus was on enhancing innate resilience rather than the kinds of deep structural or institutional reconfigurations that might undermine long-term strategies of development.

That East Asian economic fundamentals had been sound was reflected in the fact that the crisis, though unmistakably sharp and severe, was distinctly short-lived. A sequence of V-shaped recoveries was seen by all of the worst-affected countries. By 1999–2000, GDP growth rates had returned to nearly their precrisis levels in Malaysia, Korea, Indonesia, Thailand, and the Philippines, and they remained on these trajectories until the Lehman crisis of 2008–9.

The Global Financial Crisis

At the macroeconomic level, the GFC stemmed from high levels of global liquidity rooted in an unsteady balance between an overconsuming and undersaving United States and Europe on the one hand, and an underconsuming and overcapitalized rest of the world on the other (Rajan 2010, 6; Chinn and Frieden 2011). At the heart of this imbalance was huge public and private sector borrowing by the United States, ranging between $500 billion and $1 trillion per year from 2000 to 2007, along with a substantial current account imbalance for Europe. This strongly contrasted with the limited consumption and high savings rates elsewhere, particularly in East Asia. East Asia, which had appeared so vulnerable to the onrush of global capital in 1997–98, found itself a decade later as the suddenly flush banker underwriting America's and much of Western Europe's unpaid-for consumption. In this regard, the Global Financial Crisis was indeed "global" in its causation.

East Asian economies, in the wake of the AFC, had, as noted, been chastened by the demonstrated dangers of extensive foreign borrowing. Consequently most returned to domestic sources of funding to continue expanding their production of exportable goods. China, with its white hot growth in particular, but most East Asian exporting economies as well, continued policies that suppressed domestic consumption in favor of cheaper currencies and export-led growth. And as their products were gobbled up by Western consumers, East Asian governments opted to recycle their huge profits not in domestic consumption so much as in the accumulation of huge foreign reserve holdings that would provide the "self-insurance" preventing a recurrence of the AFC. These foreign reserves in turn were invested principally in U.S. and European government bonds, thus providing the inexpensive fuel that enabled debt-dependent Western consumption mediated by the sophisticated U.S. financial sector.

Starting with the Reagan administration and continuing with accelerating velocity over the next thirty years, successive U.S. administrations a-dopted policies of semipermanent debt financing as an integral component of the nation's fiscal policy. Meanwhile, financial deregulation and the lifting of capital controls underwrote the ability to borrow cheaply from overseas. Yet little of the newly incoming foreign money was utilized to enhance long-term productivity through infrastructural, manufacturing, or other productive capabilities that may have enhanced national economic resilience (Streeck 2011). Rather, borrowing centered on the political goals of holding down taxes (largely by Republicans) and slowing the speed with which social programs were being cut or privatized (largely by Democrats). Between 2001 and 2008, with Republican administrations being the chief contributors, the federal government debt nearly doubled from $5.6 trillion to more than $9.5 trillion (Pelofsky and Lawder 2008).

Meanwhile, persistently low global interest rates fueled a geometric explosion in housing prices within the United States and several European countries. The leap in prices within the United States represented a noteworthy departure from historical inflation-adjusted figures, which since 1975 had been relatively stable at around US$150,000. As prices soared, large numbers of homeowners used nominal rises in value to refinance their mortgages, drawing out equity for consumption, whether for college tuition, health emergencies, or even a new car. Low mortgage rates and rapidly rising housing prices fueled an ever-rising demand for housing, another exuberant manifestation of the conviction that "this time is different."

Importantly, even as asset prices soared, the U.S. Federal Reserve held interest rates low, further fostering the aura of "irrational exuberance." Low interest rates effectively guaranteed a floor under asset prices. In Gretchen Mortgenson's words, the U.S. Federal Reserve remained "defiantly inert and uninterested in reining in the mortgage mania" (2011, C-1). Raghuram Rajan is equally scathing. Greenspan, he argued, recognized the possibility of asset bubbles; however, he essentially "told traders and bankers that if they gambled, the Fed would not limit their gains, but if their bets turned sour, the Fed would limit the consequences" (2010, 113).

Sizzling U.S. housing prices provided both homeowners and financial institutions with the promise of unending benefits through a continual refinancing of mortgages. Particularly problematic were so-called subprime loans (Schwartz 2009). One of the many products of the financial engineering noted above, subprime mortgages allowed financial institutions to lend money at exceptionally low "teaser" rates to borrowers with dubious credit ratings (Lewis 2010; Rajan 2010, 38–41). Low monthly payments, even if guaranteed only for short periods, allowed new home buyers to move into properties with the faith, encouraged by their lenders, that housing values would rise, allowing for a spiral of refinancing deals through ever-newer mortgages. Sequential refinancing of mortgages in turn proved highly profitable for financial institutions which regularly beat the bushes for new borrowers and recurrent refinancing.

Importantly, these new mortgages were rarely held for multiyear periods by the issuing banks as traditional banks had done before financial deregulation began. Instead, mortgages became one additional instrument to be manipulated and marketed by financial engineers. Mortgages were sliced into pieces, which were then bundled together and "securitized" after which they were sold as the equivalent of AAA bonds, a financial fiction made possible by the collusion of allegedly independent ratings agencies such as Moody's and Standard and Poor's, which were paid fat fees by Wall Street firms for each deal they rated. Around 80 percent of this rapidly rising tower of mortgage debt was rated AAA (in sharp contrast to the roughly 1 percent of corporate bonds that received such a high rating). These securitized mortgages, Michael Lewis correctly notes, served as "a credit laundering service for the residents of Lower Middle Class America. For Wall Street [they were] a machine that turned lead into gold" (2010, 73).

Integral to the rising housing market and its dubious subprime funding, as well as to the subsequent global financial collapse, was one final totem of financial engineering—the newly created, and increasingly widespread, financial instrument known as "credit default swaps" (CDS) and their variant "credit default obligations" (CDO). Credit default swaps were not really "swaps" at all, but rather insurance policies, typically on a corporate bond, including mortgage backed securities, with semiannual premiums and a fixed term (Lewis 2010, 29). Essentially, they constituted low-cost bets that particular assets (including the securitized subprime mortgages) would not go into default. Since the housing market seemed to be expanding unendingly, such credit default swaps on mortgages seemed immune to any worries about default. As a result, billions of dollars in highly profitable credit-default swaps were issued by financial institutions such as the American Insurance Group's now-infamous financial products unit (AIGFP). AIGFP made $2.5 billion in pretax profits in 2005 by selling underpriced insurance on complex, poorly understood securities.

Often described as "picking up nickels in front of a steamroller" (Johnson 2009), this risky strategy proved profitable in ordinary years but catastrophically vulnerable as housing prices collapsed. Indeed, in the early days of the mortgage bond business, the biggest fear was that loans would be repaid too quickly, not that they would fail to be repaid (Lewis 2010, 7). The issuance of such CDOs within AIGFP and other firms was perceived as a no-risk license to print money. The increasingly complex and interconnected nature of CDOs and the rising number of arcane derivative products eventually created a mixture whose structure was so arcane that even investment professionals and financial regulators had a hard time comprehending it (Sheng 2009, 356; Lewis 2010, 218). American, and importantly European, financial institutions invested vast amounts of capital in such products.

This witches' brew of financial and political hubris came to its climatic boil in the United States with the collapse of Lehman Brothers on September 15, 2008. The interlinked nature of global financial markets demonstrated inherent vulnerability to the breaking of any single link. The trust among borrowing and lending institutions so critical to the financial markets evaporated once it became clear that the U.S. government would not rescue Lehman. The subsequent global freeze up in capital markets exposed the inherent fragility of the previously lauded amalgam of free flowing and highly leveraged capital, creative securitization of mortgages, unregulated derivatives, and the unmonitored pursuit of maximum profits, all laced with an unexamined optimism that asset markets would always move up (Lewis 2010; Rajan 2010; Sheng 2009). The rapidity with which global capital markets seized up and the range of countries that were threatened quickly led U.S. secretary of the treasury Henry Paulson, a longtime advocate of the unfettered markets that had suddenly proved so poisonous, to abandon his prior commitments and move quickly to bail out the troubled financial institutions by recapitalizing them through a massive injection of taxpayer money via an entity known as the Troubled Asset Relief Program (Rajan, 2010, 149). Within weeks, more than $1 trillion in government monies were allocated to the relief effort.

The GFC quickly swirled through European financial institutions as well. Numerous European financial institutions were deeply enmeshed in this system, with German, UK, Irish and Icelandic financial institutions showing the highest levels of vulnerability. German and UK banks, for example, were heavily invested in CDOs; all three of Iceland's major private commercial banks, enmeshed as they were in dubious financial products, collapsed in September 2008 and were put into receivership. Meanwhile in the United States, the housing bubble undoubtedly contributed to the GFC, as U.S. housing prices between 1997 and 2005 increased on average 75 percent; in the United Kingdom, housing prices increased by 160 percent, Spanish prices jumped 145 percent, those in Sweden rose 80 percent, and in Ireland, the number was a whopping 185 percent (Wyss 2007, 10). The difficulties in these European countries became compounded for the region as a whole as housing prices crumbled. These matters worsened as the inherent intra-European imbalances became apparent: governments in the southern parts of Europe, most notably Greece, Spain, Portugal, and eventually Italy, were exposed as having had massive levels of previously hidden public sector debts. Linked as they were to the single currency, these countries could not rely on devaluation to work their way out, thereby turning erstwhile national economic problems into a common problem for the entire Eurozone. Dealing with the pan-European problems fell heavily to the Eurozone's "northern" members, led by Germany and the Netherlands in particular, who insisted on strict austerity and fiscal discipline as a condition for economic assistance packages, most notably those offered by the European Central Bank. The result has been a dramatic slowdown in the major economies on both sides of the Atlantic.

East Asia's "Escape"

East Asia was hardly immune to the 2008–9 crisis, but within eighteen months of the Lehman meltdown, most countries from the region were in far better economic shape than the United States and Western Europe. As chief economist of Allianz Dresdner Economic Research, Michael Heise, presciently put it: "No region is immune to the financial crisis. Asian economies will also see a slowdown in growth, but not a contraction. Emerging markets in Asia will still show a considerable degree of resilience" (*Economy News*, December 12, 2008). Thus across most of East Asia, growth rates staggered and unemployment rose, but unlike the United States and most European economies, virtually all economies in East Asia gradually resumed their earlier growth trajectories by the second or third quarters of 2009.

Why did East Asia prove so economically resilient? The answer lies in three linked parts of their domestic and external political economies. First, the East Asian downturn was transmitted to the region primarily through global trade rather than as the result of close integration with global financial markets. Most East Asian economies remained heavily focused on manufacturing and exports to global markets; indeed, most continue to rely on exports for 50 percent or more of their GDP (with several such as Singapore and Hong Kong exporting amounts greater than their GDP). As global demand seized up in the wake of the shock of 2008, export-dependent economies across East Asian showed their inherent vulnerability to fluctuations in global demand. But drawing lessons from the disastrous protectionism that accompanied the global recession of 1929–32, in 2008 the major economies of the world used the newly empowered G-20 to put together packages of global fiscal stimulation that led to a resurgence in global demand, allowing

Asian exporters to resume their businesses relatively unscathed and lifting their national economies in the process.

In addition, the region's economies were greatly helped by a host of domestic reforms implemented after the AFC. Like many crises, the AFC triggered significant rethinking of prior policies across much of East Asia, including countries not so directly damaged by it (Gourevitch 1986; MacIntyre et al. 2008). The specific adjustments undertaken by national governments in response to the AFC are detailed far more extensively in the individual chapters that follow, but broadly viewed, most moves were tactical rather than strategic. In the finance area, for example, one succinct summary of changes is offered by Hamilton-Hart: key targets, she notes, were typically "restructuring, recapitalization, and regulatory change" (2008, 47). More concretely, most countries moved away from fixed exchange rates; they sponged up non-performing loans, and they strengthened regulatory controls over the financial sector to ensure greater prudence in lending practices. As Naughton comments in chapter 5, all East Asian countries, including China, "learned the same broad lessons about more prudent international policy: . . . keep the currency low enough to maintain consistent export surpluses; build up foreign exchange reserves; avoid reliance on short-term bank loans; and above all, never allow yourself to become dependent on the IMF for macroeconomic insurance."

Also important, in the aftermath of the AFC, the trade picture changed throughout the region. Most countries were able to create positive trade surpluses. In China, Japan, Korea, the Philippines, Taiwan, and Thailand, the average annual contribution of trade surplus to GDP growth turned from negative to positive between 1988 and 1996 and 1999 to 2007. Indonesia and Singapore saw enhanced positive contributions of the trade surplus over the same periods. Malaysia experienced shrinkage in its trade surplus both before and after the AFC, but the degree by which the shrinkage dragged the GDP growth rate down was narrowed to a great extent in the post-AFC years. Only in Vietnam did the contribution of the trade balance between the two periods become increasingly negative (based on author's calculations from WDI data).

Consequently, almost all East Asian countries accumulated substantial foreign exchange holdings, allowing them to move toward greater "self-insurance" against future liquidity risks. China's reserve holdings jumped nearly tenfold over the decade 1996–2006, while those of Japan and Korea leaped approximately fourfold. Most of the rest of East Asia saw similar leaps from four- to eightfold (Ruiz-Arranz and Zavadjil 2008, 21). Thus, by the time of the GFC, six of the world's largest foreign reserve holders were in Asia (China, Japan, Taiwan, South Korea, Hong Kong, and Singapore). Such strong foreign reserve positions reinforced the previous commitment of East Asian regimes to the export and savings mix that fueled their exports and underwrote U.S. and Western European overconsumption.

Investments in the region moved away from the spurious and excessive patterns that had prevailed in the run up to the crisis. The share of gross fixed capital formation as a portion of GDP declined between the pre-AFC and post-AFC periods in eight out of ten countries; investment rates after the crisis ranged from 20.6 percent (Philippines) to 29.1 percent (Korea), down from an earlier range of 21.8–38.7 percent. China and Vietnam were exceptions in this regard; between 1988 and 1996 and from 1999 to 2007, they increased their investment rates somewhat, from 31.6 percent to 37.7 percent for China and from 25.3 percent to 31.6 percent for Vietnam. As a consequence, in most of the countries, except China and the Philippines, the GDP growth rate also dropped in the wake of the AFC. In effect, the East Asian countries had come to live within their means. Still, if Japan is excluded as an especially poor performer, their average annual growth rates for 1999–2007 were still quite high, ranging from 4.6 percent in Indonesia to 10.2 percent in China. Most of Asia continued to grow more quickly than the United States (2.9 percent), the European Union (2.5 percent), Japan (1.3 percent), and the world average (3.3 percent) (based on author's calculations from WDI data).

As we and others have noted in the wake of the AFC, governments throughout the region took many other steps to create tougher financial firewalls, engage in closer monitoring of short-term capital flows, and make their regulatory systems more active and sophisticated (Grimes 2009; Pempel 2010b). In finance, there was indeed a general move toward what Hamilton-Hart has summarized as greater "market-based, competitive, and internationally open financial systems" (2008, 46). Overall, developing countries in Asia moved away from their once high reliance on bank lending for capital and became more market based; they also became more open to consolidation and the merger of their financial institutions with foreign counterparts. Yet, with the possible exception of South Korea, none of the most severely affected countries in the AFC region made wholesale moves to embrace neoliberal economics by substantial loosening of their capital markets. Across the region, these governments retained strict policy oversight and tighter regulations. Qureshi et al. examine financial regulation by geographical region and show that in the years just prior to the GFC, the developing economies of East Asia had both rising indicators of regulation as well as the regionally highest levels of absolute regulation in the four indices they examine: financial sector capital controls, economywide capital controls on inflows, foreign currency controls, and domestic prudential regulations (2011, 19). Furthermore, according to the IMF, the average share of foreign financial institutions in total domestic bank assets globally was 23 percent, whereas in East Asia it was only 6 percent (Sheng 2009, 315).

East Asian financial institutions thus remained minimally exposed to the highly risky financial instruments that were at the heart of the GFC in Europe and the United States. The financial systems of East Asia continued to be oriented toward providing investment capital for domestic manufacturing and services; they resisted (and were often prevented by the government from pursuing) extensive pursuit of profits through high-risk financial products.

Emphasizing manufacturing, exports, infrastructural development, and the fostering of a middle class, most governments in East Asia continued to focus on their real economies. Banking and financial institutions continued to garner profits largely by servicing their countries' manufacturing firms rather than in complex financial engineering. Their economies consequently remained far less vulnerable to the vicissitudes of the high-risk finance embraced by the United States and much of Western Europe. Japan, with by far the highest levels of dependence on finance in the region, was still vastly less dependent on its financial sector than other major economies.

In addition to steps that were taken within individual countries, East Asia bolstered regional ties in finance and trade, including a network of currency swap arrangements to be used in any future liquidity emergency. Begun in May 2000 as the Chiang Mai Initiative (CMI), collective capital commitments were gradually expanded to a total of $240 billion as of 2012, and the original network of bilateral swaps subsequently became the Chiang Mai Initiative Multilateralization (CMIM). Multilateralization gave the CMIM significant independence from IMF conditionality, giving the economies of the region the enhanced security of a collective safety net and an enhanced bargaining position in any future negotiations with the IMF and global financial houses. Two Asian bond markets have also been put in place, reducing the "round trip" costs of borrowing and lending in U.S. dollars (Grimes 2006, 2009; Pempel 2005 and 2010b).

Intraregional East Asian trade markets have also been deepened following the AFC. This deepening came as a consequence of both private corporate decisions and governmentally driven bilateral and minilateral free trade agreements. Prior to the crisis in the mid-1990s, the United States represented the largest or second largest export market for Japan (30 percent of total exports), Hong Kong (23 percent), South Korea (22 percent), Singapore (19 percent), Taiwan (26 percent), Malaysia (21 percent), Thailand (21 percent), and Indonesia (15 percent) (Pempel 1999b, 171). By the onset of the GFC, the U.S. share of East Asian exports had dwindled while China became the major trading partner for virtually all other countries in the region. China has become an assembly platform for its higher-wage, more technologically sophisticated neighbors within the complex of regional supply chains and production networks. These global and Asian-based multinational companies took advantage of the disparities and developmental asymmetries among the East Asian economies and blended them into what some have labeled "Factory Asia."

Consequently, when the Lehman shock struck, intra–East Asian trade totaled approximately 56 percent of all East Asia exports. Although the United

States and Europe remain the ultimate destination for many East Asian exports, particularly those produced or assembled in China, total cross-border trade since the AFC has become "more Asian," adding still another layer of insulation against extraregional economic shocks. As a result, even the global trade slowdown that followed the financial shocks proved to be short lived in its impact on the region.

In all these changes, the economies of East Asia remained largely outside the web of global financial connections that proved so toxic to the United States and much of Western Europe in 2008. As data from the Asian Development Bank demonstrate, "As of May 2008, total reported write-down and credit losses of the world's 100 biggest banks and securities amounted to 379 billion USD. Of these, Asia ex-Japan accounted for 10.8 billion USD, which is less than 3% of global losses" (2008, 25). Similarly, East Asian institutions remained largely on the sidelines as derivatives and credit-default swaps and other high-risk financial products became so seductive to their Western counterparts (Fitch Ratings 2007). The Asian proportion of capital eradicated by subprime losses was typically less than a tenth that of the United States.

To paraphrase Jeffrey Winters, as a result of such steps, to the extent that East Asian financial systems "plugged into" global financial markets, they did so with an unmistakable array of surge protectors. In the wake of the AFC, the region became far more buffered from the extreme behaviors of global capital markets, essentially opting not to privilege finance over manufacturing nor to embrace the arcane financial instruments that had become so popular (and initially so profitable) in the United States, Britain, Germany, and much of Western Europe. East Asian governments effectively joined "Gamblers Anonymous" and remained on the sidelines of the "casino capitalism" that engulfed so many of the financial institutions in the West.

As a result of post-AFC policies and their underlying approach to economic development, East Asian governments and economies enhanced the resilience in their underlying economic profiles. Tactical adjustments in a host of areas, combined with avoidance of the temptations of highly risky financial engineering left the countries of East Asia better buffered from the vulnerabilities to global capital movements than they had been in 1997–98. But, of course, as the vicissitudes of global economics has so often demonstrated, it can be very risky to thump one's chest in what may prove to be short-lived triumph.

In assessing why East Asia did so well relative to the United States and Europe during the great recession of 2008–9, two important points stand out. First, Asian governments appear to have learned from the vulnerabilities that were revealed as endemic in their collective approach to developmentalism, namely weakness in the face of unregulated and rapidly moving exogenous capital movements and a concentration on short-term profits. Consequently, as they emerged from the 1997–98 crisis, governments across the region reaffirmed their commitment to strengthening their manufacturing and export industries while increasing their trade balances, savings, and foreign reserve holdings in a collective effort to enhance their economies' resilience against any possible repeat of the vulnerabilities they had demonstrated in 1997–98. In the process, East Asian economies continued to privilege savings over spending, exports over consumption, and manufacturing over finance as the engines of their growth.

Additionally, the economies of East Asia moved closer to prudential international norms without embracing wholesale deregulation. Global financial and manufacturing firms have gained a more substantial presence across virtually all of postcrisis East Asia, but they are hardly free to engage in many of the cavalier practices tolerated among U.S., UK, German, and other financial institutions. At the same time, enhanced foreign reserve holdings, greater intra-Asian trade, financial swap arrangements, and bond funds have all been undertaken in an effort to buffer the region's economies from some of the most dangerous facets of the GFC.

Not at all coincidentally, as greater moderation and somewhat slower growth took hold across East Asia, the region, with the conspicuous exception of China, lost some of its prior magnetic attraction for the short-term speculative moves of Western investors. As Pepinsky notes in his chapter of this book, unable to guarantee themselves a good chance of massive profits, fast-moving Western capital sought other targets for high returns and backed away from their earlier Asian fascinations.

Clearly, successful economic development requires far more than just an abstract commitment to "catch-up industrialization." Though it has worked generally for East Asia, the East Asian success may well prove to have been time-dependent and thus vulnerable to as yet unseen hazards. And surely even East Asia's greatest admirers must admit that its past success, as Basri's chapter argues specifically for Indonesia, rested on not a little bit of luck. But one lesson that East Asia can offer to both the developing world as well as to the highly industrialized countries is extreme caution about minimalist government and the promises of unfettered financial markets. The massive recession of 2008–9 shows the consequences of such a course of action.

Part 1

Dealing with Crises

Continuities and Changes

2

A Tale of the Two Crises

Indonesia's Political Economy
Muhammad Chatib Basri

Prior to the 1997–98 crisis, the Indonesian economy represented one of East Asia's major success stories of economic structural transformation. The economy grew on average by 7.6 percent from 1967 to 1996. Structural transformation took place in agriculture, manufacturing, utilities, and services. In line with high economic growth and the structural transformation in several sectors, the rates of poverty declined from around 40 percent (54.2 million people) in 1976 to 17.5 percent (34 million people) in 1996. Together with Malaysia and Thailand, Indonesia was classified as a member of the second tier of newly industrialized economies (NIEs). However, the Asian Financial Crisis (AFC) in 1997 overturned the picture completely. Hill (2000b) called this situation the strange and sudden death of a Tiger economy. The AFC that hit in 1997–98 devastated the Indonesian economy, which contracted by 13.1 percent.

This economic crisis led to a series of political reforms that ended the existing authoritarian system and transformed Indonesia into the second largest non-Western democracy. This reform also brought Indonesia closer to a more open and institutionalized economic system. The management of reform in Indonesia was not easy. As the nation with the fourth largest population in the world and as the biggest Muslim nation with a secular constitution, Indonesia's economic and political reform was a complex process. Taking into account the complexity of such problems, it is clear that Indonesia faced far more substantial difficulties than Korea, Malaysia, or Thailand, which experienced the same economic crisis. None of these three countries altered their political systems radically in the wake of the crisis. By contrast, Indonesia, abandoned both its authoritarian regime and its centralized system of governance, embracing democratization and decentralization almost overnight. Indonesia's reform experience is somewhat comparable to that of the Philippines after Marcos—of course, on a different scale.

From this perspective, Indonesia has made significant progress. During the first years of the economic and political crisis, many observers pointed out the dangers of balkanization in Indonesia. Furthermore, many argued that direct presidential elections in 2004 might lead to massive violence and bloodshed as the result of intense political conflicts. Yet others envisaged the collapse of the Indonesian economy. The reality proved to be far different. Indonesia remains united, and the direct presidential election went very smoothly and was even considered the most peaceful in Indonesian history. Income per capita rebounded and surpassed precrisis levels as did GDP, consumption, and exports, although investment as a percent of GDP still remains lower than before the crisis. The debt to GDP ratio has declined substantially to less than 40 percent, inflation has decelerated, and the exchange rate is relatively stable. Corruption remains pervasive at many levels, yet even here there are some signs of improvement.

Ten years after the economic and political crisis of the AFC, Indonesia faced the Global Financial Crisis (GFC), which, in terms of scale and magnitude, was far larger than the AFC. The GFC caused economic disruption and collapse in many countries. Indonesia was obviously affected by this crisis, and its export growth declined significantly. Nevertheless, the impact of the crisis on the Indonesian economy was relatively limited compared to other countries in the region, including Singapore, Malaysia, and Thailand. This situation raises the question of why the impact of the global crisis on the Indonesian economy has been so limited? In particular, why, in contrast to the devastating effects of the AFC, were the effects of the 2008 global financial crisis so much more limited?

At least four important differences between the 1998 and the 2008 crisis account for the relatively mild effect of the GFC on Indonesia: the origin of the crisis, the exchange rate regime, policy responses, and the national political economy. The first three essentially involved economics while the fourth, and what this chapter focuses primarily on, is the linkage between domestic politics and domestic economics in how these two crises played out.

The Story of the Two Crises

The Asian Financial Crisis of 1997–98

As noted earlier, the Asian Financial Crisis that hit in 1997–98 had a devastating effect on the Indonesian economy, including an economic contraction of 13.1 percent. Figure 2.1 shows the difference between the 1998 crisis and the 2008 crisis. In the first year after the onset of the crisis, the rupiah weakened from Rp2,500 against the U.S. dollar to settle around Rp10,000, after sinking to a low of Rp12,000 (figure 2.2); meanwhile inflation jumped to 70 percent (figure 2.3). As a result of the inflation and the consequent increase in the prices of food, poverty increased substantially. The number of people living below the poverty line rose from 15.7 percent in February 1997 to 27.1 percent in February 1999 (Sumarto, Suryahadi, and Widyanti 2002, 3). The unemployment rate rose from 4.7 percent in August 1997 to 5.5 percent in August 1998, while underemployment increased from 35.8 percent to 39.1 percent. At that time, Indonesia was haunted by two related questions— when would the country begin to emerge from the crisis, and where would signs of improvement first appear?

The crisis began with Thailand. The Indonesian government responded poorly to the contagion effect of Thailand's difficulties by committing itself to several errors in policy, such as tightening the budget and raising interest rates, the combination of which eventually brought the country into even greater difficulty. Prior to 1997 there had been a lending boom in Indonesia, eventually accompanied by a high ratio of nonperforming loans (NPL) to total credit. As the economy went into a deep recession, due to contractionary devaluation, many firms faced serious distress. Because the government and the central bank tightened the budget and raised interest rates, the default rate escalated, which in turn increased capital outflow and brought Indonesia into a still deeper crisis. This experience shows that the economic

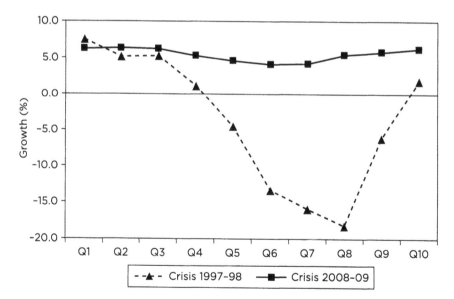

Figure 2.1 Economic growth, 1997–98 versus 2008–9. Year-to-year growth rate (%). For the 1997–98 crisis Q1 begins in the first quarter of 1997, while for the 2008–9 crisis Q1 begins in the first quarter of 2008.

Source: Calculated from CEIC database (http://ceicdata.securities.com/cdmWeb).

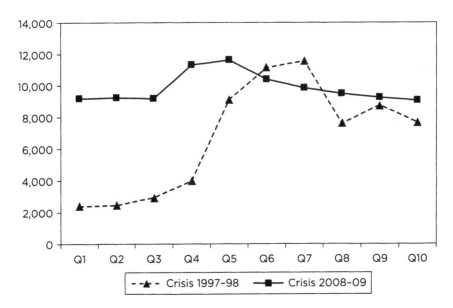

Figure 2.2 Exchange rate, 1997–98 versus 2008–9. Quarterly average (rupiah per USD). For the 1997–98 crisis Q1 begins in the first quarter of 1997, while for the 2008–09 crisis Q1 begins in the first quarter of 2008.

Source: Calculated from Bank Indonesia database (http://www.bi.go.id/en/statistik/seki/terkini/mone ter/Contents/Default.aspx).

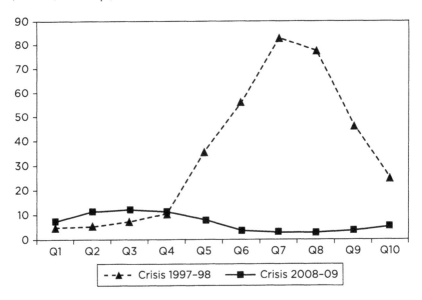

Figure 2.3 Inflation, 1997–98 versus 2008–9. Year-to-year increase of consumer price (%). For the 1997–98 crisis Q1 begins in the first quarter of 1997, while for the 2008–09 crisis Q1 begins in the first quarter of 2008.

Source: Calculated from CEIC and Bank Indonesia databases (http://ceicdata.securities.com/cdmWeb and http://www.bi.go.id/en/statistik/seki/terkini/moneter/Contents/Default.aspx).

crisis in 1997–98 centered mainly on the banking sector, financial markets, exchange rates, the problem of short-term debt, capital mobility, and the consequent political disturbances.

The Global Financial Crisis 2008

The GFC initially began in the U.S. subprime mortgage markets, but it precipitated a wider global repricing of risk that was exacerbated by the disclosure of higher than expected losses by financial institutions.[1] The balance sheet and liquidity problem in the U.S. banking sector caused a global deceleration of credit growth. In the United States, pressures in the financial sector caused a credit crunch because of the inability of the banking sector to provide credit.[2] In turn this hit the real sector and reduced both investment and consumption. Financial channels were affected by the freezing of foreign exchange liquidity that caused a liquidity shortage on international money markets as a result of the repricing of risks. This in turn could be traced to the tightening of financing conditions for emerging markets and developing countries (especially those systemic players that relied on international financial markets for funding) as well as increased funding costs from the issuance of international bonds. All of these put pressure on the balance of payments and exchange rates of the emerging markets. In addition, the many default cases in the United States caused an overabundance of cheap assets as funds from emerging markets to the United States were absorbed. This made it even more difficult for the emerging markets to obtain external funding. The result was the collapse of numerous stock exchanges and enhanced pressure on exchange rates. What was also of real concern was that the spread of the crisis had widened to sweep in many more countries covering all geographic regions, further accelerating the collapse of global markets. This was indicated by the growing integration of the global financial system as well as the existence of more and more short-term fund flows in markets, especially within the emerging markets. In addition, international trade was affected by the slower global growth, which caused a reduction in the value of exports, a drop in commodity prices, reduced remittances, increased unemployment, and even more intense trade competition (as a result of efforts to shift products that used to be exported to the United States and Europe to developing countries).

As for Indonesia, the effects of the GFC were reflected by several indicators, such as the depreciation of the exchange rates and the decline in the stock market. The rupiah exchange rate had fallen by 30 percent by the end of 2008, while the Indonesia Stock Market Index experienced a drop

---

1. This section is heavily drawn from Basri and Rahardja (2010) and Basri and Rahardja (2011).

2. This has been caused by the lack of liquidity, repricing of risk, and a greater concern about counterparty risk in interbank money markets.

of 50 percent in the same year. Banking credit growth also experienced a significant drop from 32 percent to 10 percent (Basri and Siregar 2009). In addition, banking confidence declined, as can be seen by the shrinking size of interbank borrowing and lending; this was down by 59.3 percent to Rp83.8 trillion in December 2008 from Rp206.0 trillion in December 2007 (Gunawan et al. 2009). The desire by banks to expand their funding bases at the same time that interbank rates increased caused sharp competition between banks.

It was primarily though international trade that weak global economic growth had its biggest effect, as seen in a reduction in demand for Indonesian exports starting with the fourth quarter of 2008. The drop in global demand led to weak demand for primary and mining exports, which in turn resulted in a drop in the price of commodities and mining goods. The drop in global economic growth also weakened demand for energy, leading to a decline in the global price of oil. Papanek, Basri, Schydlowsky (2009) pointed out that the collapse of exports was mainly reflected in export prices rather than export volume. In fact, the demand for primary commodity exports, especially agriculture and mining, remained relatively stable, thanks to the continuing strong demand from China and India. With natural resources accounting for more than half of Indonesia's exports, this represented a life support system for the Indonesian economy. Moreover, the depreciation of the rupiah that took place after September 2008 partially compensated for the effects of the collapse in the demand for exports. However, data show that the increase in demand due to the depreciation of rupiah (substitution effect) was still smaller than the fall in demand due to decline in income (income effect). As a result of this, all Indonesian exports experienced a drop.

As a result of this export weakness, in the fourth quarter of 2008 economic growth slowed to 5.2 percent (figure 2.1). Even so, Indonesia's overall economic growth still reached 6.0 percent, which was the highest growth in Asia after China and India.

Economic Conditions that Divided the Two Crises: Good Policy and Good Luck

The GFC of 2008–9 was, as noted, not the first crisis for Indonesia. Basri and Hill (2011) show that there had been at least six crises experienced by Indonesia—two extremely severe crises in the mid-1960s, two relatively mild ones in the 1980s, the 1997–98 AFC, plus the GFC in 2008. As for the two most recent crises, the effects of the 2008 global financial crisis, which in terms of magnitude was much larger than the 1998 crisis, were relatively limited in Indonesia. We argue that there are at least four significant differences between the 1998 and the 2008 crisis.[3] Three of the four are concerned with economic conditions and the fourth is with political economy.

---

3. This part is heavily drawn from Basri and Rahardja (2010).

The first economic difference concerns the origin of the crises. In 1998, the initial debate in the country centered on the link between currency depreciation and economic fundamentals. One view suggested that the Indonesian economy was basically as sound as it had been before, while others argued that Indonesian economy was fundamentally poor or far worse than reported by the government or other bodies such as the World Bank (Soesastro and Basri 1998). Aswicahyono and Hill (2002) pointed out that there was no clear link between the current crisis and the Krugman claim that Asian growth was a "myth," that is, that much of East Asia's dynamism had been due simply to increased mobilization of inputs such as capital and labor. They argued that the crisis in 1997–98 had mainly to do with financial markets, exchange rates, problems of short-term debt, capital mobility, and political disturbances. We have to admit, though we agree with much of the latter argument, that there was a fundamental problem in the Indonesian economy in 1998, especially in the financial sector. As pointed out by Soesastro and Basri (1998), Stiglitz and Greenwald (2003), Hill (1999), and Fane and Macleod (2004), many banks in Indonesia were very weak and had made bad loans. There had been a massive lending boom in the run-up to the 1997 crisis. The loan to deposit ratio (LDR) was more than 100 percent in 1997, and the ratio of NPLs to total credit was around 27 percent in September 1997.

On the other hand, the financial situation was relatively healthier on these fronts when the global financial crisis hit in 2008 than it had been ten years previously. The NPL ratio was less than 4 percent at the end of 2008, and the LDR was less than 80 percent, while the capital adequacy ratio (CAR) was around 17 percent. Moreover, one should not overlook the fact that the currency crisis in Indonesia began in the wake of problems affecting other countries in the region.

In 1998 the economic origins of the crisis were both domestic and external (Soesatro and Basri 1998). When the financial crisis hit Thailand in 1997, the impact on the Indonesian economy was dreadful. Thus the 1998 crisis was both homegrown and regional. In contrast, the 2008 crisis was almost entirely external; to be more precise it was triggered by the subprime crisis in the United States.

The second big economic difference involves the exchange rate regime. Prior to the Asian Financial Crisis, which hit in July 1997, Indonesia was applying the managed floating system under which there was no incentive for economic players to carry out any hedging because the rupiah constantly depreciated by 5 percent every year. When the Bank of Indonesia decided to abandon the managed floating system and adopted a free float for the currency, economic players were completely unprepared and panicked.

The situation in 2008 was far different. The free floating system had been adopted in 1997 and was continued thereafter. This had taught economic agents to live in a world of exchange rate fluctuations. Thus, unlike ten years before, economic agents had now learned how to diversify their risks and were in the habit of doing so automatically. They diversified their portfolios, and hedged their assets. Therefore, even a sudden reversal of capital inflows would have had a relatively small impact compared to what had happened in 1997–98.

The third difference involved the economic policy responses. In 1998 the Bank of Indonesia responded to the crisis by implementing an extremely tight monetary policy by raising interest rates to a very high level. Deposit account interest rates reached 60 percent in the peak crisis period. The government also implemented a liquidity squeeze. As argued by Stiglitz and Greenwald (2003), when an economy goes into a deep recession due to contractionary devaluation, many firms will go into distress. In 1998 the response of the Central Bank by raising interest rates increased the rate of private default and thereby increased the probability of capital outflows.

In contrast, in 2008 the Bank of Indonesia responded to the crisis by lowering interest rates and ensuring that there was enough liquidity in the financial system. As a result, the rate of default was relatively low in 2008, thus minimizing any negative effect on NPLs owned by the banking sector.

Table 2.1 highlights the major differences in the economic policy responses to the two crises.

TABLE 2.1
Policy responses in 1997–98 and 2008–9

The 1997–98 crisis	The 2008–9 crisis
1. Monetary policy: extremely strict. The Bank of Indonesia increased interest rates to very high levels. Deposit account interest rates reached 60 percent in the peak crisis period. The government implemented a liquidity squeeze.	1. Monetary policy: the Bank of Indonesia's interest rate was reduced by 300 basis points from 9.5 percent to 6.5 percent. Liquidity was relaxed.
2. Fiscal Policy: the original budget surplus was reversed by permitting a large budget deficit.	2. Fiscal policy: a stimulus policy was implemented. The budget deficit was enlarged and taxes were lowered.
3. Banking Health: Prudential banking regulations were extremely weak. NPLs reached 27 percent. LDR became more than 100 percent.	3. Banking Health: Prudential banking regulations were relatively tight. NPL less than 4 percent, LDR 77 percent, CAR around 17 percent.
4. Response toward banking: closure of 16 banks, which then led to bank runs.	4. Response toward banking: deposit insurance increased from Rp100 million to Rp2 billion per account.
5. Policies focused on structural reform by carrying out economic liberalizations, getting rid of monopolies, and official licensing.	5. Safeguarded relatively open trade regime.
6. Exchange rate regime: managed float. Economic players not used to exchange rate risk changes and had not carried out hedging.	6. Exchange rate regime: flexible. Economic players had become used to exchange rate risk changes.

Source: Adopted from Basri and Rahardja 2010.

Indonesia's experience during the 1998 AFC made it clear that disruption and instability in the financial sector could lead to a severe crisis of confidence. At that time, Indonesia suffered from bank runs due to such a loss of confidence. Indonesia's experience showed that the cost of allowing such a situation to happen was much higher than the cost of preventing such a loss of confidence in advance. Based on this, in 2008, the Indonesian government strongly supported immediate efforts to restore confidence in the financial sector. The minister of finance Sri Mulyani Indrawati and the governor of the Bank of Indonesia Boediono coordinated their actions to deal with the crisis. In order to monitor the crisis situation in the financial sector, the government of Indonesia (GOI) and the Bank of Indonesia (BI) set up the Financial Sector Stability Committee. Unlike the crisis in 1998, in 2008 the government was more focused on anticipating the needs and actions of the financial sector and avoided destabilizing structural adjustments. The government and the Bank of Indonesia also adopted a financial sector safety net law. The focus of control centered on efforts to monitor developments in the financial sector (including banking, capital markets, the bond market, and insurance) as well as keeping close watch on the balance of payments. Several stress tests were carried out to determine weaknesses within the banking sector as well as to examine the balance sheets of publicly listed companies in order to anticipate the effect of any depreciation of the rupiah against the dollar on debt. There was concern at that time about balance sheets and risk premiums: if depreciation worsened the balance sheets of banks and corporations, then the premium risks for the state would also go up.

Key areas for action in 2008 included:

- Ensuring the existence of liquidity in the system. The GOI and the BI took measures to ensure liquidity.
- Maintaining confidence in the banking sector by providing guarantees. The GOI and BI increased the ceiling for the guarantee on deposits from Rp100 million to Rp2 billion per account. (The political economy of this decision will be discussed later in this chapter.)
- Mitigating the impact of the financial crisis on the poorest segments of society by providing a social safety net.
- Lowering the interest rate. Unlike 1998, the BI responded to the 2008 crisis by lowering interest rates. The fifty-basis-point cut announced in the second week of January 2009, and two more fifty-basis-point reductions in the first week of February and March 2009, were steps in the right direction. The BI cut the rate from 9.5 percent in November 2008 to 6.5 percent by the end of 2009. Nevertheless, as argued by Basri and Siregar (2009), despite the BI's low interest policy, the banking sector continued to face high borrowing costs due to the agency cost problem. Banks remained unwilling to lend to each other until early 2009.

Although the effectiveness of monetary policy was limited to boosting the economy, the low interest rate policy also succeeded in reducing the probability of default by Indonesian companies which in turn helped to minimize the impact of the financial crisis on the real economy.
- Countercyclical policy through fiscal expansion.[4] The minister of finance unveiled a stimulus package for 2009 worth around Rp73.3 trillion (or around US$6.4 billion) to boost the economy amid the threat of an economic downturn. The package contained three major categories, income tax cuts, waivers of tax and import duties, and subsidies and government expenditures. In line with Keynes (1936), the aim was to stimulate spending by households and corporations, with the result that around 60 percent of the Indonesian fiscal stimulus was allocated to cover reductions in income taxes.

The factors cited above make it clear that in 2008 Indonesia survived the GFC in large part due to good economic policies and economically appropriate measures. All the same Indonesia benefited as well from a measure of good luck due to the structure of Indonesia's exports. Basri and Rahardja (2010) argue that the structure of trade is very important in explaining the difference between the 1998 crisis and the 2008 crisis. The sharp decline in exports during both crises was not something experienced just by Indonesia. A similar decline was experienced by many countries, including China, Singapore, Malaysia, and Thailand. Figure 2.4 shows how these countries experienced contractions in export growth of around 30 percent in the fourth quarter of 2008 and the first quarter of 2009.

At the same time it is important to discuss why this relatively sharp drop in exports had such a limited effect on the Indonesian economy. I argue that the effect on the Indonesian economy was limited because the contribution of exports to the Indonesian economy was relatively small compared to countries like Singapore, Thailand, and Malaysia. The total share of Indonesian exports against GDP was never much more than 29 percent, a far smaller figure than that for Singapore (234 percent), Taiwan (74 percent), and Korea (45 percent).

For one thing, Indonesia has the largest population in Southeast Asia which, together with the lag effect from the relatively strong exports in the previous three years, provided strong growth in domestic consumption during the crisis period. This delay in the growth of export sectors, however, worked to the benefit of Indonesia in 2008–9, as the crisis affected Southeast Asia mainly through export contraction. In this sense, the Indonesian economy survived the GFC thanks to a good luck rather than deliberately planned economic policies noted above.

---

4. For detail of the analysis, see Basri and Siregar (2009).

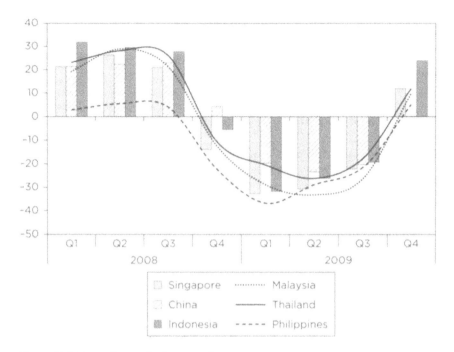

Figure 2.4 Quarterly growth of export values.
Source: Calculated from CEIC database (http://ceicdata.securities.com/cdmWeb).

Furthermore, Kimura (2005) indicates that Indonesia was far less integrated within East Asia's production networks. As a result, the effects of the global crisis on the Indonesian economy were also limited. Yet, clearly, this was not something that had been planned. Indonesia certainly would have preferred to have exports account for a larger share of its economy. But several supply side obstacles (Soesatro and Basri 2005; Basri and Patunru 2008) had already made Indonesia less competitive, thereby limiting the growth of its exports. As a result, as indicated by Basri and Patunru (2008), the Indonesian economy became more dependent on the nontradable sectors, and exports grew sluggishly. In other words, one thing that reduced the effects of the global crisis on the Indonesian economy was the good luck that came from the relatively small portion of its economy that was dependent on exports compared to its neighboring countries.

This "luck" was further reinforced by the continued strong growth of the Chinese economy. Continued Chinese growth drove the demand for commodities, and that demand remained high during the GFC. In addition, the good rainfall during 2008 also boosted agricultural production, including agricultural commodities (Basri and Hill 2011).

Thus it seems clear that Indonesia came out of the 2008 crisis so much better that it did from the crisis ten years earlier in large part due to good policies, but in several important economic areas it simply benefited from a measure of good luck. That being said, however, Indonesia's successful escape from the worst effects of the 2008 GFC had a great deal to do with the politics behind economic policymaking.

The Political Economy of Crisis Management

The most important difference between the 1998 and 2008 crisis for Indonesia lies in the areas of political economy. The political turmoil that led to the downfall of Soeharto drove the 1997 economic crisis to become far worse than it otherwise would have been, while ten years later, Indonesia enjoyed a large measure of confidence in the government.

From the beginning of the 1997–98 crisis, confidence in the Soeharto government fell quickly. Because of this there was much pressure to carry out political reforms, including widespread calls for democracy (Bresnan 2005; Schwarz 1999; Aswicahyono and Hill 2002). Political problems such as lack of transparency and loss of confidence in the government exacerbated the crisis (Fisher 1998). In the 1998 crisis, the IMF came on the scene only after the Indonesian government had tried several unsuccessful measures of its own to avoid such intervention. When first questioned about IMF involvement in the crisis, Minister of Finance Marie Muhammad stated that IMF assistance would be purely technical (Soesastro and Basri 1998), indicating the degree of doubt felt by the Indonesian president at that time. At first the government believed it would not need to accept IMF money and that consultation alone would be a sufficiently potent symbol to restore trust in the economy. On the other hand, some in Indonesia welcomed IMF involvement as an opportunity to get rid of crony capitalism, corruption, and collusion. Symbolic IMF gestures proved fruitless and consultation with the IMF turned into negotiation. The deal struck with the IMF on October 31, 1997, resulted in a US$43 billion loan, with US$38 billion from the IMF and US$5 billion from domestic sources. The government only released the main points of the agreement with no details. This first agreement had four main targets: (1) efforts to restore the soundness of the financial sector, (2) fiscal policy changes, (3) monetary policy (including exchange rate policy), and (4) structural adjustment policies. The structural policy package included tariff reductions, and flour, soybean, and garlic deregulation.

Then in early November the government liquidated sixteen banks. The first IMF package was showered with criticism. For example, Sachs (1997) questioned the tight monetary policy, asking why tightening the government budget was necessary when the crisis originated in the private sector. Sachs also wondered why the IMF didn't focus more on short-term policy, such as policies designed to improve the financial sector, rather than on long-term policies involving structural change.

In addition, it was apparent that the Soeharto government was reluctant to implement this package. Take the case of Bank Andromeda (one of the banks that was closed down by the Bank of Indonesia), which was reincarnated several weeks after its closure as Bank Alfa—a clear indication of just how unserious the Soeharto government was about economic reforms. In the eyes of the market, the Indonesian government appeared neither committed nor consistent about repairing the economy. Similarly with the deregulation of soybeans and garlic: though everything was clear on paper, many knew how things really stood, and the situation continued to worsen.

When the first IMF package was implemented, the exchange rate ranged between Rp3,000 and Rp4,000 to the U.S. dollar. There was still an opportunity to repair the economy, since rupiah exchange rates remained within a feasible range. But the ambiguous government attitude, compounded by news of Soeharto's ill health in December 1997, pushed the rupiah down still further. Finally, on January 15, 1998, a second Letter of Intent was signed between the Indonesian government and the IMF, the contents of which focused even more on structural changes than the first agreement had. In this letter the Indonesian government agreed to cancel government facilities and official supports for the national car and aircraft programs, and to revoke the monopoly enjoyed by the Clove Marketing Board.

The market was still skeptical about this agreement, and when the nomination of B. J. Habibie as the Golkar vice presidential candidate was announced, the rupiah plummeted to more than Rp17,000 to the U.S. dollar. This drop cannot be completely blamed on the political news, but must also be seen as reflecting reactions to the government's hesitation in actually implementing the IMF package.

The skepticism of the market proved to be justified, as the government issued statements that the monopoly of BULOG (Bureau of Logistics), a state-owned company which deals with food distribution and price control, would continue, as would the national car and aircraft programs. Soeharto even stated that the IMF agreement was at odds with the constitution—further proof of his government's reluctance to move seriously to implement IMF conditions. Economic and political analysis concluded that the government's argument and justification were simply rationalizations for the perpetuation of crony capitalism and favored interest groups. From an economic and political perspective, policymaking involves a process of bargaining among interest groups. President Soeharto's argument that the IMF package smacked of liberalism and thus conflicted with the constitution was thus only an effort to justify the maintenance of existing rent-seeking activities.

Indonesian economic history makes it hard to distinguish any one consistent vision or ideology guiding economic policy. Economic development during the 1970s was not primarily market oriented. The structure of exports, for example, did not typify industrialization in line with the concept of comparative advantage—a pure characteristic of free market principles. At that time, capital-intensive goods comprised a larger share of exports than did labor-intensive items and protective barriers were relatively high. Only after 1985 did the structural changes set in motion by deregulation lead to labor-intensive exports outstripping capital-intensive ones.

But this pattern did not persist for long. In practice, economic policies were reversed in the 1990s to strengthen crony capitalism and emphasize strategic industries. In other words, the ideological debate within Indonesian economic policymaking circles had not yet reached any kind of mature equilibrium. What actually happened was no more than a process of economic decision making that could be considered "rational" insofar as policy choices were most advantageous to the legitimacy of the New Order government. "Advantageous" here means choices with the lowest economic and political cost. In the 1970s, when oil dollars were available and the nationalist faction was ascendant, nonmarket and protectionist economic choices like those of a socialist, command economy were relatively "cheap" compared to promarket policies, because the government had to accommodate pressure from strong interest groups to garner political support. But by the mid-1980s, the price of oil had fallen below US$10 a barrel, thereby limiting funds available to the government. In addition, technocrats were gaining an increased political role. The result was to make the continuation of nonmarket policy choices relatively more expensive than promarket options with a more liberal bent.

The same phenomenon was evident during the 1998 crisis. Pressure from the IMF and demands for deregulation had made promarket policy choices "cheaper," and we can see the results in the IMF-mandated reforms of October and in the signed letter of intent. But subsequently the price of reform became intolerable, since it touched the interests of the rent-seeking crony capitalists and the self-proclaimed "nationalists." It was then that officials began to speak of the inappropriateness of the IMF package for the spirit of the Indonesian economy, the argument being that the IMF-proposed reforms would carry Indonesia in the direction of "liberalism."

The foregoing analysis makes it clear that Indonesian economic policy did not follow any single, unified ideological direction during the AFC. What happened was no more than a tug-of-war between interest groups mobilized around two different policy predispositions. When the role of the interventionist group increased in importance, the cost of promarket policy became too high, and policy choices moved toward government intervention. Then, during an era of crisis when the role of the promarket group gained the limelight, the cost of government intervention became too high and policy choices moved in a promarket direction. In short, there was nothing particularly profound or "philosophical" about Indonesia's framework for economic policy. What happened was only an effort to uphold the legitimacy of the regime using the most convenient ideological rationale. And this negotiation between competing policies gradually destroyed trust in government consistency. That situation held sway right up to the third IMF package, launched when the rupiah exchange rate stood at Rp8,000 to the U.S. dollar.

Soeharto stepped down on May 21, 1998, ushering in a sequence of political shifts that had a major impact on the implementation of the IMF package, leading in June 1998 to a fourth package. Unfortunately, the situation was by that time extremely serious, the exchange rate having risen above Rp10,000 to the U.S. dollar. At this level, some 70 percent of the companies listed on the JSX had to confront ratios of dollar debt to total assets of 50 percent or more (Soesastro and Basri 1998). Basri and Hill (2011) argue the crisis was mismanaged both domestically and internationally. By demanding extreme fiscal austerity and excessive policy conditionality while also displaying a lack of political sensitivity at key periods, the IMF "overmanaged" the crisis. President Soeharto, who began to lose full political control, was increasingly suspected of corruption, collusion, and nepotism with his family business partners.

Thus Indonesia faced a combination of negative forces—the loss of confidence in the government due to uncertainties about economic reforms; a drop in the core political support for Soeharto because of uncertainties about the political situation; and eventually an ever-greater need for the government to provide capital support as outflows from Indonesia escalated, until eventually making the economy collapse.

Conditions were quite different in the political economy when the GFC struck in 2008. Then, unlike the 1998 crisis, support for the government of President Susilo Bambang Yudhoyono (known colloquially as SBY) was relatively solid. Yudhoyono had been elected in 2004 as the fourth head of state after Soeharto's downfall. He was the first president elected by direct popular vote in the Indonesian history. In his presidency, he solved the conflict at Aceh and steered the economy successfully in spite of the shakiness of his power, which was based on a coalition of divergent political parties. As a result, the government was considered both legitimate and capable of controlling the situation. The general public also understood what had happened in the global economy. It was aware that the Lehman crisis was created in the United States. And as pointed out by Basri and Hill (2011), although corruption was still one of the key problems in the Yudhoyono administration, corruption charges were not directly aimed at the president. In addition, the government's economic team was also regarded as credible. Political support and a high level of confidence in the government's handling of the crisis can be seen in the news stories in the mass media. In 1998, although the media was not brave enough to criticize the government, the news that was reported was usually negative, to say the least. In the 2008–9 crisis, even though the press was very critical of the government, support for government policies in the handling of the economic crises was generally quite positive. For example, the largest newspaper in Indonesia published an article about the government-sponsored emergency financial safety net law,[5] and the media also reported that many economic analysts considered government policy to have been correct in dealing with the crisis by creating the financial safety net.[6] In short, unlike 1998, in the 2008 crisis the government was supported by the media, and this helped sustain public confidence in the economy.

One example of how effectively economic policy functioned during the 2008 crisis was the government's decision to help Century Bank. But, additionally, effective economic policy was not without periodic political clashes. The Financial System Stability Committee (KSSK) that was set up by the finance minister and the governor of BI was convinced that the collapse of Century Bank would have systemic risk for the entire economy, given the fragility of the economic situation at that time as seen by the fact that the rupiah had fallen by 30 percent. Furthermore, both the bond market and the capital market had fallen sharply, capital outflows were substantial, and there was a shrinking in interbank borrowing, as was noted above. In such a situation, the collapse of any major bank or financial institute could generate panic. Thus, even though Century Bank was relatively small and its interconnectedness to financial markets was low, the government, and in particular the BI, was concerned about the psychological impacts of even small market players. The BI's concerns were based on Indonesia's experiences during the 1997–98 crisis, when the closure of sixteen banks—which only controlled 2.3 percent of total banking assets—turned out to have had a very negative effect throughout the financial market, including large cash withdrawals by customers in other banks. This in turn rippled from the banks into other sectors.

In addition, to safeguard market confidence, as noted above, both the government and the BI implemented deposit guarantees. However, unlike other countries such as Singapore, Australia, and Malaysia, the Indonesian commitments were far short of blanket guarantees. Vice President Jusuf Kalla declined such blanket guarantees for fear of creating a problem of moral hazard. The government and the BI decided only to implement deposit guarantees to a maximum of Rp2 billion. Had there been any instability in the banking sector in Indonesia, this might have generated a migration of banking funds from Indonesia to countries where blanket guarantees were in force. Systemic risk arose because the guarantee was limited. Ultimately worries about such a risk contributed to the decision by the minister of finance and the governor of the Bank of Indonesia to provide a bailout to Century Bank in November 2008.

However the decision to bail out Century Bank generated considerable divisions among the parties. These started when the president- and vice

---

5. See *Kompas*, October 16, 2008, available at http://otomotif.kompas.com/read/2008/10/16/16551346/Atasi.Krisis.Pemerintah.Keluarkan.Perppu.JPSK.

6. See *Kompas*, October 17, 2008, available at http://nasional.kompas.com/read/2008/10/17/1513493/Ekonom:.Langkah.Pemerintah.Tangani.Krisis.Tepat; see also *Koran Tempo*, November 23, 2008.

president-elect (SBY and Boediono) started to form their cabinet several months before the actual bailout (i.e., in August 2009). At that time, some political parties, especially the Golkar Party, led by businessman Aburizal Bakrie, charged that steps taken by Finance Minister Indrawati and Vice President Boediono to bail out Century were wrong because they were based on incorrect information and that the decision would cause the state to suffer financial losses. In addition, politicians suspected that the funds to save Century Bank were being diverted to the coffers of Yudhoyono's Democrat Party and to election campaign funds for President SBY and Boediono.

The Golkar Party, even though it no longer dominated parliament, already had more than forty years as the ruling party in politics in Indonesia. It therefore usually is in the best position to take over parliament. This bailout issue was then grabbed by the opposition as a way to take over the government. Golkar, the Prosperous Justice Party (PKS), and the United Development Party (PPP), all of whom opposed the bailout of Century Bank, were also government coalition parties. Several political analysts attributed this opposition to their effort to strengthen their bargaining positions in terms of seats in the Yudhoyono-Boediono cabinet (Haris 2010). Subsequently, media and several political analysts considered this move to be aimed at creating pressure for Boediono to step down. They saw this move as being orchestrated by coordinating minister Hatta Rajasa (who was also chairman of the National Mandate Party) and Aburizal Bakrie of the Golkar Party. Both allegedly were scheming to become vice president if Boediono were to be impeached.[7] Bakrie and Rajasa denied these charges.

Apart from this, politicians who opposed the bailout of Century charged that the efforts to save it were politically rather than economically motivated and would simply help the owners of this bank because of their funding support for the campaign to elect President Yudhoyono and Vice President Boediono. Yet, when Indrawati and Boediono presented this bailout plan in October 2008, almost all parties, including the Golkar Party, supported it. Ironically, several months later when the new cabinet was being selected by President Yudhoyono after he had won the 2009 general election for the second term, and Sri Mulyani Indrawati had been reappointed as the minister of finance, political parties changed their tune, opposed Indrawati's reappointment, and began criticizing the policies being taken. Parliament called for Indrawati to resign. This despite the fact that ministers are responsible to the president, and only the president could remove them. The ensuing political pressure continued when the cabinet was being appointed during October 2009, when almost every day protesters demanded the resignation of both Sri Mulyani and Boediono. Yet the Anti-Corruption Commission (KPK)

---

7. See *Rakyat Merdeka*, December 17, 2009, available at http://www.rakyatmerdeka.co.id/news/2009/12/17/85258/Hatta-Rajasa-&-Ical-Bakal-Gigit-Jari; Metro TV News.com, February 5, 2010; *Radar Lampung*, February 6, 2010; *Indo Pos*, February 7, 2010.

never found any evidence of corruption or flow of funds from Century to pay for the Yudhoyono-Boediono campaign. The KPK even stated that there was no proof of corruption and graft in the Century bailout.[8]

In May 2010, Sri Mulyani Indrawati resigned as minister of finance because she was appointed to a position as managing director at the World Bank. Many analysts, including Hill (2010), have connected Indrawati's resignation with the political pressure related to the bailout for Century Bank in 2008. Indrawati's resignation is difficult to separate from the political tensions between her and Aburizal Bakrie, chairman of the Golkar Party. In an interview that was published in the *Wall Street Journal* (Asian edition),[9] Indrawati stated that those tensions between herself and Bakrie could be traced to 2008 when she opposed the extension of the closure of Indonesia's stock exchange amid a run on companies controlled by Bakrie. In addition, Indrawati wanted to examine the tax records of three coal mines belonging to the Bakrie family—Bumi Resources, Arutmin Indonesia, and Kaltim Prima Coal—with a total of Rp2.1 trillion in tax arrears. Bakrie denied that there were any personal problems between himself and Indrawati and that the tax case had no direct connection with him since it was a company problem and he preferred that it be settled through the courts. Indrawati's resignation was then considered by many as potentially jeopardizing the process of economic reform in Indonesia if it led to a restrengthening of the business and political strength of the Bakrie family. Indrawati was considered by many to have been the champion of reform and main pillar of stability for Indonesian macroeconomics.

What was interesting was that after Indrawati resigned as minister of finance, practically all of the protests against her and Boediono stopped suddenly, and the issue of Century was no longer a dominant issue in the media. One can see that the Century issue was more about political pressure for Sri Mulyani Indrawati to leave the cabinet than about government economic policies.

Despite this particular case of Century Bank, political support and confidence in government policy direction was strong and helped the government manage the GFC. In fact, the political tension between government and political parties really began after the GFC had largely passed, a point I will discuss below.

Key Challenges

The economic crisis in 1997 was followed by political changes that provided challenges and opportunities for the Indonesian people to undertake

---

8. *Jakarta Post*, December 9, 2010.
9. *Wall Street Journal* (Asian edition), December 10, 2009.

structural reforms that had often been neglected by past administrations. The crisis had revealed the fundamental weaknesses in Indonesia's institutional design as shown by its failure to regulate and facilitate economic activities. The institutional inability to promote policy consistency and to curb rampant moral hazard and other opportunistic behavior was the primary factor behind the collapse of the financial system in Indonesia at that time. Furthermore, unlike other Asian countries that also suffered from the economic crisis in 1997, the collapse of the financial system in Indonesia was soon followed by the collapse of its political regime.

Ten years later, institutions had been strengthened, authority was restored to government, and political life was significantly democratized. In regard to integrity, the independent status of the Supreme Audit Institution and the establishment of the KPK provided good institutional fundamentals, although they still needed to be strengthened.

Still, Indonesia needs further reforms before it can be considered substantively democratic. In addition, despite the continuation of macroeconomic stabilization, there is a growing concern about the actual implementation of reform. In the past few years, Indonesians have grumbled about how ineffective the government policies have been. Many good policy recommendations failed to be implemented simply because of ineffective institutions.

Looking forward, Indonesia has a number of hurdles it must still clear. Five of these seem particularly noteworthy: (1) demography, (2) government-party relations, (3) corruption, (4) decentralization, and (5) infrastructure development.

The demographic issue in Indonesia holds both promise and problems. Ten years after the AFC, Indonesia started to enjoy relatively high economic growth. The Indonesian economy has been entering an expansion period thanks to a demographic dividend. Until 2025, Indonesia will have a lower elderly dependency ratio than most Asian countries. This will enable Indonesia to close the gap faster with developed countries. In addition, data show that the new middle class (spending $4 per capita per day or $1,400 per year) grew from 5.7 percent (2003) to 18.2 percent (2010), or approximately 30 million people. As one can easily imagine, this new middle class will lead to a spike in demand for durable consumer goods such as motorcycles, cars, and homes. This will enable consumption to continue to be strong in Indonesia into the future. Furthermore, Indonesia has both energy and commodities whose global demand will continue to rise into the future.

However, if demographic projections are continued through 2050, the Indonesian picture is not so sunny. Mason, Lee, and Russo (2002) show that Indonesia will face an aging population by 2050. This means that after 2020–30, the aging population will continue to rise quickly. After that, the potential for high growth will decline. Therefore, Indonesia must take advantage of the current demographic bonus to ensure a period of expansion. Indonesia needs growth above 8 percent for the period leading to 2030.

To do so, Indonesia must invest in quality education and health care. Furthermore, Hausman and Rodrik (2003) emphasize the importance of new product innovations. Woo and Hong (2010) have stated that Indonesia must emphasize the role of a science-based economy. Indonesia tried in the past to leapfrog ahead, but failed, largely because the country attempted to enter high-technology sectors by producing airplanes. What the country really needs are advances in agriculture (for example, new varieties, including agro biotechnology), new approaches to water and environmental management, as well as mechanization, improvements in animal husbandry, and infrastructure that supports agriculture.

Unfortunately, the country's export products and markets remain primitive with very little advancement in these fields. An analysis of export growth between 1990 and 2008 shows that the major increases in Indonesian exports involved the same products sold to the same markets. Basically, there was no substantial introduction of new products for new markets (Basri and Rahardja 2011).

A second big problem concerns government-party relations. In the current Indonesian political system, both the president and parliament are directly elected by the people. The president's party has thus far not enjoyed a majority of the parliament. As a result, the role of political parties is becoming all the more dominant, so much so that the cabinet must have "rainbow coalitions." A president has to be realistic enough to see that his cabinet reflects political equality. He cannot simply appoint a cabinet of technocrats.

After the Century Bank debacle, the Joint Secretariat of Coalition Parties (JSCP) was set up by the president for a better coordination between the government and the parliament. JSCP is an association of the coalition parties that support the government: the Democrat Party, the Golkar Party, the National Mandate Party (PAN), the National Awakening Party (PKB), the Prosperous Justice Party (PKS) and the United Development Party (PPP). The chairman of the Secretariat is none other than Aburizal Bakrie.

However, the JSCP is not a monolithic, coherent organization. It might in fact weaken the bargaining position of any coalition party in negotiations with the government. In addition, the role of the media and civil society seems stronger today, and criticism from officials and NGOs is now continually directed at the JSCP. A free press and open information put pressure on the JSCP to not take a position or make a decision that only profits the interest of a particular entrepreneur. Nevertheless, if a common interest develops among the parties, then the JSCP will have a strong bargaining position with the government. Reform measures that implicate many private interests of politicians are likely to be challenged and become more difficult to implement. Good governance could well be the victim, and the JSCP could be an impediment to efficient national management of the economy.

Still a third future difficulty is corruption. Eradication of corruption will take a very long time to complete, but progress has been made. Basri and Hill

(2011) pointed out that many corruption cases have resulted in legislators and senior officials being fined and imprisoned as a result of actions initiated by the KPK. Thanks to the separation of powers among the executive, legislative, and judiciary branches, the judiciary system has gained significantly in influence and power. Unlike during the Soeharto era, the judiciary system is now autonomous. Corruption, however, also remains pervasive in the courts, creating uncertainty in both the legal system and in the business climate (Butt 2009).

Corruption is also still pervasive at the local level. However LPEM-FEUI (2006) argue that there has been a decline in harassment visits and bribes in some regions. The study reports that such a decline suggests that the ongoing anticorruption campaign might be having an impact at the local level.[10] Furthermore, competition between regions might also be reducing the costs of doing business in the regions. Unfortunately, national agencies such as Tax and Customs do not face similar competitive pressures, with the result that inefficiency and rent seeking in national institutions continue to be major obstacles to good governance and economic growth (Basri and Patunru 2006). While democracy has brought greater accountability and transparency, it has not directly reduced corruption (Basri and Hill 2011)

A fourth problem that Indonesia has to deal with is the issue of decentralization. Decentralization, for example, has created incompatibilities between centralized government policies and the role of local government. Basri and Hill (2011) argue that there is a principal-agent problem in which the agent (local government) need not obey the principal (central government) because the local government is now directly elected by its own constituencies. As a result, the central government is less able to enforce rewards and penalties on the local government. Although the amount transferred by the central government to the regions is quite significant, it does not necessarily improve the infrastructure or lower poverty incidence in the regions. Basri and Hill (2011) also point out that despite the many benefits of decentralization, the system is still a work in progress and that, owing to local capture, the political marketplace is not yet able to weed out poorly performing subnational governments.

Fifth, and finally, Indonesia's long-term economic development must confront the problem of infrastructure. In an archipelago such as Indonesia, transaction costs, especially in logistics, are relatively high compared with continental countries. This has been well documented by various research reports. The prices of commodities such as sugar, flour, and cement in eastern Indonesia (Nabire) are three times higher than in Java. This large price difference reflects the high costs of shipping and supply due to the poor

---

10. It is also possible, however, that local government officials have had sufficient experience with the new environment such that the corruption becomes more institutionalized.

distribution system (Basri and Rahardja 2010). For instance, inefficiencies at Indonesia's numerous harbors make transport costs more expensive, especially for export-oriented and import-based industries (Patunru et al. 2007). The cost of transporting goods from Warsaw to Hamburg, a distance of 750 kilometers, is only half the cost of sending goods from Makassar to Enrekang in Sulawesi, a distance of only 240 kilometers (USAID 2004). The cost of logistics in Indonesia amounts to 14 percent of total production costs, far higher than, say, Japan where it is only 5 percent (LPEM-FEUI 2005).

Trade logistics—the capacity to integrate domestic economies and connect domestic economies with international markets through the dispatch of goods—is an extremely important factor in realizing a country's economic growth potential. However, Indonesia should equally hesitate to commit fully to regional production networks because businesses might suffer immediate losses and benefits remain elusive. The right choice is to maintain openness along with a better integration of the domestic market.

Compared with the Asian financial crisis of 1997–98, the impact of the 2008 global crisis on the Indonesian economy was relatively limited in spite of the fact that the effects of the latter crisis were much larger than the 1998 crisis in terms of magnitude. I have argued that at least four differences divide the two crises: the origin of the crisis, the exchange rate regime, policy responses, and the overall situation of the political economy. First, in 1998 the economic origins of the crisis were both domestic and external, while the 2008 crisis was almost entirely external. Second, prior to the 1997–98 crisis, Indonesia applied the fixed exchange rate system but replaced it with the free floating system after the crisis. Third, economic policy responses were different. Beside the change in the exchange rate system policy mentioned above, the Indonesian government took extremely tight monetary and fiscal policies in 1998 but more relaxed policies in 2008. In 2008, the government also took more flexible and prudential policy concerning banking and trade than in 1998.

In addition to these good policies, I have argued that "good luck" in trade conditions played an important role in the 2008 crisis. Because of the delay of Indonesia's integration into the global and regional networks of production, its trade dependence was lower than other Southeast Asian counties. In consequence, impacts through trade shrinkage of the global financial crisis were much smaller for Indonesia.

While highlighting all those factors, I have focused primarily on the role of Indonesia's domestic political economy during these two crises. The political turmoil leading to the downfall of the Soeharto regime drove the 1998 crisis to become far worse while a larger measure of confidence Indonesians had in their government helped it handle the 2008 crisis in a calm and positive manner. Lest I leave an unduly optimistic picture of Indonesia's political and economic future, however, I have closed with an assessment of several major hurdles that Indonesia must deal with in the coming years: demography, government-party relations, corruption, decentralization, and infrastructure.

Ten years after the 1998 crisis, Indonesia is not immune from another financial crisis, but the ability of Indonesia to manage the economic crisis in 2008 at least shows that the country and its governing elites have learned a number of lessons from what went wrong in 1998. The 1998 crisis helped the country to survive the 2008 crisis. Problems remain for Indonesia's longer-term economic development, but the country is clearly in a far stronger position to move forward than it was a decade ago.

Unraveling the Enigma of East Asian Economic Resiliency

The Case of Taiwan
Yun-han Chu

For my generation of central bankers, the rapid growth of cross-border financial transactions and international capital flows is one of the most important economic developments we have experienced over the past 30 years. . . . Large and sudden inflows of foreign capital lead to exchange rate overshooting, loss of trade competitiveness, domestic credit booms and asset price bubbles, all of which can elevate systemic risks and create financial fragility. It is little wonder that the subject of capital account liberalisation remains highly contentious.
—Perng Fai-nan, governor of the Central Bank of the Republic of China, in *The Banker*, August 30, 2010

The case of Taiwan offers the key to a systematic understanding of the elements defining the economic resiliency of East Asia, not just individual East Asian economies but the regional economy as a whole. Some political economists have suggested that the reason why most East Asian economies managed to cope with the Global Financial Crisis (GFC) of 2008–9 more effectively than other regions lies in the transformation of their domestic institutions and policies after the 1997–98 financial crisis. Taiwan's experiences will show that this view offers only a partial, if not simplistic, explanation.

First of all, not all the postcrisis institutional changes and policy adjustments turned out to be conducive to strengthening financial stability and economic adaptability. Some East Asian economies had been pressured by the United States and the IMF to adopt wide-ranging neoliberal prescriptions—fiscal austerity, deregulation, liberalization, and privatization—after the 1997–98 crisis. The results of these domestic adjustments along the neoliberal line were mixed. In some areas, they strengthened a country's economic vitality as well as the economy's overall international competitiveness. In other areas, they actually made these societies more vulnerable to external financial shocks. So we have to unbundle the experiences of the postcrisis reform and transformation and their varying economic consequences very carefully.

Second, the Taiwan case also demonstrates that many elements underwriting its economic resilience had deeper roots. They have been fostered by a set of entrenched institutional arrangements and established policy orientations over the long run. Many factors that had accounted for Taiwan's outstanding shock-absorbing capability during the 1997–98 regional crisis were still in place and remained crucial when the government was called on to cope with the much more severe GFC of 2008–9. So it was not the case that Taiwan upgraded its economic capability to withstand the external shocks by undoing its past policies and institutional arrangements after the regional crisis. On the contrary, Taiwan managed to retain the bulk of these long-running sources of economic resilience despite the tremendous external pressures and relentless efforts by neoliberal advocates to dismantle these "outdated" policy practices in the name of financial liberalization and internationalization during the decade-long interval between the two crises.

Third, the two crises and the circumstances under which they occurred were very different in character. So we have to look for some new elements that had not been of much relevance in accounting for Taiwan's superior capacity in coping with external economic shocks in the first case but became quite important this time around. In particular, I argue in this chapter that part of the reason why most East Asian economies managed to cope with the GFC of 2008–9 more effectively than other regions lies in the transformation of not just their respective domestic institutions but the region's overall geoeconomic configurations, ideological milieu, and institutional arrangements.

Most noticeably, over the decade-long interval, all major East Asian economies have worked together to strengthen the resiliency of the regional economy as a whole. In so doing, they collectively created an enabling environment that in turn strengthened their individual capability to cope with the 2008–9 GFC. This is in stark contrast with the regional environment of the late 1990s, which had been truly unforgiving, as all East Asian economies suffered from the downward spiral of competitive currency devaluation and financial contagion, victimized by the predatory tactics of the hedge funds and speculative investors, leaving them at the mercy of international lending agencies that were based outside the region and insensitive to their needs of focusing on essential policies and protecting the most vulnerable. In a nutshell, in the aftermath of the regional financial crisis, East Asian countries concluded that *they must all hang together, or assuredly they shall all hang separately.*

Taiwan in Comparative Perspective

It has become received wisdom that Taiwan was one of the few Asian economies that had emerged from the 1997–98 East Asian financial crisis relatively unscathed. The damage to the island economy was mild by regional standards. The growth momentum was slackened but not disrupted. In 1998, Taiwan's economic growth rate was dragged down to 3.5 percent, and the island suffered a 9.4 percent drop in exports, the worst performance since 1983. But this record was by far more admirable than the rest of the region. In contrast, South Korea's economic growth rate had dropped to –5.7 percent in 1998. More important, Taiwan registered a successful recovery from the shock. The island's economic growth rate increased to 6.0 percent and 5.8 percent in 1999 and 2000 respectively.

Taiwan's economic resilience was put under the most strenuous test during the 2008–9 GFC. Like all other export-oriented East Asian economies, Taiwan's dependence on trade through global production networks and export-led growth strategies left the island highly vulnerable to the sharp contraction of demand from the North American and European economies. Taiwan's economy slumped into recession in the second half of 2008. Its real GDP, following a growth rate of 6.0 percent in 2007, registered a meager 0.7 percent growth in 2008 and contracted 1.8 percent in 2009 primarily due to a record 19 percent drop in the total exports. This amounted to the worst economic contraction since 1951.

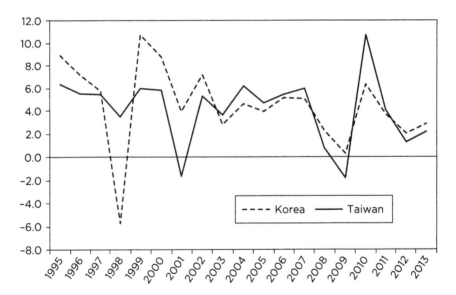

Figure 3.1 GDP growth rate of Taiwan and Korea, 1995–2013.

Source: IMF 2013.

Much like many other emerging economies in the region, Taiwan turned out to be more resilient than the rest of the world and emerged poised to lead the global economic recovery. By the first quarter of 2010, not only had Taiwan exited the recession, it recovered the entire loss in output that had occurred during the so-called Great Recession. Taiwan registered an astonishing 13.11 percent (annualized) growth in the first quarter of 2010 and a remarkable 10.76 percent for the year (Directorate General of Budget 2014). This makes Taiwan's recovery superior to that of South Korea, which managed to bounce back at a 6.3 percent growth in 2010 (IMF 2013).

More impressive is the resilience of Taiwan's banking sector, which weathered the GFC relatively unscathed despite the wider economy suffering its worst recession on record. Its conservative, consolidated balance sheet position ensured that it was well placed to navigate the turbulent global economy, which remained under the threat of a double-dip recession and the debt crisis of some weaker European economies (Fast Market Research 2010). So the island's shock-absorbing capability turned out to be once more quite respectable, albeit no longer as outstanding as it had been.

In a way, the story behind Taiwan's economic rebound after the 2008–9 GFC is not significantly different from other vibrant East Asian economies. Most economists identify at least five common elements contributing to the stronger than expected economic rebound of the East Asia economies.

First, the region was relatively well insulated from the global financial meltdown, as it had inherited relatively healthy financial systems prior to the subprime loan crisis and built up a huge foreign reserve as a hedge against a replay of the 1997 regional financial crisis. Asset bubbles were either not alarmingly threatening, or they had been contained well before the current crisis, as in the case of China. Second, the degree of foreign participation in their banking sector was comparatively much lower. On average, American and European banks accounted for about 10 percent of the total net worth of the East Asian banking sector while the figure for Latin America is 35 percent and for Eastern Europe 49 percent (Hishikawa 2003).

Third, most East Asian economies have shown considerable resilience, thanks in part to high household savings during good times on which they could fall back during lean times without having to make drastic cutbacks in private consumption. Fourth, the macroeconomic fundamentals were quite healthy in most East Asian economies. Except for Japan, most governments were not heavily indebted, and they still enjoyed spare fiscal capacity to borrow and spend. So most East Asian governments and central banks responded to the GFC with decisive and firm fiscal and monetary actions. Last, but not least, the region's resilience should be attributed to the rapid turnaround in the region's larger, less export-dependent economies. Although adversely affected, China and India were not in recession. Their huge domestic sectors helped cushion the impact as exports constituted just 35 percent of China's GDP and 22 percent of India's. In particular, China has emerged as the region's new locomotive of growth, as during the later 2000s it rapidly became the top export market for its neighboring economies, including Japan, South Korea, and Taiwan.

In addition to these common elements, Taiwan's shock-absorbing capability was also enhanced by a set of structural characteristics that are quite exceptional in comparison with other East Asian emerging economies. First, Taiwan's economic vitality is built on a more decentralized industrial structure. Small- and medium-sized enterprises (SMEs) still account for more than 75 percent of the total employed workforce. SMEs in Taiwan have formed comprehensive horizontal and vertical industrial networks through cooperation and division of labor among themselves and with large enterprises, creating an efficient and flexible industrial clustering. Over the last decade, both South Korea and Taiwan have achieved levels of technological capabilities that rival those of the advanced countries. In South Korea these capabilities are concentrated in a small number of relatively larger firms, *chaebol*. In contrast, they are spread across a large number of relatively smaller firms in Taiwan (Etemad and Lee 2001).

Second, Taiwan was more insulated from the external financial shock because the island's economic growth has been financed almost exclusively by domestic savings. A combination of high savings rate and higher efficiency in capital utilization has allowed Taiwan to generate excess savings and become one of the major sources of foreign investment in East Asia. The gross value of the foreign assets owned by Taiwan's private sector has consistently exceeded its external liabilities.

The island has become more vulnerable to the sudden movement of foreign portfolio investment as the share of the stocks owned by foreign institutional investors of the total market values of Taiwan Stock Exchange has steadily increased from less than 4 percent in 1977 to 25 percent in 2007. This, however, is still lower than the average level of 35 percent observed in South Korea before the 2008–9 crisis. In addition, Taiwan's Central Bank always stands ready to cope with any sudden massive outflow of speculative capital as it is empowered to introduce capital controls and has accumulated an exceptionally large foreign reserve, the world's third largest after China and Japan.

Third, most of Taiwan's big enterprises maintain a sound corporate financing structure that allows them to withstand any credit crunch during economic downturns. The debt-to-equity ratios of Taiwanese enterprises large and small are among the lowest in the world. The average ratio of large enterprises is about 100 percent, while the ratio of SMEs is around 150 percent. This is because Taiwan's financial sector is uniquely characterized by the coexistence of a conservative banking sector and a dynamic capital market. As a result, high-growth firms raise capital mainly through rights issues and initial public offerings, instead of bank loans.

A full understanding of Taiwan's exceptional economic resilience, however, requires more than just an economic analysis. What is also required is an analysis of the political underpinnings of these economic structures, macroeconomic policies, development strategies, and regulatory regimes. In this chapter, I argue that elements of the island's economic resilience have been fostered by a set of entrenched institutional arrangements and established policy orientations. In the final analysis, these have been embedded in Taiwan's particular security environment, political structure, and internal power configuration (Chu 1999).

The Historical Roots of Taiwan's Economic Resilience

In Taiwan, most elements of economic resilience had been nurtured during the four-decade-long reign of a hegemonic party. Under the political dominance of the Kuomintang (KMT), the state's development strategy and policy guidelines for macroeconomic management, more than anything else, had fostered a decentralized industrial structure, the module of domestically financed growth, and the dualistic nature of its financial sector. Under the KMT's long political tenure, the state's long-standing policy guideline for macroeconomic management was characterized by its overriding concern over monetary and financial stability as well as fiscal conservatism. Also, its established pattern of industrial targeting was in part designed to address the deficiency of the SMEs in financing and R&D. In response to the challenge of globalization, the state had chosen a sequence of financial liberalization that gave priority to deregulating the domestic capital market over internationalization, that is, foreign participation. Despite the trend toward an integrated global financial market, the state had been keen to safeguard its ability to set monetary targets by preventing the internationalization of the local currency and controlling the volatility of cross-border movement of short-term capital. Amid the trend of politicization of economic policymaking that came with the island's democratization, the state had managed to protect the autonomy of the monetary authority and contain the erosive effect of "money politics" on the health of the banking sector through institutional adjustments.

These established policy guidelines and long-term development strategy have taken root, as they were embedded in a set of institutional arrangements and entrenched ideological orientations. These prevailing structures regulated the power relations among different economic agencies within the overall state apparatus and constrained the scope of political participation by business, labor, and other interest groups in economic decision making. These entrenched ideological orientations, which reflected the collective memories and learning that the incumbent elite had acquired over a long period of time, set the parameters for policy discourse and deliberation within the state apparatus. At a more fundamental level, the incumbent elite inherited, established, maintained, and adjusted these institutional arrangements and policy orientations to cope with the changing security environment and to meet the twin challenge of globalization and democratization.

These institutional arrangements and ideological orientations are not immutable, but they have had strong staying power. These prevailing structures were kept largely intact despite the rapid indigenization of the KMT's power structure during the 1990s, because they helped sustain the incumbent elite's steering power over the national economy as well as its ability to deliver desirable socioeconomic outcomes. They were steadily weakened but not abandoned even after the KMT lost its grip on power in 2000, because the political risk of dismantling these prevailing structures to the Democratic Progressive Party (DPP) outweighed its expected utility.

Another longstanding institutional characteristic of Taiwan's economic decision making involves the privileged status of the Central Bank of China (CBC) within the overall state apparatus. The CBC is formally a part of the cabinet but in practice, the governor of CBC is always handpicked by the president rather than the premier. The bank occupies a unique position in the state apparatus because it is at the same time a part of the economic bureaucracy and a part of the national security apparatus, which falls under the exclusive purview of the president. As a result, the CBC has long occupied the commanding heights of the state economic bureaucracy. The governor of the CBC is always considered the most senior economic minister. The CBC has been staffed by elite technocrats, who enjoyed a prestige unmatched by any other economic ministry. The governor of the CBC is not subject to cabinet reshuffling, as the position is protected by a four year renewable term. In fact, most governors stayed on for long periods, much longer than the cabinet.

The CBC is more than just a monetary authority. It is also entrusted with an extensive regulatory authority over the banking sector and capital market. According to the Central Bank Act, the first two operational objectives of the bank are to (1) promote financial stability and (2) guide sound banking operations. The act also empowers the CBC with a variety of monetary policy instruments, including targeted prudential measures, and authorizes the CBC to maintain an orderly foreign exchange market and conduct targeted financial inspections. During the 1980s and 1990s, the CBC's supervisory and investigative authority overlapped with the Ministry of Finance (Yen 1998). The Ministry of Finance traditionally played second fiddle to the CBC as far as banking regulation is concerned. Many finance ministers were themselves former deputy governors of the CBC. The bank was able to overrule the Finance Ministry, which deals with the constituencies in the financial sector more directly, over the sequence and timetable of financial deregulation and internationalization. The CBC also traditionally served as a check on the expansionist tendency of the planning technocrats by setting limits on the use of credit policy in industrial targeting. The steering power of the CBC over the banking sector was further buttressed by an array of state-owned banks that virtually monopolized the first-tier banking, that is commercial banks that accounted for more than two-third of the total outstanding loans and discounts before the opening up of the banking section in 1992. Until 1992, private participation was limited to the second-tier money banks consisting of regional savings and loans, city credit cooperative associations, and credit departments of farmers' and fishermen's associations at the grassroots level. During the authoritarian years, the governor of CBC usually had more say than the premier in the appointment of senior bank officials (Chen 1998, 64). As a result, the CBC was able to pull a number of disciplinary strings controlling the lending policy of state-owned banks, through the rediscount window, financial inspection, and appointment power.

This arrangement was originally designed to prevent a replay of the disastrous hyperinflation and currency crisis of 1947–48, which had contributed to the defeat of the KMT leadership by the Communist regime in 1949 (Chen and Haggard 1987). The CBC was entrusted with the authority to protect the island's economic stability in the name of national security and for the political security of the KMT regime.[1] The CBC became the institutional embodiment of the incumbent elite's overriding concern for monetary and financial stability. During the 1970s, the two oil shocks and the crisis of diplomatic derecognition, which functionally replaced the fading memory of the civil war, reinforced the political rational for a privileged and autonomous CBC.

Under the steering authority of the CBC and the Finance Ministry, for almost four decades the Nationalist government has invariably maintained a positive real interest rate, minimum public-sector foreign debt, small fiscal deficit, a fixed exchange rate pegged to the U.S. dollar, restrictions on the convertibility of the New Taiwan dollar (NTD), a rigorous regulatory regime over financial institutions, and a conservative ethos that permeated the entire banking sector. State-owned banks almost always demanded collateral for their loans. Most state-owned banks have maintained their capital/asset ratio above 12 percent, much higher than the International Bank of Settlement's 8 percent requirement. Also, Taiwan's reserve requirement has been among the highest in the world.

Furthermore, to contain the encroachment of political cronyism, the CBC and Ministry of Finance imposed on local financial institutions a strictly limited scope of deposit/loan operations and geographical span and a requirement to redeposit their surplus reserves in designated state-owned banks. Also the CBC and Finance Ministry stood ready to close down insolvent local financial institutions through forced mergers and acquisitions. With these controlling measures, the CBC and Finance Ministry were able to keep the nonperforming loan ratio of the overall banking system at a sustainable level.

---

1. Between 1949 and 1961, as a temporary measure, the Bank of Taiwan actually performed the function of the central bank. After 1961, the Central Bank of China was reinstated as the Nationalist government retreated from its goal of "recovering the mainland."

Also the KMT elite stuck to the principle of fiscal conservatism for more than three decades. The central government regularly generated fiscal surplus year after year during much of the 1970s and 1980s and the outstanding public debt was kept at a minimum. This rigid fiscal discipline was steadily loosened during the 1990s as the KMT elite came under competitive electoral pressure and yielded to the pent-up demand for the expansion of social entitlement programs. However, the KMT still put a legal cap on the central government's borrowing power. Under the Public Debt Law, the central government's new borrowing each year was kept to no more than 15 percent of the annual budget and was specifically earmarked for fixed capital investment (rather than current consumption).[2] Also the total outstanding public debt is not allowed to exceed 40 percent of the current GDP. Thus, on the eve of the first power handover of 2000, the central government's total outstanding debt was still less than 24 percent of the GDP and well below the legal limit. In addition, the KMT handed the DPP a fiscal reserve of about NTD$280 billion, the equivalent of 2.7 percent of the GDP in 2000, a reserve accumulated over the previous decade (Chen 2007).

The deregulation of the financial sector of the late 1980s and early 1990s was prompted by economic exigency. A series of ominous economic signs, the mushrooming of underground financial institutions, a bubble in the real estate and stock market, and a rapid deterioration of private sector investment, compelled the government to take decisive measures to overhaul the anachronistic financial sector. Since 1989, the government has introduced a series of measure to deregulate the banking sector. The fixed interest rate scheme was abolished. New licenses for commercial banks were issued to qualified private investors. Regional savings and loans were upgraded to medium business banks. Restrictions on the operation of foreign banks were relaxed. However, the privatization plan for state-owned commercial banks, the centerpiece of the banking reform, was held off until mid-1998. By the time the KMT handed over power to the DPP in 2000, the government still effectively controlled eight of the top ten commercial banks, which accounted for more than 60 percent of the total net worth of the entire banking sector.

Another long-standing policy objective adamantly pursued by the CBC was minimizing the island's vulnerability to external shocks. The CBC consciously built up Taiwan's shock-absorbing capacity to withstand diplomatic shocks, escalation of military tension in the Taiwan Strait, or any conceivable economic exigency. During the 1980s and 1990s, the government had built up not only a huge foreign reserve but also an exceptionally large oil and food reserve. A big cushion was justified as Taiwan would have to survive on the basis of self-help. Since 1978, Taiwan was no longer a member of IMF and

---

2. However, under extraordinary circumstances, such as wars, major natural disasters, and epidemics, the government is allowed to introduce special budget bills that are exempted from this provision.

World Bank. It could not count on an international rescue package in a time of currency crisis, nor bilateral emergency loans from its security partners. With dwindling diplomatic recognition, official foreign reserves have almost become a benchmark measure of Taiwan's self-confidence.

This mentality explained why the CBC was very hesitant to remove foreign exchange controls despite a soaring trade surplus since the early 1980s. It put off foreign currency deregulation until mid-1987, when the US trade representative started putting the undervalued NTD in the political spotlight, when the current account surplus reached a staggering 19 percent of GNP, and when the accumulation of the trade surplus and domestic savings started to wreck havoc on the real estate and stock markets. In July 1987, the CBC finally decided to remove most restrictions on private holdings of foreign exchange and to nurture the growth of a foreign exchange spot market and later futures market. However, the CBC still applied a panoply of monitoring schemes and continued to intervene heavily to prevent excessive short-term fluctuation. The restrictions on the futures market were lessened only gradually. The foreign exchange derivative positions of all domestic banks were still under strict supervision by the CBC. More important, the CBC resolved to prevent an internationalization of the local currency. The Central Bank continued to prohibit domestic banks from offering local currency accounts for their customers abroad and restricted the outbound movement of the NTD. In essence, the CBC was keen in curbing the growth of an offshore foreign exchange market of the NTD. In so doing, the CBC was able to retain its position as the sole market maker of NTD. Furthermore, the foreign borrowings for Taiwan's banks were traditionally low, because the CBC restricted banks' holding/owing foreign assets/liabilities. Despite the flooding of cheap yen into the international money market during much of the 1990s, Taiwan's domestic banks did not engage in heavy short-term foreign borrowing, or the so-called "carry trade," nor did they participate actively in the global financial markets.

Bowing to U.S. pressure, Taiwan's stock market was opened to foreign institutional investors around early 1991. Under the influence of the CBC, the Finance Ministry imposed strict investment caps on foreign investors. Initially, each foreign institutional investor could invest up to US$50 million and the total quota was set at US$2.5 billion, which represented only about 2 percent of total market capitalization. Each institution was allowed to buy up to 5 percent of a single company and total foreign ownership of a company was limited to 10 percent. Also to prevent rapid capital inflows and block off the entrance of hedge funds, the qualified foreign institutional investor (QFII) system was established in 1992. Only reputable and well-established foreign banks, insurance companies, and funds management companies could apply to be QFIIs. Further the Central Bank introduced reporting procedures regarding foreign portfolio investment to track the activities of QFIIs. As part of the down payment during the WTO negotiation with the United States, the Finance Ministry was compelled to raise the investment cap step by step. On the eve of 2007–8 financial crisis, the capital ceiling for individual foreign institutional investors was raised to US$600 million. The cap on ownership of individual foreign institutional investors in any listed company was set at 15 percent and no more than 30 percent for all foreign investors.

The island's economic resilience was put to a rigorous test when the PRC employed a saber-rattling strategy in the summer of 1995 and March 1996. During the first missile crisis, the stock market lost about a third of its total value. And the local currency dived by 9 percent. The CBC intervened heavily to support the NTD. The Finance Ministry was instructed to set up a stock market stabilization fund. All government-run investment funds and retirement funds were required to buy in. Managing the missile crisis, as it turned out, functioned as an unintended rehearsal for the East Asian financial shock a year later.

At the zenith of the one-party authoritarian rule, the KMT relied on a proven formula for maintaining the entrenched political dominance of the mainlander elite, the émigré group that fled to the island after it was defeated by the Chinese communists on the mainland in 1949, at the national level and for controlling a limited popular electoral process implemented at local level. The development of Korean-styled conglomerates had not been possible for the first three decades of the postwar era. The mainlander elite discouraged concentration of wealth for both political and ideological reasons. The myriad of SMEs that flourished around the state-sponsored export-oriented industrialization strategy enabled the KMT to broaden its social base since the emerging industrial structure addressed both the growth and equity issues with a high degree of effectiveness. More important, the monopoly or near-monopoly of the state-owned enterprises (SOEs) had preempted private participation in the financial sector, public utility sector, and most of the capital-intensive industries from the very beginning.

For the first four decades of the postwar era, business was politically weak, because big businesses had depended on the state for essential economic resources. The private sector lacked the organizational and ideological endowments for autonomous collective actions. More important, the state had been relatively strong vis-à-vis private business, because the state was endowed with a centralized political authority, an oversized military and administrative apparatus, and a huge array of SOEs. The political ascent of the business elite was not fully actualized until the end of the 1980s. With the death of the last strong man, Chiang Ching-kuo, in 1988, the cohesion of the party's central leadership deteriorated and the pace of democratization increased. The personnel turnovers, the split within the party leadership, and the new democratic institutions provided the business community with a strategic opening for gaining more recognition in the party power structure.

The emerging political clout of the business elite weakened the autonomy of the state economic bureaucracy, and economic officials were compelled to embrace a probusiness outlook. During Lee Teng-hui's tenure, some private capitalists, in particular, the chairmen of the three largest business organizations, were recruited to serve on the KMT's Central Standing Committee, the formal decision-making organ of the party. Furthermore, the trend of liberalization and privatization in the 1990s created a raft of rent-seeking opportunities for big business groups to seize the economic resources that were carved out of state-dominated sectors. Financial service liberalization, telecommunication deregulation, and state-enterprise privatization were among the most profitable areas. In other words, the KMT government in the 1990s had to keep a precarious balance between taking into account distributional considerations and committing to developmental goals.

Nevertheless, during the tenure of Lee Teng-hui, the influence of special business interests over the economic policymaking still had its clear limits. The KMT central leadership still maintained the commanding heights on economic decision making while entrusting technocrats with sufficient policy autonomy. The KMT, being an oversized, richly endowed, and autocratically governed political machine, still provided the institutional foundation for the undisrupted political dominance of its national leadership over both local factions and big business. While catering to the demands of distributional coalitions, the KMT managed to insulate a development-oriented policy network from power peddling.

The economic planning technocrats were encouraged by the overall success of the past development strategy, which relied more on SMEs than big business as agents of industrial upgrading and technological innovation. The industrial upgrading strategy of the 1980s and 1990s did not discriminate against SMEs. On the contrary, the state economic bureaucracy was keen to address the deficiencies of SMEs: through public-funded R&D support and technological transfer, the provision of venture capital, and a lending guideline that stipulates that all medium business banks must extend at least 60 percent of their outstanding loans to SMEs. The planning technocrats were still able to channel resources into targeted sectors and incubated high-tech start-ups. The CBC and Finance Ministry economic technocrats still had a decisive say in devising the priority and timetable of deregulation and liberalization as well as the design of the new regulatory schemes and mechanisms (Chu 2007a).

In a nutshell, as long was there was no alternative power pact in sight, the KMT elite could effectively use its unabated staying power and incontestable ability to make long-term policy commitments and construct an unequal partnership with the business elite, under which the party-state elite set the limits on influence-buying and policy contestation.

Domestic Transformation during the DPP Era

Most of the adjustments in development strategies, policy priorities, and institutional arrangement that took place during the ten-year interval between the two crises were propelled less by the lessons learned from the 1997–98 regional financial crisis than by the political earthquake brought about by the historical power rotation after the 2000 presidential race.

Since Taiwan emerged from the 1997–98 regional financial crisis largely unscathed, there was no compelling reason or the political urge to change course. On the contrary, the credibility of some long-standing policy objectives and institutional arrangements, in particular the independence of the Central Bank and its core mission of preserving the country's monetary and financial stability, as well as the due diligence of the regulatory agencies supervising the banking and insurance sector, had been reinforced by their proven track record.

However, the terms of the public discourse in Taiwan were nevertheless dominated by those favoring the neoliberal policy prescriptions being vigorously promoted by the IMF and the United States and being followed by many East Asian governments in the aftermath of the financial crisis. On Taiwan, many foreign financial institutions, business leaders, and neoliberal economists criticized the technocrats' complacency and urged the government to introduce sweeping liberalization and deregulation measures. They warned that Taiwan could miss the boat as other East Asian tigers turned the crisis into an opportunity for wide-ranging reform.

Some of the neoliberal agenda was adopted by the incoming DPP elite, which had long ridiculed the KMT's past practice as party-state capitalism. However, the Chen Shui-bian administration selectively adopted some of these prescriptions less because of its intellectual rationale, and more because they fit his political strategy to dismantle the institutionalized ties between the KMT and the business community. In some cases, reform measures were adopted also because they provided Chen's family and closest allies with new opportunities for collecting political rents.

The DPP had been highly critical of the KMT's impregnable control of state corporatist arrangements and condemned the collusive relations between state and the business elite. The DPP as a long-time opposition party did not have any preexisting institutionalized channels of interaction with business interests. Nevertheless, as their political standing steadily rose, prominent individual DPP politicians cultivated their personal ties with business donors, and increasingly with like-minded business tycoons.

Under Lee Teng-hui's leadership, KMT-owned enterprises were transformed into holding investment companies, which were heavily involved in joint ventures with domestic business groups having large-scale investments in land speculation, public construction, mass transportation, banking, and insurance. Once Chen Shui-bian took over the presidency, his administration was determined to tear apart this interlocking network and replace KMT-centered institutionalized collusion with a president-centered spoils system.

Elected as a minority president, Chen had a deep sense of political insecurity and a survival instinct that led him to grab as many resources as possible to consolidate his rule.[3] The personnel reshuffle of the top positions in the partially privatized state enterprises and state-controlled banking and financial institutions became an important route for the DPP government to break up KMT influence and extract political rents (Chu 2005). Chen handpicked pro-DPP figures to replace senior technocrats in almost every state-controlled enterprise, including steel, electricity, public utilities, mass media, petroleum, airlines, sugar and salt refining, as well as telecommunications. The privatization of SOEs and banks provided another conduit for the DPP government to cajole private capitalists into the new alliance based on an exchange of favors.

In the name of consolidating Taiwan's banking sector, which had been deemed too saturated with small players and lacking the necessary scale and know-how to compete internationally, the Financial Holding Company Law was enacted in 2001. This opened the door for cross-market business and spawned a series of planned mergers and acquisitions. For effective supervision over the new financial holding companies, a new cabinet-level independent supervisory agency, the Financial Supervisory Commission, was created in 2004 to unify several previously separate regulatory authorities with respective responsibility over securities markets, banking, and insurance.

In theory, the chairman of the new commission is protected with a fixed term and should be free of political influence. But in practice Chen appointed his political protégé to head this new supervisory body. Later on, it turned out that Chen and his wife were deeply enmeshed in the deals of financial consolidation. Most of the emerging private financial groups were the natural allies of the DPP, as they had been overshadowed by the state-owned banks under the KMT tenure for too long. Unfortunately, Chen was more interested in soliciting wealth for his personal coffer than cultivating new business allies for the DPP. As a later judicial investigation revealed, in exchange for huge kickbacks, the first lady was involved in virtually every dubious merger and acquisition deal that involved the shares of state-owned banks or enterprises being transferred to a handful of business tycoons who had thronged into the president's residence for private audiences with her. .

What Chen Shui-bian's wife could deliver was pressure on the minister of finance to offer her favorite business donors the controlling shares of state-own banks at below-market price and instructions to the chairman of the Financial Supervisory Commission to expedite the review and approval process over these merger and acquisition deals. These dubious deals enriched a few of the island's wealthiest families and enabled them to build up their financial conglomerates at a faster speed. However, the overall health of Taiwan's

---

3. Chen Shui-bian was elected in March 2000 with only 39 percent of the popular vote. The KMT did not lose power as the consequence of its record of economic management or its developmentalist philosophy. The KMT lost its grip on power primarily because the KMT was split into two camps, and the 2000 president election became a three-way race.

financial sector remained largely intact because these privately owned financial holding companies were still under the vigilant daily supervision of the various bureaucratic arms of the Financial Supervisory Commission, including the Bureau of Monetary Affairs, the Bureau of Securities and Futures, the Bureau of Insurance, and the Bureau of Examination, all of them staffed by senior career civil servants and beyond the immediate reach of the president and his wife.

The scandal of bribe taking broke out in the early part of Chen's second term and ignited a devastating political storm. Chen Shui-bian's political credibility never recovered. The KMT-controlled parliament put many of the planned auctions of the shares of the state-owned banks on hold. The chairman of the Financial Holding Company was removed from office over corruption charges. The DPP-initiated financial reform was abruptly truncated. So when the KMT returned to power in 2008, the government still owned three of the top ten commercial banks and maintained effective control over another four. The combined net worth of these seven state-owned or state-controlled big banks still accounted for more than 43 percent of the total network of the entire commercial bank sector (see table 3.1).

After the 2000 regime turnover, the institutional foundations of the developmental state were significantly damaged and the underlying logic of economic decision making was overturned. First of all, the tradition of a strong state ended, as Chen Shui-bian won the 2000 presidential election with only 39.3 percent of the popular vote, followed by James Soong's 36.8 percent, and the KMT's Lien Chan's 23.1 percent. In addition, because Chen faced a KMT-dominated parliament, the syndrome of "divided government" not only crippled the DPP government throughout its eight-year reign but also undermined the coherence of the state-centered economic policy network (Wu 2007).

First, institutionalized channels of interest intermediation no long functioned as they had. The KMT-sanctioned elite business groups were no longer recognized as the privileged spokesmen of the business community as new pro-DPP organizations were promoted by the Chen administration. Encompassing corporatist organizations became fragmented and the state-sanctioned policy consultation mechanisms frayed across the board (Lee and Chu 2008). Established institutional arrangements for industrial planning and their developmentalist orientation were gradually eroded by the political confusion and uncertainty of severe and protracted political gridlock and partisan bickering.

Second, the morale of the economic bureaucracy was severely damaged. The Chen Shui-bian administration had an innate distrust toward the established bureaucracy, which they believed had long been the KMT's stronghold. President Chen and his premier openly criticized the "old bureaucrats" for being numb, arrogant buck passers. Many senior technocrats opted for early retirement due to their disagreements with DPP political appointees

TABLE 3.1
Taiwan's top fifteen banks by net worth (as of June 2010)

Ranking		Ownership	Net worth (million of NTD)	Share of total
1	Bank Of Taiwan	State-owned	231,753	11.7%
2	Mega International Commercial Bank	State-controlled	151,199	7.6%
3	China Development Industrial Bank	State-controlled	129,200	6.5%
4	Chinatrust Commercial Bank	Private	120,956	6.1%
5	Taiwan Cooperative Bank	State-owned	112,612	5.7%
6	Land Bank Of Taiwan	State-owned	101,898	5.1%
7	Cathay United Bank	Private	90,993	4.6%
8	First Commercial Bank	State-controlled	90,192	4.5%
9	Hua Nan Commercial, Ltd.	State-controlled	84,158	4.2%
10	Chang Hwa Commercial Bank	State-controlled	83,675	4.2%
11	Taipei Fubon Commercial Bank Co., Ltd.	Private	82,640	4.2%
12	Citibank Taiwan Limited	Private	78,129	3.9%
13	The Shanghai Commercial Savings Bank, Ltd.	Private	72,452	3.6%
14	Bank Sinopac Company Limited	Private	63,355	3.2%
15	Taishin International Bank	Private	56,535	2.8%
Total of top 15 banks			1,549,747	78.0%
Total of state-owned and state-controlled banks			855,487	43.1%
Total of all 23 banks			1,986,849	

Source: Financial Supervisory Commission 2011.

over controversial policies. Politically motivated appointees took over strategic positions that were supposed to be reserved for nonpartisan technocrats in the developmental state apparatus. This only suppressed the morale of the economic bureaucracy even more. The rupture between the new regime and the established bureaucracy triggered the inevitable demise of the developmental state apparatus, which became increasingly unable to map out a comprehensive development strategy and implement it consistently and with longer-term vision.

Furthermore, the antagonism between the DPP government and the business community, especially the high-tech industry (the backbone of Taiwan's competitiveness), grew considerably as the latter's pleas for normalizing trade relations with Beijing, lifting bans on direct transportation, relaxing rigid entry controls for mainland Chinese visitors, and abolishing the 40 percent cap on Taiwanese investments in China fell on the deaf ears of the DPP government. In the end, the DPP government's ideological bias against closer economic ties with mainland China accelerated capital flight and an exodus of high-tech firms and talented professionals. The Taiwan stock market was hit by waves of strategic decapitalization as more and more listed companies chose to scale down their registered capital. Foreign multinationals also opted out and scaled down their operations. Most alarming was that Taiwan was becoming increasingly marginalized in the region. Just as China emerged as the principal architect of the region's multilateral institutions with the launch of the AEASN-China Free Trade Agreement and the inauguration of the East Asia Summit, Taiwan became the only economy in the region without a normal economic relationship with the mainland (Chu 2007b).

Between 2000 and 2008, Taiwan's economy registered many disappointing years with sluggish growth and a slew of poor statistics. Among the East Asian tigers, Taiwan trailed Singapore, Hong Kong, and South Korea on all essential economic indicators. Taiwan's Stock Exchange fell off the world's "top fifteen" list in terms of size of market capitalization and off the world's "top ten" list in terms of trading volume. By the end of 2005, the dollar-denominated per capita income of South Korea for the first time overtook that of Taiwan.

The independence of the Central Bank became the only institutional pillar supporting Taiwan's economic resiliency that remained largely intact during the DPP era. Perng Fai-nan was appointed by Lee Teng-hui to head the Central Bank in 1998, and Perng became the only KMT-affiliated senior economic official that was retained by Chen Shui-bian for the entire eight-year DPP reign. Lee Teng-hui, who still exerted considerable influence behind the scenes during Chen Shui-bian's first term, was a strong advocate for retaining Perng.[4] Lee convinced Chen that the reputation of Governor Perng and his elite staff had become the embodiment of Taiwan's monetary and financial stability, and it was simply too risky for the DPP government to replace him.[5] Furthermore, Chen Shui-bian's agenda of Taiwan independence and the ensuing escalation of political tension in the Taiwan Strait made the Central Bank's role as the guardian of Taiwan's shock-absorbing capacity even more compelling.

---

4. For some insider analyses of Lee Teng-hui's influence over cabinet reshuffling during Chen's first term, see a special report published in *China Times*, available at http://forums.chinatimes.com/report/abian2000/personel/89040204.htm, and a report published by a pro-DPP online news media, available at http://big5.southcn.com/gate/big5/www.southcn.com/news/hktwma/shizheng/200201230503.htm.

5. *Global Finance* magazine rated Perng Fai-nan as the world's best central banker in 2005. In 2009, he became the world's only central banker winning the "A" rating for five consecutive years.

Nevertheless, the Central Bank was pressured to soften its opposition to opening up Taiwan's capital market even wider for foreign investors. The DPP government was keen to attract foreign institutional investors to fill the void created by the exodus of domestic investors who precipitated a torrential capital flight from Taiwan to mainland China and overseas tax havens after the DPP took office. Following the removal of the investment cap and the lifting of most restrictions on foreign ownership of listed stocks between 2000 and 2001, the QFII system was finally abolished in October 2003. Foreign institutional investors are exempted from investment caps and faced no quota restrictions.

However policymakers at the Central Bank were fully aware of the fact that unfettered financial liberalization and unbridled international capital flows could have put Taiwan's financial stability at risk. To deal with the potential hazard, the Central Bank applied a full array of monitoring mechanisms tracking the activities of foreign investors and it did not hesitate to introduce temporary capital controls whenever the situation required. It also continued to use all possible measures to tame the volatility in the currency market and steadily built up Taiwan's foreign reserve to hedge against the sudden exodus of speculative capital and other conceivable economic exigencies. To alert the political leaders and mass media about the risk of financial instability, in 2006 the Central Bank introduced an early warning system. It issued Financial Stability Indicators every six months, and starting in June 2008 the system was upgraded to a fully fledged, semiannual Financial Stability Report.

In summary, most of the postcrisis institutional adjustment and policy changes taking place in Taiwan did not bode well for the island's economic future. The island's economic competitiveness as well as its growth momentum was significantly undermined by the political shock and ensuing political turmoil brought about by the 2000 power rotation. The resultant realignment of government-business relations also substantially hampered the autonomy of the state economic bureaucracy and diminished its developmentalist orientation as well as its capability. Nevertheless, the legacy of an independent, resourceful, and proactive central bank, whose reputation and credibility had been strengthened by its record of steering the island safely through the regional financial crisis as well as cross-strait crises, was preserved. The legacy of prudential financial regulation was also largely kept intact with the concentration of regulatory authority in a new cabinet-level supervisory commission, despite the meddling of Chen Shui-bian and his family during the privatization of state-owned banks.

Coping with the 2008–9 Global Financial Crisis

In many ways, Taiwan was more vulnerable to external economic shock in 2008 than during the previous financial crisis. First of all, the state has lost much its steering capability and its coherent ideological orientation. Over the previous decade, the government has failed to foster the growth of new export sectors. This made the island's exports excessively concentrated in electronics and information technology products. Also the government has not incubated Taiwan's IT producers into world-class brand-name companies. The lion's share of these exports suffered from commoditization pressures with their profit margin shrinking over time. Second, after years of sluggish economic growth and a series of sweeping tax cuts under the DPP rule, the government's fiscal health steadily deteriorated. By the end of 2008, the central government's tax revenue constituted less than 14 percent of the GDP, and the Finance Ministry had to raise additional income equivalent to 9 percent of the GDP through borrowing, collecting fees and fines, and selling off state-owned assets in order to balance the books. Third, the SOEs that had been an important policy instrument for industrial upgrading during the 1980s no longer played a significant economic role. Under the prevailing ethos of neoliberal reform of the 1990s, the bulk of SOEs in the manufacturing sector were privatized. The share of SOEs to the gross fixed capital formation has declined from more than 30 percent around early 1980s to less then 10 percent since 1999. Last, Taiwan's capital market was on longer insulated from external financial shock. The foreign institutional investors accounted for almost a quarter of the total market capitalization.

However, comparatively speaking there were still enough cushions in place. Taiwan's Central Bank still held enough reserve capacity to cope with economic turbulence. The ratio of nonperforming loans of the entire banking sector was kept below 1 percent of the total outstanding loans. Taiwan's banking sector was also largely free of shadow banking activities featuring financial engineering, leveraged trading in derivatives, and off-balance-sheet transactions. The overall foreign exposure of Taiwan's financial sector in terms of its asset and liability position was still quite low. On the eve of the Lehman Brothers collapse, Global Insight in its authoritative Banking Risk Rating Service ranked Taiwan as one of the emerging economies with the lowest risk, second only to Saudi Arabia, in terms of capital/asset ratio, liquidity, and risk/liability management (*Taipei Commercial Times* 2008). In a way, the backwardness of Taiwan's banking sector turned out to be its source of resiliency during the global financial meltdown.

Third, with the return of the KMT and its statist mentality, Ma Yingjeou and his economic team were not hesitant in applying a strong dose of extraordinary measures. The Central Bank slashed the discount rate by 2.375 percentage points in seven cuts from September 2008 to March 2009 and extensively expanded the scope of its repo facility operations to provide financial institutions with enough liquidity. Most noticeably, the government offered a blanket guarantee for all deposits in insured financial institutions by their full amount until the end of 2009. This extraordinary measure not only effectively stabilized the market and restored the confidence of depositors but also attracted a lot of capital inflow as wealthy Taiwanese were anxious to extricate their savings from foreign stock markets, overseas asset management accounts, and troubled American banks.

The government also set up a Special Task Force on Facilitating Enterprises to Obtain Operational Funds to help small and medium enterprises (SMEs) to weather the economic storm. In particular, the government cajoled the banks to undertake extraordinary leniency, such as adjusting the rate of mortgage loans and corporate loans monthly instead of quarterly or semiannually without additional renewal fees, automatically extending commercial loans by six months for corporations that faced financial difficulties but still operated normally and paid loan interest as scheduled, and temporarily loosening collateral requirements on margin loans to ease selling pressure from margin calls.

At the height of the global financial meltdown the government issued a temporary ban on short-selling of one hundred fifty listed shares below the previous day's closing price, suspended borrowed and margin stocks from short-selling, and narrowed the percentage fall limits of share prices and instructed state-owned financial institutions and the four government-managed funds to purchase blue-ribbon stocks to stabilize the stock market.

The KMT government also expedited the passage of a special budget through the KMT-controlled parliament to inject NTD$500 billion into the economy through expanding investment in public works, offering every citizen a consumption voucher valued at NTD$3,600, and launching short-term employment programs. The KMT government also introduced a controversial tax cut by dramatically lowering the ceiling of the estate and gift tax rates from 50 percent to 10 percent in order to attract capital remitted abroad.

Most significantly, the KMT government restored business confidence with its conciliatory approach to cross-strait relations. With a clearly-defined objective of seeking closer economic ties and greater political mutual trust across the strait, the new approach consists of five components. First, the Taiwan government proceeded with a series of high-level dialogues with the mainland Chinese government. Second, it engaged in a rapid movement toward normalization of trade and investment relationship. Third, it proposed the acceleration as well as the deepening of economic integration and cooperation. Fourth, it searched for a modus vivendi aimed at avoiding zero-sum competition and head-on collision in the international arena. Finally, it proposed intensification of bilateral social contacts and cultural exchanges. The momentum of cross-strait rapprochement culminated in the signing a cross-strait Economic Cooperation Framework Agreement (ECFA) in June 2010.

It was politically safe for the KMT to reverse the DPP's confrontational approach, because the end of Chen Shui-bian's political tenure saw a marked shift in public opinion in favor of a normalized economic relationship with mainland China. The majority of Taiwanese citizens have come to recognize and accept the new reality: China has emerged as the second largest consumer market in the world, the largest source of tourist spending in the region (surpassing Japan), and an increasingly important source of foreign direct investment. It was no longer only business owners of export-oriented sectors or people with transportable skills and investment capital who favored closer economic ties with the Chinese mainland leaving most people working in inward-looking sectors on the island to suffer from outbound capital flow, brain drain, and industrial hollowing out. Increasingly, in the eyes of Taiwan's general public, mainland China was no longer just a manufacturing platform or the most popular destination for Taiwan's outbound investment but potentially an important source of tourist spending, investment capital, and consumer demand. The list of potential beneficiaries has grown significantly to include sectors such as real estate, medical services, finance, hotel and catering, fishery and farming, mass media, entertainment, and culture. This amounts to a large-scale realignment of Taiwan's social forces around the issue of cross-strait economic integration, with the KMT firmly occupying the centralist ground. Thus Ma Ying-jeou's electoral victory was an expression of a broad-based social coalition that includes many potential beneficiaries who look forward to a political rapprochement across the Taiwan Strait.

A massive amount of private investment capital started flowing back to Taiwan beginning with the second half of 2008, giving the local stock market and property market a strong and timely lift. Taiwan popped up again on the radar screen of foreign multinational firms that suddenly found new possibilities for incorporating the island into their Greater China strategy. The island's service industry benefited significantly with the arrival of mainland Chinese tourists, whose numbers started out with 0.62 million in 2009 and jumped to 1.68 million in 2010. The intensified economic ties also enhanced the spillover effect of China's RMB4 trillion economic stimulus, which generated some timely buying which helped to save Taiwan's LCD monitor and major appliances producers which had been on the brink of bankruptcy. The signing of the ECFA enabled the island to unleash its full potential in exploiting the expanding business opportunity in mainland China, which has been emerging as the new buyer of last resort. The signing of the ECFA is also expected to remove the major political obstacle preventing Taiwan from negotiating free trade agreements with ASEAN countries and other trading partners. In a nutshell, the rapprochement in cross-strait relation has brought Taiwan considerable "peace dividends" just as the island was battered by the worst economic contraction in its history as a result of the slackening global demand for its high-tech exports.

To sustain the island's growth momentum over the long run, the government is taking a two-prong strategy—to promote emerging industries to address the twin challenges of overconcentration (in semiconductors, notebook computers, LCD monitors, and handsets) and the diminishing profit margin that Taiwan's IT industry is facing and to channel investment capital and human resources into some key rising industries to diversify the island's overall structure of export. For the former, the government identified three forward-looking IT-related industries—cloud computing, smart electric vehicles, and green buildings—in all of which Taiwan is poised to become a significant global player. For the later the government is placing its best hope on six rising industries—high-end agriculture, biotechnology, green energy, travel and tourism, medical care, and cultural and creative enterprises.[6] Among the six, the last three (which are all service-related) industries have the greater potential for generating employment opportunities. The government has implemented the Taiwan's Service Industry Development Plan since 2009 to help the local service industries to upgrade their international competitiveness and their share in the global services trade. The success of the plan requires not just directing more R&D investment toward the service sector and a timely adjustment in the structure of Taiwan's higher education but also a stable and cooperative relationship with mainland China, whose urban consumers constitute the most promising overseas market for Taiwan's services trade.

The Transformation of the Region

An important reason for Taiwan's ability to cope with the 2008–9 GFC was a more enabling regional environment. The ideological milieu and the cooperative institutional arrangements in East Asia changed markedly between the two crises.

In the aftermath of the 1997–98 regional financial crisis, East Asian countries were motivated to seek mutual assistance through bilateral or regional arrangements. As a result, major East Asian economies have expanded their bilateral currency swap mechanisms and increased the share of their bilateral trade that is settled in local currencies rather than U.S. dollars. Also, under the auspices of ASEAN Plus Three (APT), two regional financial cooperation initiatives, the Chiang Mai Initiative Multilateralization (CMIM) and the Asian Bond Markets Initiative (ABMI), are well underway. The CMIM established a framework of mutual assistance among APT countries to address each others' short-term liquidity difficulties. The ABMI initiative was designed to promote the local currency bond markets and enhance the recycling of regional savings toward developing regional bond markets.

At a special meeting held in Phuket in February 2009, APT members agreed to increase the size of the CMIM by 50 percent from US$80 billion to US$120 billion, and to develop a more robust and effective surveillance

---

6. These strategies are developed and implemented by the newly established Executive Yuan Invest in Taiwan Task Force headed by the deputy premier. Please refer to http://invest taiwan.nat.gov.tw/library/main_eng_general.jsp.

mechanism to support the operations of the CMIM. In their May 2009 meeting in Bali the finance ministers of APT reached agreement on all the main components of the CMIM, including the individual country's contribution, borrowing accessibility, and the surveillance mechanism, and decided to implement the scheme before the end of the year. At the Bali meeting, the finance ministers also reiterated their pledge for expanding the role and function of Asian Development Bank (ADB). A planned capital enhancement will augment ADB's capital base to an appropriate level. A Credit Guarantee and Investment Mechanism (CGIM) will be established as a trust fund of the ADB to support the issuance of local currency-denominated corporate bond in our region (Chu 2009).

While there is not yet a formal mechanism for coordinating their exchange rate policy, Asian central bankers have strengthened the regional network for dialogues and consultation through such mechanisms as the Executives' Meeting of East Asia-Pacific Central Banks and the annual meetings of the South East Asian Central Banks (SEACEN) Board of Governors.[7] With growing consensus over the need to harness the volatility of currency markets, an implicit regional monetary mechanism has gradually merged with renminbi and yen functioning as the twin anchorage for a synchronized and orderly currency adjustment. As a consequence, Asian economies have collectively created a more enabling environment that in turn strengthened their individual capability to cope with the GFC.

Also, regional economic integration has accelerated with the launch of ASEAN-China Free Trade Agreement in 1999 and the inauguration of East Asia Summit in 2005. Strong growth in China and India has provided additional impetus for intraregional trade. Over the last decade, world trade has been growing approximately 10 percent annually while intra-Asian trade has been galloping at 20 percent. All East Asian economies have reorientated their trade so that their dependence on the U.S. and European market was partially lessened and substituted by the growing consumption power of emerging economies. In particular, China's formidable spare fiscal capacity for antirecession expansion and its insistence on a slow and orderly appreciation of its currency has injected the region with an important stabilizing force during the Great Recession of 2008–9.

Last but not the least, the political backlash against IMF-imposed austerity measures and its underlying ideological bias has precipitated a growing awakening among the East Asian policy thinkers (Crotty and Lee 2005). They have become more vocal about the flaws and biases in the U.S.-dominated multilateral institutions of global economic governance and the U.S.

---

7. The Executives' Meeting of East Asia-Pacific Central Banks is composed of central banks and monetary authorities of Australia, Mainland China, Hong Kong SAR, Indonesia, Japan, Korea, Malaysia, New Zealand, Philippines, Singapore, and Thailand. The SEACEN Board of Governors is composed of sixteen central banks and monetary authorities from East Asia.

policymakers' complacency in prolonging the unsustainable global economic imbalance. Asian political leaders have come to question the policy credibility of the IMF, whose invasive policy prescriptions were blamed in the region for having exacerbated the 1997–98 meltdown. East Asia as a whole has become more confident of its own philosophy and policy preference in maintaining the balance between state and market, between economic openness and social protection, and between competition and equity. More and more Asian leaders, perhaps with the exception of Japan, also began to question the legitimacy and effectiveness of the G8, the IMF, and the World Bank, since their rules of representation and decision-making no longer reflected the weights and new responsibilities of emerging economic powers from East Asia and other regions. The proposal for the creation of a regional monetary fund and a vibrant regional bond market sent a strong signal to the world that the region was ready to walk out of the intellectual tutelage of the IMF and United States.

While most East Asian economies, with the exception of China, were pressured to lift restrictions on their capital accounts over the last decade, policymakers in the region also became more aware of what kind of hazards that speculative capital flows might bring. East Asian policymakers have learned from each other, especially from countries that suffered the most from the 1997–98 financial crisis (such as Thailand and South Korea) and countries that had emerged from the previous financial crisis relatively unscathed (such as China and Taiwan) (Singh 2000). Increasingly it has become a shared understanding among East Asian policymakers that surging short-term capital inflows can overheat an economy, speed up growth of bank credit and money supply, and create speculative bubbles in stock markets and the real estate sector. Once the bubbles burst, sudden financial reversals result in a breakdown in the financial system.

Over the last decade most developing countries in the region have insured themselves through managing exchange rates and building huge currency reserves. In this way they hope they have protected themselves against the tempests of currency speculation and never again will need the emergency lending windows of the IMF. More and more East Asian policymakers recognized the imperative to build up their risk management capability in an increasingly riskier environment brought about by U.S.-engineered financial globalization and U.S.-indulged global economic imbalance. Many of them have equipped themselves with monitoring mechanisms for tracking the cross-border movement of the speculative capital and scrutinizing the balance-sheet of their banking institutions and large corporations, in particular the foreign liquidity of large banks (McCauley and Zukunft 2008). All these policy measures and institutional capacity had saved Taiwan from a financial crisis in 1997–98.

Although Taiwan is not a full member of this emerging East Asian community, it is fully embedded in this more enabling regional environment. So Taiwan has benefited indirectly but substantially from the region's newly installed stabilizing mechanisms. The fact that many other Asian monetary authorities had emulated Taiwan's policy-induced risk-managing capacity after the 1997–98 crisis simply enhanced the credibility of the island's central bank and reinforced its prudential approach to regulating short-term capital flow and curbing the harmful volatility in the foreign exchange market. During the GFC, because most of the neighboring economies were also fully armed and ready to rein in the predatory hedge funds and market speculators, the task of warding off speculative attacks on New Taiwan dollars proved to be much easier. Taiwan's monetary authority no longer feels the pressure to defend itself for applying vigilant capital controls, because this time around many other emerging economies were doing virtually the same in their efforts to tame the capital and property markets (K. Singh 2010).[8]

During much of the 1990s and early 2000s, policymakers at Taiwan's Central Bank were the lonely advocates for prudential regulation over short-term capital flow and the foreign exchange market. They fought hard against the rising tide of financial liberalization. They not only had to face political pressures from abroad, especially from the United States and the IMF, but also the prevailing intellectual current that discredited all forms of government control over cross-border capital movement. Their philosophy and practices were repeatedly ridiculed by local neoliberal-minded economists and pro-business mass media and commentators as being too conservative, parochial, and backward.

Then the GFC brought about a sea change in the ideological arena. Overnight the mainstream economists became speechless as their intellectual enterprise crumbled like a house of cards (Krugman 2009). Overnight all Asian policymakers came to recognize the inherent vulnerabilities and systemic risks in the existing international monetary system. They became confident and bold enough to take issue with their counterparts in the United States and Europe. They rebuked the view that a savings glut from Asian surplus nations was the main culprit of the global crisis. Instead, they pointed out that central banks in the developed world were complacent about the gigantic risks that asset price bubbles posed to the real economy of jobs, production, savings, and consumption and that the U.S. Fed's repeated efforts to contain the damage of the bursting bubble on the real economy through aggressive easing of interest rates merely delayed the necessary structural adjustment and market correction and produced bigger asset price bubbles and aggravated the problem of "moral hazard."

Even the IMF is nowadays reversing its long-standing view (IMF 2010b).[9] By the time of the 2008–9 Icelandic crisis, the IMF endorsed the use of capital

---

8. Temporary capital controls are imposed by Indonesia, South Korea, Brazil, and Russia.

9. A recent paper prepared by the Strategy, Policy, and Review Department of the IMF stated that "in certain cases countries may consider price-based capital controls and prudential measures to cope with capital inflows."

controls under exceptional circumstances. By February 2010 the IMF fully reversed its earlier position, saying that capital controls can be useful as a regular policy tool even when there is no crisis to react to, though it still cautions against their overuse (*Financial Times,* June 10, 2010). Influential voices from the ADB and World Bank also joined the IMF in advising that there is a role for capital controls.

At long last the prudential approach that Taiwan's central bankers have stubbornly and adamantly adhered to for the last three decades has been vindicated for its intrinsic merit. Taiwan's monetary authority finally has found a more hospitable soil at home for cultivating its philosophy and policy practices. No episode better illustrates the sea change in the market of ideas on the island than a weekly column by the editor of *Business Weekly,* Taiwan's top business magazine. In her column, the editor openly apologized to Governor Perng Fai-nan for ridiculing his decision to shut down the Non-Deliverable Forward market for NTD at the crest of the regional financial crisis eleven years ago as "an inconceivable move to turn back the clock. . . . We were too naïve and too much indoctrinated by the surrogates of Wall Street then" (Kuo 2009).

Reacting to Financial Crises

Institutional Path Dependence in Korea and Thailand

Yasunobu Okabe

After the 1997 Asian financial crisis (AFC), South Korea (hereafter Korea) and Thailand, both of which had suffered great losses, were able to restructure their financial sectors. Following the internationally standardized menu of restructuring measures, the countries disposed of nonperforming loans (NPLs), increased their capital base, and realigned the banking sector. Their restructuring improved the health of the banking sectors and minimized the adverse effects of the global financial crisis (GFC) of 2008 on their financial markets.

Although the two countries adopted similar measures after the AFC, they displayed markedly different vulnerabilities to the GFC. Korea, which had performed better than Thailand in the financial restructuring and therefore expected to weather the GFC better, was more severely affected and driven to the brink of a second financial crisis in 2008. This chapter will address the reasons for this contrast from the perspective of path dependence, focusing on different paths of formation and restructuring of the financial systems in the two countries.

Korea and Thailand differed greatly in the post-AFC restructuring and impacts of the GFC, but they share many common external conditions. First, the two countries fell into a similarly serious crisis in 1997–98 and were required to undergo liberal financial reforms in exchange for the IMF rescue package. Second, although their export and GDP growth were adversely affected by the economic downturn during the GFC, their exposure to toxic assets was low because local banks had not invested heavily in U.S. subprime loans. By comparing the Korean and Thai experiences, we will be able to clarify the importance of domestic factors, especially the different institutional configurations of their respective financial systems.

Although the progress of their financial reforms and the impact of the Lehman shock drew broad scholarly attention, the differences between the two countries have been largely ignored. Hamilton-Hart surveys the post-crisis financial reforms and the subsequent trajectories of the banking systems in Indonesia, Korea, Malaysia, and Thailand (Hamilton-Hart 2008). However, the main focus of that research is on how much the banking systems had changed in all four in the decade after the AFC, and not on how such changes affected each country's vulnerability to the GFC. Ghosh also only discusses the improvement of bank soundness and efficiency, and the general trend of financial intermediation in East Asia after 1997 (Ghosh 2006, 63–72).

While several economists did examine the impact of the Lehman shock with a focus on East Asian resilience, few paid due attention to the different degrees of external vulnerability among the East Asian countries, and none have shed light on the differences between Korea and Thailand (Dowling and Rana 2010; Bhaskaran and Ghosh 2010; Saw and Wong 2010).

I rely on the path dependence approach to explain how the external vulnerability of the two countries was affected by the post-1997 financial restructuring. I also discuss how their ways of restructuring were shaped by their pre-1997 financial systems.

Liberalization and the Onset of the 1997 Crisis

Institutional Persistence and Change

Prior to the financial liberalization that occurred in the 1980s and 1990s, the financial systems in Korea and Thailand stood in a sharp contrast to one another. Korea had formed a system that could be characterized as "rent-for-enterprises," while Thailand had a "rent-for-banks" system.

In Korea, the powerful state controlled the banking sector and intervened to mobilize both domestic and external financial resources to promote manufacturing industries. To this end, the state supplied financial rent to *chaebol* enterprises through various measures, including the maintenance of low real interest rates, the guarantee of debt, allocations of credit and externally borrowed money, the subordination of the central bank to the proindustry government, and the adoption of moderately expansionary fiscal and monetary policies (Choi 1993; Woo 1991).

In Thailand, on the other hand, the state opted for less intervention into the powerful private banking sector. The government did protect the existing banks by restricting new entries, but beyond that avoided interventionist policies in deference to private banks' desires for fiscal balance, money supply control, and de facto central bank independence, all of which were regarded as important to avoid inflation and lower real interest rates (Doner and Unger 1993; Suehiro 2005).

Once firmly established, institutions have a strong tendency to persist (Krasner 1984; Pierson 2004). This institutional resilience is true even in cases where institutions disappear as formal organizations, as actors in an effort to secure previously beneficial patterns in the face of uncertainty sometimes accept existing patterns as guidance for future behavior (Goldstein and Keohane 1993, 13–17). The characteristics of the current financial systems in the two countries can therefore be understood as reflections of the power and interests of stakeholders—namely the states, banks, and industrial enterprises—that have persisted since the formative period.

The path dependence tendency notwithstanding, institutions do change as the success or failure of existing institutions transform the interests and power of the concerned actors. First, under new domestic and external circumstances, the existing system may not be able to continuously function properly and satisfy everybody; disenchanted or dissatisfied actors will therefore demand transformation of the system. Second, changes in the balance of power among stakeholders may lead to actors' efforts to readjust the system to the new balance of power, or to recover the former balance of power. Third, formerly absent players, including both domestic and external actors, may appear and make new demands for change.

In short, institutions create both continuing and transforming tendencies. The balance between persistence and change is deeply affected by political processes developed among stakeholders.

The Korean Case

In Korea, a serious move toward systemic transformation began during the 1980s in the form of liberalization of the domestic financial market. Serious concern regarding inflation and corporate debts spread among political and bureaucratic leaders. Technocrats in economic ministries especially feared that the accumulation of NPLs held by big corporations could cause a debt crisis. Leaders also worried that inflation caused by financial repression (accomplished by keeping interest rates lower than their market equilibrium levels) was destabilizing the economy (Cho and Kim 1997, 42). The Chun Doo-hwan government also recognized mounting public criticism of government favoritism of the chaebol, and therefore sought to rectify the image of a cozy relationship between the government and big business (Lim 2003, 48; Zhang 2003, 75).

Joining these domestic pressures was the external demand for financial-market liberalization as pressure from OECD, IMF, and the U.S. government became stronger after the late 1980s. The Kim Young-sam government (1993–98), longing for OECD membership, felt an especially strong pressure to hasten reforms (Haggard 2000, 37).

The process of liberalization began in the domestic market. The national banks were privatized throughout the 1980s. However, to avoid the dominance of chaebol over the privatized banking sector, the government imposed an 8 percent limit on ownership by any single shareholder in 1982. The limit was then tightened to 4 percent in 1994 (Bank of Korea 2006, 18). In addition, the government continued to supervise the banks by controlling the appointments of top executives and offering them subsidies (Park and Kim 1994, 192, 196).

While chaebol were excluded from the banking sector, they nevertheless had enough resources and reputation to establish nonbank financial institutions to raise money domestically and externally. The expansion of exports led by big business and the democratic opening in the latter half of the 1980s also strengthened chaebol power, and their influence on public policy was enhanced as politicians and political parties increasingly relied on financial contributions from big corporations (Kang 2002, 153–54, 158–66).

The financial policy of the government was therefore constrained by the expanding influence of chaebol. The interest rate was liberalized only in a very gradual manner because higher interest rates would raise the already heavy debt burden on the chaebol corporations (Choi 1993, 49–51; Chung 1994, 115). Chaebol influence also affected the order of the liberalization of international capital transactions. In 1994, short-term capital transactions were liberalized, preceding the liberalization of long-term capital accounts such as equity investment and foreign direct investment (FDI). This sequence perfectly fit chaebol preferences for obtaining easy short-term capital to expand their export-oriented production while excluding the possibility of foreign intrusion into their lucrative businesses. While public opinion was usually critical of the privileged status of chaebol in Korea, chaebol could count on a common aversion to foreign capital intrusion.[1]

Before the AFC, technocrats in the Kim Young-sam government intended to rectify the debt dependence of chaebol enterprises to avoid a debt crisis similar to the one experienced in 1979–81. Taking advantage of financial deregulation and liberalization, chaebol enterprises could now finance their businesses with corporate bonds, equity, and/or short-term foreign borrowing instead of bank credits. This made chaebol more independent of the government. They competed vigorously to raise money and invest in heavy and chemical industries. However, given the excessive supply of semiconductors and shipbuilding in the international market, the increase in labor costs, and the technology lag behind advanced industrial countries, this competition only led to excessive investment (Haggard 2000, 55) and lower

---

1. Lee Kyu-sung, who served as minister of finance (1988–90) and minister of finance and economy (1998–99), writes: "[Before the AFC] in Korea, FDI was being impeded by restrictive investment policies and widespread ambivalence and suspicion among the general public" (Lee 2011, 118).

profitability, thereby aggravating chaebol indebtedness. The average corporate debt ratio (total liabilities/stockholders' equity) in the manufacturing sector reached as high as 317.1 percent in 1996 and 396.3 percent in 1997 (Bank of Korea 2000).[2]

The failure of chaebol firms such as Hanbo Steel and Kia Motors triggered the crisis. Fingers point at the Kim Young-sam government for its lack of consistency and speed, which caused a decline in the rollover ratio of short-term foreign capital and brought about capital flight (Dooley and Shin 2000, 157). The massive capital outflow was, of course, precipitated by the well-known double mismatch of short-term foreign borrowing (Yoshitomi and Ohno 1999; Park 1998, 29).

The Thai Case

Financial liberalization was delayed in Thailand, but the factors that precipitated the reform were similar to those in Korea. Government technocrats in Thailand identified functional deficiencies in the existing financial system, but unlike in Korea where inflation and corporate debts were the main problems, the primary problem in Thailand was a broadening gap between savings and investment. To meet the expanding demand for business financing, government officials attempted to develop a local bond market and enhance foreign-capital intake (Suehiro 2005, 39; Bank of Thailand 1992, 331–32). This policy also sought to satisfy the increasing international demand that Thailand comply with trade-related obligations under the GATT Uruguay Round agreements and to implement capital-account liberalization as demanded by the World Bank, IMF, and the U.S. government (Pasuk and Baker 2002, 164–65; Zhang 2003, 113, 129–30).

At the same time, criticism against oligopolistic business groups dominated by big commercial banks mounted gradually. As the polity was democratized, the government felt a growing necessity to tackle this problem.[3] Newly emerging firms and local entrepreneurs sought financial liberalization to reduce the cost of raising money. Big banks, however, opposed the competition-enhancing liberalization of interest rates. Furthermore, the Thai Bankers' Association, together with the Bank of Thailand (BOT), resisted the deregulation of foreign entry into the banking sector, fearing it would destabilize the banking system and intensify competition (Zhang 2003, 120–24).

---

2. Chaebol counted on the government to consider them too big to fail and come to their rescue as it had done during the previous crises, creating a moral hazard. Hahn concluded in his statistical analysis that the bigger a chaebol is, the more its investment behavior is risk-taking (Hahn 2000).

3. Tharin Nimmanhemin, former minister of finance (1992–95), interviewed by author, February 20, 2009.

As a compromise, foreign capital transaction was freed in 1993 only in the offshore market. By this measure, foreign entries into the financial market were avoided. However, short-term foreign money did not stay in the offshore market, but rather flooded the domestic market in massive quantities.

In contrast to what happened in Korea, domestic banks and finance companies in Thailand invested the incoming money in real estate and securities. The Thai financial institutions had not developed enough capacity for financial intermediation under the long-term government protections and sought quick profits in the nonproductive sectors. This practice led to an asset bubble, the same double mismatch of short-term foreign borrowing (Ammar 2005, 72, 80), and the conspicuous default of several finance companies and banks. However, the government continued to rescue ailing nonbanks and commercial banks (Thitinan 2001, 118–25, 194–95), thus exacerbating the problem incurably.

Financial Restructuring

Postcrisis Restructuring Measures

There are three main actions that can be taken in order to restructure after a serious financial crisis (Claessens et al. 2001; Honohan and Klingebiel 2000). They are (1) to dispose of NPLs through the establishment of public and/ or private asset management corporations, (2) to recapitalize ailing or failed banks by injecting public, private, and/or foreign funds, and (3) to realign the banking sector through nationalization, private merger and acquisition, and/or the invitation of foreign banks. The third task is connected to the second because recapitalization is deeply related to the ownership structure and the government-bank relationship.

While the completion of these tasks is common for crisis-ridden countries including Korea and Thailand, the approach can differ with regard to the role of the government in the process. For instance, a government-led approach was taken in Korea, while a market-driven approach was adopted in Thailand. This section will reveal that path-dependent institutional constraints were prominent during the period immediately following the crisis, while the influence of change-seeking political forces receded (at least temporarily) due to the crisis.

The Korean Case

Korea's financial restructuring featured strong and prompt government initiative and substantial acceptance of the entry of foreign capital. The Kim Dae-jung government set up the Financial Supervisory Commission (FSC) to lead the restructuring process. This commission did not hesitate to fund the disposal of bank NPLs through the government-established Korean Asset Management Corporation (KAMCO) as well as the recapitalization of the ailing banks. The public funding that was injected from 1997 to 2003 amounted to approximately 30 percent of GDP in 2002 (Lim and Hahm 2004, 20, 22). In concrete terms, the government nationalized two banks, injected public funding into nineteen other banks to support their efforts to reduce NPLs and to strengthen their capital bases, and closed down five banks (and thirty merchant banks).

Under government supervision, several of these ailing banks were merged with or purchased by relatively healthy local banks or by foreign capital. The government approved 100 percent bank ownership by foreigners and raised the single shareholder ceiling from 4 percent to 10 percent in 2002 (Bank of Korea 2006, 18) in order to enhance the incentives for foreign investors. As a result of the bank realignment, the number of banks decreased from thirty-three in 1997 to eighteen in 2006, including five government-run banks (Bank of Korea 2006, 19, 22, 32).

The government also launched corporate reforms by which the largest chaebol were eventually forced to exchange their businesses ("Big Deal") to cut down excess capacities. Smaller chaebol were compelled to liquidate insolvent businesses under the guidance of government-supervised banks ("Workout"). The government further ordered the five largest chaebol to lower their debt-equity ratio to below 200 percent by the end of 1999 (Mo and Moon 2003, 128–33).

Existing literature mentions several reasons why the Kim Dae-jung government was able to take such a radical approach in the face of powerful chaebol forces and the labor pressure against employment reduction. First, Kim Dae-jung had always been in the opposition and had no chaebol connections (Haggard 2000). Second, as there was a general feeling that chaebol were responsible for the crisis, resistance from them was relatively weak. Third, the national crisis was so profound that the general public as well as political parties supported the reforms (Jung 2001, 17–18; Lim and Hahm 2004, 15).

These factors, however, do not explain why the Kim government came up with such interventionist policies to realize neoliberal reforms. This can be understood only by taking into account the institutional legacy of the Korean financial system. The state at one time managed the banking sector and credit allocations; virtual control by the state persisted even after bank privatization.

The institutional persistence of the financial system is reflected in the structure of bank supervising institutions. The FSC, the new leading coordinator for restructuring, was integrated into the ministerial hierarchy dominated by the Ministry of Finance and Economy (MOFE) (Lee 2004, 157; Kim and Lee 2006, 415–16). Most of the executive officials of the FSC also came from the MOFE. For example, Lee Hun-jae, the first chairman of FSC

(1998–2000), started his career in the Ministry of Finance (MOF) and experienced financial crises in the 1970s. His successors were also career officials from the MOF or MOFE.

Under the precrisis Kim Young-sam government, these technocrats considered the possibility of introducing prudential regulations, lowering debt financing by the private companies, reducing the risk of short-term borrowing, and improving international competitiveness of the Korean banks by reducing their number. Their ideas were never put into practice, however, because they could not gather political support for these measures, which could damage chaebol and bank interests at least in the short term.

The political climate was drastically altered by the crisis, and an opportunity was then made available for serious reforms (Kim 2002, 219). Consequently, the MOFE willingly intervened in the financial market not only to promptly solve the NPL problem and implement bank recapitalization but also to scale up the size of the financial institutions.

Once the reforms started, the government increased its control over the banking sector by raising the stockholding of the banks through the injection of public funds (Jung 2001, 16). At the beginning of 2001, the government owned 21.7 trillion won of commercial bank equities, which represented 48 percent of the total equities of all financial institutions in Korea (Lee 2002, 163–64). The personnel network connecting the MOFE and banks also contributed to the government control of the banks. The network was built on *amakudari*, or postbureaucratic career appointments of MOFE officials to the banks.[4] Such government ownership and networks smoothed the merger of banks and the resolution of NPLs.

Another institutional legacy of the Korean financial system was the continuing limitation of chaebol ownership of banks. The government faced a dilemma choosing between chaebol and foreign investors for the money necessary to recapitalize fragile banks and to reprivatize the nationalized banks. The government chose foreign capital (Kim and Lee 2008, 176; Mo 2008, 268), because during the early postcrisis years the public aversion to the chaebol was greater than that against foreigners. The government, however, was cautious enough to also limit the foreign ownership of individual financial institutions for fear of nationalist backlash.[5]

---

4. For instance, in March 2007, a former vice minister of MOFE assumed the presidency of Woori Bank, one of the four largest banks (see http://www.woorifg.com/, August 15, 2007). Woori Bank was newly founded in 2001 after the merger of four small- and medium-sized banks under the government initiative.

5. Public criticism against foreign investors soon mounted because people believed that foreigners were able to purchase the Korean banks at a bargain price thanks to the huge amounts of public money helping to save the banks (Kim and Lee 2008, 176). This opposition to foreign capital was evident in the news report about the suspicion of the illegal acquisition of Korea Exchange Bank by Lone Star Funds, an American equity fund, in 2003 (*Korea Times*, March 13, 2007).

The Thai Case

In contrast to the Korean case, Thai financial restructuring was characterized by gradual and private sector–led reforms and a very limited acceptance of foreign capital. Unlike the Kim Dae-jung government, the Chuan Leekpai government did not play an active role in financial restructuring. The government did establish the Financial Sector Restructuring Authority (FRA) in 1997 and closed down fifty-six finance companies and liquidated their assets.[6] It also nationalized four small and medium-sized banks. However, it did not take forceful measures with regard to the big banks; private banks were left to act on their own initiative in disposing of NPLs and strengthening their capital bases.

Under the Announcement for Comprehensive Financial Restructuring of August 14, 1998, the government planned to inject 300 billion baht for bank recapitalization. In practice, only ten financial institutions participated in the plan, and only 70.63 billion baht, or 23.5 percent of the original budget, was spent before the December 2000 deadline. Large private banks such as Bangkok Bank, Thai Farmers Bank (currently Kasikorn Bank), and Bank of Ayudhya did not participate in the plan and opted instead to recapitalize on their own through the stock market (Veerathai 2003, 26–31).

The market-driven approach was also taken in the disposal of NPLs. The Chuan government established the Corporate Debt Restructuring Advisory Committee (CDRAC) to foster debt-restructuring negotiations among private companies but did not form a public entity to force the disposal of NPLs. Instead, it allowed private banks to set up their own asset management companies (AMC). As a result, the speed of NPL reduction was naturally slow. To quicken the process, the Thaksin Shinawatra government, which came to power in 2001, shifted to a government-led approach and established a public Thai Asset Management Corporation (TAMC) similar to Korea's KAMCO (Veerathai 2003, 73–76). Nevertheless, it turned out that 80.5 percent of the NPLs transferred to TAMC came from state-owned banks and their AMCs, rather than privately owned ones (author's calculation from TAMC 2002).

In contrast to what happened in Korea, there was no large-scale realignment of the banking sector (except the nationalization of some small and medium-sized banks), and foreign investors were allowed to buy only small and medium-sized banks. The share of foreign banks in the Thai banking sector was as a result only 4.3 percent in 2005, while the corresponding figure for Korea was 55.6 percent (World Bank 2007a).[7] The oligopolistic structure of the banking sector remained unchanged in the postcrisis period.

---

6. Those disposed assets amounted to 14.3 percent of the total assets of all financial institutions, including commercial banks, approximately 18 percent of GDP (FRA 2002, table 1.2.1; Veerathai 2003, 14).

7. Here "foreign banks" are defined as banks in which more than 50 percent of the shares are owned by foreigners.

The Thai government adopted this private sector-led approach and limited the entry of foreign capital because of the resurgence of institutional constraints on the financial system. This resurgence of the institutional legacy is partially explained by the weakening of change-seeking political forces and a political deadlock caused by Chuan's multiparty coalition. The emerging firms and small and medium-sized local entrepreneurs—all potential supporters of anti–big bank policy—were hard hit and weakened by the crisis. Their loss was deepened when the government implemented the austere IMF-sponsored monetary and fiscal policies and conducted a fire sale of local assets to foreigners (Hewison 2005, 315–16). As a result, these business interests could not exert political pressure on the government to enact policies (such as the speed-up of the NPLs disposal and a greater foreign bank participation) that contradicted the preferences of big banks.

Chuan's Democrat-led government was formed by eight factionalized parties and was reshuffled four times (Chambers 2008, 316, 318). After each reshuffling, ministerial posts were redistributed to parties and factions that sought to control resources under each ministry's jurisdiction. Thanks to this large number of veto players, economic policymakers consequently faced a deadlock (Doner 2009, 129–30).

Relieved from change-seeking political pressures and taking advantage of the political deadlock, officials of the Ministry of Finance (MOF) and the BOT simply reinforced their traditional behavior of nonintervention. The Thai officials apparently felt more comfortable with a market-centered approach even in the postcrisis years. In an interview with the author, a BOT director said anonymously that the Thai government adopted the market-led approach, in contrast to the government-led approach of Korea, due to the difference of "culture."[8] A former codirector of the MOF Fiscal Policy Office said that he was not sure that government initiative would be more efficient than private initiative in tackling financial restructuring.[9]

The second institutional legacy of the Thai financial system was the oligopolistic structure of the commercial banking sector and its preference for limited government intervention in the financial market, except for the policy of excluding foreign competition. Even after the AFC, assets of the five biggest local banks (out of around fifteen) continued to surpass 70 percent of the total banking sector assets; four of these five banks were private. Such private dominance of the financial market was markedly different than what was observed in Korea and contributed to the influence of private banks over the government policy for recapitalization, NPL disposal, and foreign entry into the market. Consequently, as mentioned above, large private banks owned by founder families and their close friends did not participate in the

---

8. Anonymous director of the BOT, interviewed by author, February 27, 2007, Bangkok.
9. Veerathai Santiprabhob, interviewed by author, January 31, 2007.

government plan for recapitalization, because top bank executives worried that the government might intervene in their lending practices and demand their resignation.[10] Neither did Thai bankers want government involvement in the NPL problem, as they preferred to solve it by their own initiative even if the speed of the rectification was slower as a result.

Finally, both the banking sector and the Thai government were averse to any foreign dominance of the financial market. Lacking antibank sentiment equivalent to the anti-chaebol feeling among the general public in Korea, the Thai government did not have strong public support to seek foreign capital for its efforts to restructure. Consequently, while allowing foreign investors to participate in the recapitalization of small and medium-sized banks, the government did not approve majority ownership of major banks by foreigners.[11] When foreign shareholders were allowed to increase their stocks in large banks such as Kasikorn Bank and Bangkok Bank, their stocks were nonvoting shares. Many restrictions were also imposed on foreign bank operations. In fact, a Japanese banker in Bangkok complained to the author that acquiring the status of a local bank would not be worthwhile since foreign-dominated banks were subject to stricter supervisions by the BOT.[12] For example, even if foreign-owned banks acquired the status of local banks, they were not allowed to open any more than four branches.

Different Impacts of the GFC

Financial Systems on the Eve of the GFC

The financial restructuring in Korea and Thailand contributed to the recovery of the banks' health and stability in both countries. Both countries gradually improved the capital adequacy ratio (CAR) and the NPL problem in the post-AFC years. Between 2001 and 2007, the CAR ratio increased from 11.7 to 12.3 in Korea and 13.3 to 14.8 in Thailand, while the share of NPLs fell from 3.4 to 0.7 in Korea and 11.5 to 7.9 in Thailand during the same period (IMF 2007; 2010a). These improvements helped the recovery of bank lending. However, the speed of the recovery was much greater in Korea than in Thailand. In fact, Korean bank lending—loans and discounts—constantly increased in the post-AFC years, while Thai bank lending turned upward only in early 2002 (figure 4.1).

---

10. Ibid.; and Twatchai Yongkittikul, secretary general of the Thai Bankers Association, interviewed by author, February 9, 2007.

11. The Financial Institutions Act that was approved by the National Legislative Assembly in 2007 allows BOT to give permission to foreigners for shareholding of banks up to 49 percent. Over 49 percent shareholding of a bank by foreigners is permitted only when Ministry of Finance considers it necessary for stabilizing the bank.

12. Anonymous executive of a Japanese commercial bank operating in Thailand, interviewed by author, February 8, 2007.

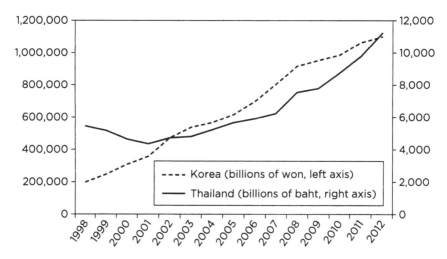

Figure 4.1 Bank loans in Korea and Thailand, 1998–2012 (end of year). Banks in Korea are commercial and specialized banks. Loans include discounts. Banks in Thailand, including foreign banks, are total commercial banks.

Sources: Bank of Korea website, http://ecos.bok.or.kr/flex/EasySearch_e.jsp; Bank of Thailand website, http://www.bot.or.th/English/Statistics/EconomicAndFinancial/ExternalSector/Pages/StatExternal Debt.aspx.

The loan/deposit rate was again greater in Korea than in Thailand. Thai lending behavior was quite conservative, most likely due to the slow pace of NPL disposal. Their loan/deposit rate was below 100 percent in 2000–7, which means that the banks loaned less than what they received as deposits (figure 4.2).[13] The ratio exceeded 100 percent only in 2008. In Korea, the loan/deposit rate exceeded 100 percent as early as 2004 and reached almost 140 percent on the eve of the GFC (figure 4.2).

The capacity of financial intermediation of the banking sector also differed in the two countries. Although the proportion of direct finance (e.g., stocks and other equities) rose in corporate financing in both Korea and Thailand, the dependence on financial loans was much higher in Korea than in Thailand. The flow-of-funds data from the Bank of Korea and the NESDB of Thailand show that in the former, the average share of loans in total corporate net financing was 36.5 percent annually in 2002–5. The equivalent figure for Thailand was –7.4 percent, which means that repayments were larger than new borrowing.[14]

Finally, the Korean banking sector showed more stability than its Thai counterpart. The Bank Z-score is a useful proxy for banking stability: it scores higher when the return on asset (ROA) is higher, the capital adequacy rate

---

13. Possibly the rest of the deposit was invested in safer assets such as government bonds.

14. Calculated from data retrieved from Bank of Korea website (http://ecos.bok.or.kr/ flex/EasySearch_e.jsp) and Thailand's National Economic and Social Development Board website (http://www.nesdb.go.th/Default.aspx?tabid=333).

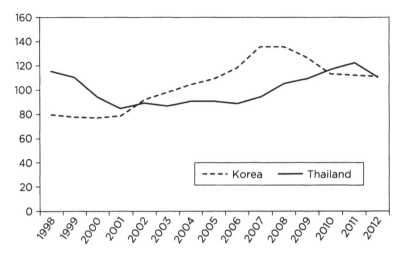

Figure 4.2 Loan/deposit ratio of commercial banks in Korea and Thailand (%). Information about Korean banks comes from author's calculation. Banks in Korea are commercial and specialized banks. Loans include discounts. Banks in Thailand, including foreign banks, are total commercial banks.

Sources: Bank of Korea website, http://ecos.bok.or.kr/flex/EasySearch_e.jsp; Bank of Thailand website, http://www.bot.or.th/English/Statistics/EconomicAndFinancial/ExternalSector/Pages/StatExternal Debt.aspx.

is greater, and/or when the standard deviation of ROA is smaller (which means less volatility of return).[15] According to a dataset provided by the World Bank, the annual averages of Bank Z-scores for 2002–8 were similar in Korea and Thailand: 6.67 for the former and 6.20 for the latter.[16] However, Korean scores generally moved in an upward trend: 3.2 (2002), 8.0 (2004), 6.7 (2006), and 9.6 (2008). By contrast, Thai scores were quite volatile: 7.0 (2002), 4.7 (2004), 8.2 (2006), and 4.7 (2008). In short, whereas the health and stability of banks in both countries improved, the recovery of bank lending and its contribution to corporate finance were more successful in Korea than in Thailand. This is the result of speedier restructuring through state-led measures in Korea. Ironically, however, when the GFC hit Asia, Korea was impacted far more seriously than was Thailand. Korea actually was driven to the brink of a second financial crisis in 2008 while effects on Thailand were minor.

15. The Bank Z-score is estimated as (ROA+equity/assets)/sd(ROA). I am grateful to Jean-Claude Maswana for his suggestion to use this score. Here sd(ROA), the standard deviation of ROA, is estimated as a five-year moving average. A higher z-score indicates that the bank is more stable.

16. See World Bank website, http://econ.worldbank.org/WBSITE/EXTERNAL/EXTDEC/ EXTRESEARCH/0,,contentMDK:20696167~pagePK:64214825~piPK:64214943~theSite PK:469382,00.html.

Several researchers point to external factors in their explanations of the impact of the crisis on each country. For instance, Chalongphob and Somchai pointed out that external debts and exposure to subprime loans were low in Thailand, while Shin and Takayasu argued that the unexpected shift of foreign money in the wake of the Lehman shock was critical for the Korean crisis (Chalongphob and Somchai 2009; Shin 2010; Takayasu 2010). According to an IMF report, Korean banks had very little direct exposure to the troubled U.S. credit instruments (IMF 2010a, 62). The main cause of the new crisis in Korea was the accumulation of short-term foreign debts and their sudden outflow—the same phenomenon that occurred during the AFC. To understand why the same failure happened not in Thailand but in Korea, where the financial restructuring progressed much more deeply and quickly, we again need to refer to the institutional legacies of the financial systems.

The Korean Case

Somewhat ironically, it was the active lending behavior of the refurbished domestic and foreign-owned banks that caused the renewed external vulnerability of the Korean economy.

As seen in figure 4.1 and figure 4.2, Korean banks, freed from the NPL burdens, increased their lending in the 2000s and raised the loan/deposit ratio from 100 percent (2004) to nearly 140 percent (2008). In order to supplement the shortage of deposits,[17] banks increasingly depended on foreign borrowings. Table 4.1 shows that Korea's total external liabilities rose from $225.2 billion at the end of 2006 to $365.1 billion in the third quarter (Q3) of 2008, just before the Lehman crisis occurred. Half of this, or $189.6 billion, was in the form of short-term debts. The largest short-term debtors were domestic banks and domestic branches of foreign banks, which held short-term debts amounting to $65.4 billion and $93.9 billion respectively (the sum total represented 43.6 percent of the whole external debt in Q3 of 2008). Domestic banks and domestic branches of foreign banks took out these short-term loans to finance both the investment by residents in foreign funds and shipbuilders' contracts.

On the one hand, foreign portfolio investment boomed in the middle of the 2000s, reaching $56.44 billion in 2007.[18] This boom was precipitated by two factors. First, Korean depositors, unsatisfied with low deposit interest rates, shifted their assets to foreign investment funds as well as the capital market. Second, the scope of the tax exemption on dividend income extended to overseas listed shares during 2007–9 (Takayasu 2010, 187). Asset

---

17. In fact, Korean households shifted some of their financial assets from deposits to portfolio investments against a background of an investment boom in 2006–7, to the extent that commercial banks fell short of funds in won (SMBC Seoul 2009, 15).

18. Bank of Korea website, http://ecos.bok.or.kr/flex/EasySearch_e.jsp.

TABLE 4.1
External debt of Korea, 2006–8 (billions U.S. dollars)

Gross external debt	2006	2007	2008 Q1	2008 Q2	2008 Q3	2008 Q4
Total	225.2	333.4	358.2	366.6	365.1	317.4
Short-term	113.7	160.2	174.2	176.8	189.6	149.9
Total debt of domestic banks	82.1	109.0	118.3	126.5	122.1	97.0
Short-term	44.3	54.6	60.5	66.7	65.4	42.6
Total debt of domestic branches of foreign banks	54.4	83.9	92.6	84.2	97.4	72.4
Short-term	51.8	79.3	87.8	80.4	93.9	67.8
International reserves / short-term debt (%)[a]	210.1	163.6	151.7	146.0	126.4	134.2

Source: Bank of Korea website, http://ecos.bok.or.kr/flex/EasySearch_e.jsp.
  [a] Author's calculation.

management companies that managed foreign funds, fearing won appreciation, hedged exchange risk by making forward contracts with domestic banks and foreign bank branches. These banks subsequently augmented short-term foreign borrowing to adjust their position.

On the other hand, against the backdrop of the worldwide shipbuilding boom between 2003 and 2008, Korean shipbuilders received orders equivalent to US$215.1 billion as of November 2008 (SMBC Seoul 2009, 5).[19] The shipbuilders also hedged exchange risk by making forward contracts with banks, which in turn increased short-term foreign borrowing.[20]

Although these foreign debts were actually guaranteed by foreign currency that those asset management companies and the shipbuilders would be paid in the future, such heavy dependence on short-term foreign debt made both domestic banks and foreign bank branches vulnerable to liquidity risks and changes to external financial conditions, despite little exposure to subprime assets (Shirai 2009, 34).

To make the situation worse, the government's prudential regulation was lenient for foreign bank branches. Domestic banks were strongly pressured to offset their debts with foreign currency-denominated assets so that their foreign exchange (FX) position was squared. In contrast, foreign bank branches were left without any such obligation (Shin 2010, 179). As a result,

---

19. Their order book amounted to 67.02 million cgt (compensated gross tons) at the end of December 2008, representing 36.7 percent of the world's total orders that year, the largest national share. See Clarkson Research Services, excerpt from Nexans, Shipbuilding White Paper, December 2008. Available at http://www.nexans.us/Corporate/2009/wp_shipbuilding 2008.pdf).

20. As shipbuilding generally takes two to four years from contract until delivery, it was necessary for Korean shipbuilders to hedge exchange risk.

foreign banks' short-term debts piled up rapidly and exceeded those of domestic banks after 2006 (table 4.1). A major cause of the renewed upsurge of short-term debts resides in the framework of financial regulation dominated by the Ministry of Strategy and Finance (MOSF). Since the Bank of Korea (BOK) does not have autonomous status in Korea, there was no chance of a course correction of misjudgments by the MOSF.

When capital inflows into Korea declined under the worldwide subprime loan crisis, the Korean won sharply depreciated (almost 30 percent in one month). At the same time, the ratio of international reserves to the short-term foreign debt fell rapidly from more than 200 percent in 2006 to 126.4 percent in Q3 of 2008 (table 4.1). At this point the Korean economy was only able to avoid the second financial crisis through a $30 billion currency swap approved by the U.S. Federal Reserve Board in October 2008.

The Lee Myung-bak government, which took power in February 2008, established the Financial Services Commission (FSC) to replace the Financial Supervisory Commission (former FSC) and granted it full authority concerning financial regulations (Park 2010, 55, 59). Under the new regime, the function of the MOSF's Division of Financial Policy was theoretically transferred to the new FSC. In practice, the MOSF, as the primary coordinator of all economic policies, continued to strongly influence financial matters (Park 2010, 58). Just like the former FSC, the new FSC is associated with the MOSF by appointments of ex-ministerial officials. The chairman, the vice chairman, and one of the five commissioners of the new FSC are former high-ranking officials of the MOF, MOFE, and MOSF who share similar technocratic career paths.[21]

Under the current regime, the BOK plays an important role in maintaining financial stability and managing the payment and settlement system and emergency liquidity provision to banks as the lender of last resort. For the same purpose, the BOK is responsible for providing information on the economy, financial markets, and financial institutions. However, the BOK's authority in financial regulations is not clearly defined. While the FSC Act recognized the FSC as a guardian of financial stability, the BOK Act did not explicitly include the maintenance of stability as one of its missions. The Financial Supervisory Services (FSS), the executive hand of the FSC, acknowledged only small roles for the BOK and frequently refused to provide the BOK with information collected through their supervisory operations (Park 2010, 59).[22]

Without an independent supervisory body, the MOSF overlooked the risk of short-term foreign debts creeping into the country through forward

---

21. See FSC website, http://www.fsc.go.kr/eng/ab/ab0401.jsp.
22. This refusal to provide information was confirmed by an anonymous high-ranking official of the BOK in an interview with the author. This official also said that the FSC and the FSS had often rejected BOK requests for joint supervisory operations that are allowed by the BOK Act (Seoul, February 10, 2010).

contracts. A high-ranking BOK official informed the author that the central bank unofficially called the government's attention to the increasing debts before the Lehman shock. However, government officials, particularly those within the MOSF, did not listen to the BOK warning.[23]

The MOSF paid little attention to the short-term debts mainly for two reasons. First, the government allowed a rapid increase in short-term borrowing by the banks in the belief that the banking sector was now on a much stronger foundation after the successful financial restructuring with broad foreign participation. Although big chaebol firms strengthened their self-financing capability during the restructuring period, smaller enterprises and households still depended heavily on bank credits and welcomed the expansion of financial resources in the market.

Second, the government did not ask foreign banks to square their position with foreign currency-denominated assets because it wrongly believed that their assets were mostly held in foreign currencies and that their main offices were powerful enough to help their subsidiaries in times of crisis (Shin 2010, 179–81). A part of the problem originated in the fact that the post-AFC policy of the Korean government was highly permissive to the entry of foreign capital. Such a liberal policy contributed to the rapid recovery of the Korean banking sector but simultaneously proved to be highly risky without a robust mechanism to rectify policy misjudgments of the national regulatory agency. In Korea, the agency's excessively optimistic expectations were disappointed by the large capital flight by the foreign banks.

The government-led financial system was quite effective in the quick and deep financial restructuring after the AFC. However, it turned out to be still vulnerable to external financial turmoil during the GFC because incorrect judgments by the government could not be rectified by any independent supervisory body.

The Thai Case

In Thailand, as mentioned above, both the government and banks were reluctant to accept state interventionism in the financial market, which made the restructuring process slow. The delay of the restructuring in turn strengthened the conservative and risk-averse behavior of the banks. This behavior was also reinforced by the painful experience of the AFC (Chalongphob and Somchai 2009, 3). Thus the external exposure of Thai banks was kept low and consequently helped Thailand escape from the subprime loan crisis. The Thai baht remained relatively stable as a result.[24]

---

23. Anonymous high ranking BOK official, interviewed by author, March 4, 2011.

24. Between December 2007 and November 2008, the exchange rate of baht against the U.S. dollar depreciated by 8.3 percent while the Korean won depreciated by 96 percent. The depreciation rates were 16 percent in Indonesia, 17 percent in Malaysia, and 8 percent in Singapore (Shirai 2009, 35).

TABLE 4.2
External debt of Thailand, 2006–8 (billions U.S. dollars)

Gross external debt	2006	2007	2008 Q1	2008 Q2	2008 Q3	2008 Q4
Total	70.0	74.4	80.3	78.9	78.8	76.1
Short-term	27.2	34.0	38.6	37.7	37.7	33.6
Total debt of banks	6.7	6.4	6.8	7.7	7.2	7.2
Short-term	3.2	4.0	4.3	5.3	4.5	4.5
International reserves / short-term debt (%)[a]	245.8	257.1	285.2	280.6	271.7	330.3

Source: Bank of Thailand website, http://www.bot.or.th/English/Statistics/EconomicAndFinancial/
ExternalSector/Pages/StatExternalDebt.aspx.
  [a] Author's calculation.

In fact, Thai banks did not hold as much short-term foreign debt as their Korean counterparts prior to the Lehman shock (in Q3 of 2008). According to table 4.2, the amount of this short-term foreign debt was US$4.5 billion, representing only 5.7 percent of the total external debt (compared with 43.6 percent for Korean banks). Although half of Thailand's external debts were short-term, they were fully covered by the international reserve. The ratio to short-term foreign debts reached as high as 271.7 percent in Q3 of 2008 (compared with Korea's 126.4 percent).

Furthermore, while one small bank, ThaiBank, needed to be recapitalized in 2008 because of high exposure to subprime-related toxic assets such as collateralized debt obligations (CDOs), most of the banks were only marginally exposed. The banking sector's exposure to foreign assets was 1.2 percent of total assets as of August 2008, and only 0.04 percent of total assets were related to CDO investment (Bank of Thailand 2008).

The low dependence of Thai commercial banks on short-term foreign borrowings and their limited exposure to the toxic assets can be explained through an examination of banks themselves and the bank regulators. Commercial banks' lending behavior, as mentioned above, was very conservative, due to the slow pace of financial restructuring and their experience in the AFC; they hesitated to have a finger in subprime loans. The bank regulators also learned lessons from the financial crisis of 1997 and reinforced their conservative policy stance. For instance, the BOT strengthened the regulation and supervision of commercial banks during the 2000s. Both domestic and foreign bankers found that the BOT was very conservative and eager to control everything related to banking. In an interview conducted by the author, a Thai banker said that the BOT was much more concerned with bank soundness than lending to real sectors.[25] According to a Japanese banker operating in Thailand, the BOT does not permit the self-assessment of NPLs by

---

25. Anonymous source, interviewed by author, September 2, 2011.

commercial banks, a practice widely accepted in the world today.[26] The Thaksin government, which had a more interventionist tendency than its post-AFC predecessors, did try to weaken the BOT regulations, but its attempt was averted by the September 2006 coup. After that, the BOT regained its authority and even succeeded in consolidating its legal independence in 2008.

Conclusion

This chapter has traced the continuity and change of the financial systems in Korea and Thailand in relation to the two grave crises: AFC and GFC. As the path dependence approach argues, institutions, once firmly established, have a powerful tendency to persist. However, as success or failure of the existing institutions transform the interests and power of the concerned actors, and as the existing system comes to be perceived as poorly functioning or unsatisfactory as a result, they may be put under strong pressure to transform.

In Korea, the "rent-for-enterprises" financial system, characterized by strong government intervention and the absorption of rent by chaebol firms dominating the nonbanking sectors, faced challenges from technocrats, democratic forces, and foreign investors. As a result, deregulation and liberalization of the financial market were realized during the 1980s and 1990s. However, due to the strengthened chaebol influence, the reforms sharply expanded foreign debts taken by banks and other financial institutions.

By contrast, Thailand had a "rent-for-banks" financial system in which the state took a hands-off policy, except for measures to exclude foreign banks and to maintain macroeconomic stability. The biggest beneficiaries were oligopolistic private banks. By the early 1990s, this system faced multiple problems, including a saving-investment gap, increasing antipathy against oligopolistic business groups, and foreign demand for liberalization. As the political parties became more influential, government policy became more expansionary and interventionist. As a compromise between conservative banks/technocrats and emerging forces, the liberalization of the financial sector took the form of opening offshore markets, which brought enormous foreign-money inflow and the debt crisis.

Ironically, the serious financial crisis in 1997–98 helped the resurgence of traditional institutional configurations of the financial systems in both countries: the interventionist state and chaebol firms that expanded outside of the banking sector in Korea, and the conservative state and oligopolistic banks in Thailand. The restructuring of the banking sector was speedy and deep

---

26. Anonymous source, interviewed by author, August 30, 2011. In addition, the same Thai banker cited in Footnote 25 said that BOT is usually slow to permit new financial products that commercial banks develop.

in Korea thanks to active and decisive government intervention, but was slow and shallow in Thailand.

Ironically, the successful restructuring encouraged the propensity of banks in Korea to borrow foreign money, while the slowness of the Thai restructuring only reinforced conservative lending and borrowing behavior. Furthermore, the institutional legacies that reasserted themselves during the period of restructuring reinforced positive foreign borrowing by Korean banks and timid borrowing by Thai banks. In Korea, the central bank lacked regulatory authority and so the misjudgment of the finance ministry regarding the behavior of domestic branches of foreign banks could not be rectified in time. As a result, Korea almost came to the brink of another financial crisis in 2008. In contrast, GFC's adverse effect on the Thai financial market was minimal, partially because the central bank of Thailand successfully resisted the Thaksin government's pressures and rigidly regulated the financial market.

This examination demonstrates that institutions matter, even in the highly globalized world. Global financial forces may increasingly compel smaller countries to deregulate and liberalize their financial markets so that they are congruent with global standards. These smaller economies are especially vulnerable in a severe global crisis. Under such conditions, they are further forced to adapt their domestic system to the global rules. Offering a warning about such expectations, I have shown in this chapter how financial systems with different institutional characteristics adapt themselves differently under similarly strong international pressures for liberalization and in similarly severe financial crises. The path dependence approach is correct in its insistence on institutional stickiness.

However, as the Korean experience showed in 2008, such institutional stickiness does not always contribute to strengthening the firewall against capricious flows of global money. On the contrary, it can put the entire national economy at risk when national regulators make serious misjudgments regarding the behavior of financial market players.

China and the Two Crises

From 1997 to 2009
Barry Naughton

On first look, China appears to have been relatively less affected than
other countries by both the Asian Financial Crisis (1997–98) and the Global
Financial Crisis (2008–2009). China was not the epicenter of either crisis; it
responded relatively effectively to both, and it managed to sidestep the worst
impact of both crises. Chinese resilience has long been a theme of accounts
of the 97–98 Asian Financial Crisis (AFC). Sharma (2003, 252), for example,
characterized China as "the domino that did not fall" in that crisis. Strong
performance through the Global Financial Crisis (GFC) fed a broader sense
of self-confidence that is affecting every aspect of China's policy and relation
with the world. As Ming Wan points out, "To many in China, the country's
stronger performance during the crisis vindicates its choice of development
model" (2010, 532). It is tempting to think that China has been only marginally affected by these external crises, and that it marches to a different drum,
to a cadence driven by its own vast domestic market and its own internal
political dynamics.

On closer look, however, each crisis had a profound impact on China,
and there are important parallels between the two. Chinese leaders have paid
close attention to the potential impact of external crisis, and have responded
quickly, and on occasion massively, to the challenge of external crisis. During
the earlier AFC, China tried out a domestic stimulus package that had an important impact on its performance. Ten years later, in the GFC, the response
was an order of magnitude bigger, and deployed even more decisively. In that
sense, the relatively successful responses to the AFC can be seen as a trial run
for the more ominous GFC.

It is only when the crisis response is embedded into a broader account
of China's institutional and policy evolution that we can begin to uncover
the deeper significance of these crises. Each of the two crises gave impetus

to significant institutional change in China. In general, crises tend to serve as change accelerators. In interpreting the Chinese experience, the crucial additional observation is that each crisis at first left the general orientation of policy unaltered even as it sped up and intensified the pace of policy-making. As a result, each external crisis led to an apparent overshooting: the existing policy instruments were used much more vigorously, and this crisis-impelled intensification of policy ultimately could not last. As crisis conditions faded, the crisis response began to appear somewhat excessive in retrospect. Certain measures that had been seen as absolutely necessary began to seem quaint and were quietly discarded. However, it must also be acknowledged that some crisis measures, taken in haste, became ingrained into the institutional and political economy fabric. The ultimate impact of crisis turns out to be full of ironic twists and unanticipated consequences. In the end, it is the crisis *and the extreme measures taken in response* that determine the long-run impact of the crisis.

Looked at from this perspective, the ultimate impact of the two crises appears increasingly distinct and indeed almost opposite. In the case of the AFC, China at first accelerated the pace of institutional reform, in line with Premier Zhu Rongji's approach to the economy. After a new administration took over in 2002–3, the overall policy orientation gradually shifted: the pace of institutional change slowed dramatically, while macroeconomic policy settings gradually became less appropriate to the changing external environment but also ensured that the Chinese had plenty of reserve ammunition to deal with any subsequent crisis. These choices set the stage for China's response to the GFC. When the GFC arrived, China's response reflected a set of policy choices that were almost the reverse of those made in the face of the AFC. Institutional reforms were nonexistent, while the stimulus response relied on direct government action and co-optation of the banking system to support those government-sponsored activities. The consequences of those choices have been profound and continue to echo through current Chinese policy choices and debates.

The first two sections of this chapter describe and analyze China's response to the Asian and then Global Financial crises. The discussion tracks commonalities and differences in three dimensions: immediate macroeconomic crisis response, institutional adaptations, and trade and exchange rate policies. What emerges is that while the immediate macroeconomic response was similar in both crises, the institutional adaptation was very different, and in some respects opposite. The AFC accelerated institutional restructuring, while the GFC inhibited it, and led instead to a bloat of stimulus-supported sectors and projects. The third section delves more deeply into the institutional implications of China's response to the GFC, showing that—in contrast to the situation after the AFC—China was left with an overdue agenda of postponed restructuring. In the fourth section, I examine the path from the AFC to the GFC and beyond, arguing that three separate strands link the two crises, which are woven together in ways that are sometimes unexpected. The final section examines the state of the Chinese political economy in 2013: after successfully managing two external crises, the Chinese economy now faces accumulating problems from the maladaptation of domestic institutions, a maladaptation that is not unrelated to the crisis response.

China's Response to the Asian Financial Crisis, 1997–98

Like nearly everyone, the Chinese were caught by surprise by the AFC. The crisis began the day after the long-anticipated resumption of sovereignty over Hong Kong on July 1, 1997. On July 2, Thailand was forced to abandon the peg of the Thai baht to the dollar, and as a result the baht depreciated 17 percent on that day. For the first several months of the crisis, Chinese policymakers mainly focused their attention on Hong Kong, which was vulnerable in the initial phases of the crisis. In fact, the full force of the crisis hit Hong Kong in the fall, when the very large and very international Hong Kong Stock Exchange came under speculative attack. During this period the benchmark Hang Seng index fell from its precrisis peak of 16,800 to almost 9,000, including two days in late October when the Hang Seng index fell more than a thousand points in a single day. Ultimately, the Hong Kong government abandoned its long-held policy of nonintervention and organized a coordinated market rescue program. The government invested the equivalent of HK$110 billion (about US$12.5 billion) in the market from foreign exchange reserves, while the large blue-chips and Chinese government firms listed on the market engaged in big stock buybacks. The PRC government actively supported the Hong Kong effort, although probably with a relatively modest financial commitment. Within a few months, capital returned to the Hong Kong market, and the situation was stabilized (Jao 2001). The experience showed that the Chinese government was willing to intervene in markets and also probably taught Chinese policymakers a lesson about the wisdom of intervening early and forcibly. The episode also provided raw material for a narrative of national solidarity, in which Chinese people in the mainland and in Hong Kong stood together to defeat international speculators (personified in this case by George Soros).

In fact, Chinese policymakers had their hands full with domestic economic problems. Earlier in the decade, the policy stalemate between conservatives and reformers had been broken with the aid of Deng Xiaoping's "Southern Tour" of 1992. Major economic reforms had taken place, but they had been accompanied by a tremendous initial surge of inflation. The top economic policymaker, Zhu Rongji, had been struggling to bring down the inflation rate, while also preparing the ground for the next wave of economic reforms. When the AFC arrived, Zhu was finally close to his goal. After twenty-one straight quarters above 5 percent, the rate of inflation had been brought down below this "red line" for the first time in the second quarter of 1997 (figure 5.1). Monetary restraint was paying off, and the economy seemed to be close to a "soft landing," controlling inflation without too excessive a cost in terms of foregone growth.

Disinflation, combined with a new attitude toward state ownership, was already driving a dramatic downsizing of the Chinese state sector. In 1996, more than 7 million workers had been furloughed from Chinese public enterprises, and the question was whether this punishing downsizing would continue. The arrival of the AFC was thus exceedingly unwelcome, since it created a serious dilemma for Zhu Rongji: to what extent should he allow the downward pressures of the AFC to continue to slow the Chinese economy? In the end, Zhu maintained the policy course. The number of newly furloughed workers remained above 5 million annually through 2000, and furloughed workers either found new jobs outside the state sector, transitioned to retirement, or remained unemployed (Naughton 2007, 185–89). By the end of the process, the number of workers in traditional state-owned enterprises had declined by two-thirds, and the total employed by publicly owned enterprises of all kinds fell by about 40 percent. A crucial step—perhaps *the* crucial step—in

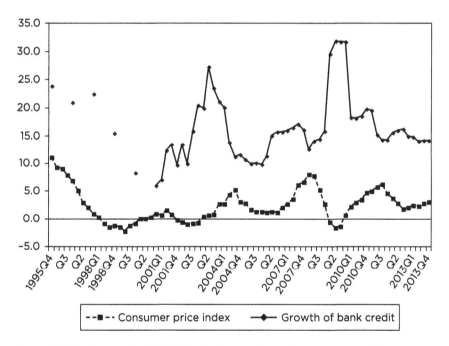

Figure 5.1 Credit growth and CPI inflation: increase from the same quarter of the previous year (%).

Sources: The data on credits are from http://www.pbc.gov.cn/publish/diaochatongjisi/126/index.html; CPI inflation from National Bureau of Statistics of China accessed at http://data.stats.gov.cn/workspace/index?m=hgyd.

the transition to a market economy had been achieved. In the long run, then, the AFC fit into a process of domestic transformation, painful but necessary for the country's economic progress.

Of course, the policy response was not that simple. Zhu Rongji did not immediately perceive the threat to China's domestic economy from the AFC, and it was not until the very end of 1997 that Chinese policy began to adapt fully to the consequences of the AFC. Since monetary policy had been effective in controlling inflation, and had just recently achieved a degree of credibility, the decision was made to maintain restrictive monetary policy but loosen fiscal policy. China had generally kept its budget deficit below 1 percent of GDP, but the deficit was now allowed to inch higher in 1998, and expand to 1.9 percent in 1999 and 2.5 percent in 2000. As figure 5.2 shows, nearly all the increase in fiscal effort ultimately showed up as increased physical infrastructure investment. For the first time, China's core physical infrastructure investment surged above 8 percent of GDP, creating a precedent for later policy. More broadly, a campaign was launched to "keep growth at 8 percent," which gave government officials a certain amount of leeway to initiate projects, pressure companies to restrain layoffs, and exaggerate their reported production figures. In the event, 1998 GDP growth was officially reported at 7.8 percent, although subsequently as China's statisticians were revising GDP and growth rates upward for other years, they quietly lowered the 1998 rate to 7.3 percent.

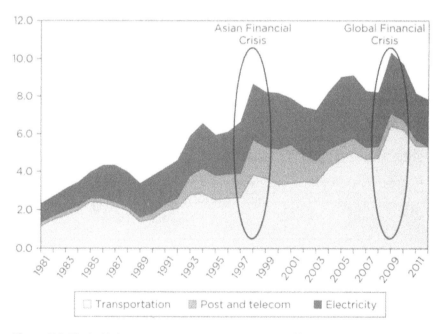

Figure 5.2 Physical infrastructure investment: share of GDP (%).
Source: National Bureau of Statistics of China (2013), 168–69 and earlier volumes.

The best-known Chinese policy response to the AFC involved doing nothing. That is, China maintained the value of its currency, the RMB, pegged at 8.28 to the U.S. dollar, while the crisis-effected economies were devaluing substantially. China's willingness to avoid competitive devaluation was positive and contributed to the stabilization of the overall situation. In fact, China did not have to bear a great deal of pain to carry out this policy, because a number of astute policy choices in the preceding years had greatly improved China's overall economic position. During 1993–94, China had dramatically opened its economy, welcoming foreign investment for the first time and unifying the existing dual exchange rate. Exchange rate unification had involved a substantial overall devaluation, since the new rate was close to the old unofficial swap market rate. Since then, inflation had been gradually pushing up China's real exchange rate, but nevertheless China's imports had grown slowly, declining as a share of GDP through 1998. The same tough macroeconomic policies that had been lowering inflation and driving state sector restructuring were also limiting demand for imports. Export growth, in the meantime, had kept pace with GDP growth, so that China began to run large trade surpluses, more than 4 percent of GDP, in 1997 and 1998 (figure 5.3). Finally, foreign direct investment had surged, with inflows surpassing 4 percent of GDP annually after 1993. This policy configuration steadily replenished China's foreign exchange reserves, which had finally grown to a reasonably safe level, reaching 100 percent of annual imports in 1997 for the first time (figure 5.3). With a substantial export

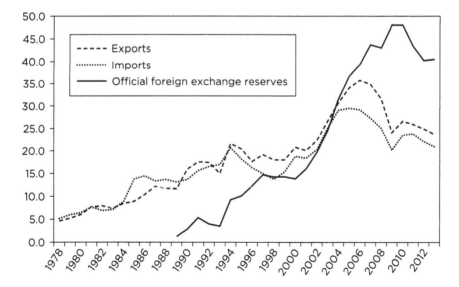

Figure 5.3 Exports, imports, and official reserves: share of GDP (%).

Sources: National Bureau of Statistics 2013, 224 for exports, imports, and exchange rates; 44 for GDP. Data on foreign exchange reserves are from State Administration of Foreign Exchange, available at http://www.safe.gov.cn.

surplus and adequate reserves, it was not hard for China to wait out the crisis with a fixed rate.

In short, China's direct macroeconomic responses to the AFC were prompt and appropriate, but basically moderate. Compared to later interventions, their scale reflected the fact that China had far less skin in the game. Trade was already moderately large as a share of GDP, but not as large as it would be ten years later. China's financial system was still largely closed, so risks of financial contagion were insignificant. There was some capital outflow, and capital controls were tightened somewhat, but the decline in reserves was quite manageable. Most crucially, with a comfortable trade surplus and a balanced budget, China was not constrained to adopt procyclical policies of austerity or monetary contraction, as were the worst-hit Asian economies. For China, the AFC was a major challenge, but not an emergency. China could roll out a modest stimulus to help offset the external downturn and—given reasonable economic health of its main developed economy export markets—wait out the rest of the crisis. This meant that policymakers could keep their eyes fixed on longer-term strategic priorities, including domestic restructuring. Since Premier Zhu Rongji had already decided that it was worth absorbing some pain to pursue state-sector restructuring, the costs of the AFC could be absorbed without throwing away the policy credibility that had already been achieved at substantial cost.

Despite the relatively modest direct impact of the AFC on China, one of the most important results was the lesson China learned about vulnerability. In one sense, China learned the same broad lessons about more prudent international policy that the most directly affected crisis countries learned: keep the currency low enough to maintain consistent export surpluses, build up foreign exchange reserves, avoid reliance on short-term bank loans, and above all, never allow yourself to become dependent on the IMF for macroeconomic insurance. In another sense, the lesson China learned about vulnerability was a lesson about its own systemic features that could easily lead it into crisis. As Steinfeld (2008, 188) points out, "The cautionary note—indeed alarm—heard in China was not about the risks of capitalism but, rather, about those of socialism." The financial difficulties experienced by banking systems throughout East Asia convinced Chinese leaders that their own banking system was even more precarious than they realized, and desperately needed restructuring and recapitalization. The collapse of the majority of the Korean *chaebol* convinced policymakers that the largest state firms could not simply be made into national champions through investment and expansion, but instead needed radical reform and corporatization. The harshness of global competition seemed to strengthen the conviction of China's top leaders that China needed to enter the World Trade Organization (WTO) in order to consolidate and protect its status as one of the world's leading trading economies.

The results of these lessons were soon apparent in Chinese economic policy. In November 1999, China finally reached agreement with the United

States on their bilateral accord that paved the way for Chinese entry into the WTO in December 2001. China followed up the WTO commitment with a productive set of initiatives for economic engagement with other Asian countries, especially its ASEAN neighbors. The Chiang Mai Initiative to establish a swap mechanism for foreign exchange reserves among the ASEAN countries plus China, Japan, and Korea was begun in May 2000, and China then followed up by unexpectedly proposing an ASEAN-China Free Trade Agreement in December of the same year (Sheng 2003). This action signaled the beginning of a period of proactive, economically based "good neighbor" policies that marked most of the first decade of the twenty-first century, including the ASEAN-China FTA itself, which came into effect at the beginning of 2010. Equally significant, China set about restructuring its banks. First, China wrote off trillions of RMB in bad loans; then injected trillions of RMB of government money into the banking system. On the foundation of these improved balance sheets, foreign strategic partners were solicited to take stakes in the healthiest banks. With strategic partners lined up, the better banks were then restructured and listed on the Shanghai and Hong Kong stock markets. It was an impressive, costly, and professionally executed effort. China pumped about 28 percent of GDP into its banking system in this period, counting only the first wave of large commercial banks (Ma 2006; Naughton 2007; Walter and Howie 2012). Perhaps most strikingly, China had recognized that the banking system could not be used indefinitely as a prop for inefficient and loss-making state-owned enterprises. After the state enterprise sector was downsized, the next step was to bring the state banks out of their near-insolvent position, restructure their incentives, and give them the opportunity to adapt to a more competitive economy. China came out of the AFC determined to continue with multisided reforms that made its economy more productive and more resilient.

China's Response to the Global Financial Crisis (2008–9)

A decade later, China confronted a new external crisis. There were some odd parallels with the earlier crisis. The GFC hit—with the collapse of Lehman Brothers and AIG on September 15, 2008—shortly after China finished staging the Beijing Olympics in August. The Olympics had been long anticipated in China as a symbol of China's emergence, and was certainly the biggest national celebration since the return of Hong Kong in 1997, just on the eve of the AFC. Again, the external crisis also hit just as a domestic program of inflation fighting and macroeconomic contractionary policies were beginning to bite (discussed below). In comparison with the earlier crisis, China's response to the global crisis of 2008–9 was unusually bold and decisive. In retrospect, it is clear that the decisiveness of the crisis response reflected an unusual combination of conditions: the threat was exceptionally clear, and

China was unusually well positioned to respond. At the front end, the global crisis produced an unusually high level of consensus among policymakers, so they had little trouble agreeing on policy. Moreover, it was obvious to Chinese policymakers that globally the crisis was being taken very seriously, and that the threat to China was substantial. Moreover, China was in a good position to respond largely because of the prudent policies first set in place after the AFC. Foreign exchange reserves were large: with almost $2 trillion in reserves, China had 170 percent of 2008 imports (figure 5.3). The government budget was also balanced; the state-owned enterprise sector had returned to profitability after its restructuring at the turn of the century.

Perhaps most important, the Chinese banking system was in a strong position. The difficult and protracted process of bank reform, recapitalization, and restructuring that had been carried out between 2003 and 2006 had left the banks with reasonably strong core capital and low burdens of nonperforming loans (NPLs). By the eve of the 2008 financial crisis, NPLs in the system had officially been brought down from crisis levels to below 5%, a tolerable level. (CBRC 2009: 36; cf. Lardy 1998; Brandt and Zhu 2007). The bank reform process had finally reached the most troubled bank, the Bank of Agriculture, which was restructured at the end of 2008 (but not listed on the stock market until August 2010, due to the impact of the crisis). Thus the last reform launched by Zhu Rongji had finally reached conclusion after years of effort and billions in costs. In essence, then, China was in a strong economic position because of strong fundamentals and prudent macroeconomic policies, but even more so because it was reaping the benefits of difficult and thorough reforms carried out in the 1990s and early 2000s.

The Chinese response to the global financial crisis can be dated precisely. On November 5, 2008, a joint meeting of the State Council and the Politburo—the highest governmental and Communist Party bodies—decided on a RMB4 trillion (US$586 billion) stimulus investment program. That money, equal to 12.5 percent of 2008 GDP, was to be spent beginning immediately and with utmost urgency, putting shovels in the ground as quickly as possible. Outlays were to begin during the fourth quarter of 2008 and to be expended through the end of 2010. This decision marked the unambiguous beginning of the full crisis response.

In fact, the stimulus decision marked a remarkable turnaround in Chinese policy. Only five months earlier, China's central bank had still been trying to slow the economy in order to fight inflation. As figure 5.1 shows, Chinese inflation had soared during 2007 to truly worrying levels. On June 25, 2008, the last of a string of increases in bank reserve requirements had taken effect, restricting money supply by requiring commercial banks to keep more funds on deposit with the central bank, and pushing the rate to a historic high of 17.5 percent. Overall, the Chinese economy had been in a period of overheated expansion for some time. In the middle of the decade, exports grew dramatically (figure 5.3), and GDP growth accelerated (table I.1). The

Chinese economy and the inflation rate were both accelerating during 2007 in a way that was fundamentally unsustainable: GDP growth hit 14.2 percent for the year, and inflation rose above 8 percent, the highest rate in more than a decade.

The economic data highlight how different developments in China had been during the period between the AFC and the GFC compared to those countries hit hard by the AFC. The crisis countries experienced a sustained drop in GDP growth and a decline in investment rates that lasted through the 2000s (Park, Shin, and Jongwanich 2009). This was not true at all for China, where investment rates inched steadily upward and GDP growth accelerated. Indeed, China was the primary beneficiary of the round of global growth acceleration that made 2003–8 the period of the most rapid expansion of the global economy certainly since the 1960s and perhaps ever. For China, GDP growth stayed above 10 percent from 2003 onward, before hitting stratospheric levels in 2006, 2007. Under these circumstances, the attention of the Chinese central bank understandably turned to fighting inflation and moderating growth. The fixed rate with the U.S. dollar was loosened in July 2005, and then from November 2007 bank officials, for the first time since the beginning of reforms, allowed the RMB to appreciate substantially against the dollar (about 1 percent per month). Yet still the global bubble grew. As the Chinese central bank was tightening monetary policy, the U.S. Federal Reserve Board was expanding the U.S. money supply, pumping dollars into the system in an attempt to avert collapse. Global oil prices followed Fed policies, climbing at an accelerating pace through the first half of 2008, until they reached US$145 per barrel on July 3, 2008, which proved to be the peak. By far the world's largest importer of commodities, the Chinese economy was quite exposed to the rapid increase in commodity prices that took place during 2007–8, and this made the fight against inflation fiendishly difficult.

The pain felt in the domestic economy from anti-inflation policies was immediate. When macroeconomic policy shifted to inflation-fighting, in November 2007, the stock market promptly collapsed. At historic highs in November 2007, the Chinese stock market in the subsequent six years (through the end of 2013) has never recovered to even one-half of this peak. When the political leadership permitted the RMB to appreciate at a reasonably rapid rate, exporters screamed that they were squeezed between rising wages and soaring commodity prices, on the one hand, and a higher currency on the other. Real estate developers protested as property prices came down. Both lobbied Beijing intensively. The Chinese leadership stayed the course until July 2008, and then began to back away from anti-inflationary policies. It was hard for them to tell how rapidly economic conditions were deteriorating, with the Beijing Olympics going on in August and events taking place in New York with no precedent. Gradually, over five months, policy shifted 180 degrees: appreciation was halted, some export tax rebates were revived, and the People's Bank of China (PBC) changed course and began to cut interest rates. Of course, these five months, between June and November, were the months in which the global financial crisis rippled out from New York, as stresses in the U.S. markets erupted and the collapse in global markets began after October 1.

When China's top leaders did decide to act, they rolled out a stimulus program heavy on infrastructure investment. The program's initial price tag of RMB4 trillion was translated by international press reports into a precise-sounding US$586 billion, but this was in reality just a big, round number, not fleshed out with concrete projects or programs. Since 2009, the RMB4 trillion stimulus program has come to serve as a shorthand designation for the Chinese response, but it is in some respects extremely misleading. It gives the impression that the Chinese response was predominantly fiscal, carrying out an infrastructure investment program orchestrated by the central government. However, this was far from the case: the response was primarily monetary (rapid expansion of credit), which funded initiatives organized by local governments. Moreover, the "transmission process" that got money flowing into the economy was highly politicized, relying on Communist Party channels to convey commands with urgency, rather than standard financial channels (Naughton 2009; see Lardy 2012 for a very different interpretation). These characteristics would have substantial implications for the long-run effects of the stimulus response.

Of the initial RMB4 trillion, the central government committed to directly fund RMB1.18 trillion, about 30 percent of the overall program. Moreover, the program was written to include some RMB1 trillion that had already been committed for reconstruction after the devastating May 2008 Sichuan earthquake. Of the remaining RMB3 trillion, 60 percent was earmarked for transport and energy infrastructure, 33 percent for smaller-scale infrastructure (such as affordable housing, environmental projects, and village projects), and the rest for technological upgrading, health, and education. The National Development and Reform Commission (NDRC) head Zhang Ping stressed that none of the investment was going to ordinary industrial sectors, which were widely thought to have surplus capacity. As figure 5.2 shows, China's overall infrastructure effort did increase substantially, jumping about 2 percentage points of GDP in 2009.

In fact, the real action was going on behind the scenes. Joint with the State Council meeting, there was a Communist Party Politburo meeting, which is where the real power lies in China. When an authoritative document on the stimulus was issued, it was sent out from the Party Politburo through party channels. This document, Central Document No. 18 of 2008 has never been published, since, like many central Party documents, it was considered secret and was thus only distributed through internal party channels. However, we have a good idea of the contents from indirect sources. Central Document No. 18 and the accompanying draft from the top planning agency, the

NDRC, specified ten policy measures, including a RMB100 billion increase in government investment for the fourth quarter 2008, injunctions to loosen monetary policy, and increased bank credit to support investment and small businesses. By far the most important element of Central Document No. 18 was the general sense of urgency that was displayed, which was reiterated by officials in the following weeks. When the NDRC met on November 10 to allocate the first tranche of the RMB100 billion, it declared that for all government agencies, "the absolutely most important economic work is to urgently implement the center's increased investment and other measures to increase domestic demand . . . [and] make every second count" (NDRC 2008). The decision to send the document down through party channels added to this sense of urgency, conveying the sense that it was permissible to overturn ordinary obstacles to spending the money.

This action on the part of the central authorities was complementary to one of the most basic characteristics of the Chinese system. Local governments throughout China typically have a virtually inexhaustible demand for local infrastructure and construction projects. This is because local government officials have a distinctive incentive system, in which they are evaluated for promotion largely on the basis of their performance in regional economic growth. Confronted with the need to make a difference in their locality, attract attention from superiors, reward friends and clients with lucrative projects, and make a name for themselves before they move on (typically in three to six years), local government leaders have a strong demand for investment projects. Local governments typically have a "wish" list of projects they would like to undertake, and thus an insatiable demand for investment projects. When the central government solicited local projects for inclusion in the stimulus plan and, even more important, when it slackened the financing constraint that had long held back ambitious local politicians, it triggered a flood of new projects. Thus Central Document No. 18 initiated a structured bargaining process between the center and the localities (Xiao 2009). The center first signaled the type of projects it wanted locals to propose and gave the provinces a rough idea of the amounts they might expect, based on the province's population and its historic degree of reliance on central government investment, plus extra consideration for regions with high minority populations and big cities. The provinces then responded with a list of proposed projects.

Local governments were eager to seize this opportunity. Within days, local governments were convening meetings to propose projects and strategize over Central Document No. 18. For example, Shandong Province called a special meeting on November 11—only six days after the announcement—where the provincial governor urged attendees to "seize the favorable opportunity created by expansionary fiscal policy and the 'appropriately loose' monetary policy" (Qiang 2008). Meetings like this were initially being held in all the provinces, and then later in thousands of counties and hundreds of cities across China in mid-November (Naughton 2009). This process certainly displayed its strengths, for it elicited a rapid start to tens of thousands of investment projects. In an interesting discussion of crisis responses, Kanbur (2009) makes a distinction between those that are easy to ramp up but hard to wind down (like food subsidies), versus those that are hard to ramp up but relatively easy to wind down (such as public works projects). It is a peculiarity of the Chinese system that public works projects are much easier to ramp up than in a "normal" economy. In the event, Chinese local officials revealed that they had "shovel-ready" projects on the shelves they could quickly pull down and put into operation. Within a month, eighteen out of thirty-one total provinces had proposed projects with a total budget of RMB25 trillion, more than 80 percent of annual GDP (Huo et al. 2009). With this embarrassment of riches, it was easy for the NDRC to award project approvals with quick and rudimentary inspection of documents. The result was that the resource mobilization was much more rapid in China than in most countries. In the United States, for example, the maximum impact of the early 2009 fiscal stimulus bill did not occur until the second quarter of 2010, eighteen months after the crisis hit. In China, it was possible to observe the initial effects of new and accelerated projects in the Chinese economy within weeks, and certainly in the first quarter of 2009.

None of this was possible without a funding mechanism. While the fiscal impulse was significant, it pales beside the financing needs of the vast array of projects local governments wanted to start. In fact, the only possible source of funding of this magnitude was the banking system. The central government had already prepared the ground for a substantial mobilization of credit resources (and an associated relaxation of credit standards). Interest rates and reserve requirements were lowered. These explicit policies designed to ease provision of credit were mixed with the urgency and politicization of the stimulus itself. Together, these measures sent a powerful signal to banks that they were expected to ramp up lending quickly and suggested to bank loan officers that they would not be held accountable for loans that might later turn sour.

Inevitably, the banking system responded with a flood of lending. As figure 5.1 shows, bank lending exploded during the early months of 2009. During the first quarter of 2009, total bank loans outstanding increased by a whopping RMB4.6 trillion. This can be put into perspective in two ways: first, the increase in bank credit during the first three months of 2009 was more than the total planned RMB4 trillion investment stimulus package, which had been intended to stretch over more than two years plus one quarter; second, if we roughly calculate what ordinary credit needs would have been during the first quarter of 2009, then the *excess* credit above normal just in this one quarter was equal to 10 percent of annual GDP. This is a huge amount of credit to be injected into an economy in a short time. Credit creation stayed high in the second quarter as well before gradually being brought down to earth. There are various ways to calculate the total Chinese stimulus effort during all of 2009, but it was certainly huge. One illustrative calculation puts the amount of bank lending above "business as usual," plus special bond financing and fiscal deficit, at a total 20.7 percent of GDP in 2009 (Kroeber 2010, 27). The consolidated government budget swung into a deficit, equal to 2.3 percent of GDP in 2009, including most of the special bond issuance. Thus the explosive growth of bank credit provided the bulk of the Chinese stimulus response. It was primarily a monetary response, not a fiscal one, and it was driven by the state-owned banking system.

By comparison, in the United States, the Federal Reserve Board also dramatically increased its lending, holding US$1.2 trillion more in assets on its balance sheet in mid-April 2009 than a year earlier, an amount equal to more than 8 percent of 2008 GDP of US$14.5 trillion. But this was an attempt to offset a collapse in credit extended in other parts of the economy, whereas there was no such collapse in China. The U.S. fiscal stimulus was of comparable magnitude to the expansion in the Federal Reserve Board balance sheet, so that total stimulus response peaked at around 15 percent of GDP. The Chinese stimulus was thus larger proportionately than the U.S. stimulus, and delivered much more promptly. As a result, by mid-year 2009, there was already unmistakable evidence that employment had stabilized in China, and that output was beginning to recover. China was arguably the first economy to have recovered from the global financial crisis, and the derived demand for commodity imports was crucial in stabilizing the global economy at the end of the first quarter in 2009. Official GDP growth was ultimately tagged at 9.2 percent in 2009, during the midst of the most profound global economic crisis of the era (table I.1).

The Institutional Impact of the Global Financial Crisis Response

In order to create the vigorous stimulus described in the previous section, Chinese leaders had to adapt existing institutions for new purposes. The most immediate and profound impact was on local governments. Local governments in China are not permitted to borrow directly from banks themselves, so they must establish development corporations or other quasi-independent agencies to actually do the work. This process carries obvious moral hazards, and in normal times the central government monitors it fairly closely. However, in 2008–9, the central government relaxed its oversight over these development corporations and actively encouraged local governments to expand them. The resulting so-called local government funding or investment "platforms" (*rongzi pingtai*) were allowed to qualify for loans and issue certain kinds of corporate bonds that would count as paid-in capital (Naughton 2009). These special provisions were designed for projects that were approved by the government as part of the stimulus investment program, but they spread quickly and local government funding vehicles proliferated.

Governments at all levels, empowered by the massive flow of money through the system, soon moved into more assertive forms of industrial policy. At first, this was part of central government crisis management. In February 2009, "Industrial Revitalization Plans" were issued for ten sectors, mostly traditional industries that were struggling with declining orders, excess capacity, and substantial losses. Although justified by crisis conditions, these plans authorized financial support for specific firms and envisaged desirable market structures for two- and three-year time horizons. This newly interventionist spirit in Chinese industrial policy soon spilled over into plans for high-technology and strategic emerging industries (SEIs). The SEIs were composed of twenty high-technology industrial sectors seen to be emergent in the postcrisis period. Noting that governments everywhere were stepping up their investment in new energy, environmental, and information technologies, the Chinese government gradually assembled their own aggressive support programs into an overall framework during 2009. Ultimately, the SEI program declared that its objective was to raise the share of this cluster of industrial sectors from under 4 percent of GDP in 2010 to 8 percent in 2015 and 15 percent in 2020. A commonly articulated Chinese perception was that the impending emergence of fundamentally new high-tech industries gave China the opportunity to get in on the ground floor. Without powerful incumbents to lock them out of dynamic and profitable positions, China could "occupy the commanding heights of the new technological revolution." In this view, aggressive government intervention in the short run could have important long-run benefits.

The Chinese crisis response thus gradually began to shape large and long-term policy decisions. In fact, the Chinese premier Wen Jiabao, in his 2010 *Government Work Report*, which is an authoritative official document, summarizes the lessons learned from the global crisis and China's response: "In the past year, vigorously responding to the global financial crisis . . . we came to the following conclusion: while continuing to . . . let market forces play their basic role in allocating resources and stimulate the market's vitality, we must make best use of the socialist system's advantages, which enable us to make decisions efficiently, organize effectively, and concentrate resources to accomplish large undertakings" (Wen 2010).

This formulation specifically equates the market and the centralized deployment of administrative and political resources. Wen's assessment amounted to a major reevaluation of Chinese policy principles, following decades in which the importance accorded to the market in determining the allocation of resources had steadily increased. The novelty in this formulation is the most important aspect, and only one part of it is new: the emphasis on the centralized deployment of resources. This in fact was the lesson that the Chinese leadership drew from the crisis response of 2009.

What we see from this quote is that the initial institutional and systemic impacts of the GFC response were precisely the opposite of those of the AFC response. Under Zhu Rongji, the response to the AFC was to continue the pressure on the state sector and increase the resolve to open, reform, and institutionalize the reformed system. Under Wen Jiabao, the GFC response was to strengthen the state sector, legitimize increased government steerage of the economy, and bring the financial sector back under government tutelage as an instrument of government policy. One piece of evidence for this interpretation is a statement by Huang Mengfu, head of the All-China Federation of Industry and Commerce. Huang is by merit of his position the designated spokesman to the Communist Party from the private business sector. He declared in September 2009 that "in certain regions and sectors, we've observed the phenomenon of the state advancing at the expense of the private sector . . . we will pay a serious price for this." In the years after the GFC, Chinese policymakers were clearly heeding Wen Jiabao's lesson, and not Huang Mengfu's remonstrance.

Stated broadly, although the stimulus worked, it was costly. At a minimum, it halted and temporarily reversed the decades-long trend for the state to retreat from the economy and for private and nongovernmental actors to play a greater role. This was harmful not primarily because the state sector is "inefficient" or "backward," but rather because these actions profoundly disrupt the incentive structure that applies to both private and public actors. As long as the scope of the state sector was basically known and the trend both inside and outside the state sector was toward more profound marketization, individuals were rewarded for maximizing incomes and minimizing costs according to market-determined prices. However, when the scope of the state sector becomes indeterminate, and administrative interventions repeatedly redraw the boundary between state and private, then individuals are forced to devote time and resources to anticipating and manipulating government actions. This new environment changed calculations and increased costs. More important, it increased rent-seeking opportunities and produced many more inefficient outcomes.

Stimulus policies undermined the integrity of the financial system in more direct and immediate ways. First, banks relaxed their concerns about risk and loosened prudential standards, making massive loans to government clients. This represented the sudden abandonment of the difficult process of upgrading banking standards that had been underway since 1997, a process which had taken a large leap forward with the bank recapitalization and restructuring accomplished primarily in 2003–6. Bank budget constraints had gradually become "hard" (binding), but now they had suddenly become "soft" again. For fifteen years, banks had been allowed to write off trillions of RMB of NPLs. The stimulus surge of bank lending not only created fears of new NPLs but also fears that the government could no longer credibly demand that the banks be responsible for their own profits and losses. Thus the whole incentive environment of the banking system was weakened.

Second, the government more or less intentionally expanded the number of financially unsound local government investment corporations, as described previously. Not for the first time, financially flimsy (and sometimes shady) local government investment corporations proliferated in the Chinese economy. Estimates of the total value of debt owed by these corporations start at 20 percent of GDP and range upward from there. While it is entirely possible for the Chinese government to absorb an additional 20 percentage points of GDP worth of debt without threatening its fundamental financial stability, it represents a significant setback on the road to a healthy, market-compatible financial system.

It can be seen that the vigorous Chinese response to the GFC was dependent on some of the most deeply ingrained, but least functional, features of the Chinese political economic system: the responsiveness of local officials to the opportunity to invest, the willingness of actors at all levels to return to "soft budget constraint" conditions, and the lack of real independence of the banking system in the face of renewed politicization. While all of these features propelled the stimulus impulse, they also resurrected some of the most serious shortcomings of the prereform Chinese economic system. Economic policy was driven by a top-down mobilization of the system via Communist Party channels. Its effectiveness relied on unleashing the "expansion drive" in the system—that is, the built-in tendency for political and bureaucratic actors at all levels to claim public resources to invest in their own projects (and careers). Thus the fact that the system was highly responsive to a top-down call to quickly ramp up investment should not be too surprising; this is, after all, exactly what the system had been set up to achieve. Over decades of economic reform, these systemic defects had never disappeared, but they had been increasingly subordinated to market forces.

In their response to the GFC, Chinese leaders displayed a surprising willingness to discard the hard-won achievements of earlier reforms. In fact, it was an almost cavalier disregard for those achievements. The Chinese stimulus was not a careful technocratic response; it was an all-out mobilization than opened a Pandora's Box of complex effects. The reason why the response to the stimulus policy was extraordinarily rapid and effective is that it was achieved by bringing back to life some of the worst features of the Chinese system. It revealed the deep structure of the Chinese political economy, even as it intensified some of the aspects of the system. It also created a legacy of complex problems that confront the subsequent Xi Jinping–Li Keqiang administration, which are discussed in the final section.

Connecting the Dots: From the AFC to the GFC and Beyond

Considering the dual crises from the Chinese standpoint, we should stress three relationships that connect the AFC and GFC, each with implications for the present. First, the crises were linked by a successful set of policies that dealt with the immediate challenge of both the AFC and the GFC. Certainly, China's economic performance was impressive, and neither crisis seemed to slow China's astonishing growth very much. Moreover, both crises have provided material for a narrative of success, one that is picked up and repeated by official Chinese news outlets. Thus the AFC led China to take effective measures, to fight off speculative attacks on Hong Kong, and to emerge as a responsible power in the Asia region. China's success in confronting the GFC has not only enabled its breathtaking economic growth to continue—thus dramatically increasing its weight in the global economy—it has also given the Chinese leaders an unprecedented sense of self-confidence, combined with a profound disillusionment about the United States and its liberal economic models.

However, the second relationship between the two crises should make us much more cautious about this simple narrative of success. In this second relationship, the institutional characteristics of the two crisis policy responses can be seen as virtually opposite, mirror images of each other. In the late 1990s, at the onset of the AFC, China was undergoing a "transition recession," similar in kind but still milder in effect than the transitions experienced by other postsocialist countries (Kolodko 2000). The transition from socialism inevitably leads to a fall in measured output, but different approaches affect the size of the transitional recession. China, by deciding to develop market-oriented production institutions *first* and dissolving the bureaucratic economy *second*, had helped minimized its transitional recession and converted it instead into a "growth recession." But it was impossible to reduce those costs to zero, and China was in the midst of that difficult process when the AFC hit.

As we have seen, the initial response to the AFC contributed strongly to a deepening of that reform process. However, it also ironically set the stage for a subsequent weakening of commitment to that process. Steinfeld (2008, 188) argues that "a twenty-year-old reform agenda, one that since the late 1970s had tentatively and instrumentally employed market mechanisms to sustain socialism, was in the aftermath of the AFC peremptorily and unceremoniously ditched. In its place, sweeping marketization—capitalism, in effect—was embraced at considerable political and social risk." Looking back from the perspective of the second decade of the twenty-first century, it is clear that this conclusion was premature. From 1992, when Deng Xiaoping pulled China out of the post-Tiananmen reaction and kick-started reforms, until November 1999, when China signed off on terms for its membership into the World Trade Organization, an extraordinary series of systematically deepening economic reforms transformed China into what was fundamentally a market economy. In this context, the AFC of 1997–98 was a bright punctuation mark, signaling the entry into a climactic stage of reform, in which state-owned enterprises were closed down on a massive scale and unemployment surged temporarily. However, in the years following the AFC, this deepening reform did not continue. Instead, once the bank restructuring conceived under Zhu Rongji was completed, reforms slowed dramatically. Indeed, if we adopt a relatively strict definition of reform as "a change in economic system that lowers barriers and subjects new areas to market competition," there have been no major reform initiatives in the decade since bank restructuring. China has thus fallen short of embracing sweeping marketization, much less capitalism.

The primary concerns of China's leaders during the 2002–12 Hu Jintao–Wen Jiabao administration shifted away from market reform and toward social policy that would ameliorate some of the negative outcomes of the reform process. The early years of the Wen Jiabao administration saw important steps to lower rural tax burdens, increase agricultural procurement prices, and provide subsidies for grain farmers. These policies were clearly motivated by a desire to moderate the increasing inequality of the 1990s, especially the urban-rural gap that had remained stubbornly wide. Further policy initiatives ensued in a wide range of social arenas: education, health insurance, and housing policy, to name a few. Obviously such a list does no more than give a flavor of recent decision making, and the reality in each field is complex (see Naughton 2011). Nonetheless, the impetus behind these policy measures clearly lay in the inequalities and imbalances that accompanied the reform process as a whole. Such measures can be seen as complementary to market-oriented reform, essential to making a market economy function better and more fairly.

Yet it is unmistakable that the adoption of these measures was accompanied by a shift away from reliance on the market and toward the increased use of direct government intervention in the economy. By the early 2000s, a palpable "reform fatigue" affected Chinese society, as unemployment, inequality, corruption, and a broken social contract were associated in the public mind with the reform process. To a certain extent, because the AFC deepened China's growth recession, it contributed to this reform fatigue. In that sense, it may also be implicated in the backlash to reform that slowly developed during the 2000s. A consequence of this backlash was that policy-makers ceased demanding market-conforming solutions to solve social and developmental problems. In a range of fields from housing policy, health insurance, to technology and industrial policy, we see a renewed willingness to resort to direct government intervention to achieve social and political goals. As argued above, by the time the GFC hit, China's policy had already been reoriented away from market reforms, and it was easy to rely on an intensification of direct government action to deal with the immediate challenge. Thus the institutional impact of each crisis response was the mirror image of the other.

The reinterpretation of the policy agenda in the post-AFC period gradually altered the way in which the concern about external vulnerability was reflected in actual policy choices. In particular, the peg of the RMB exchange rate to the U.S. dollar became an inflexible touchstone of external policy. Maintaining exchange rate stability in the face of devaluation pressure was a decision widely praised in 1997–99. Chinese policymakers proceeded to hold the peg in place another six years, until mid-2005. During that time, China's export competitiveness exploded, on the heels of successful domestic reforms and WTO membership (formally begun in December 2001, with many provisions phasing in over the subsequent two to three years). The result was soaring exports, a widening trade surplus, and steady accumulation of foreign exchange reserves (figure 5.3). Not surprisingly, this policy elicited substantial international criticism, not least from the United States, and the Chinese response to the criticism was telling: Chinese government officials bristled at foreign, especially American, criticisms of their exchange rate policy and dug in their heels on national sovereignty grounds. At the same time, thoughtful Chinese economists pointed out that misaligned and inflexible exchange rates were creating imbalances that were ultimately costly to the Chinese economy (Yu 2007). An initially constructive policy of exchange rate stability gradually became an obstacle to China's smooth adaptation to rapidly changing economic conditions.

In a broader sense, the quality of Chinese economic policymaking began to decline as the commitment to marketization and reform waned after 2003. The decision to maintain a fixed and undervalued exchange rate led to a variety of interrelated problems. These problems have been analyzed most cogently by Lardy (2012): as China accumulated reserves in the mid-2000s, the tendency for the domestic money supply to expand could only be partially restrained, at great effort, by central bank sterilization. As a result, inflationary pressures steadily built, and the monetary authorities were only able to periodically restrain them. As figure 5.1 shows, cycles of inflationary pressure steadily pushed up the overall price level (after the economy moved out of the deflationary period associated with the AFC itself). Concerned about the financial health of the banking system (which had only recently been rehabilitated), policymakers responded by keeping caps on deposit interest rates, which increasingly resulted in negative real interest rates for China's savers. "Financial repression" resulted, in which the financial system implicitly taxed the household sector for the benefit of the corporate sector. These policies restrained the growth of household income by directly reducing interest income to China's high-saving households. Moreover, low interest rates on bank loans reduced the demand for capital market alternatives to the banking system and tied firms (especially state-owned firms) more closely to the state-owned banks. The saving and investment options of Chinese households were highly restricted, especially after the stock market collapse of 2007, and housing became one of the few outlets for household saving. In the absence of forward progress on marketization, imbalances arose that were not subject to the automatic reequilibration of the market. Thus while China's immediate reaction to the AFC was to intensify market-oriented reforms, the longer-term response involved a steady deemphasis of market-conforming policies, and the gradual buildup of renewed institutional and macroeconomic distortions in the economy.

This leads us to the third relationship between the AFC and the GFC: the 1997–98 AFC and the Chinese response contributed to changes in the global economy that in some respects set the stage for the 2008–9 global crisis. China's post-AFC policies contributed to the global imbalances that were part of the environment out of which the GFC grew. It is not that Chinese policies caused the GFC; there is more than enough blame for the GFC in U.S. macroeconomic policies and regulatory lapses. However, Chinese policies *enabled* U.S. policy mistakes because of the two main channels through which Chinese exchange rate policy influenced the United States. First, sustained Chinese government demand for U.S. treasuries (for its official foreign exchange reserves) helped keep long-term interest rates low. Second, maintaining a fixed RMB–U.S. dollar exchange kept Chinese export prices low, contributing to lower U.S. prices and restrained U.S. inflation. Both these effects suggested to the U.S. Federal Reserve Board that U.S. monetary policy was not "too loose." As a result, U.S. policymakers maintained a policy stance that, in retrospect, most economists believe to have been excessively expansionary (see Taylor 2009 for an alternative view). This expansionary excess contributed to inflating the housing bubble, the bursting of which was the proximate cause of the GFC. In this sense, China's role in the lead-up to the GFC was no different from that of the other East Asian economies, all of which began to run long-term trade surpluses and accumulate foreign exchange reserves after the AFC. However, China was the largest single actor in this story, and thus serves as one of the primarily links between the two crises. Asian current account surpluses were the mirror image of U.S. deficits, and the willingness of the Asian economies to keep their surpluses in low-yielding U.S. treasuries fed the hubris at the U.S. Federal Reserve Board who believed that there were no bubbles, just an adjustment to a "global savings glut," and thus delayed regulatory and prudent macroeconomic responses until they were too late (Coulibaly and Millar 2008).

There is no unambiguous connection of cause and effect in these relationships. All we can say with confidence is that Chinese policymaking allowed for increasing distortions in both domestic and international economic relationships through the mid-2000s. When the GFC did come (due to American mismanagement), the cautious—some might say excessively cautious—trade and currency policies of China put it in a relatively secure position. Reserves were certainly ample, and domestic financial conditions still reasonably secure. Like other countries that had accumulated reserves during the good times of the 2000s, China weathered the GFC in reasonably good shape. Thus the policies that emerged out of the AFC set up policymakers to respond to the GFC effectively and in a manner completely consistent with their existing policy orientation. By 2008, Chinese policymakers, led by the Premier Wen Jiabao, had already dialed down their commitment to market reform and begun to stress achievement of social and economic goals through direct government action. Some of these government actions included a new health insurance and medical delivery scheme, which was on the cusp of adoption as the GFC hit. Another included an activist technology policy that had been steadily developed in the wake of the 2006 tech-sector reevaluation as outlined in the document, *Medium and Long-term Plan for Science and Technology Development* (State Council 2006). In this context, China's policymakers approached the challenges of the GFC from the standpoint of government planners: they believed in direct government action and moved quickly to put government programs in place that would directly support the sectors and households affected by the global crisis. The result was a further increase in the level of direct government intervention in the economy.

As such, the initial response to the GFC echoed the response to the AFC by intensifying the existing policy orientation of the existing leadership. Zhu Rongji's reformist impulses were extended by the AFC; Wen Jiabao's interventionist tendencies were extended by the GFC. In a sense, this is not surprising since China is a large country with an extraordinarily complex and sometimes tensely negotiated domestic political equilibrium. Thus external events, even rapidly moving and potentially dangerous external events, are filtered through a complex domestic political environment. Leaders such as Zhu Rongji or Wen Jiabao, having achieved political positions that enable them to carry out large-scale agendas to which they are personally committed, are not likely to abandon them in the face of external events. Instead, they adapt those agendas to new circumstances, which often involves making that agenda more radical or extending it into new areas. But by the same token, the radicalization of the agenda creates fertile ground for a subsequent backlash. Policy responses to crises are not necessarily sustained after the first few years, particularly when a new administration takes power.

Coming immediately out of the GFC, Chinese self-evaluation was overwhelmingly positive. The stimulus program produced tremendous benefits, which were shared between China and the rest of the world. Within a few years, though, policymakers and the public began to acknowledge the increasingly obvious costs of the crisis response. Around the world, most countries were by the end of 2013 engaged in unwinding the extraordinary measures taken to cope with the crisis. Fiscal stimulus was being unwound to restore confidence in future government finances, especially in Europe. Extraordinary interventions in financial markets were also being unwound, especially in the United States. However, China has been at variance with these trends, as can be seen in three dimensions. First, the credit-based stimulus impulse China launched in 2009 has not been systematically drawn down. Figure 5.1 portrays a mixed picture, showing credit growth coming down from rates greater than 30 percent to the range of 15 percent, close to historical norms. In fact, after 2010, credit continued to grow rapidly, but much of the credit growth came outside the formal banking system, in the so-called "shadow banking" system. During 2012, more than half of total social credit came through these channels. One good indicator is provided by the indebtedness of local governments. Despite a major effort begun in 2010 to restructure and reduce local government debt, this debt has stayed high and actually increased. According to a report of the National Audit Office, debt of province, city, and county governments amounted to RMB10.6 trillion in mid-2013. Moreover, the debt load had grown at an annual rate of just below 20 percent since the end of 2010, and most of the increase had come outside traditional bank lending channels. By a broader definition of central and local debt, including contingent liabilities, debt was RMB30.3 trillion, or about 52 percent of projected 2013 GDP (Chinese National Audit Office 2013; Wang 2013). The problem is not so much that China's government debt is unsustainably large, but rather that extraordinarily rapid credit growth triggered by the GFC has still not been brought under control. This kind of financial excess shows up in asset bubbles, which are continuously being created, most precariously in the housing sector.

A closely related phenomenon is observed in the real economy where the investment rate has remained extraordinarily high. The stimulus response to the GFC pushed the rate of investment to an unprecedented 47 percent of GDP in 2009. In subsequent years, despite repeated statements of the need for more balanced growth, the overall investment rate has actually edged up, maintaining an astonishing 48 percent of GDP on average in 2010–2012. However, as figure 5.2 shows, pure infrastructure investment has come down from its 2009 high, while other forms of investment have more than taken up the slack. Massive investment has become the main driver of the Chinese economy, and the government has made little progress in reducing this overreliance on investment. The crisis-driven changes to the "rules of the game" are a major part of the problem—they give government officials and state-owned enterprises control over a larger volume of resources than before and reduce the accountability of both officials and financial institutions. These changes inevitably soften budget constraints, reduce individual risk, and encourage even larger investments. The extraordinary credit expansion and investment effort unleashed during the GFC are thus still shaping the Chinese economy. In this sense, China's stimulus measures have proved to be quite hard to wind down (Kanbur 2009). In the macroeconomic, investment, and financial arenas, the post-GFC period has continued through at least the end of 2013.

Finally, China has continued to embrace the extraordinary expansion of government intervention that was adopted during the crisis. To be sure, this expansion predates the crisis, but as we have shown above, the crisis led to a further intensification of the direct government role in the economy. So far, the Chinese government has not scaled back its effort in any of these areas. Thus China has continued to embrace the full panoply of social insurance and industrial policies that were ramped up during the crisis. The continued emphasis on "strategic emerging industries" in 2013 has been especially striking, since a number of these programs (e.g., solar panels) have run into serious economic problems. This has occurred at the time when most market economies have been reemphasizing the lines that divide government from the market and committing to a speedy government withdrawal from the market.

Yet if China is still wrapped up in its crisis-response phase, there are signs that significant changes are on the horizon. Indeed, it is entirely possible that the 2010–13 period will come to be seen as an era of overshooting following the response to the GFC. Since late 2012, a new administration has been in charge of China's economy. Xi Jinping, the new Communist Party leader, and Li Keqiang, the head of the government, immediately upon taking office, began talking of the need to revitalize the economic reform process. In November 2013, an important party meeting (the Third Plenum) committed to a new program of wide-ranging reforms to be overseen by Xi himself. Although this process is in its infancy as of the end of 2013, the leaders have already decisively parted company with the policy orientation of the Hu–Wen administration. In the party resolution that came from this meeting, a key theme was the need to clarify the distinction between the functions of government and the market, and to "greatly reduce the direct allocation of resources by government" and let the market play a "decisive role" in resource allocation (CCP 2013). Although it may seem purely semantic, this dramatic shift of emphasis is in fact a reversal of the "lesson" that Wen Jiabao drew in 2010 (quoted earlier). In Wen's formulation, the market's role in resource allocation had been "basic" but taken for granted, and needs to be supplemented by decisive, large-scale government deployment of resources. The new leadership has announced a dramatic shift toward a market-driven policy model. To be sure, a great deal of work still needs to be done to flesh out these rhetorical commitments and ensure effective implementation.

The Xi Jinping administration is still dealing with the legacy of the GFC and the Chinese response, but that response no longer seems natural, inevitable, and right. Rather, the crisis response may have been excessive and certainly carried on for too long, leaving a legacy of hard-to-resolve problems. Ten years ago, in 2004, the Wen Jiabao administration was gradually but steadily moving away from the reform commitments of the Zhu Rongji era, commitments that had been solidified by the AFC. Today, in 2014, the Xi Jinping–Li Keqiang administration is gradually moving to reinstate some elements of that reform agenda. How far will they go? How thoroughly will they reassess the costs and problems of the previous administration? It is too early to tell, but it is clear that as of the end of 2013, the Chinese leadership is moving out of the postcrisis period and into a new era where more policy options (old and new) are being seriously considered.

The challenges are formidable. Complicating the policy options is the fact that China is reaching a crucial turning point in its development process. Since the 1980s, China has been undergoing a full-fledged growth miracle, with average annual GDP growth rates slightly above 10 percent per year. This extraordinary growth dynamism is part of what gave the Chinese economy such enormous resilience in the face of the two crises. However, China is reaching the end of this miraculous growth phase and entering a middle-income status in which growth rates are unlikely to ever again surpass 8 percent in a given year. As table I.1 showed, growth in 2012 has already slid below 8 percent, almost reaching the low point recorded in 1998 during the middle of the AFC. Almost certainly, this is the new "normal," since labor force growth has slowed dramatically and upward pressure on unskilled wages is now substantial. Under these conditions, efforts to keep the growth rate above 8 percent would be risky and unlikely to succeed.

The challenge to Chinese policymakers is to transition to a sustainable growth path, to maintain something like 6 percent annual GDP growth per year over the next decade. Such an outcome would be extremely positive. Indeed, an increasingly middle-income China with a much better educated workforce and huge diverse domestic market will create a completely new type of economic miracle if it can sustain growth and transformation at that pace. However, such a transition will not be easy. Indeed, the experiences of Japan and Korea, examined elsewhere in this volume, shows that it is extremely difficult to make the transition out of the miraculous growth phase and into a new phase of sustainable middle-income growth.

Chinese policymakers thus face the extraordinary challenge of adapting to long-run slower growth while rebalancing the economy and reviving market-oriented economic reforms. In the long run, these objectives are completely consistent and indeed mutually reinforcing; in the short run, many difficult choices have to be made and opposition to change overcome. The leadership has committed itself in principle to a new round of economic reform, but actual implementation has scarcely begun. What will determine the success of the endeavor? Policymakers must carry out the restructuring of the financial system thoroughly and with determination. They must accept lower growth rates while a healthier economic model is developed. They must scale back direct government intervention and allow greater space for dynamic Chinese private businesses to move into new areas. They must put local governments on a sounder financial footing in order to allow them to withdraw from land and commercial markets. These things are difficult but not impossible. We may find that in the future, these actions are portrayed as the inevitable rectification of extreme policies, the end set of extraordinary measures that are no longer necessary. The crises, in this interpretation, are finally over.

Part 2

Toward a Second East Asia Miracle?

6

Political Business and External Vulnerability in Southeast Asia

Thomas B. Pepinsky

The Global Financial Crisis (GFC) of 2008–9 represents a landmark event for the advanced industrial economies. In island Southeast Asia—Indonesia, Malaysia, the Philippines, and Singapore—the GFC will be remembered as an external shock that generated a lot of worry but few direct costs. This is in stark contrast to the crisis of 1997–98, which in the region toppled one authoritarian juggernaut (Indonesia), dealt a near-fatal blow to another (Malaysia), and frightened the remaining two countries, both of which had enjoyed strong growth in previous years. The 1997–98 financial crises in Southeast Asia generated a voluminous literature on their origins and consequences, most of which emphasized how political economy factors played a central role in explaining why the crisis unfolded across the region in the way that it did. Southeast Asia's "noncrisis" of 2008–9 raises the question of whether political and economic reforms after the 1990s crises have shielded island Southeast Asia from the current economic crisis.

The answer to that question is no. Rather, island Southeast Asia has weathered the current crisis primarily because of more subtle changes in exchange rates and domestic regulation alongside broader changes in investor beliefs about the viability of these countries' political and economic systems. In this chapter, I outline some of the lessons that we can draw from a comparison of these two international financial crises and their effects in island Southeast Asia. My focus is on political-business relations and the politics of external vulnerability in these four countries. The central lesson from the two crises is that the pathways from tight political-business relations to vulnerability to international contagion during global or regional financial crises—which I gloss here as "external vulnerability"—are subtle and complex. Alone, neither domestic political economy factors nor international economic integration are sufficient to explain the course of these two crises in island Southeast

Asia. Further, not even the conjunction of domestic political economy factors and international economic integration explains the course of the two crises. Rather, to understand why the Asian Financial Crisis (AFC) of 1997–98 was so devastating for Southeast Asia while the GFC was so minor, we must focus on the more subtle interactions of incentive structures, regulatory regimes, and global economic conditions.

In advancing this argument, I challenge existing explanations for external vulnerability in the AFC and beyond that focus on broad political economic factors such as "corruption," "crony capitalism," "moral hazard," and related factors (see also Chang 2000; Weiss 1999). In this sense, the argument in this chapter complements Chu (this volume), who also holds that East Asia's resiliency cannot be explained by political or institutional reforms that have been enacted since the AFC. However, my argument differs in the relatively greater emphasis that I place on changing investor perceptions about the propriety of political-business relations in island Southeast Asia, as well as their interactions with the technical policy choices by national governments.

The central lesson from the four country comparison is that whatever pathologies we can identify in the political economies of small, open, developing economies such as those in island Southeast Asia, it is by no means the case that they generate external vulnerability—even in the small, open, developing economies that are often thought to be most vulnerable to volatile international conditions. There is no shortage of reasons to worry about the economic prospects of these four countries. Tight political-business relations in Indonesia, Malaysia, the Philippines, and arguably even Singapore continue to produce important political and economic problems. Nowhere in Southeast Asia do political-business relations approach a "laissez-faire" model of capitalism; instead, I characterize political-business relations in contemporary Indonesia and the Philippines as "rent seeking," in contemporary Malaysia as "collusive," and in Singapore as "regulatory." In various ways, each of the four island Southeast Asian economies faces serious problems of efficiency, equity, corruption, and cronyism. These raise fundamental questions about the long-term sustainability of these countries' developmental trajectories. Their having withstood the GFC does not deny these problems. But it does indicate that the existence of tight political-business interactions does not generate external vulnerability in the ways that a cursory reading of the literature on the 1997–98 crisis might suggest.

In the following section I briefly review the state political-business relations in island Southeast Asia prior to 1998. While the links between politicians and business interests were tight throughout the region during this period, political-business relations produced very different kinds of external vulnerability in each of the four countries under consideration. I then examine the record of political and economic restructuring in the wake of the crisis, which I rate to have been significant in Indonesia but little more than cosmetic in the other three. From there, I argue that Indonesia's reforms had nothing to do with protecting it from the 2008–9 financial crisis; as there were no significant reforms in the other three countries, such reforms could not have helped them either. I conclude with a commentary on what political economists and regional specialists should infer about the role of political business, cronyism, and related issues in explaining country vulnerability to financial crises.

Business and Politics in the 1990s

Southeast Asia's economic performance in the early- and mid-1990s was no less than spectacular when viewed against previous decades' lackluster performance and the relatively difficult post-1980s adjustments in Africa and Latin America. Singapore, which had already enjoyed its postindependence transformation into a regional manufacturing hub, sought to lay the groundwork for a second economic transformation through innovation and services. Indonesia, Malaysia, and the Philippines had undertaken difficult reforms in the late 1980s in response to the global economic slowdown earlier in that decade. These reforms, coupled with relative political stability and a fundamentally open orientation to the global economy (especially in Indonesia and Malaysia), enabled each to take advantage of the global upswing of the 1990s through the export of commodities and manufactured goods. Strong GDP growth followed as shown by figure 6.1.

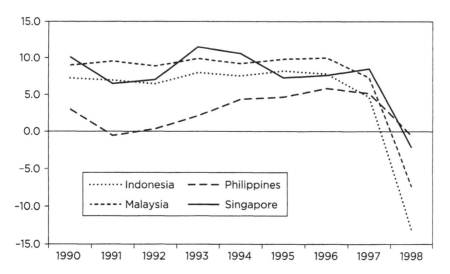

Figure 6.1 GDP growth rate of four Southeast Asian countries, 1990–98 (%).

Source: IMF 2013.

There was no shortage of attempts to link developing Asia's economic success to various paradigms and schools of thought about economic development. For liberals, island Southeast Asia represented the victory of capitalism over the dirigiste policies that were once popular in the region, and of globalization over autarky and national developmentalism (World Bank 1993). For institutionalists, island Southeast Asia confirmed that institutions play an essential role in directing and managing the dislocations inherent in economic transformation in a globalized world (Abrami and Doner 2008, 230–38). For neo-Marxists and other structuralist critics of developing Asia's quasi-developmentalist regimes, what appeared to be the foundation for long-term economic development was little more than capital accumulation by powerful economic actors, which masked serious problems of equity, access, and participation for most citizens (Rodan et al. 2005).

Reality did not quite confirm any of these perspectives. While none of these economies were dirigiste in any meaningful sense of the word, neither did regimes create the sorts of unfettered free markets that classical liberalism might have expected would be necessary to generate sustained economic growth in what had formerly been quite backward regions. Indonesia, Malaysia, and the Philippines were hardly developmental states in the way that Singapore, South Korea, and Taiwan were. And while all countries fell short in important ways in providing access to the fruits of economic development to all, the 1990s did see substantial improvements in material well-being for most citizens of these countries. Importantly, all of this was accomplished under political regimes that fell short of basic standards for democratic quality, from the military-bureaucratic New Order regime in Indonesia to the mobilizational hegemonic party regimes in Malaysia and Singapore to the messy and elite-dominated young democracy of the Philippines.

What is clear is that during this period of rapid economic growth, deep connections between political and business elites flourished. In every country, political elites used economic policy as a tool for consolidating or maintaining political authority. This happened in different ways in different countries, and this has important consequences for the way that the AFC unfolded across island Southeast Asia. But the commonality across them is that growing economies provided regimes with ready access to cash to fund development schemes (which generated performance legitimacy) and crony enterprises (which generated elite compliance) alike.

In Indonesia, the New Order regime had responded to the oil shocks and general economic slowdown in the 1980s with a round of privatization and deregulation (Soesastro 1989). Combined with the country's relative openness to trade and foreign investment, this provided the foundation for nearly a decade of rapid economic growth. Politically connected entrepreneurs in both the Chinese Indonesian and indigenous *pribumi* business community were well positioned to capitalize on the new economic opportunities afforded by deregulation and privatization. These opportunities allowed connected figures to nurture their large and diversified business empires that penetrated nearly all sectors of the Indonesian economy. In exchange for favorable regulations, choice tenders, and political protection, entrepreneurs provided the cash and business opportunities that financed the New Order regime, including off-budget activities associated with the military and the bureaucracy as well as Soeharto and his immediate family. This hierarchical model of political-business relations can best be described as "predatory." All of this was supported by substantial inflows of foreign capital eager to take advantage of the country's booming economy. Capital inflows were in turn encouraged by a pegged (and overvalued) exchange rate, an open capital account, financial deregulation, and an implicit understanding at home and abroad that the government would maintain these policies indefinitely (Hill 1999).

Malaysia too responded to crises of the 1980s with privatization and deregulation. And like Indonesia, Malaysia had long embraced foreign trade and investment as key engines for growth (some infant-industry protectionism notwithstanding). But Malaysia's economic structure along with its configuration of business interests and political power differed from Indonesia. Economically, Malaysia entered the 1990s with a much more developed financial system, including a stable and relatively liquid equities market. Politically, Malaysia's Barisan Nasional regime relied on the support of the country's indigenous *bumiputera* (primarily Malay) majority, whose economic status had not yet caught up with that of the country's ethnic Chinese minority even after decades of economic and political favoritism. This meant that more so than in Indonesia, Malaysia's political elites distributed the fruits of economic growth broadly among the country's indigenous masses, fostering Malay participation in the equities market in particular but also taking care to nurture the nascent Malay entrepreneurial class (Gomez and Jomo 1999). This more interconnected form of political-business relations—without the dominant executive found in Indonesia—can best be described as "collusive." As in Indonesia, favorable policies generated broad support for the regime among its key constituents. Foreign capital attracted to Malaysia's growing economy and stable political system—again, under a pegged and overvalued exchange rate with an open capital account and a liberalized financial sector—further supported growth in the 1990s.

Indonesia and Malaysia each saw GDP growth far exceed 5 percent per year throughout the early and mid 1990s. The Philippines saw much more modest growth until the middle of the decade, and never reached the same dizzying pace seen elsewhere in the region. While there are undoubtedly many factors that help to explain the Philippines' relatively slower growth, from a political economy perspective, the central factor explaining slower growth was the interaction of new and fragile political institutions with an unstable and confusing business environment. Unlike Indonesia and Malaysia, the Philippines saw the end of its authoritarian regime in the 1980s; in the subsequent decade the administrations of Corazon Aquino and Fidel Ramos worked within a new democratic political order. Two legacies of the prior authoritarian period remained, though. One was political instability, visible through several unsuccessful coup attempts, the privatization of security for the country's elites, and sustained infighting among various political factions. The second was the Filipino economy's continued domination by relatively small and insulated group of economic elites (the "oligarchs") whose influence penetrated regulatory institutions, yielding a "rent-seeking" form of political-business relations. Together, political instability and "patrimonial plunder" made the Philippines a relatively less attractive foreign investment destination that its neighbors (Hutchcroft 1999). A more restricted capital account and a less overvalued exchange rate reinforced this, especially in comparison to the stable and highly open economies elsewhere in the region.

Political business in Singapore in the 1990s followed a still different trajectory. The Singaporean political system shares a number of features with Malaysia, including a dominant party (the People's Action Party) that has adopted a mobilizational strategy for maintaining power. But cognizant of its shortage of human and natural resources, and sensitive to its strategic location along an important trade route, Singapore's leaders have consistently embraced trade and foreign investment since independence. Doing so has meant capitalizing on the strong legal and administrative institutions that it inherited from the British to provide an institutional environment that foreign companies find attractive in terms of stability, legal certainty, and the ease of doing business. In this way, Singapore parlayed its history as a free trade port into a position as a regional hub for manufacturing, trade, and services. This does not mean that politics and business do not mix in Singapore—quite the opposite, the links between the two are tight and include many personal links between politicians and business elites (Hamilton-Hart 2000). But legal and regulatory authorities have not been captured by particularistic interests in the way that they have been elsewhere in the region, producing political-business relations in Singapore that can be described as "regulatory." Foreign capital flowed into Singapore just as in Indonesia and Malaysia, but this was to take advantage of good economic institutions rather than to capitalize on strong growth and financial deregulation under open capital markets and a pegged exchange rate.

By 1996, the signs of overheating in developing Asia were apparent, if ignored by most market participants and governments alike. Chinn (2000), among others, has found evidence that the rupiah, ringgit, and peso were overvalued, although the extent of this overvaluation was not severe. Foreign debt inflows were large relative to GDP, especially in Indonesia and Malaysia (see table 6.1), while inflows of portfolio capital and foreign direct investment reached substantial portions of each country's GDP (see table 6.2).

While inflows of foreign debt and equity investment are themselves not dangerous, the problem for Indonesia, Malaysia, and to a lesser extent the

TABLE 6.1
Ratio of net inflow of debts to GDP, 1991–96 (annual average)

	Long term	Short term	Private nonguaranteed
Indonesia	2.33	1.99	1.35
Malaysia	2.65	1.98	2.37
Philippines	1.48	0.85	1.07
Singapore	n/a	n/a	n/a

Source: Author's calculations from World Bank 2013.

TABLE 6.2
Ratio of net inflow of investment to GDP, 1991–96 (annual average)

	Foreign direct investment	Private excl. FDI	Total private
Indonesia	1.63	2.34	3.97
Malaysia	6.65	5.18	11.83
Philippines	1.7	2.18	3.88
Singapore	8.83	−3.02	5.87

Sources: Author's calculations from Asian Development Bank 2000 and IMF 2010c.

Philippines lay in the way that they were intermediated into the domestic economy. In Malaysia they fed the rapid expansion of the Kuala Lumpur Stock Exchange (KLSE), whose market capitalization exceeded 200 percent of GDP by the beginning of 1997 as individuals and corporations alike—encouraged by the regime—sought to grab a piece of the country's growth. In Indonesia they coursed through the country's conglomerates and their financial institutions to feed a rapid increase of domestic lending, much of which made little regard to fundamental viability of the ventures being funded so long as they fulfilled political needs. In the Philippines similar patterns prevailed, if to a smaller extent due to the country's more modest performance (Hutchcroft 1999). Figure 6.2 charts private sector credit growth in the four economies, making clear both the rapid growth in private sector credit and its size relative to GDP prior to 1998. Exchange rates played a key role, as market participants appear to have believed that there existed implicit government guarantees about future exchange rate trajectories. This encouraged market participants to discount exchange rate risk in Indonesia and Malaysia, something which would later prove devastating when the crisis hit. Only in Singapore did prudential authorities manage the inflow of foreign capital in a way that would ultimately prevent a painful financial reversal.

This, then, was the state of affairs in island Southeast Asia in early 1997. Political-business relations were close in all four major economies, but they varied in ways that would affect the build-up of external vulnerability. Stable, cooperative political-business relations in Indonesia and Malaysia, predatory

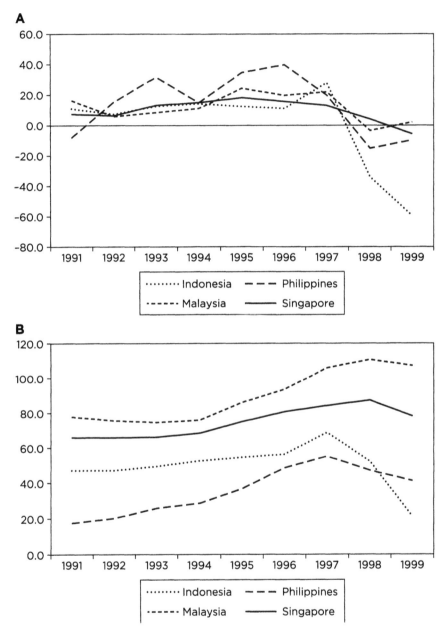

Figure 6.2 Private sector credit: Credit growth calculated in constant prices (panel A) and credit as a percent of GDP (panel B).

Source: Author's calculations from Asian Development Bank (2000).

in the former and collusive in the latter, and enabled by external economic policy settings and a lack of independent regulatory oversight, fed booming economies that attracted large inflows of foreign capital. Stable, cooperative political-business relations in Singapore, combined with strong legal and regulatory institutions, led to strong economic growth that also attracted significant capital inflows, but which was far less vulnerable to sudden changes in investor sentiment or to the exchange rate. Unstable politics and elite rent seeking was the hallmark of political-business relations in the Philippines and led to the capture of regulatory institutions by powerful business interests and discouraged the type of capital inflows seen elsewhere in the region.

The Asian Financial Crisis and Postcrisis Reforms

The aforementioned patterns had important implications for these economies' vulnerability to sudden external shocks such as that which accompanied the Thai government's decision to float the baht in June 1997. The baht float represented the end of the common belief that East Asian currencies were fundamentally sound, most basically in the sense that governments could not be forced to abandon their managed exchange rate regimes. Coming on the heels of the bursting of a property bubble in Thailand, it also encouraged investors both at home and abroad to reevaluate the fundamental viability of the pattern of rapid growth fed by capital inflows in the region. Thereafter, investors became concerned with future growth trajectories in developing Asia, and began to pull back from their former eagerness to feed these economies' appetite for foreign capital. By September 1997 the rupiah, ringgit, and peso had been allowed to float. The combination of downward exchange rate pressure and rising concerns about the quality of outstanding loans and investment projects quickly became a self-reinforcing cycle: investors concerned about future exchange rate movements held off from investing or divested altogether, which exposed the fragility of existing financial systems to changes in investor sentiment, which of course further damaged investor sentiment. The subsequent course of the crisis from this point forward is well known and need not concern us here, aside from the observation that the very factors that had previously undergirded rapid economic expansion—in Indonesia and Malaysia especially—now proved to be the very factors that made the crisis so severe.

Indonesia's crisis was the most dramatic, and the one most often marshaled as evidence of the ways in which political-business relations can produce external vulnerability (Robison and Rosser 1998). The rupiah float in August 1997 exposed the extent to which private foreign borrowing had gravitated toward short maturity structures and failed to take into account foreign exchange risk. So long as the domestic economy continued to grow, and so long as the government would protect the rupiah, borrowers had every incentive to seek cash overseas at favorable terms in order to invest at home, and no incentive to hedge their borrowing against possible currency movements. After the float, borrowers found themselves having to pay back loans that were growing increasingly expensive at the same time that their profit-making opportunities at home were disappearing. Banks and other financial institutions reacted by hoarding what funds they had, which in turn starved the entire economy of working capital. This meant that nearly all sectors of the Indonesian economy, not just those directly exposed to foreign capital inflows, found themselves in crisis.

Politically connected business interests, who had themselves helped to create the now-collapsed system, placed enormous pressure on the regime to find a policy solution that would bring the crisis to an orderly close. However, the main feasible policy solutions—deinternationalizing the rupiah and closing the capital account, or alternatively raising interest rates and slashing public expenditures to establish credibility—were viewed as unpalatable by important subgroups within the business community. Indonesian firms with fixed assets (many of which had informal ties with the military or to the first family) sought to reflate the economy under a closed capital account, while largely ethnic Chinese-owned firms with mobile assets scrambled to protect their ability to send cash overseas (Pepinsky 2008a). Fierce battles over adjustment policy within the regime put various factions of the business community in direct competition with one another, which had the consequence of dividing the regime itself. Wild policy swings and Soeharto's perceived inability (or refusal) to comprehend the seriousness of the crisis before him did not help. In the end, it took the ouster of Soeharto, the complete collapse of the financial system, an IMF bailout, and two years of painful adjustment before the country would see growth resume. Few could have imagined that the high-flying New Order economy would crash so hard, so quickly.

In nearby Malaysia the crisis unfolded a bit differently. Unhedged foreign currency borrowing never reached the levels in Malaysia that it did in Indonesia, but Malaysia's far more developed stock market allowed Malaysian firms to rely on equity financing to a far greater degree than could Indonesian firms. Inflows of private short-term capital, most of which targeted Malaysian equities markets, reached 43 percent of total capital inflows in 1996 (Tourres 2003, 24). The ringgit float was seen as confirmation that the Malaysian economy's prospects were less promising than previously thought, prompting foreign investors to divest and leading to the collapse of share prices on the KLSE and the rapid growth of nonperforming loans in the domestic financial sector. As in Indonesia, this made the crisis a truly national problem, and produced broad pressure on the regime to bring the crisis to an orderly close while avoiding the most painful consequences of the investment slowdown.

Popular outrage at economic dislocation combined with simmering grievances at the regime's authoritarian rule almost spelled the end of Prime
Minister Mahathir Mohamad's government. However, a broadly popular
adjustment package—which repegged the ringgit at a modestly overvalued
rate and banned all outflows of short-term capital—allowed the regime the
breathing space to engineer a relatively quick and robust recovery. The contrast with Indonesia is instructive (Pepinsky 2009). The Malaysian regime's
constituents in the business community were far less divided in terms of asset
profiles than were the New Order's supporters. Important fractions of the
ethnic Chinese Malaysian business community with mobile assets rejected
Mahathir's adjustment measures, but due to their longstanding marginaliza-
tion from politics, this was politically inconsequential. The Malay masses were
likewise largely supportive of the adjustment package that they received, and
this afforded the regime some leeway to crack down on the country's first
truly panethnic opposition movement in order to prevent regime change
(Pepinsky 2008a). Shielded from international markets, political and business elites were able to protect their business interests in a way that preserved
the essential logic of Malaysia's political economy.

The Philippines in the 1990s never reached the heights of growth fed by
capital inflows seen in Indonesia and Malaysia. The corresponding economic
downturn accompanying the 1997–98 crisis was therefore simply not as substantial as in either of the two other countries (Noland 2000). But the Philippines did face an acute crisis, forcing a peso float and some painful orthodox
stabilization measures. MacIntyre (2001) rates decision making in the Philippines to have been more successful than that in Indonesia or Malaysia due to
the country's relatively (but not completely) insulated democratic political
institutions, which allowed the Ramos administration to cut spending and
the Central Bank (BSP) to raise interest rates (two policies that were bitterly
resisted by key constituencies in both Indonesia and Malaysia). Perhaps due
to the fractionalization of the post-Marcos political economy, it is more difficult in this context to speak of meaningful cleavages in the country's business community that shaped the course of the country's adjustment. But as
Hicken (2008) observes, crisis management may have been the high point
of the Philippines' economic performance since the fall of Marcos. We will
touch on to this point later when returning to the politics of external vulnerability in that country.

Singapore's experience differs altogether from the others. Singapore did
register negative GDP growth in 1998, so in that sense it was clearly affected
by the AFC. Exporters to the region as well as the travel and leisure industries, which all depend on strong performance in Singapore's neighbors, suffered the most. But this was a small setback for the region's most developed
economy. Prudent regulation of the financial sector prior to the crisis helped
to restrain both the excessive growth of domestic credit and its exposure to

currency movements, while also keeping domestic banks better capitalized than their neighbors (Ngiam 2001). These basic features of the Singaporean financial system meant that there was little reason to doubt the long-term viability of the Singaporean economy, even though its short-term prospects dimmed along with its neighbors. Politically, the shallow crisis, which the regime could quite credibly blame on factors external to its own control, created few problems for the regime. Still, Singapore's reliance on overseas workers (who have no political voice) means that the burdens of adjustment to difficult economic circumstances can always be externalized to noncitizens, reducing Singaporeans' own grievances with the regime. This likely helped the Singaporean regime to manage the political consequences of the relatively small amount of retrenchment that did take place.

To summarize: the 1997–98 crisis was devastating in Indonesia, serious in Malaysia, challenging in the Philippines, and shallow in Singapore. What of subsequent changes in political-business relations in these four countries? The simple answer is that political-business relations in Indonesia did change in important ways, but these changes have not redressed most of the fundamental challenges facing that country. In the remaining countries, political-business relations do not appear to have changed in any appreciable way at all.

The collapse of the New Order and the return of electoral democracy to Indonesia was a sea change for Indonesia's political economy. At the basic level, many of the formerly high-flying conglomerates suffered heavily during the crisis, although most have been reformed in some fashion. The Soeharto family no longer occupies the heights of the Indonesian economy. There have been some halting attempts to prosecute former corruptors. Bank Indonesia and the Ministry of Finance have plainly improved the country's financial regulatory environment, although from a very low base. But the major difference is not the identity of the main players in the business community (aside from the oldest father figures, they are mostly still around), or the fact that they try to direct policy in ways favorable to their long-term business interests (naturally they still do), but rather the logic of political business relations in the democratic era. A common refrain among old Indonesia hands in the business world is that under the Soeharto regime at least one knew how to get things done: pay someone at the top of a pretty clear political-economic hierarchy. That old hierarchy has been replaced by a web or network of crony connections, one that is far more unclear, unpredictable, and saddled with individual bottlenecks that can discourage the types of stable political-business relationships that flourished under the New Order (Pepinsky 2008b). It is certainly no longer the case that a powerful political executive can demand concessions and patronage from his or her subordinates in the business world. Elections have become witness to lavish spending by various candidates and their business allies seeking to gain political power. The spring 2010 ouster of Finance Minister Sri Mulyani Indrawati shows that big business interests can still throw their weight around (Baird and Wihardja

2010). To reiterate, there is no doubt that corruption, collusion, and cronyism continue in Indonesia's democratic era, and that powerful business groups have weathered the crisis remarkably well (Robison and Hadiz 2004). In that sense, political-business relations are just as concerning as ever. But they are different. Whether or not that difference is consequential for Indonesia's external vulnerability is a subject to which I return in the next section.

In Malaysia, the Philippines, and Singapore, however, political-business relations continue under the same form that they did prior to the crisis (Hicken 2008; Pepinsky 2008b). In Malaysia, this is because the regime was able to adopt policies that protected the existing distribution of political and economic power—that was quite literally the entire point of adopting these policies. This meant that the crisis was not a fundamental break in the Malaysian political economy, for although some key players in the business scene changed (most notably, Anwar Ibrahim and his corporate allies disappeared), the logic of the system remained intact. In the Philippines and Singapore the crisis also did not represent a fundamental break, but this is more obviously the case because the crises were either relatively minor (the Philippines) or almost nonexistent (Singapore). Indeed, Singapore's political and business elites continually recall their country's insulation from the AFC as prima facie evidence of the viability of the political-economic system that they have created.

A summary description of changing political-business relations in the four countries appears in table 6.3. As the entries in the table make clear, meaningful change in political-business relations has only occurred in Indonesia, while in the remaining three countries old patterns continue to prevail.

I describe political-business relations in Indonesia as "predatory" during the 1990s owing to the massive amount of political power under in the New Order executive and the tight links between it and most substantial business enterprises within the country. The implication is not that Soeharto or his family had unlimited power; quite the opposite is true. Rather, it is that to a greater degree than anywhere else in the region, Soeharto was able to prevail on business connections to act in a manner which was consistent with furthering his regime's political survival. The contrast with Malaysia—whose political-business relations I describe as "collusive"—helps to make this point clear. The executive retained substantial involvement in the economy, and politicians' links to the private sector were tight. But the commanding

TABLE 6.3
Political-business relations in Southeast Asia, 1990s and 2000s

Decade	Indonesia	Malaysia	Philippines	Singapore
1990s	Predatory	Collusive	Rent seeking	Regulatory
2000s	Rent seeking	Collusive	Rent seeking	Regulatory

heights of Malaysia's economy were less concentrated in the hands of a small and insulated economic elite than was the case in New Order Indonesia, which gave private enterprise in Malaysia a different kind of political voice.

The Philippines and Singapore differ from both of these countries in the 1990s—Singapore because its regulators were then (and today still are) much *more* autonomous than those in Indonesia and Malaysia, and the Philippines because its regulators have always been much *less* so. I describe Singapore's political-business relations as "regulatory" because of the clear ability of regulators and financial authorities to identify and implement policies with a minimum of interference from private interests. The other end of the spectrum is the Philippines, where I describe political-business relations as "rent seeking" in the sense that regulatory bodies have proved simply unable to implement effective policies that ran counter to the interests of the oligarchs. This is the outcome, moreover, that has obtained in Indonesia today in the wake of the collapse of the New Order.

The four labels in table 6.3 offer an interesting parallel to Kang's (2002) typology of state-business relations in emerging economies. For example, both he and I would consider Indonesia in the 1990s to have been "predatory" and the Philippines throughout this period to have been "rent seeking," and for largely the same reasons. However, the analytical purpose of these two typologies differs in important ways. Table 6.3 is, following Elman (2005, 297), a descriptive typology of the four cases to serve as a "descriptive characterization" of "what constitutes" each type. In the context of this particular argument, table 6.3 proposes a shorthand description of the overall pattern of political-business relations that we observe in these countries. Kang's typology, by contrast, is explicitly causal: each type is an equilibrium outcome that emerges from the interactions between business and the state. In that sense, Kang's is an explanatory typology that "makes predictions based on combinations of different values of a theory's variables" (Elman 2005, 297). Kang argues, for example, that "rent seeking" is a pattern of corruption that emerges when business is concentrated and the state is fractured, making the form of corruption the dependent variable and state coherence and business concentration the two independent variables. My argument is agnostic about the causes of rent seeking as a pattern of political-business relations in Indonesia and the Philippines, and instead asks whether or not political-business relations can be understood as an independent variable that explains external vulnerability.

To summarize, in none of the four countries is it accurate to describe political-business relations as "laissez-faire" in the sense of an idealized liberal market economy where private interests have no ability to shape policy.[1] Instead, the political economies of each of these countries feature regular

---

1. Kang (2002, 17) adopts a different view of laissez faire capitalism in which "neither state or business is powerful enough to take advantage of the other."

interactions between political and business elites. The nature of these interactions varies, yielding different policy outcomes and different kinds of external vulnerability, as described above.

Surviving the GFC

Fast forward ten years to 2008. Viewed relative to the AFC, the GFC will register as little more than a blip. The economies of island Southeast Asia did not grow nearly as quickly prior to the crisis, averaging a bit less than 5 percent growth per year from 2002 to 2008 as compared to above 6 percent from 1991 to 1996. And what growth crunch did occur was on an entirely different scale than the 1997–98 crises: the two hardest-hit economies, Malaysia and Singapore, registered negative growth of less than 2 percent in 2009, while Indonesia and the Philippines never trended negative at all, and all four rebounded healthily in 2010 (see figure 6.3).

The differences between the AFC and the GFC in Southeast Asia run deeper than just this simple comparison of growth rates. In 1998 both Indonesia and Malaysia experienced twin currency and banking crises (although Malaysia's authorities would dispute the latter), and in addition, the Philippines experienced a currency crisis. Only Singapore faced neither unsustainable currency pressure nor a banking crisis. In 2008–9, none of the four countries experienced either a currency crisis or a banking crisis. Exchange rates vis-à-vis the U.S. dollar in both crisis periods help to demonstrate the substantial differences between these two crises in terms of the countries' external financial relations (see figure 6.4).

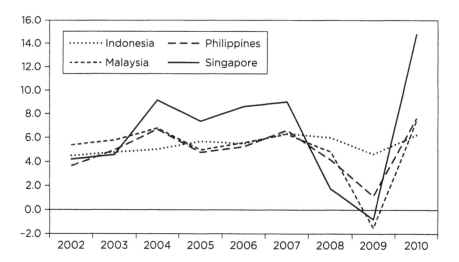

Figure 6.3 GDP growth rate of four Southeast Asian countries, 2002–10 (%).
Source: IMF 2013.

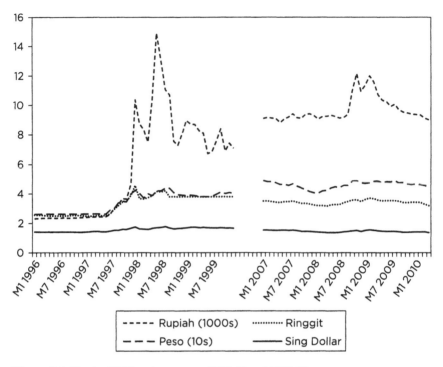

Figure 6.4 Nominal USD exchange rates, 1996–99 and 2007–10.
Source: IMF 2010c.

Absent a currency crisis or a banking crisis, what then explains lower growth in 2008–9 in island Southeast Asia? The lower growth rates in Indonesia and Philippines, and the relatively shallow contractions in Malaysia and Singapore, can be attributed almost entirely to the collapse of exports to, and investment from, the developed world. It is important to note here that these are factors that are largely outside of the control of governments in Southeast Asia (Pepinsky 2012). Collapsing demand in the United States and Europe for exports from emerging economies simply removed much of the market for exports from island Southeast Asia's economies. Likewise, as foreign investors shifted their investment emphasis to safety and security over profit, capital inflows to island Southeast Asian economies slowed. Figure 6.5 charts the downturns in FDI inflows (in panel A) and net portfolio flows (in panel B) experienced by the island Southeast Asian economies in 2008–9.

The question that remains is, Why did the fall in exports and collapse of foreign investment in these four countries not result in the same sort of currency and financial meltdown in 2008 as had occurred in 1997. After all, the AFC began as a mere currency shock, and it was only after currency movements and capital outflows exposed the rot at the heart of Indonesia's and Malaysia's economies that shocks degenerated into full-blown crises. In 1997

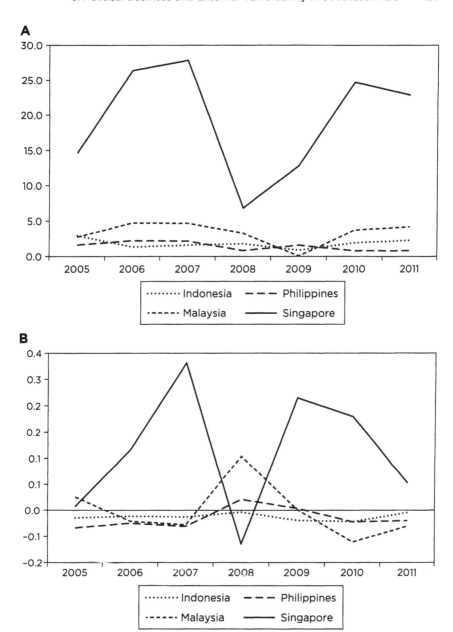

Figure 6.5 FDI (panel A) and portfolio investment (panel B), 2005–11 (% of GDP).

Source: Author's calculations from World Bank 2013.

currency depreciation exposed external vulnerability, which led to capital flight, which in turn fed currency depreciation that exposed external vulnerability still further. Given the right conditions, a reversal of capital inflows and a trade shock could have initiated similar dynamics in 2008–9.

There are several possible reasons why this has not occurred. The first possible reason is that the current economic downturn is generated by "pull" factors in the advanced economies drawing capital out of, and trade away from, these economies. That is, events outside of island Southeast Asia are responsible for the slowdown in growth. We can contrast this with a crisis generated by "push" factors in the emerging economies, as was the case during the AFC. In that case, at the heart of the crisis were problems in domestic economic management (although this is certainly a point of debate, see Winters 1999). While this distinction is useful for helping to distinguish between two sorts of causes of economic downturns, in numerous circumstances the very absence of capital or trade can expose external vulnerability, as was the case in Latin America in the 1980s (where oil price shocks and high interest rates led to a series of emerging market crises) and in the Baltics and parts of Eastern Europe in 2008. We might then rephrase the question as: Why were there no push factors in 2008–9?

A second answer is that the economies entered the crisis in a better position to insulate themselves from the vagaries of international markets than they did in 1998. In this regard, the evidence is mixed. A strong reserve position, relative to foreign debt, helps authorities to ward off currency pressures, which are often the proximate trigger for what later become systemic financial crises. Figure 6.6 shows reserves to external debt ratios in 2008 were indeed twice those of 1997 in Indonesia and the Philippines, suggesting that a stronger external position may have helped these two economies. But a far stronger reserve position was not sufficient to protect Malaysia in 1997.

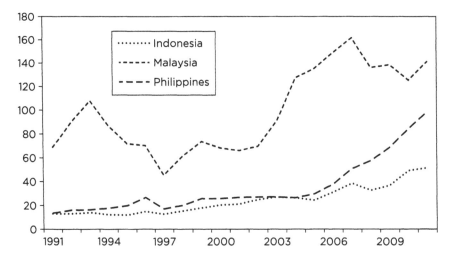

Figure 6.6 Reserves/total external debt, 1991–2011 (%).

Source: World Bank 2013.

These figures indicate that reserve accumulation may have been beneficial for helping to withstand the current crisis, but certainly was not sufficient to withstand all crises given a sharp deterioration in investor sentiments.

A third possibility is that the former crisis countries have undergone a fundamental change in their domestic political economies that has eliminated the root causes of external vulnerability. If this were true, we would expect to see that Indonesia, Malaysia, and perhaps the Philippines had experienced changes in the very basis of political-business relations. Table 6.3 above provides a brief overview of such changes, and the evidence is mixed at best. It is true that Indonesia has experienced just such a transformation. It is also true that Singapore, which in neither period experienced a true financial crisis, has maintained the very same "regulatory" political economic structure that helped it to withstand the AFC. For now, let us bracket the issue of whether changes in Indonesia's political-business relations from "predatory" to "rent seeking" actually caused it to withstand the Great Meltdown of 2008–9 unscathed. There is much to learn from the other two cases of Malaysia and the Philippines.

Recall that Malaysia experienced a severe crisis, but not one that produced a dramatic transformation of its "collusive" political economy, while the Philippines experienced a relatively shallow crisis that authorities were able to bring under control with some ease. If a transformation of political-business relations is a necessary condition for withstanding the external shock of the Great Meltdown of 2008–9, then we would expect that Malaysia and the Philippines would have fallen victim again to the current crisis. Yet this quite plainly has not occurred. Instead, we see in Malaysia that the same policies of interethnic redistribution that generated close ties between Malay business elites and the county's political elites, and which incentivized its political elites to use promises of economic empowerment to attract support from ordinary Malays, have not generated external vulnerability. This is even more striking given the country's fragile political situation in late 2008 and early 2009, where a newly emboldened panethnic opposition threatened to unseat the ruling Barisan Nasional regime (B. Singh 2010). Political-business relations—even in periods of high political drama—cannot explain both external vulnerability in 1997 and the lack thereof in 2008.

The case of the Philippines, alongside the case of Indonesia, also gives lie to the suggestion that "healthy" political-business relations are either necessary or sufficient to withstand external shocks. It should be uncontroversial that the state of political business in Indonesia and the Philippines is far from healthy—"rent-seeking" political-business relations correspond to a domestic political economy in which regulators have scant ability to formulate or implement meaningful policies that run counter to the interests of powerful economic elites. Yet we do not observe even a hint of an externally oriented crisis in either country, and in fact, in each country it is precisely those highly problematic internal markets that have provided a cushion against the trade and investment shocks of the current crisis.

One way to visualize these points is to consider investors' perceptions of the extent to which countries' political-business relation were "risky," in the sense that they represent a threat to the ability of investors to realize profits from or to count on the safety of their investments. If political-business relations, conceived of in broad terms, explain investor sentiments, which in turn explain external vulnerability, we should expect to see that it is in those countries and periods where investors view political-business relations to be most problematic that crises occur. It is certainly difficult to compare the extent to which this is true across countries or across time, and even more difficult to separate the investment risk due to political-business relations from the risk due to other factors. But some suggestive data do exist. The consultancy Political Risk Services provides yearly ratings of "political, economic, and financial risk" for a number of countries (PRS Group 2013). Its political risk ratings capture subjective evaluations of corruption, bureaucratic quality, and the rule of law with respect to investment risk, all of which should clearly reflect the state to which political-business relations themselves directly influence external vulnerability. The evolution of these ratings over time for the four economies of island Southeast Asia appears in figure 6.7.

Comparing across countries alone, there is suggestive evidence that political risk may influence external vulnerability, for Singapore rates as less risky than do the other three economies. But looking within countries and across

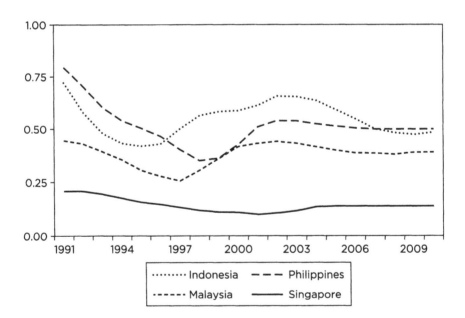

Figure 6.7 PRS political risk ratings, three-year rolling averages, 1991–2010. Index inverted so that 0 = "least risk," 1 = "most risk."

Sources: Author's calculations from PRS Group 2013 and Teorell et al. 2013.

time, that pattern breaks down. Political risk in Indonesia, Malaysia, and the Philippines as ranked by PRS not only fell throughout the 1990s, it was lower in the 1995 for all three countries than it was in 2008. Yet of course we know that politics contributed in a basic way to these economies' vulnerability—or lack thereof—to the AFC, as discussed in the previous section. Figure 6.7 accordingly suggests a simple conclusion: if the nature of political-business relations in a country is problematic, it is not because it directly generates external vulnerability, but rather because it can at times generate specific pathologies that are themselves the direct causal antecedents of external vulnerability.

This brings us to the fourth possibility for island Southeast Asia's insulation from the current crisis, the one which I consider the most compelling. This possibility is that there is no single root cause of external vulnerability that can be identified within the broad heading of political-business relations or related political economy issues. Instead it is the interaction of various specific interrelated factors—among them, incentive structures, regulatory regimes, and global economic conditions—that generate external vulnerability. This, in other words, is a plea for a more careful analysis of the factors that lead from external vulnerability to crises than can be recovered from a focus on the broad headings of corruption, cronyism, or political-business relations.

Abstracting away from the particulars of any one case in island Southeast Asia, there were four central factors at play in the AFC: exchange rate misalignment, asset price bubbles, rapid capital inflows, and lax prudential regulation. These are summarized in table 6.4.

These factors interacted to produce the severe crises in Indonesia and Malaysia. Lower amounts of inflows behind a lower degree of capital openness,

TABLE 6.4
Policies, investors, and external vulnerability

		Indonesia	Malaysia	Philippines	Singapore
Capital inflows	1996	High	High	Moderate	High
	2007	Moderate	Moderate	Moderate	High
Financial regulation	1996	Poor	Fair	Fair	Good
	2007	Fair	Fair	Fair	Good
Exchange rate misalignment	1996	Yes	Yes	Yes	No
	2007	No	No	No	No
Investor sentiment	1996	Positive	Positive	Tentative	Positive
	2007	Tentative	Tentative	Tentative	Positive
Net external vulnerability	1996	High	High	Medium	Low
	2007	Low	Low	Low	Low

and the absence of a clear asset price bubble, shielded the Philippines to a certain degree. Active and careful prudential regulation helped Singapore to avoid a crisis altogether. One might respond that these four conditions were in fact epiphenomenal on one or two deeper political factors—regulatory capacity and state autonomy are two common arguments (Weiss 1999). But again, the comparison to the present period is instructive, because only in the Indonesian case is it possible to argue that there has been any change in either regulatory capacity or state autonomy.

Looking to island Southeast Asia in January 2008, how did conditions compare to January 1997? Prudential regulation has undoubtedly improved in Indonesia and Malaysia, which each have "endorsed the major international financial standards governing bank regulation" (Hamilton-Hart 2008, 47). But there remain problems at the implementation stage due to the pressure of connected firms to avoid arms-length oversight of their activities: political-business relations, in particular pertaining to financial policy, remain collusive in Malaysia and have veered towards rent seeking in Indonesia. From the perspective of the proximate causes of external vulnerability, more interesting is the fact that although capital openness remains high, prior to 2008 there had been no massive inflow of capital to any of the island Southeast Asian economies that paralleled the early- to mid-1990s. Moreover, asset price bubbles were nowhere in evidence. Exchange rates in 2007 were not obviously ripe targets for speculative attacks, something which was clearly true in both countries (and the Philippines as well) in 1996.

Viewed alongside Singapore and the Philippines, it is probably impossible to boil down the absence of these risk factors in 2008 to a single difference between Indonesia and Malaysia in 1997 and 2008. But if there were such a factor, it is probably the change in investors' beliefs about the propriety of the patterns of political-business relations in these two countries. In other words, the same configuration of political-business relations in Malaysia that sympathetic observers had imagined to be "just right" has been appraised with far more caution in the wake of the AFC. In Indonesia, most investors probably do not favor a return to the New Order's political and economic system (although some certainly do), but there is no doubt that Indonesia's political economy is considered by many to be standing in the way of the type of rapid economic growth seen in the 1990s. Investors' opinions about Indonesia are therefore best described as "tentative" whereas they were once clearly "positive." In the Philippines, the same political-business relations that discouraged massive capital inflows in the 1990s continued to do so in the 2000s. The increase in perceptions of political risk in Indonesia, Malaysia, and the Philippines that appears in figure 6.7 following the crisis indicates the changes in investor sentiment about the propriety of political-business relations. The Malaysian case is most revealing, for perceptions of political risk increased *even though nothing else about the country's collusive political economy changed*. Singapore's insulation from the AFC, which resulted in no appreciable change in political risk as measured in figure 6.7, explains its continued strong performance since then.

In sum, the sole obvious difference between Indonesia and Malaysia in 1997 and 2008 is in *beliefs* about their domestic political economies—today, they are *believed to be* less like Singapore, and more like the Philippines, than they were in the 1990s. Investor beliefs play a central role in explaining rapid economic overexpansion of the type seen in Indonesia and Malaysia in the 1990s. This overexpansion then interacts with and reinforces the very pathologies inherent in each political economic system, which in Indonesia and Malaysia were problems of regulation, exchange rate settings, and asset price bubbles. As the Philippines demonstrated in 1998, one way to avoid a crisis is to avoid the boom preceding it. The experiences of all four island Southeast Asian economies in 2008–9 are a contemporary parallel.

Political Business and External Vulnerability

At this point we can draw together the various strands of the argument that I have advanced in this chapter. Three island Southeast Asian countries suffered from crises in 1997–98, whereas none of them did in 2008. In Indonesia and Malaysia, the 1997 crises were severe, whereas the crisis in the Philippines was painful. In all three crisis-affected countries, there were clear indications that various aspects of these countries' domestic political economies were instrumental in explaining both why the crisis took place and why it became as severe as it did.

However, the experience of the GFC calls into question the relationship between political business and external vulnerability during periods of global or regional financial distress. Instead, the course of the current crisis in island Southeast Asia has been determined primarily by the extent of trade and investment ties to the industrial economies. This is a trade and investment shock, nothing more. The puzzle is that this is just a trade and investment shock amidst a period of unprecedented global financial turmoil. History shows that any sort of economic shock might have degenerated into a generalized financial panic, and that domestic politics usually affects how this happens. This can be the case in predatory systems such as that of New Order Indonesia, in collusive systems such as Malaysia, and in rent-seeking systems such the Philippines. But absent the very precise technical conditions found during the AFC—rapid capital inflows, asset price bubbles, and misaligned managed exchange rates—none of these "unhealthy" political-business relations created the sorts of external vulnerability seen in the late 1990s. Indonesia's predatory political-business relations have become more like the Philippines' rent-seeking political-business relations, but that change is not responsible for Indonesia's relative insulation from the crisis. Malaysia's collusive political-business relations have not changed, so they cannot explain both Malaysia's vulnerability to the earlier crisis and its insulation from the current one.

There is a plausible argument that rigorous prudential regulation in Singapore explains why it was vulnerable to neither the AFC or to the Great Meltdown of 2008–9. It would be convenient if we could attribute the absence of crises in island Southeast Asia today to increases in regulatory oversight or state capacity in the former crisis countries too. It is true that financial regulation in Indonesia today is indisputably better than it used to be,[2] and Malaysia's regulators have been keen to avoid repeating the earlier crisis. But in neither case can we argue that prudential oversight has contained political business. Rather, the very existence of the earlier crises in island Southeast Asia has produced important changes in how these countries interact with the global economy. With investors chastened by the collapse of 1997–98, there was no massive inflow of mobile foreign capital to any of the economies in island Southeast Asia prior to 2008. Actors at home and abroad no longer had unrealistic expectations about future exchange rate movements. In a world in which investors are skeptical about the prospects for sustained and rapid economic growth under the sorts of political-economic systems found in Indonesia, Malaysia, and the Philippines, the precipitating conditions for the type of cross-border financial contagion seen in 1997–98 will be absent.

There are theoretical and practical implications to the experiences of island Southeast Asia in 2008–09. Theoretically, the issue is how to understand when and how political-business relations generate vulnerability to international financial contagion. Responding to the many arguments that moral hazard originating in active political interference in the economy caused the AFC, Ha-Joon Chang (2000) observed that cronyism did not appear to be deteriorating prior to the crisis in the 1990s. Nor did changes in the extent and nature of cronyism in Thailand and South Korea have any obvious relationship to the onset of the crisis. These facts make it hard to sustain the belief that cronyism, which he calls a "permanent feature of these countries," could have explained the crisis in and of itself. Indeed, the massive expansion prior to the crisis "seems to be good proof that irrational euphoria can take hold during a financial mania" (Chang 2000, 780). This is not to deny that cronyism mattered in 1997, but that its effects on external vulnerability are conditional on how cronyism interacts with economic policies and international conditions.

The implications of this discussion are similar. We should not attribute the absence of the crisis in Southeast Asia during the current period of international financial instability to some sort of change in political-business relations, an improvement of financial regulation or state capacity, or any similarly broad political economy factor. There has been nothing even close

---

2. I thank Yuri Sato for emphasizing this point.

to approaching a convergence of political-business relations in Indonesia, Malaysia, or the Philippines on what we might call the "Singapore model" of a regulatory state. The implication is that when understanding the general question of how political-business relations generate external vulnerability, we must attend, first, to the specific mechanisms that link private interests to public policies. From there, we must understand the relationship between economic policies and cross-border economic linkages. There is precious little analytical purchase in the broad question of whether corrupt or crony-dominated economies are more likely on average to fall victim to international financial crises.

Practically, we would like to offer some reassurance to Indonesian, Malaysian, and Filipino policymakers that they have done things that help them to avoid crises. We would like to tell policymakers elsewhere that the Indonesian, Malaysian, and Filipino governments have lessons that they may apply to their own countries. But the record of noncrises in Southeast Asia during 2008–9 does not offer much beyond what we already knew from 1997–98. At the heart of the matter is how countries manage their financial integration with the global economy. We learned in 1997–98 that Ronald McKinnon's (1993) admonition that financial liberalization should follow the establishment of robust markets and regulatory systems, and that capital account liberalization should only follow after financial liberalization was complete, was all too painfully true. The AFC showed the consequences of massive capital inflows under managed exchange rates that fed asset price bubbles in a politically manipulated market for credit. Indonesia, Malaysia, and the Philippines have not solved the problems that political-business relations created earlier, they have avoided the symptoms of unhealthy financial market expansion partially because political-business relations are today perceived to be so problematic.

And finally, I should observe that throughout this discussion I have set the bar very low for defining success. In essence, I have argued that the conjunction of changing investor perceptions of the viability of domestic political-economic systems and different policy settings that followed the crisis have protected the island Southeast Asian economies from experiencing this crisis right now. But other crises loom in island Southeast Asia. Indonesia and the Philippines are experiencing what might be considered a "slow crisis" of democratic underperformance in economies plagued by corruption, cronyism, and bureaucratic incompetence. Malaysia is confronting the challenge of transforming its economy to higher value-added production and services while protecting the perquisites of power and favoritism that undergird the country's political economy. Even Singapore struggles to create the conditions where innovation—which its leaders have identified as the future of Singaporean growth—can flourish; it also faces a generation of Singaporeans who are simply less loyal to the People's Action Party's vision of what Singapore is than their grandparents were, as well as an growing postethnic cleavage between long-settled Singaporeans and new immigrants. These are problems that speak to the viability of long-run development trajectories rather than to vulnerability to short-term financial volatility.

The long-term growth prospects for all four economies here will depend on their ability to escape what has been termed the "middle income trap" (see Doner this volume; Gill and Kharas 2007). Doing so will require the development of flexible yet capacious economic institutions that can identify globally competitive sectors and industries with growth potential. To do this successfully, policymakers must be insulated from the constraints of short-termism or political interference. Nothing about the current political and economic institutions in Indonesia and the Philippines seems appropriate for those tasks. Malaysia has developed a range of institutions that are in principle well-suited for active and effective industrial policy, but the political constraints identified above still abound. Singapore is a high-income country and so the middle income trap does not apply. Yet it is not clear how the region's most advanced economy will be able to turn the corner from trade, processing, and services to build an economy based on knowledge and in-novation. This difference between island Southeast Asia's short-term success in managing the crisis of 2008–9 and the long-term uncertainty in nurtur-ing sustained economic growth is striking, and no government in the region views the absence of a crisis today as enough to make up for the bigger chal-lenges that these economies face.

Success as Trap?

Crises and Challenges in Export-Oriented Southeast Asia

Richard Doner

Since the 1997 Asian Financial Crisis (AFC), the middle-income and approaching-middle-income countries of Southeast Asia substantially increased their reliance on exports (World Bank 2012). As such, one would have expected them to be especially vulnerable to the 2008 recession. And indeed, in May 2009, the IMF's deputy managing director concluded that Asia's growth deceleration had been sharper than in other regions, with GDP in Asia, excluding India and China, falling by almost 15 percent. This contraction, he argued, resulted from the region's "integration with the global economy" (Kato 2009). Yet only three months later, *The Economist* (August 15, 2009, 69), trumpeted "Asia's Astonishing Rebound" and highlighted the 10 percent average growth rate of the region's emerging economies, led by industrial production's impressive recovery. And while not at pre-1997 boom-year levels, subsequent growth rates in Southeast Asia were quite healthy, resulting in Thailand joining Malaysia in upper-middle income status (World Bank 2011b). The region's countries have also made significant progress on a number of millennium development goals, including poverty reduction (ADB 2000).

Can this rebound translate into long-term, sustained growth? Viewed through the lens of one low-income-but-growing country (Vietnam) and two middle-income countries (Malaysia and Thailand), I argue that there are reasons for concern. Without innovation-promoting institutional reforms, growth in these countries will be constrained by competition from low-wage, low-productivity rivals on the one hand, and by entry barriers to high-wage, high-productivity producers on the other. This perspective follows recent arguments that avoiding "middle-income traps" involves shifts from diversification to specialization and from investment to innovation-led development (Gill and Kharas 2007; Yusuf and Nabeshima 2009). These moves in turn require different kinds of firm-level competencies, especially involving technology. Some such competencies result from firm-specific features, such as leadership, that respond to market competition (Lall 1992). But many are a function of innovation-supporting collective goods, such as technical training and standards, that rarely emerge naturally from the market. They require incentives and new forms of interest coordination, that is, institutional capacities, typically involving public and public-private, as well as purely private activities.

I suggest that the emergence of new institutional capacities, and thus technology-supporting collective goods, has been stunted by the middle-income countries' otherwise successful responses to the 1997 and 2008 crises, and the political consequences of these shifts. These responses, which relied largely on macroeconomic measures and financial sector reforms, as well as a proliferation of free trade agreements and participation in global production networks, alleviated pressure for systematic improvements in technology-related capacities, such as research and development and technical training. They perpetuated a broader development strategy that, while resulting in impressive GDP growth rates and diversification, has encouraged capital-intensive, foreign-dominated manufacturing and weak intra- and intersectoral linkages. While reducing poverty quite significantly, this pattern of mild disarticulation has in turn spawned conditions that undermine sustained growth in the face of competition from both low-wage/low-skill and higher-wage/higher-productivity rivals.

It has done so in several, related ways. First, it has dampened broad, private sector demand for the kinds of collective goods required for movement to higher-income activities. It has done so in part by strengthening the position of foreign firms in export-oriented manufacturing, firms with limited interest in the public provision of innovation-related services such as technical training, and in part by encouraging the growth of migrant, casual, and other forms of informal employment that allow domestic firms to avoid higher-skill activities and discourage worker investment in skill development. Second, it has weakened labor's political and economic role in the development process. This is of concern because it runs counter to the labor-inclusion experiences of not only in the corporatist states of Western Europe but also of what some have called "micro-corporatism," as in the East Asian newly industrialized countries (NICs) (Jeong and Lawler 2007). This has, in turn, contributed to widening income gaps in Southeast Asia (Chongvilaivan 2013). Third, it has both reflected and contributed to relatively fragmented political and bureaucratic institutions. Such fragmentation in turn has allowed for the persistence of domestic business groups relying on family ownership/control and diversification rather than developing core competencies necessary to compete with low-wage and low-skill rivals (Suehiro and Nateneapha 2004, 91).

My argument, in sum, is that, by promoting low demand for skills, labor exclusion, and weak development-related institutions, successful adjustments to prior crises constitute a trap. The corollary to this argument is that movement beyond middle-income status will occur only when political leaders are faced with significant threats that amount to crises.

Theoretical Approaches to Growth Divergence

Development Stages, Development Challenges, Institutional Capacities

Recent scholarship has explored the significant but declining role of sectoral diversification for economic growth. Evidence suggests a U-shaped pattern in which diversification increases roughly through middle-income, after which further growth involves greater growth in fewer sectors, with the shift occurring at roughly US$9,000 per capita GDP (Imbs and Wacziarg 2003). This line of thinking is consistent with scholarship on "middle-income traps" noted above. Countries ranging from lower middle-income Philippines, Indonesia, and Thailand to upper middle-income Malaysia have grown through diversification. They have effectively mobilized resources for investment in new activities that have raised national incomes (Waldner 1999, 163). Their ability to do so was based on (1) institutional arrangements that allowed them to overcome both information and coordination failures inherent in new, risky activities, and (2) factor endowments, raw material exports, and low-wage labor. What they have not successfully done is to develop technological strengths and innovation capacities. The resulting risk for the middle-income countries lies in being squeezed by lower-wage rivals such as Vietnam while finding it difficult to compete with higher-wage and higher-productivity producers, such as Taiwan (Somchai 2010).

Continued growth, the argument goes, will require becoming more specialized in the sense of being more efficient and "deeper," that is, with more domestic linkages, in a smaller number of sectors (Imbs and Wacziarg 2003). This process, which can also be understood as *upgrading*, requires relying less on investment and more on innovation understood as the diffusion of technology—a product, process, or practice—that is "new," not necessarily to the world, but to a particular firm or group of firms. It requires absorptive capacity—an endogenous, cumulative learning process in which local producers recognize the value of new technology, assimilate it, and apply it to commercial ends (Cohen and Levinthal 1990).

Some argue that firms will develop such technological capabilities on their own through competitive emulation of best practices under pressures of market mechanisms (Pack 2000). At some point in the diversification process, wage levels rise beyond levels competitive with low-cost rivals. Assuming an open trade regime, this will, the argument goes, encourage moves into labor-saving technical changes that shift the relative scarcity and prices of capital and labor, and induce innovation-related investments by firms. But the adoption and development of technology is fraught with market imperfections and failures, such as long gestation periods subject to unpredictable and path-dependent learning processes, uncertain demand, lack of complementary inputs, and poaching of skilled personnel by competitors. As a result, competitive pressure from superior imports is rarely if ever sufficient to overcome such problems (Rodrik 2007, 107).

The expansion and deepening of firms' capabilities thus requires broader packages of incentives and support (Pietrobelli and Rasiah 2012). These include testing and standards services, vocational and technical training, foreign direct investment (FDI) screening and monitoring, improved infrastructure (e.g., IT logistics), trade regimes that encourage upstream-downstream linkages, market development, and research and development diffusion. One source of such incentives and support might be multinationals and their broader global value chains. But absent significant incentives from host countries, even the most innovative multinational subsidiary typically retains functions such as training, process innovation, and product development in-house, if not at home. Indeed, as Lall (1992) argued, multinationals tend to transfer innovations, not innovation processes, to host country sites.

In sum, the need to promote technology absorption and new, efficient inputs poses difficulties well beyond the uncertainty and risks characterizing any new investments. Consistent with endogenous growth theory, these difficulties require going beyond a broad-brush, one-size-fits-all agenda to address specific policy reforms aimed at the particular challenges in specific countries at particular development stages (Pritchett 2003). Their information requirements are higher; they require the involvement of multiple parties in extended implementation chains; and they pose tough distributional challenges. Addressing these upgrading challenges requires significant institutional capacities: consultation, monitoring, and credibility (Doner 2009).

The Politics of Institutional Origins and Evolution

What accounts for the presence/absence of such institutional capacities? Writings by economists are either silent on the issue or, more typically, fall back on hopeful appeals for democracy, governance, and/or able and corruption-free leaders (Rodrik 2004, 19–20). These solutions are problematic: the link between regime type and development is suspect; the emphasis on governance suffers from both questionable measures and probable endogeneity problems; and while a focus on leaders highlights the political elites' role as "principals" in raising the profile of industrial transformation and in promoting institutional reform, it simply begs the question of political leaders' motivations. A more useful approach begins from the finding that institutional change emerges out of the rough and tumble of politics (Bates

1995). But why would political leaders pursue difficult but growth-promoting institutional reforms rather than channel largesse to key constituencies—typically economic elites interested in easy profits through speculation and rent seeking?

Two related factors seem important: labor inclusion and crises. Past experience suggests that some form of labor inclusion is necessary for the shift from middle- to upper-income status in most developing countries (i.e., those not endowed with immense stores of valuable natural resources). Such inclusion is, in turn, at least in part a function of crisis—defined here as ongoing and imminent threats to political elites.

Labor as a Growth Partner

Scholarship on the industrialized world has demonstrated numerous developmental benefits of various forms of labor inclusion (Katzenstein 1985). Consultation with labor can discourage inflation (by tying wage increases to productivity), encourage workers to invest in company-specific skills, and reduce tendencies to engage in disruptive forms of protests by providing workers with some degree of security against arbitrary layoffs and other types of punitive actions. In Western Europe, these benefits occur with active, organized labor movements in corporatist arrangements that find few if any direct counterparts in East Asia, whether in Japan or in the NICs, where labor's political position is decidedly weak.

But if labor has been absent from Japanese-style corporatism in terms of peak bargaining (Pempel and Tsunekawa 1979), unions have been active at the enterprise level, and numerous forms of joint consultation, including quality circles, have been widespread in Japanese firms, especially the larger ones (Cole 1979). And while labor in the East Asian NICs has been subordinated and even brutally repressed (Deyo 1989), it has not been ignored. Instead, linking developmental goals and nationalist sentiments, political leaders in the NICs combined "strategic repression" with broad-based public goods, including very significant investments in human capital (Gallagher and Hanson 2009; Freeman 1993, 2). Popular sectors were de facto growth partners benefiting from compensatory measures that helped not only to foster a consensus on difficult shifts of production factors but also to make that shift an efficient one. The move to export-led growth in the East Asian NICs prompted leaders to improve labor's access to high-quality, especially technical, education, even as elites remained more resistant to extensive social insurance schemes seen in other regions (Haggard and Kaufman 2008). Indeed, in Singapore and South Korea, labor has been an active participant in ongoing productivity improvement efforts (Yuen and Lim 2000; Lee 1998).

As I argue below, such emphasis on improving human capital, in some cases involving labor in the process, contrasts sharply with the relative neglect of such issues in the middle-income countries of Southeast Asia (Yusuf and Nabeshima 2009). This neglect is not a function of ignorance or indifference, but rather of differences in threats or crises facing political elites (Doner et al. 2005).

Crises

Much of the now-extensive scholarship on crises and their impacts focuses on sudden-onset economic shocks and their consequences for macroeconomic reform (Nelson 1999; Corrales 1997). Although this literature is useful for recognizing significant cross-national variation in response to similar crises, it is of limited utility when it comes to the kinds of upgrading challenges central to escaping the middle-income trap. Its emphasis is on reforms such as exchange rate shifts or fiscal reforms that, relative to upgrading, can be achieved with the "stroke of a pen" (Naim 1994). While they often do have distributional consequences, these first-generation reforms exhibit neither the need for coordination and long time horizons, nor the kinds of time-, place-, and sector-specific information required by second-generation reforms in health and education, much less the third-stage measures inherent in technology absorption and upgrading (Nelson 1999). Thus economic crises as "shocks" might trigger "blips" of reform, but they are unlikely to constitute the kinds of ongoing and severe threats leading to investment of political resources required to address the challenges of upgrading.

This chapter's core argument is that several related sets of factors have moderated such severe threats in Southeast Asia, thus enabling these countries to avoid the tough policy and institutional changes required for upgrading. First, their heretofore successful export strategies, many of which are based on multinational corporation (MNC) dominated global production chains, have required neither indigenous innovation capacity nor domestic linkages. Second, large informal labor forces (bolstered by migrant labor) undermine labor's capacity for collective action, reduce pressure on wages and productivity, and lead to growth-inhibiting inequality. The result is that political elites (or local industrialists) do not view technology promotion, including effective education, as key to survival. These patterns predate but have been intensified by successful responses to both the 1997–98 and 2008–9 crises. Although such factors are less problematic for lower-income Vietnam than for Malaysia and Thailand, we do see their impact in the Vietnam case, as described in the following section.

Development Trajectories and Responses to Crises

Low Income—Vietnam

Development Performance

Vietnam's growth over the past twenty years has been impressive, described by one observer as "booming out of a poverty trap" (Pritchett 2003, 142).

There is general agreement that this growth has resulted from freeing up "enormous reservoirs of unused or underused resources, especially labour in the rural sector" (Riedel and Turley 1999, 11). GDP per capita grew at almost 7 percent per year from 1993 to 1998, with the country probably meeting most of the Millennium Development Goals ahead of schedule (Dapice et al. 2008, 41). But by the early years of the twenty-first century, concerns emerged as to the sustainability of this trajectory. Below we trace the key stages of the country's reform and then suggest that the political logic of these stages conforms to the framework presented in the previous section.

Reform Strategies and Stages
COMMAND ECONOMY
The country's initial, postwar strategy was development via a socialist command economy. Under the Five Year Plan (1976–80), this involved full socialization, including nationalizing industry and suppressing private trade; movement from small-scale to large-scale production; and integration of the North and South. The effort was doomed by a lack of state capacity in areas such as information gathering and monitoring, as well as by a failure to provide new modes of production and distribution to make up for the newly suppressed private activities.

In response, illegal markets exploded and state-owned enterprises (SOEs) went outside the plan to procure inputs ("fence breaking"). Although these local deviations from the plan probably moderated the crisis' impact, they also reflected a political problem—namely, a deterioration of public confidence in the party-based political leadership. Leaders had a stark choice: "Rescue the Plan by strengthening enforcement, which in the existing conditions was sure to make matters worse. . . . or save the economy and recover public support by sanctioning some of the adaptations that had already occurred" (Riedel and Turley 1999, 15).

MARKET RETRENCHMENT
Leaders selected the latter option. The second Five Year Plan (1980–85) involved some relaxation of controls and the introduction of a contract system. The overall package included abolition of price controls, unification of exchange rates leading to a fivefold devaluation of the dong, raising civil servants' salaries, introduction of a contract system in agriculture, expansion of family farms through long-term leases, and reforms for SOEs that included cutting their budgets while granting them greater autonomy on pricing, production, and investment decisions. However, this did not constitute a clear reform path. Along with greater autonomy for local initiatives and recognition of the need for nonsocialist sectors, various forms of regulation and taxes weakened small business in services and trade.

This awkward compromise between pressures from below and a desire for recentralization had significant, positive results: food production increased, although it seems to have been a short-term response to growth in household plots. Further, the reforms resulted in speculation, corruption, smuggling, a flood of sideline activity, inflation due to increased wages for officials, subsidies, and a significant spike in the budget deficit (Riedel and Turley 1999). When combined with growing resistance to centralized restrictions on local initiatives, especially in the South, the compromise was not sustainable.

Doi Moi

These problems prompted a new set of reforms—*doi moi* (renovation)—approved by the Sixth Congress in 1986. These included enhanced SOE autonomy, permission of small-scale private traders, and elimination of the state's monopoly over foreign trade. They provided the basis for changes at the margins, including cutting differences between official and market prices, ending rationing for many commodities, ending checkpoints on internal trade, and establishing the legal bases for foreign investment and trade. Yet again, these initial reforms were partial and couched within a clear reassertion of the government planning apparatus, government control of SOEs, and the maintenance of a dual pricing system. In sum, the initial stage of *doi moi* offered incremental changes. But these were fraught with tensions that contributed to increased budget deficits, triple-digit inflation, and pockets of famine (due to a poor harvest in 1987).

REFORM INTENSIFICATION

The response was an acceleration of the pace and expansion of the scope of *doi moi* in 1989. The leadership ended the two-tier price system, set interest rates at real positive levels, devalued the dong to rates close to market rates, equalized tax rates across economic sectors, cut public sector expenditures, freed up agricultural prices, and relaxed foreign exchange and trade rules. These measures amounted essentially to a Washington Consensus–type shock therapy in which the government moved to get out of the way of private producers (Riedel and Turley 1999, 22). The results were impressive: GDP growth rates increased, inflation declined, savings increased, investment doubled, and Vietnam shifted from a rice importer to a rice exporter. Exports overall rose and diversified, based in part on low wages and competitive exchange rates (Agosin 2007, 31).

Yet by 2000, there were questions as to the sustainability of this growth. A competitive exchange rate and free trade for exporters could facilitate strong outcomes for simple import-intensive exports such as garments. But if firms were to "graduate to a more diversified and higher value-added mix of products," they would require measures such as equipment modernization in the upstream textile industries, fewer barriers to private firm growth, and supply-side measures such as training and innovation schemes. These in turn require institutions, such as "a single, demand-driven, industry-responsive association which could overcome important market failures and enhance industry efficiency" (Hill 2000a, 294 and 297).

Such institutions barely existed as of 2000. Indeed, moving into the twenty-first century, Vietnam faced a number of challenges if growth was to be sustained: falling foreign investment due to poor infrastructure; dominance of the financial sector by large, state-controlled banks heavily involved with SOEs; a weak fiscal system; and reform of the state enterprise sector which, at the end of the 1990s, accounted for more than half of industrial output and contributed one-fourth of state revenues (Beresford 2008; Leung and Riedel 2001; Painter 2003, 31). State-owned enterprise reform was especially difficult: as the only economic entities with clear property rights, they soaked up investments, dominated export quota allocation (which they often could not fill), and generally crowded out smaller, private firms.

This problem did not go unnoticed, and in 1994 the government initiated a transformation of the SOEs into diversified, *chaebol*-like "General Corporations." Painter argues that this model has confused control and accountability because it was imposed top-down and because, in some cases, the composition of the conglomerates defied economic logic. There was, however, a political logic that reflected fragmentation within the state itself: the very incoherence of the reform, along with the "diffusion and sharing of power and authority," enabled the transition to be managed "to accommodate external pressures while also . . . preserving the state's ability and integrity as it pursues its long-term programme of *doi moi*" (Painter 2003, 39).

HINTS OF AN EARLY MIDDLE-INCOME TRAP?

This may have been an overly optimistic view. Writing in 2008, even before the current global crisis really hit, observers expressed not just skepticism but downright alarm at Vietnam's trajectory. As of May 2008, price inflation and the fiscal deficit were high, FDI inflows had slowed, and the trade deficit had dramatically increased (FETP 2008, 1–2; Dapice et al. 2008).

Equally alarming was rising inequality: the country's Gini coefficient rose to 0.41 in 2004, up from 0.35 in 1998, with rural–urban income gaps especially wide (Dapice et al. 2008, 41, 43; Frizen 2002; Gill and Kharas 2007). This led to charges that despite Vietnamese claims of pursuing a NIC-type strategy of industrialization and growth with equity, the country's growth trajectory, policies, and institutions are in fact closer to those of Thailand, Indonesia, Malaysia, and the Philippines, whose growth "began to slow down and plateau when they reached a level of development such as Vietnam will attain soon" (Dapice et al. 2008, 43).

Two contributing factors were of special concern: the expansion of a private banking system without adequate supervisory institutions (FETP 2008, 10–11), and persistent problems with the General Corporations (former SOEs). Despite the state-inspired consolidation, these groups have retained influence over key sectors and exhibited weak performance even as they soak up a majority of credit and investment allocations and suffer from debt-to-equity ratios that surpass even those of the Korean *chaebol* (Dapice et al. 2008, 30). Rather than *chaebol,* the Vietnamese groups seemed to be following the Southeast Asian pattern of heavy dependence on "domestic markets for low-value added goods and on speculation and financial engineering . . . [leading to] domestic vested interests that eventually became a serious obstacle to industrialization and national competitiveness" (Dapice et al. 2008, 47–48).

How then do we account for Vietnam's initial reform stages and subsequent institutional lethargy, as reflected in an inability to reform the General Corporations?

Crises and the Politics of Reform

Explaining Vietnam's reform initiatives requires acknowledging a sort of reform spillover in that the impact of earlier changes contributed to reform through the 1990s: the incremental retreat from collectivization, the expansion of private plots, and the emergence of a contract system built on early, less-noticed moves to private plots in the north (Kerkvliet 2005). Nevertheless, looming crises and the threat of significant losses, or the absence of such pressure, constituted the core driver for policy change. Consider first the factors influencing reform initiatives: Vietnam's shift from a command economy to initial reforms in the early 1980s was clearly a response to various threats regarding food shortages, concerns over aid, a trade embargo, and Khmer Rouge raids from the west. The subsequent shift to *doi moi* in the mid-1980s was moderate and incremental. This reflected the achievements of initial reforms, along with generous Soviet support. Intensification of *doi moi* in the late 1980s occurred only with the collapse of the Soviet Union and loss of broader socialist support. The resulting loss of access to cheap inputs for agriculture and the SOEs exacerbated internal economic problems, such as inflation. These pressures pushed the leadership not only to undertake significant policy changes, but also to initiate complementary institutional reforms, ranging from moderate shifts in property rights to support for business associations.

These same incremental steps also contributed to a weakening of reform efforts. Greater autonomy without state support for technology-related investments led the General Corporations to pursue noncore activities, to rely on credit and protection, and to avoid "the more uncertain task of technological upgrading and becoming internationally competitive" (Beresford 2008, 232, 227–228). But underlying the lack of government pressure for better performance was the fact that earlier urgency was replaced by "a sense of complacency and satisfaction with the status quo" (Dapice et al. 2008, 2). In addition to the success of prior reform efforts, this satisfaction was a function of the relatively moderate pressures facing Vietnam up to 2008. Owing to an earlier "minicrisis" in 1996, Vietnam avoided some of the worse impacts of the Asian crisis by its imposition of controls over trade, investment, and financial flows (Leung and Riedel 2001, 19). More recently, it has not suffered from significant foreign exchange shortages. Despite the country's significant fiscal and trade deficits noted above, foreign exchange has been financed by large capital inflows, which rose from US$9.4 billion in 2006 to US$15.7 billion in 2007, amounting to 15.4 percent and 22.7 percent of GDP (FETP 2008, 5). Vietnam has also benefited from high prices for its commodity exports—crude oil, marine products, rice, coffee, rubber—which dominate its list of largest export earners.

The ability to take "the easier way out" seems to have both reflected and reinforced the particular structure of Vietnam's political leadership. In addition, the way that structure channels newly available resources seems important. Malesky et al. (2009, 1) argue that, in contrast to China's more unified leadership, Vietnam's leadership is essentially a "diffused troika" representing different views of the roles of the party and military and of the benefits of private sector growth and global integration. These divisions require broader policymaking coalitions, which in turn motivate leaders "to provide equalizing transfers that limit inequality growth among provinces." What is especially significant for our purposes is that these equalizing transfers are channeled through well-established patronage networks. Although reducing inequality, these transfers seem to follow more of a political logic than an economic one. Unlike in the East Asian NICs (Kang 2002), there seems to be no separation of export-oriented, efficiency-based sectors from those subject to extensive patronage. As a result, "there is reason to suspect that Vietnam's architecture privileges equality over long-term growth prospects by choking off development in its economic engine" (Malesky et al. 2009, 26).

Further, Vietnam's export market advantages seem fragile. WTO membership, despite some phaseout conditions of the Agreement on Textiles and Clothing (ended in 2005), has not provided Vietnamese producers with the extent of production experience enjoyed by most ASEAN countries. Also the global crisis has constrained demand from Vietnam's largest export market, the United States, which accounts for more than 20 percent of Vietnam's exports.[1]

The question, then, is whether these tougher conditions will be sufficient to overcome the kinds of patronage networks noted above. If not, the risk increases that Vietnam—an aspiring middle-income economy—will remain stuck in a Southeast Asian pattern of reliance on "low-cost labor and natural resource exploitation" (Dapice et al. 2008, 7), but that it will do so without the more extensive diversification, the vibrant private sectors, and the sophisticated financial sector of the more advanced middle-income countries.

---

1. Next in terms of importance are Japan (13.7 percent), Australia (7.4 percent), China 6.9 percent), and Germany (4.5 percent) *CIA World Factbook—Vietnam* (2008).

Middle Income: Malaysia and Thailand

Despite their significant differences on dimensions such as ethnic makeup and politics, population, and religion, Malaysia and Thailand share important features, especially in contrast to the East Asian NICs. Below, I trace the developmental outcomes, policies, and institutions common to these two middle-income countries. I argue that relatively similar levels of threats, involving resource endowments, external pressures, and domestic considerations, are necessary to explain both their strengths and their challenges.

Development Performance

As noted at the beginning of this chapter, Malaysia and Thailand are in most respects—income growth, structural change, export growth, diversification, and poverty alleviation—striking economic successes.[2] Their records are less impressive in two other areas: income distribution and economic upgrading. The sources of this inequality are uncertain, but at least three merit note: the expansion of the FIRE sector (finance, insurance and real estate); increasing skill premiums and widening wage dispersion as a result of trade, liberalization, and globalization; and associated labor market reforms resulting in growing informal sectors (Gill and Kharas 2007, 290–291; Packard and Nguyen 2013; Chongvilaivan 2013).

The two countries have also seriously lagged the NIC's level of upgrading, that is, combining increased value added with efficiency, local linkages, and technological capacities (Yusuf and Nabeshima 2009; UNDP 2007; Gill and Kharas 2007). To be sure, higher value-added products have become more prominent in the two economies, as reflected in the growing percentage of medium- and high-tech products in manufacturing exports. But this record is marred by limited local inputs, high trade dependency, and in some cases, denationalization. Local producers account for little of the value, as reflected, for example, in the high trade deficits characteristic of mid- and high-tech industries, and the general lack of indigenous suppliers in industries such as Malaysia's semiconductors and Thailand's disk drive and automotive production (Doner 2009; Mckendrick et al. 2000).

An important puzzle, then, is the gap between the advanced nature of these two countries' export structures and the much more modest technological levels in their production processes (Lall 1998). As relatively high wages in Malaysia and Thailand require a shift to competitive advantages resulting from knowledge and spillovers, rather than merely resources and labor costs, these capacities remain modest, especially in historical and comparative perspective: a 2003 analysis concluded that Thailand's capacities for exploiting technology and generating innovation, as well as the commitment

---

2. On the region's impressive diversification relative to the Latin America and the Caribbean, see Agosin (2007, 31, table 5).

to building such capacities, lag significantly behind what they were in the NICs at similar stages in their development (Bell et al. 2003, 4). Although Thai and Malaysian rates of growth and degrees of diversification remain above world and developing country averages, these weaknesses in technology and innovation raise broader concerns about the sustainability of their growth (Intarakumnerd et al. 2002; Yusuf and Nabeshima 2009, 3). I suggest below that these weaknesses are in part a function of the labor market structures, especially the informal sectors, resulting from these countries' otherwise successful development strategies.

Reform Strategies and Stages

Several common elements in Malaysian and Thai growth strategies stand out. First, beginning in the early 1970s, both countries shifted from a combination of import substitution industrialization and commodity-based exports to export promotion emphasizing manufactured goods. The results were reflected in the striking shift in the composition of each country's exports (ADB, various years). Second, these shifts were complemented by increasingly open financial sectors, as well as liberal trade and investment regimes. Both countries have gradually reduced tariffs (although, as discussed below, this reduction has been uneven and incremental). Whereas Malaysia has been much more reliant on FDI inflows than has Thailand, both countries' development approaches have been "embedded in regional and global innovation systems, and . . . [their] primary linkages to sources of innovation are through MNC internal technology transfers" (Felker 2001, 139–140). Third, both have generally practiced cautious macroeconomic management (Rasiah 2001).

Fourth, however, in addition to these otherwise Washington Consensus–like strategies, both countries' states have intervened to alter the sectoral composition of their economies and deepen their technology levels and linkages. As suggested by their impressive diversification, state efforts were quite successful in the former. Research on Thailand's tourist, sugar, textile, auto, and rubber industries, as well as on the country's impressive macroeconomic performance, demonstrates the success of state-supported, sector-specific promotion efforts by public and private sector institutions, including ministries, the Board of Investments, sectoral institutes, and business associations, to address information, coordination, and related risk problems (Doner 2009).

Similar efforts took place in Malaysia, albeit with less even results. Promotion was successful in the cases of rubber and palm oil, as well as in electrical and electronic products, which became the main export component of Malaysia's manufacturing sector. But in autos, Malaysian promotion efforts have remained more domestically oriented and resisted the shift to the extensive FDI-supportive policies that Thailand adopted after the 1997 crisis, policies that have made Thailand the automotive hub of Southeast Asia (Doner and Wad, forthcoming).

As suggested by our earlier review, however, neither has done well on linkage and technology promotion, *despite* awareness of the importance of upgrading by both governments. Thailand's auto industry and Malaysia's electronics industry nicely illustrate these weaknesses. Both industries are successful export hubs, operating within global value chains. This creation of efficient "clusters" is a very significant achievement. But as a recent World Bank report notes, the actual tasks performed in these clusters are typically of low complexity, "often involving only the assembly of final products. Import content is high, and in the case of Malaysia a substantial fraction of the labor in industry is also imported" (World Bank 2010, 12). In fact, these clusters are primarily *logistical* (i.e., they reduce transactions costs in production) rather than technological (which capitalizes on spillovers of research and development between different players in the supply chain).

Overall, both countries' technology and innovation policies suffered from key strategic weaknesses. Among these are a focus on product innovation rather than the process innovations that were more feasible, given the MNCs' control of product development; and a tendency to separate state-based research and development from firm-level innovation processes. Also notable were a failure to integrate science and technology policy into broader economic policies, that is, industrial policy, investment policy, trade policy, and to a lesser extent, education policies; weak technology financing strategies; and relative neglect of policies to encourage technology diffusion (Felker 2003). These policy problems have continued from the 1990s to the present, and they are reflected in persistent *institutional* weaknesses in Malaysian and Thai technology-promotion efforts.

Crises and the Politics of Reform
These weaknesses in real economy upgrading are especially striking relative to both countries' strengths in macroeconomic policy and financial reform. How do we explain this variation? My answer, noted at the beginning of this chapter, hinges on the degree of pressures—threats—facing political leaders. In the rest of this section, I assess this argument through the lens of three major crises as well as what might seem at first glance to be outliers.

1980s CRISIS
Both countries were hit hard by falling prices for agricultural commodities, oil price hikes, and cyclical declines in electronics in the mid-1980s.[3] GDP growth slowed and even fell. Both countries' foreign indebtedness had risen, with Thailand's exceeding that of the Philippines; Thailand was forced to borrow US$542 million from the World Bank, thus becoming the world's fifth largest recipient of bank funds at the time. As a long-time observer

---

3. This discussion draws on Rasiah (2003) and Doner (2009, chapter 4).

noted for Thailand, "No previous Thai government had been under the kind of severe and sustained economic pressure that now brought the technocrats to the conclusion that a thoroughgoing shift to an export orientation could no longer be delayed" (Muscat 1994, 195).

These pressures stimulated important stabilization measures, reforms in trade administration, devaluations, and infrastructural development that helped both countries emerge from the crisis in good shape. Thailand became the poster child for successful World Bank–type economic reform in these areas. But reform *initiatives* did not stop with macroeconomic measures. Thailand also initiated an effort to improve the basic competitiveness of local producers and to reform the enclave-nature of foreign dominated manufacturing. This took the form of proposals for tariff reform and the creation of a Restructuring Committee (RESCOM) and, subsequently, an Industrial Linkage Program designed by the Board of Investments (BUILD) to match indigenous suppliers with foreign firms.

Equally significant is what did *not* occur. Thailand's RESCOM was largely ignored and eventually abandoned. BUILD ended up as little more than a state-sponsored database of local suppliers largely neglected by multinationals. In the area of trade, export-oriented reforms were grafted on to protection for local suppliers of raw materials and intermediates and for local downstream firms producing for the domestic market. In addition, the country's overall tariff levels actually increased in the 1980s, even as the government proclaimed its export orientation. And while tariff rates declined in the 1990s, they remained high relative to those of other large developing countries. The result was a combination of rising effective rates of protection for upstream firms, most of which were locally owned, and countervailing export subsidies for downstream firms, most of which were foreign owned. Added to this protection were local content requirements in the automotive and agricultural machinery industries and a set of specific business taxes and tariffs that discouraged linkages between final exporters and domestic suppliers. Finally, as Felker has argued, Thai business itself resisted efforts by Thailand's Board of Investment to take advantage of new FDI inflows with promotion criteria more focused on technology development (Felker 2001, 142–143). In Malaysia, meanwhile, technology promotion efforts were "not much more than government wish lists" (Felker 2003, 144).

Three factors—facilitated, to be sure, by the reforms noted above—moderated pressures that likely would have pushed further institutional development. First, both countries initially used their resource endowments to moderate balance of payments problems. This seems to have been especially important for Malaysia, where new petroleum contracts provided significant revenues (Rasiah 2003, 66). Second, both benefited significantly from rapidly rising FDI inflows, especially from Japan and the East Asian NICs (Gomez and Jomo 1999, 292; Doner 2009, chapter 4). Finally, the availability of large reserves of unemployed workers, including migrant labor, attracted foreign firms and reduced pressure to devote resources to upgrading-related activities such as technical and vocational training. In Malaysia's booming electronics industry, the use of migrant labor grew from just over one thousand in 1990 to more than forty-six thousand in 1996, roughly 10 percent of the workforce (Henderson and Phillips 2007, 91; Rasiah 2003, 50).

1997 Asian Financial Crisis

Haggard (2000, 1) labels the 1997–98 Asian crisis a "singular event in the region's postwar economic history." The magnitude did, however, vary by country. Although Thailand and Malaysia were among the four most seriously hurt (along with South Korea and Indonesia), Malaysia was the least hard hit and responded with the most heterodox policies: Prime Minister Mahathir abandoned Malaysia's currency peg in July 1997 but avoided IMF borrowings, fixed its exchange rate, and imposed capital controls. However, Malaysia did not go it alone. Its ability to sustain capital controls without IMF help reflected the availability of other funds (Haggard 2000, 83–84). Domestically, the government was able to draw on funds from Petronas (the national oil company), as well from the Employee Provident Fund. Externally rebuffed by international financial markets, the government drew heavily on funds from the Export-Import Bank of Japan. A final, important part of this story has to do with the size and the "dispensability" of Malaysia's foreign workforce. Many of the workers in the worst hit sectors, especially construction, were migrants who "simply left the country; in effect, *Malaysia exported a substantial part of its unemployment*" (Haggard 2000, 196, emphasis added).

Thailand was harder hit: more than 3 million people were pushed into poverty; the country was in a state of insolvency; and the government accepted the IMF's second-largest-ever support package—US$17 billion.[4] In addition to financial sector reform, the government responded with aggressive efforts to improve productivity in both agriculture and industry. This took the form of an ambitious and corporatistlike Industrial Restructuring Program (IRP). But by 2001, the IRP was abandoned by newly elected Prime Minister Thaksin. Thailand's ability to avoid the challenging upgrading tasks proposed in the IRP was a function of two factors. One was a devaluation-induced jump in exports, which in turn helped improve the balance of payments, increase foreign exchange reserves, and stabilize the baht. And, as in Malaysia, foreign funds were important: Japan's "Miyazawa Fund" contributed US$1.5 billion for development and the Asian Development Bank (ADB) put in another US$300 million for agriculture. Subsequently, Thaksin himself announced an ambitious and explicit upgrading effort, aimed at technology, linkages, and clusters and bolstered by an aggressive plan for

---

4. Unless noted, this discussion draws on Doner (2009, 125–30).

educational and bureaucratic reform. His government, overthrown in 2006, implemented few of these initiatives, instead relying on export-driven growth and baht stabilization that facilitated the use of state credits to stimulate demand and fuel clientelist politics.

The availability of migrant workers also discouraged serious efforts in areas such as education and training. While Thailand's recovery may not have "benefited" from as large a large migrant workforce as did Malaysia's, by 2000 Thailand had "become deeply dependent on legal and illegal foreign migrant workers" (Suehiro 2008, 272; Huguet and Punpuing 2005). It is also evident that the rural sector has provided a "labor sink" and, since 1999, that Thai growth has been driven by "the increasing employment of its large reserves of underemployed labor in the rural sector" (Lauridsen 2002, 158). The crisis stimulated more flexible labor market policies that expanded the legal scope for part-time, contract, temporary, and other forms of informal employment. As Lauridsen (2002, 113) noted, "Crises and reform have bred informalization."

2008–9 Crisis

The region's rebound in the wake of the recent crisis seems to have resulted from several factors. First, as other chapters argue, relatively healthy financial sectors (due to post-1997 reforms of financial supervision, corporate governance, and so on) have facilitated aggressive monetary and fiscal stimulus programs. Thailand and Malaysia, as well as Taiwan, South Korea, and Singapore, have "all had a government boost this year of at least 4 percent of GDP" (*The Economist*, August 15, 2009). Malaysia's ability to provide such financing is in part a function of natural resource revenues: oil and gas now account for around 40 percent of government revenues (NEAC 2010, 131–132). The longer-term challenge involves sustaining the recovery without the expansionary policies fueling asset-price bubbles. Doing this will require letting exchange rates rise, but this will hurt exports; and exports are, of course, another key component of the recovery in Malaysia and, more strikingly, in Thailand.

Although a critical strength, the countries' export performances conceal two weaknesses: extensive reliance on exports and on unskilled, informal (temporary, contract) labor. As the World Bank (2010, 1) warned, "The Thai economy runs on a single engine: external demand." A major challenge for both countries is thus to expand internal demand. But this has been difficult in light of the country's lack of upstream linkages with the potential to absorb labor and persistent inequality. In Thailand, inequality is reflected in a strikingly small middle class. And while a recent ADB report highlighted the rise of an Asian middle class and the fact that Thailand and Malaysia were among the five Asian countries with the largest middle classes (as a percentage of population), the ADB also highlighted the fragility and overall vulnerability of these middle classes (ADB 2010, 32–33).

In addition, both countries have increased their dependence on unskilled and temporary/contract labor. This is reflected in Archanun et al.'s findings that, following the 1997–98 crisis, "many enterprises . . . adopted a more flexible employment system for production in which firms hire both permanent and temporary workers at the same time. In addition, they usually run overtime to enhance their capital utilization rate and to avoid any possible over-investment problems" (Archanun et al. 2010, 109). The rise of unskilled labor is equally notable in Malaysia due to a combination of brain drain by ethnic Chinese and an undereducated domestic population (NEAC 2010, 42–60). Significant informal sectors have contributed to this low-skill equilibrium.

In Thailand, the level of informality has increased over the past ten years, with the informal sector estimated at well over 60 percent of the entire workforce and even a significant portion of those with college education—30 percent— estimated to work in the informal sector, especially in small shops and eateries (Amornivat 2013). Malaysia's informal sector is much smaller than Thailand's, between 8–9 percent (Department of Statistics 2013).

Migrants, often unskilled, are important for both economies. For Malaysia, official sources estimated that semi- and unskilled migrant workers accounted for 13.9 percent of total manufacturing workers and fully 10 percent in electronics in 2000. As such, the electronics industry is running a close second to construction as the largest user of migrant labor, with most migrants in electronics working as contractual production employees (Henderson and Phillips 2007, 92). Encouraged by immigration policies favoring low-skilled and cheap labor, foreign labor accounted for more than a third of the growth in total labor supply from 1990 to 2005, with over 90 percent of these low-skilled, contract workers. One estimate is that the number of migrant workers might have reached 2 million in 2006, roughly 20 percent of the formal labor force.[5] For Thailand, estimates of migrants range from 2 million to as high as 4 million, well over 5 percent of the labor force in 2005, contributing to 7–10 percent of value added in industry and 4–5 percent of value added in agriculture (ILO 2007; Youngyuth and Prugsamatz 2009, 4).

Research points to several related, negative consequences of large informal sectors, especially those with sizeable numbers of migrant workers. One, stressed in the Malaysian literature, is wage depression (Tham and Liew 2004; Wad 2009). This in turn discourages investments in higher value-added activities requiring more skilled labor and thus to reduced potential technology spillovers from foreign investors. Ironically, this may also inhibit labor

---

5. Personal communication from Donna Turner on October 16, 2009. See also Turner (2005). Many migrants to Malaysia come from neighboring Indonesia. According to the World Bank, the Malaysian-Indonesian migration corridor "contains the second largest flows of undocumented workers—after the one between the US and Mexico" (World Bank 2007b).

absorption despite overall growth. In Thailand, GDP growth is driven by exports, and most of those exports are driven by a few sectors with relatively high import components but low employment (Sethaput 2010). The result is a tendency for "wageless growth" that, in the long run, will undermine efforts to develop a middle class and to reduce inequality.

This emphasis on informality and reliance on migrants also has institutional and political consequences. Institutionally, it seems to discourage the emergence of public, private, and public-private rules and organizations designed to promote skills development. Bryan Ritchie has effectively documented the extensive fragmentation characterizing workforce development agencies in both Thailand and Malaysia (Ritchie 2010, 100–106). Reliance on a large informal workforce weakens labor's potential for organizational cohesion and thus political influence. This not only reduces the possibility of pressure on employers to raise wages and potentially, as a result, to invest in productivity measures such as technical training; it also deprives both business and government of active interlocutors with whom to develop such programs. Turner (2005, 58) argues that migrant labor contributes to a segmented labor force that in turn promotes a "low wage regime," where local unions make little effort to organize, and "where little is invested in training and technological advances."

The further implication, reflected in the earlier-noted work on Western Europe, is that weakly organized labor is associated with inequality. This last point is speculative, but it is consistent with the conclusion that well-organized social groups are necessary for broad public goods: "Democratization without well-organized social groups may lead to modes of political competition that promote inefficient policies, targeted at narrow groups at the expense of the poor" (Keefer 2009, 663–664). It is also consistent with the rise of inequality in Malaysia and Thailand, noted earlier. The challenges to long-run political stability are evident in Thailand's intensifying conflict between "red" and "yellow" shirts, and labor's vulnerability to populist appeals having little to do with improvements in skills and productivity.

Conclusions and Key Questions

This chapter has explored the factors accounting for the success and limitations of Southeast Asian responses to economic crises through the lens of one low, but rapidly developing income country, Vietnam, and two middle-income countries, Malaysia and Thailand. My overriding concern has been to explore the potential for sustained economic growth. In the case of Vietnam, this speaks to the capacity for further, efficient diversification necessary to move further into middle-income status. For Malaysia and Thailand, it involves the capacity for upgrading as the basis for movement out of middle-income status. I have argued that two "demand" factors: (1) significant pressures on political elites, and (2) some form of labor inclusion—whether in the form of a macrocorporatist bargain, a more enterprise-level "microcorporatism," or a "growth partnership" in which labor is repressed organizationally but strengthened with educational and other job-related resources—are necessary if the institutional capacities required for upgrading are to be "supplied." Differences with regard to these factors are key to explaining the weaknesses of the otherwise successful Southeast Asian cases relative to the East Asian NICs (Jiminez et al. 2012). In the conclusion, I wish to address challenges to this analysis.

Threats as Stimuli to Institutional Development and Upgrading

The emphasis on threats as necessary for the creation of upgrading-related institutions and growth partnerships suffers from two methodological weaknesses. One is that the threat variable is dichotomous: a country is either threatened or is not. The second weakness is that our cases lack "variation on the independent variable." That is, since neither Vietnam, Malaysia, nor Thailand, at least at the national level, confronted significant threats, it is difficult to conclude that the presence of such threats would have stimulated institutional strengthening and upgrading. We can address both of these weaknesses by expanding our cases in two ways: through within-country observations that allow us to see the impact of even moderate threats, and through comparisons with other national cases (Doner and Wad forthcoming; Doner et al. 2005).

Foreign Investment as Alternative to Threats

What of the potential for improved skills and upgrading as a result of investments by multinational corporations? There are exogenous and endogenous obstacles to such productive spillovers. On the exogenous side, their access to global suppliers allows MNCs to avoid the resource-consuming efforts to promote skill-based domestic suppliers. Further, in industries such as electronics and autos, firms tend to be capital intensive. Thus electrical and mechanical machinery and automotive goods account for more than a third of Thailand's exports but employ well under 5 percent of the labor force (World Bank 2010). And finally, FDI-linked options are more "compressed" (Whittaker et al. 2010). Changes in production technology and social relations that occurred over a century and a half in the United Kingdom, some fifty years in Japan, and a few decades in the NICs, now occur more rapidly and, in some cases, simultaneously. In addition, the disaggregated nature of global production chains means that, unlike South Korea, Japan, and Taiwan, countries such as Malaysia and Thailand have fewer if any opportunities to develop complete, national production structures (i.e. upstream, midstream, and downstream) in industries that also have the potential to be globally competitive.

As a result, taking advantage of FDI requires ever-more assertive FDI promotion strategies, a deepening of the kinds of institutional capacities reviewed earlier in this chapter, and an educated workforce. Yet the overall strategy of Malaysia and Thailand is what one World Bank study labeled "passive FDI-dependent learning" that has engendered little of the spillovers assumed to flow from the presence of foreign producers (Yusuf and Nabeshima 2009, 59). Underlying this passive approach is the fact that political elites, unencumbered by resource constraints and/or some form of organized labor, have found it acceptable to cede key industrializing roles to multinationals who pay decent wages but employ relatively few workers and develop few linkages to local suppliers (Van der Hoeven and Saget 2004, 204).

Indigenous Business Demand for Upgrading

Large, indigenous, diversified business groups have played key development roles in Southeast Asia, as they have in Latin America (Suehiro 2008, chapter 9). But diversification by Latin American "grupos" minimizes their need to develop deep, core competencies that would increase their focus on technology absorption and transfer, and thus their demand for technical personnel (Schneider and Soskice 2009). Commodity booms, as well as the opportunity for profits in nontradable sectors, have further weakened pressures for technology development by local groups in Southeast Asia (Dixon 2010).

Potential for Labor Inclusion

The possibilities for more active labor inclusion in Southeast Asia seem limited by a number of factors. One, emphasized earlier, is the availability of a segmented and relatively low-skilled migrant workforce. A second is that the shift from mass, Fordist-type production to more flexible or "diversified quality production" reduces labor cohesion and thus leverage (Eichengreen and Iversen 1999). A third is the weakness of labor-party linkages. Labor's role in promoting productivity increases and overall stability in industrial relations seems to be facilitated by union links to encompassing yet competitive political parties. The case of Singapore would seem to provide positive support for this contention, whereas the more fragmented party system of Thailand (Brown 2004), and the ethnically flavored parties in Malaysia, illustrate the results of a lack of such a party.

In light of labor's organizational weakness, combined with fragmented political parties and access to foreign exchange from commodity and low-skill manufactured exports, the most feasible option for labor is continued reliance on clientelist links, whether of the ethnic type, as in Malaysia, or of the more populist type, as in Thailand under Thaksin (Pasuk and Baker 2008). These kinds of arrangements provide few incentives or institutional bases to address the tough challenges of technology absorption and upgrading. Whether such patterns develop in Vietnam, a country with a traditionally move active labor movement, remains to be seen.

8

Japan

The Political Economy of Long Stagnation
Keiichi Tsunekawa

When the economic crisis hit East Asia in 1997–98, Japan was already in a deep recession that had begun with the bursting of its own bubble economy in the first half of the 1990s. Japan's economy looked to be recovering by the middle of the 2000s but found itself hit by the Global Financial Crisis (GFC) more seriously than the United States, the epicenter of the crisis. Japan's annual GDP growth rates for 1999–2007, 2008–9, and 2010–12 were 1.3 percent, −3.3 percent, and 2.0 percent. The corresponding figures for the U.S. were 2.9 percent, −1.6 percent, and 2.4 percent (IMF 2013).

Up until the mid-1990s, Japan was the undoubted economic leader in East Asia. In many respects, Japan's developmental strength was the precursor of many later-developing East Asian countries. It achieved long-term super-high growth based on massive investments in manufacturing and the export of manufactured goods, a pattern followed by other East Asian countries. The development of industrial sectors was largely dependent on technologies imported from the United States and Europe but then improved on in Japan, resulting in better product quality and production efficiency.

With its private firms demonstrating a high capacity to improve product and process technologies, the Japanese economy escaped the "middle income trap" analyzed by Doner for several Southeast Asian countries, instead growing into an advanced industrial country. However, Japan's trajectory thereafter demonstrates that even a high-income country risks falling into its own trap, one in which continuous growth is impeded by serious market uncertainties compounded by difficulties of sustaining technological innovation and intense contradictions in public policies.

An early sign of such troubles emerged during the 1980s when Japan started to implement many market reforms under strong U.S. and European pressures, liberalizing trade and investment and deregulating financial and other business activities. These reforms jeopardized the established practices and institutions designed for coordination of interests among market players and between market and nonmarket players. Political democracy made this interest coordination even more complicated and difficult. Similar difficulties in interest coordination have emerged in other East Asian countries as their polities have become more open and democratic. The basic question that Japan has faced for the past quarter century and other East Asian countries may face in the future is how to develop a new mode of interest coordination in a globalized economic environment so as to allow continuous technological improvement or innovation ensuring satisfactory economic growth, even if such growth is not as high as before.

This chapter analyzes the fundamental causes of the Japanese stagnation from a political economy point of view. It shows that the economic difficulties of Japan cannot be explained by economic logic alone. Political factors have played a crucial role in shaping economic developments in Japan. This chapter, however, does not intend to disprove economic explanations so much as to offer an alternative interpretation focusing on political factors.

This chapter uses Korea as a reference for comparison. Korea shares with Japan many of the experiences of a typical East Asian developmental state but its economic performance since the Asian Financial Crisis (AFC) has been much better than Japan's.[1] The Korean case consequently helps to highlight the sources of Japanese difficulties.

The chapter is structured as follows. Section 1 will review the existing literature, which tries to explain Japan's long-term stagnation from two contrasting angles: the supply-side view and the demand-side view. I argue that both views miss the mark and point out that the real problem is that Japan's political economy has fallen into a trap in which any policy, whether supply side or demand side, cannot be pursued for a long enough period to prove its validity. Japan's continual policy fluctuations have heightened market uncertainties, obstructing both investment and consumption for an extended period of time. To examine the underlying reasons for Japan's continual policy swings, section 2 first lays out the nature of the developmental state that brought such high growth to Japan in the earlier decades. It shows that the developmental state in Japan was in practice accompanied first by dense clientelist networks on top of which were subsequently overlaid additional welfare-state programs. By the early 1980s, this mixture of competing policy agendas undermined the overall strength of public finance while also worsening economic relations with the United States. Consequently, Japan saw the emergence and strengthening of neoliberal policies, which started to

---

1. Authors differ in their judgment on which states deserve to be called developmental (World Bank 1993, 7; Rodan et al. 2005). Southeast Asian countries except Singapore are regarded as less developmental than Northeast Asian countries. Nobody disagrees that Japan and Korea were the most typical cases of the developmental state.

weaken the preexisting developmental, clientelist, and welfare-statist orientations. The result was policy uncertainty combined with a decline in the support base for the ruling conservative party and the emergence of a huge group of nonpartisan voters willing to swing widely from election to election based on short-term issue considerations.

Section 3 will examine how the intensified political competition made the fluctuation among different policy agendas a perpetual characteristic of Japan's political economy, which in turn impeded both investment and consumption and prolonged the economic stagnation caused originally by the bursting of the bubble economy and aggravated by the AFC. Section 4 is dedicated to the analysis of Japan's political economy after Koizumi's ascent to power and his systematic efforts to break the longstanding logjam among competing policy goals of the ruling Liberal Democratic Party. Koizumi was relatively persistent in his neoliberal policy stance, and the Japanese economy achieved a certain recovery as a result. Investment and consumption, however, remained low and the economic growth of Japan became deeply dependent on export growth. The GFC consequently hit Japan particularly hard as a result of its impact on global export markets. In addition, the crisis reactivated the intense political competition and subsequent policy vacillations that had plagued Japan for nearly two decades.

Section 5 summarizes the three historical sections to demonstrate how the specific nature of the postwar state ultimately brought about Japan's long economic stagnation. It will also touch on the change in the nature of technological innovation in Japan and how that too aggravated market uncertainties in Japan.

Section 6 compares the Japanese case with the Korean experience. It shows that a more decisive policy shift occurred in Korea due to that country's different political and institutional configurations, which in turn were generated by different experiences during the developmental state phase. The chapter concludes by suggesting that the minimum condition necessary for Japan to regenerate its economy would be a political realignment of political parties that would present more consistent and clear-cut policy options to the electorate and that the political system be reformed to guarantee greater longevity for its elected officers.

Explanations for Japanese Stagnation

In explaining Japan's long-term stagnation, the overwhelming majority of scholars—both economists and political scientists—take the supply-side view. One typical view offered by Yasuyuki Todoh (2010) argues that a return to substantial economic growth will occur only through productivity improvement brought about by technological and managerial innovation. Such innovation will only emerge out of global competition and the acquisition of the best technologies and know-how from wherever they are available. Therefore, existing Japanese impediments against free trade and investment must be lifted.

Many political economists and political scientists concur with this view although their arguments often have a more institutionalist flavor. Such arguments contend that the relational institutions characterizing the developmental state—the main bank, cross-shareholding, the horizontal and vertical business networks, long-term employment, and close government-business consultations—which had helped or at least did not obstruct high economic growth in the early postwar period—came to impede the formation of new patterns or institutions more appropriate for the highly competitive global market that Japan increasingly faced. Typical in this line of argument is Kozo Yamamura's view (2003) that the "cooperation-based capitalism" of Japan is institutionally inferior to the "market-driven capitalism" of the United States in a world that has entered the breakthrough phase dependent on a new technological paradigm.

In contrast, Pempel (1998 and 2010a) and Kingston (2004) focus on the wastefulness of the clientelist institutions that continue to protect noncompetitive producers like small constructors, farmers, and/or retailers as the main source of Japan's economic weakness.

Rosenbluth and Thies (2010) also blame governmental protection of noncompetitive sectors but their main targets are the longstanding developmental institutions mentioned above. Unlike Yamamura, they argue that these institutions only helped maintain ineffective industries and service sectors under government protection and therefore created inevitable difficulties when Japan faced international pressures for liberalization.

Authors like Richard Katz (2003a) and Leonard Schoppa (2006) do not distinguish between developmental institutions and clientelist institutions, blaming both for the difficulties faced by the Japanese economy. The former argues that protection of backward sectors and labor market inflexibility are the key culprits slowing the revival of the Japanese economy. Schoppa adds that the inflexibility of the labor market, the binding subcontracting networks, and the high cost of regulated services and inputs all force Japanese enterprises to increasingly choose the "exit" strategy of shifting their production abroad.

In comparison with such supply-side explanations, there are fewer supporters of demand-side explanations. Mari Osawa (2011), for instance, argues that excessive deregulation and pursuit of "small government" jeopardized job security and weakened the social safety net in Japan. As this happened, income distribution deteriorated and domestic consumption shrank, causing the economy to lose an important engine of growth. To substantiate her contention, she cites an OECD study (Jones 2007) that compares the member countries in terms of the reduction of poverty rate through national tax and social benefit systems. In mid-2000s, Japan, among the OECD countries, recorded the second lowest reduction of its poverty rate through tax and social benefits superseded only by Mexico.

This demand-side view was shared by the first two Democratic Party of Japan (DPJ) administrations (2009–11). In the *New Growth Strategy* announced in June 2010, the DPJ government rejected economic policies based on public works (clientelism) as well as those which place a disproportionate emphasis on productivity (neoliberalism). It criticized "excessive market fundamentalism" and proposed "the third way" by which to realize innovation and growth through "enlargement of employment and demand" in sectors such as social welfare services and environment/energy (Japanese Government Cabinet Office 2010b).

The demand-side view is rather defensive vis-à-vis the powerful supply-side view because it does not show how demand expansion assures sustained growth through productivity improvement in existing and new economic sectors. The supply-side view, however, is also based on a shaky assumption, namely that once market-oriented reforms are fully implemented, the Japanese economy returns to the growth path. In practice, they give little evidence to substantiate their contention. The fact that old relational institutions have ceased to bring about high economic growth does not automatically mean that their elimination and a full conversion to the American-style arms-length capitalism guarantees renewed (and sustained) growth.[2]

Instead of discussing the relative merits of these two economic explanations, this chapter attempts to present an alternative interpretation that the real problem Japan faces today is not the lack of neoliberal or aggregate-demand policy but rather policy fragility in which economic policy zigzags so rapidly and inconsistently that any policy, either more neoliberal or more interventionist, is never sustained long enough to test its validity. As a result, high uncertainty has lingered in the domestic market for many years, impeding both investment and consumption. The change in the nature of the technological innovation pointed out by Kozo Yamamura is an additional factor that could further deepen market uncertainty. Policy fluctuations and technological change together seem to have obstructed the previously effective practice in which market players committed resources with implicit long-term perspectives and guarantees.

This chapter will also argue that the main causes of Japan's policy drift are the catchall nature of the main political parties and the existence of a huge group of nonpartisan voters, both of which prevent the creation and consistent pursuit of any single set of economic policies. These contradictions emerged long before the AFC and have persisted over the two major global crises. The source of these contradictions is found in the specific process of formation and transformation of the developmental state in postwar Japan.

---

2. Dore (2000) casts doubts on the contention that the Japanese-style relational capitalism is inferior to the American model in every industrial sector.

Mixed Nature of the Developmental State and Its Consequence

When Chalmers Johnson (1982) first formulated the idea of the "developmental state" in Japan, he emphasized the role of the state bureaucracy (MITI in particular) and the industrial policies the national bureaucracy allegedly orchestrated to transform the country's industrial structure and enhance the nation's international competitiveness. He also highlighted the role of a variety of institutions—lifetime employment, *keiretsu* groups, subcontracting networks, company financing that restricted shareholders' influence, the government-controlled financial system, and the like. All of these were regarded as helpful for the rapid economic growth of postwar Japan. Johnson, however, rejected any cultural explanation for these institutions, insisting that they were products of private firms' and the government's responses to social and economic conditions during the period following World War I and the Great Depression. Tetsuji Okazaki concurs with Johnson in the view that institutions such as mechanisms to encourage worker participation, weak stockholders' roles, and exclusive bank-firm relations were products of conscious government policies designed to mobilize financial and human resources for Japan's war efforts (Okazaki 1994, 374). Such developmental institutions were then reinforced by postwar reforms such as the dissolution of the *zaibatsu* business groups and General Headquarter's policy to utilize the existing bureaucracy (except for the military and a part of the police) to govern Japan.

It is not necessary to repeat a detailed explanation of the above-mentioned institutions. It is sufficient to point out that these institutions served to guarantee that Japanese manufacturers enjoyed stable long-term relations with the government on the one hand and relevant market players (banks, subcontractors, and workers) on the other, thus allowing them to make their investment and production decisions not for the short-term profitability of shareholders but for long-term growth of the firms (and in the process, to catalyze the overall growth in the country's GDP).

These institutions fit perfectly with the kind of catch-up industrialization characterized by Yasusuke Murakami (1996) as "decreasing average cost" manufacturing. Japanese firms imported the world's most modern technologies and added smart improvements to products and production processes so as to efficiently produce goods whose marketability had been fully tested in the advanced industrial countries. Anticipating market availability, they rushed to invest and produce. To do so, however, they needed access to huge financial resources, which they could not raise by themselves. They also needed close coordination and long-term cooperation with other market players to avoid excessive competition, to improve product quality and production processes on a continuous basis, to reduce the risk of failures stemming from high indebtedness, and to ward off the danger of takeover by quick-profitability-oriented outsiders. The aforementioned institutions served to meet these needs.

Serious economic inefficiencies were created far less in big manufacturers and their subcontractors, all pillars of the developmental state, and far more in the sectors dominated by small producers. The developmental state was consolidated in postwar Japan in parallel with the formation of the clientelist networks because the probusiness political order was secured under democracy only by votes provided by farmers and the numerous other small producers of goods and services. In the immediate postwar years, facing a sudden upsurge in the power of a radical labor movement and the political challenge from leftist parties, neither conservative politicians nor business leaders moved to embrace the European style corporatist accommodation between big labor and big business in the interest of industrial peace. Instead, they sought probusiness stability by strengthening clientelist connections with farmers and other self-employed people. Kabashima (2004, 14–16) and Pempel (2010a, 234–39) argue that these extensive clientelist networks were vital to the maintenance of political stability and policy consistency, and these in turn contributed to economic growth and the expansion of fiscal resources, which became available for redistribution from Japan's economically competitive to its noncompetitive sectors. Clientelist policies and institutions and developmentalist policies and institutions reinforced each other.

Clientelist policies, however, reached their limit by the 1970s because the economy had matured and the growth rate inevitably declined, a trend precipitated by currency revaluations and by the first oil shock, which heavily hit the Japanese economy due to its high dependence on imported energy resources. However, clientelist policies were not reduced accordingly. On the contrary, they continued to expand under Kakuei Tanaka's heavily public-work oriented government.

Furthermore, during the same decade, programs designed to expand social welfare were also enhanced. Formation of the welfare state in Japan had begun in 1961 with the introduction of universal medical insurance and old-age pensions, but these were expanded in the 1970s when pension benefits were raised and indexed to inflation, and when copayment for medical services was reduced for family members and abolished for people over seventy years old (Shinkawa 2005, 55–56, 72–73).

It was the prospect of a serious decline in its electoral support and the need to refurbish its popularity that led the LDP government to introduce generous policies enhancing clientelist and welfare-state benefits. The demographic transformation brought about by rapid industrialization and urbanization was crucial to explaining this phenomenon. Among the electoral base of the LDP, the primary-sector population declined sharply from 41 percent to 18.3 percent between 1955 and 1970. It further declined to 10.8 percent in 1980 and 7 percent in 1990 (Japan Statistics Bureau 2013a, table 198-a).

In turn, the great majority of Japan's working population was by then salaried employees in the secondary and tertiary sectors. The LDP, to continue to win comfortable majorities within the Diet, needed to appeal to these urban salaried voters while at the same time not losing its traditional support base of small producers. Consequently, the LDP, instead of fighting against the welfare state agenda, which leftist opposition parties had taken advantage of to gain control in many important local governments, embraced such policies as part of its own agenda. The result was the simultaneous expansion of clientelist and welfare policies. The LDP consequently became a catchall party.

Thanks to these policies, the LDP succeeded in maintaining its traditional support base. Yet, it was not similarly successful in organizing the welfare-state beneficiaries into a firm support base because most recipients were diverse and amorphous individuals from cross-cutting sectors, occupations, and localities who could not be easily organized into special interest groups parallel to the longstanding clientelist groups at the heart of LDP support, like agricultural cooperatives or shopkeepers associations. Still, the enhanced clientelist and welfare policies contributed to the recovery of LDP popularity by 1980. Such a recovery, however, was realized only through the imposition of heavy burdens on the government budget. As table 8.1 demonstrates, the share of central government expenditure (general and special accounts) in GDP increased from 18.2 percent in 1970 to 29.6 percent in 1980. The Fiscal Investment and Loan Program (FILP) expenditure funded by the national postal saving and insurance revenues also expanded from 4.8 percent to 7.4 percent of GDP. As the GDP growth rate almost halved in the 1970s there was a concomitant decline of revenue growth and the national debt inevitably ballooned. In 1980 it accounted for 32.6 percent of the general account, while in 1970 its share had been a mere 4.2 percent.

In the face of this alarming expansion of the public deficit, a strong call for budget discipline rose among leaders of the internationally competitive sectors and their labor unions, the Ministry of Finance, a part of the LDP, and some national newspapers and academics. The de facto coalition of big business, small producers, and welfare beneficiaries that had supported the mixed agendas of developmentalism, clientelism, and welfare-statism saw its first serious sign of fissures. Under strong pressures from the Second Provisional Council for Administrative Reform, which preached the virtues of "small government," rice price subsidies and social security benefits were curtailed.

These measures indicate that during the 1980s a neoliberal orientation clearly began to replace pure developmentalism while clientelist and welfare expenditures started to be restricted. As a consequence, by 1990 the national bond issue was reduced to 10.6 percent of the general account, a drop of 22 percentage points from 1980 (table 8.1).

During the 1980s and early 1990s, the LDP government also faced strong American pressures for market openings that would require retrenchment

TABLE 8.1
Public expenditure and national debt

	Expenditure of central government	FILP	Accumulated national debts	National bonds issued	Redemption & interest payment
	% of GDP			% of General Account	
1960	19.6	3.6	–	0.0	1.5
1970	18.2	4.8	3.7	4.2	3.7
1980	29.6	7.4	28.6	32.6	12.5
1990	26.0	7.7	37.0	10.6	21.6
2000	39.7	8.7	72.0	37.0	25.8
2005	45.7	3.4	104.3	36.6	22.4
2010	41.9	2.9	132.8	44.3	22.4
2012	51.0	3.1	148.5	49.0	24.3

Sources: Calculated from Japan Statistics Bureau 2014, tables 3-1, 5-3, and 5-9; Yano Tsuneta Kinenkai 2006, tables 3-3, 9-11, 9-19, and 9-22; MOF 2011, 2012 and 2013a.

of developmental institutions as well as the curtailment of clientelist measures protecting small producers. In practice, the institutions of Japan's developmental state had already been weakened due to the spectacular rise in the financial power of individual private enterprises on the one hand and the diminution of policy tools to control foreign-exchange transactions and foreign investments on the other. If certain developmental institutions such as cross-shareholding, enterprise unionism, and subcontracting networks persisted, it was mostly because market players themselves accepted these institutions as their own. How much they would continue to use them subsequently depended on their own corporate judgments, not on any government decision.

In contrast, the Japanese government was compelled to respond to the American challenges to its clientelist policies since it was evident that government measures continued to protect noncompetitive sectors vis-à-vis foreign competitors. The Japanese government belatedly agreed to abandon its import quota system for beef and oranges in 1988 (MAFF 2007, 1, 5). In the retail business, the LDP government reduced the restrictions against large-scale stores in 1990–91 in spite of fierce opposition from small shopkeepers and their patrons within the LDP (Kusano 1992, 24; Schoppa 1997, 175).

These measures could not help but weaken the existing clientelist ties between small producers and the LDP. At the same time, as discussed above, the nation's welfare-state beneficiaries were too amorphous to replace small producers as a new and dependable support base for the LDP. Furthermore, the generous welfare policies adopted in the early 1970s were too short-lived for the LDP to gain any permanent advantage. For example, as a part of the deficit curtailment effort, the copayment by elderly patients which had been abolished in 1973 was reintroduced in 1982;[3] premiums for medical insurance were raised and pension benefits were curtailed in 1984–85 (Miyamoto 2008, 108–109). Welfare beneficiaries were disappointed by the LDP before they had formed a tight allegiance to the party.

The general criticism against LDP rule erupted in 1989 when the LDP government, aiming at strengthening the long-term fiscal base of the government, forcefully introduced the 3 percent consumption tax. Voter anger resulted in the historical defeat of the LDP in the following House of Councilors election. The LDP lost its majority in the upper house, a situation that lasted for the following quarter of a century.

Japan's major political parties, including the Japan Socialist Party (JSP), then the largest opposition party, were also losing traditional supporters while being unable to forge stable relationships with any new voting blocs. Taniguchi (2012, 154–65) found that the newly emerging "modern non-partisans," unlike traditional voters who were just indifferent to politics, consciously distance themselves from specific political parties but also have a stronger interest in politics, tend to go to the poll more frequently and vote according to party performance.

According to opinion surveys conducted by NHK, the national broadcasting corporation, the number of people who claimed to support no party increased from 32.2 percent in 1983 to 37.8 percent in 1988, 40.7 percent in 1993, 52.3 percent in 1998, and 56.9 percent in 2003 (NHK Hoso Bunka Kenkyujo 2004, 106). The same tendency is indicated by polls by *Yomiuri* newspaper (2002, 497–501), according to which nonpartisan voters expanded from 28.8 percent in March 1988 to 38.0 percent (March 1993) and 54.3 percent (March 1998). Weakening ties between political parties and the electorate was not just an urban phenomenon. The same NHK opinion surveys demonstrate that between 1988 and 2003, support for the LDP dropped more sharply in villages, towns, and cities with less than 100,000 population than in bigger cities. The number of floating voters increased concomitantly in less-populated regions (NHK Hoso Bunka Kenkyujo 2004, 108–109). These figures reflect the reality that winning elections was getting more difficult every day.

Neoliberal Upsurge, AFC, and Policy Drift

The expansion of nonaligned voters, together with the postbubble economic stagnation and the revelation of a series of corruption scandals between the late-1980s and the mid-1990s, made political competition even more intense

---

3. Furthermore, wage earners who had been exempted from payment for medical insurance-covered services were now required to pay 10 percent of the total expense (Estevez-Abe 2008, 217–18).

during the 1990s. In the process, the LDP split and lost power to a multiparty coalition led by Morihiro Hosokawa in August 1993, thus ending its thirty-eight years of consecutive dominance. It regained power ten months later but only as a member of a coalition government headed by a Socialist prime minister. Not until January 1996 did the LDP recover the premiership under Ryutaro Hashimoto. Facing a tough electoral landscape, LDP politicians had strong incentives to enhance clientelist and welfare-statist policies in an effort to recover their electoral strength.

However, under the severe economic conditions following the bursting of the bubble economy, pressures for neoliberal reforms from big business and their allies in the government were mounting simultaneously. The neoliberal drive was precipitated by the U.S. government, which continued to demand liberalization and deregulation of the Japanese market, all challenges to the developmental and clientelist institutions that were so integral to Japan's political economy. As Japan's economic recession deepened and dragged on, these institutions were challenged by neoliberals as raising business costs in Japan. They argued that market deregulation would lower costs and help reactivate the Japanese economy. Responding to this neoliberal logic, every cabinet after the Hosokawa administration announced hundreds or even thousands of targets for deregulation as a part of their economic reactivation policy. Such targets covered a number of sectors including large-scale retail business, production and distribution of alcoholic and petro products, the electric power industry, and the telecommunication industry (Tsunekawa 2010).

In the financial sector, new deregulation measures aiming at dismantling a variety of the developmental institutions that had supported long-term connections between banks and firms were gradually implemented throughout the 1980s and 1990s and were brought to completion in 1998 by the so-called financial Big Bang. In that year, all remaining restrictions were removed over foreign-exchange transactions and crisscrossing investments among financial subsectors (Asako et al. 2011, 121; Hashimoto et al. 2011, 398–99).

The deregulation of labor markets was another neoliberal effort that curtailed an important developmental institution. When the Law on Dispatched Workers was first implemented in 1986, it covered only sixteen job categories such as secretarial services, software development, and accounting. By the 1996 revision of the law, however, the job categories into which temporarily dispatched staff could be employed were expanded to twenty-six. In 1999, a negative list scheme was introduced, and all sectors except five became able to hire dispatched workers.

In addition to this general surge in neoliberal policies, the long-lasting stagnation made it increasingly difficult for Japanese firms to maintain their established relations with *keiretsu* firms, subcontractors, or employees. As a result, the practice of cross-shareholding and subcontracting began to shrink during the 1990s, although many important firms including Toyota and Matsushita (Panasonic), as a matter of corporate strategy, sought to maintain such relational institutions as much as possible. The share of long-term stockholding (both mutual and one-way) dropped from 63.6 percent in 1990 to 43.2 percent in 2000 (METI 2003, table 13–24). Small and medium-sized enterprises that worked as other firms' subcontractors decreased from 55.9 percent in 1987 to 47.9 percent in 1998 of all SMEs (Small and Medium Enterprise Agency 2000, table 2261). The share of "regular" workers who enjoyed long-term employment contracts dropped from 83.6 percent in 1985 to 74.0 percent in 2000, while employees with short or temporary contracts increased from 16.4 percent to 26.0 percent (Japan Statistics Bureau 2013b).

Clientelist institutions were challenged as severely as developmental institutions. In the negotiation leading to WTO, the Japanese government finally agreed to a gradual tariffication of rice imports and the dismantling of its rice control system (Francks et al. 1999, 101). New measures were adopted in 1995 to enhance the liberalization of the domestic rice market, which culminated in the abolition of the Food Agency in 2003 (MAFF 2004).

Public works programs benefiting both big and small construction firms became another major target for retrenchment because the economically stimulative effects of such public works were increasingly less visible following the bursting of the bubble economy and consequently they could no longer be justified given the heavy fiscal burdens they entailed. Public works spending peaked in 1995–96 and turned downward thereafter. The Hashimoto administration (January 1996–July 1998) decided to reform FILP to inject greater financial discipline into the use of resources collected by the Agency for Postal Services.[4] As a part of the reform, the Public Corporation for Housing and Urban Development was reorganized to terminate FILP's construction operations for public housing. The reform began to be implemented in 2001. Almost half of the decline in the FILP budget between 2000 and 2005 can be explained by the drop of expenditures for housing (Yano Tsuneta Kinenkai 2006, table 9-22).

Welfare programs were also curtailed in response to neoliberal influences. The pension benefits and premiums were revised every five years to the disadvantage of the beneficiaries. Furthermore, the pension eligibility age was raised gradually from sixty to sixty-five. The copayment for medical services by the insured was also raised from 10 percent to 20 percent (Shinkawa 2005, 313, 338).

However, neoliberal measures to deregulate market activities and to curtail distributive and redistributive programs met fierce resistance from the affected sectors and ministries as well as their political patrons. Because

---

4. By the 1998 reform (effective April 2001), the Finance Ministry was prohibited from directly transferring financial resources from postal savings, life insurance, and pension funds to public corporations and banks. Instead, FILP projects implemented by these entities would be financed either by the issuance of their own bonds in open markets or by FILP bonds issued by the Ministry of Finance (Cargill and Yoshino 2003, 152–53).

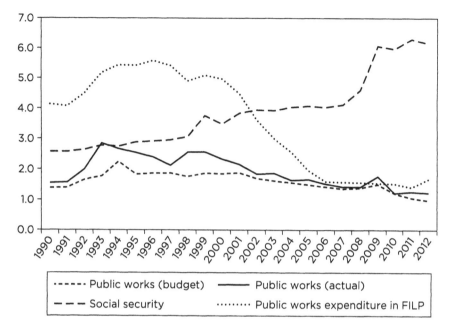

Figure 8.1 Share of expenditures in GDP (%). The actual and budgeted spending for public works and the social security numbers cited here are from General Account expenditures of the central government. The FILP numbers cover six items: housing, infrastructure for living environment, national land preservation and reconstruction, roads, transportation and communication, and regional development.

Sources: Calculated from Japan Statistics Bureau various years and MOF 2013a and 2013b.

political competition among parties was intense regardless of who was prime minister, virtually all Japanese governments had little choice but to vacillate between neoliberal pressures on the one hand and clientelist or welfarist pressures on the other. To placate voter discontent, governments, both LDP and non-LDP, made many compromises that clashed with neoliberal prescriptions. For instance, the government passed a law in 1994 earmarking 6 trillion yen (US$60 billion) for the agricultural sector. The huge sum to be spent over six years was offered as a side payment to alleviate farmers' opposition to the WTO agreement (Francks et al. 1999, 100). Furthermore, though the government agreed in 1999 to allow rice imports, the tariff rate on rice was kept prohibitively high. The government also decided in 1996 to spend 685 billion yen of public money to rescue the bankrupt housing finance companies in which agricultural cooperatives had a huge investment (Muramatsu 2005, 28–29).

The neoliberal pressure against public works spending faced similarly strong counterpressures from politicians. Opponents were emboldened by the unusually lukewarm policy of the Finance Ministry toward fiscal discipline. The Finance Ministry, fearing that large-scale rescue operations would expose the seriousness of the situation and destabilize the financial system, hesitated to use public money to rescue commercial banks.[5] Instead, the ministry expected that expansionary measures would eventually succeed in reactivating the economy and gradually solve the nonperforming loan (NPL) problem, relieving itself from having to take any responsibility for the financial mess (Tanaka 2005, 210). An expansionary policy equally suited the interest of LDP politicians who needed resources to distribute to their clients. Consequently, in every year following 1992, special stimulus measures were adopted by a succession of governments (Komine 2011a, 441). The results are reflected in figure 8.1, which gives figures for public works. Between 1992 and 2000, actual spending exceeded the general account budget for public works by a large margin. In addition, the FILP expenditure for public works, as a share of GDP, also increased between 1992 and 1996.

Alarmed by the recurring expansion of fiscal deficits and believing that the Japanese economy was on a firm track of recovery, the Hashimoto administration raised the consumption tax in April 1997 from 3 to 5 percent and announced a fiscal structural reform the following month. In late November of the same year, the reform plan was enacted into a law, which aimed at, among other things, lowering the 1998 general account budget to levels lower than for 1997 and lowering the fiscal deficit to 3 percent or less of GDP (Komine 2011b, 65–66). As mentioned previously, Hashimoto was also eager to enforce deregulation measures, including the financial Big Bang.

Hashimoto's neoliberal effort, however, was short lived because in the same November that the Fiscal Structural Reform Act passed the Diet, two major securities companies and one big bank went bankrupt and the financial sector of Japan was thought to be facing a "systemic crisis." This crisis coincided with the outbreak of the AFC. However, Japan's crisis was not caused by the AFC but by the prolonged NPL problem in the domestic financial sector. In June 1997, a month before the collapse of the Thai baht, Japanese bank lending to all Asian countries except Japan itself was in a range of merely 3.2–7.1 percent of their outstanding loans.[6]

Notwithstanding, the AFC certainly deepened the sense of crisis in Japan. One day after attending the ASEAN+3 summit on December 16, 1997 in which Asian leaders talked about measures to deal with the crisis, Hashimoto announced that his government would introduce special tax cuts to avoid

---

5. Actually, Prime Minister Miyazawa proposed using "public assistance" to cope with the NPL problem as early as August 1992. Finance Ministry bureaucrats stoutly opposed the idea (Sugita 2005, 63, 77).

6. All foreign claims by Japanese banks (on the immediate borrower basis) to Asia and the Pacific countries totaled US$132 billion (BIS data from http://www.bis.org/statistics/cons stats.htm). Total outstanding loans by Japanese banks (covering only their banking-business account and converted into USD by the exchange rate of 114.4) were US$4.16 trillion (Bank of Japan data from http://www.stat-search.boj.or.jp/ssi/cgi-bin/famecgi2). If city banks' loans alone are counted, Japanese bank lending to Asia and the Pacific on June 1997 was 7.1 percent.

Japan's becoming the source of a global depression. His government further adopted a special stimulus package amounting to 16.7 trillion yen in April 1998 (Komine 2011b, 67). As a result, the ratio to GDP of the general account expenditure for public works, which had shrunk in 1996 and 1997, shot up in 1998 (figure 8.1). However, the economy continued to be depressed with the political result that the LDP was badly defeated in the House of Councilors election in July 1998. In addition, two major investment banks went bankrupt in October–December 1998. To cope with the political and economic crises, in November 1998 the incoming Obuchi administration launched a 23.9 trillion yen package called Emergency Economic Measures (Tanaka 2005, 203, 207–208). According to Kingston (2004, 124), 120 trillion yen was spent for the purpose of economic reactivation between 1992 and 1999, almost 60 percent of which was directed to public works.

The neoliberal targeting of welfare-state expenditures was more successful than the efforts to cut public works. Pension and health insurance benefits were indeed reduced. However, the cuts were not big enough to compensate for the increase in expenditures due to the aging of society. Consequently, as seen in figure 8.1, welfare-state expenditure as a share of GDP increased steadily between 1990 and 2012.

In short, public policy in the 1990s was full of contradictions. On the one hand, deregulation/liberalization and supply-side reforms aiming at dismantling the developmental, clientelist, and welfare-state institutions were implemented in response to the increasing influence of neoliberalism. As a result, during the 1990s, the developmental state was seriously undercut and the clientelist and welfare-state benefits were partially curtailed. However, the political necessity to win elections led many politicians to defend clientelist and welfarist policies and institutions, thus leading to larger public spending for small producers and welfare beneficiaries. Such measures would have required tax increases to refurbish government revenues, which had been in a long-term decline under the low-growth economy. Fearing adverse reactions from the electorate, however, the governments avoided such tax increases in favor of the issuance of national bonds to cover the increasing costs for social security and public works. Table 8.1 shows the devastating impact of the combination of spending expansion and revenue constraint on the health of government finance. The expenditure of the central government, which had decreased from 29.6 percent in 1980 to 26.0 percent in 1990 of GDP, leaped up to 39.7 percent by 2000. The accumulated national debt reached 72.0 percent of GDP in 2000, double the level in 1990.

Neither the partial dismantling of the developmental, clientelist, and welfare-statist institutions nor the sporadic expansion of public spending were sufficient to bring about the recovery of Japan's stagnant economy. The average annual growth rate was a mere 1.2 percent during the 1990s, down from 4.6 percent during the 1980s. As shown in figure 8.2, thanks to the repeated introduction of stimulus packages, the contribution of government

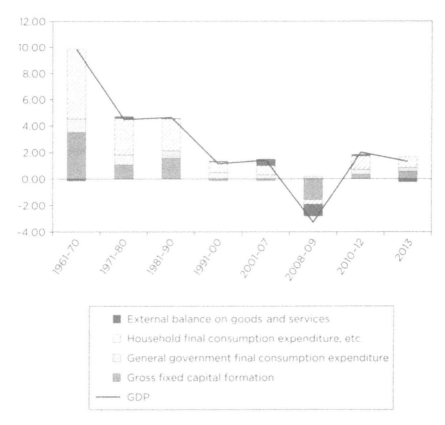

Figure 8.2 Japan's GDP growth rate and its components (% increase, annual average).

Sources: World Bank database available at http://databank.worldbank.org/data/home.aspx and Japanese Government Cabinet Office 2014.

consumption did not decrease in any significant way between the 1980s and the 1990s. In contrast, the contribution of household consumption decreased significantly. Alarmingly, gross fixed capital formation made a zero or negative contribution to the growth rate during the 1990s. These trends signify that both investors and consumers were extremely cautious during the final decade of the twentieth century.

Koizumi Reforms and Reversal

When Prime Minister Koizumi took power in April 2001, he declared his intention to return to the fiscal structural reform policy. He succeeded in establishing his image as a tough and uncompromising leader and, by doing so, gained enormous popularity among the electorate. Such popularity made it possible for him to take advantage of prior reforms in the electoral system,

party financing, and administrative institutions, all of which had been implemented between 1994 and 2001, and use them to strengthen his power both
within his party and within the government. He used this in part to crush
resistance from vested interests opposed to neoliberal reforms. In order to
impose fiscal discipline on public work programs, the Koizumi administration reorganized the four public highway corporations into one public corporation and six semiprivate companies in 2005; he also privatized the Japan
Post as four separate companies in 2007 (Uchiyama 2007, 66, 74–75, 102).
As a result of such reforms, the government expenditure for public works,
especially that of FILP, slowed considerably as shown in figure 8.1, and the
expansion of national debt was halted as seen in table 8.1.

Pension benefits were also curtailed and the copayment for medical services was raised from 20 percent to 30 percent although expenditures for
social security did not show any sign of decrease due to the aging of society
as noted above.

Furthermore, the Koizumi administration cut deep into the fabric of the
developmentally based labor relations by allowing manufacturing firms to
temporarily employ workers sent by staff-dispatching companies. The share
of dispatched and fixed-term workers in the total workforce thus increased
from 4.2 percent to 11 percent between February 2001 and March 2007,
while the share of regular workers in long-term employment dropped from
72.8 percent to 66.3 percent during the same period (Japan Statistics Bureau
2013c).

Figure 8.2 demonstrates that the average GDP growth rate in 2001–7, during the first six years of which Koizumi was prime minister, saw a glimmer
of improvement compared with the preceding decade. However, household
consumption did not improve at all, while gross fixed capital formation continued to be a drag on the growth rate. The recovery is explained mainly by
the expansion of the national trade surplus.

If capital formation is disaggregated, we see that private investment in
plant and equipment showed some signs of recovery after 2003, presumably
thanks to Koizumi's supply-side measures (figure 8.3). However, the expansion of private plant and equipment investment was insufficient to compensate for the contraction in public investment and stagnating private housing
investment. This latter stagnation is explained by the continuing sluggishness of household expenditure.

Voters at the time, tired of policy drift and the long economic stagnation,
were certainly attracted by Koizumi's style of uncompromising leadership,
although most did not like the shrinkage of welfare and other public benefits
and the loss of regular jobs. Consequently, when Koizumi left office in September 2006 and when his successors could not demonstrate equally decisive
and astute leadership, the Japanese voters quickly turned against the LDP
government and its neoliberal reforms. The revelation of the loss and omis-
sion of tens of millions of individual social security records in February 2007,

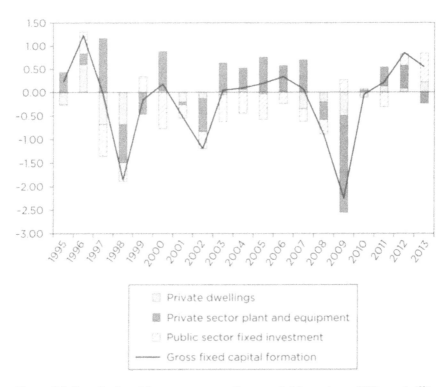

Figure 8.3 Contribution of three components of gross capital formation to GDP growth (%).
Source: Calculated from Japanese Government Cabinet Office 2010a and 2014.

though having nothing to do with Koizumi's reforms, contributed to the sense that the LDP was negligent toward people's welfare and became a severe blow against the party. In the House of Councilors election held in July 2007, the LDP won only 37 seats (out of 121), or 12 seats fewer than three years before, while the rival DPJ won 60, or 10 seats more than in the 2004 election.

The LDP government faced a further blow when the GFC hit. Although the exposure of Japanese banks to the "toxic" derivatives, so pervasive in the United States and much of Western Europe, was low, the overall economy was impacted through the severe contraction in global trade, which, as shown in figure 8.2, led to a sharp downturn in Japan's economic recovery. Figure 8.2 also demonstrates that the decline of gross fixed capital formation was even more conspicuous. In 2008, as seen in figure 8.3, all three components of capital formation dropped sharply. Private investment (plants, equipment, and housing) further contracted in the following year. The growth of public investment, in contrast, turned positive in 2009 thanks to government stimulus policies. Between August 2008 and April 2009, the LDP government launched four stimulus packages amounting to 27.4 trillion yen of direct spending by the national government (Asako et al. 2011, 144–45). As a result, fiscal discipline was lost and the general account dependence on deficit financing once again started to increase, reaching 51.5 percent in 2009 (MOF 2011).

These extravagant spending efforts, however, could not deter the deterioration of the LDP's popularity. It lost heavily in the House of Representatives election of August 2009 and the LDP government was replaced by the DPJ-led coalition government in September 2009. In that election, the DPJ criticized the rise in poverty and inequality allegedly brought about by the "excessively market-oriented" policies of the LDP governments. The DPJ's election slogan was "people's lives are the first priority."

Interestingly, the DPJ election manifesto was written by Ichiro Ozawa who had been an LDP leader until the party's split in 1993. He took a page from the LDP's electoral playbook of promising clientelist and welfarist generosity, except for the DPJ's deemphasis of public works. Besides public works programs, however, the manifesto promised other distributive and redistributive programs such as a children's allowance, fuel tax reduction, free access to highways and to high-school education, along with farm income compensation (DPJ 2009). Some DPJ leaders are known to have a neoliberal orientation, but their influence was muted during the first two DPJ administrations. After taking power, the DPJ started to implement its promised programs, and it also enhanced unemployment benefits and social protection. The party also sought to revise the Law on Dispatched Workers so as to reduce the ease with which firms could employ "dispatched workers," thus attempting to facilitate their "regularization."

The popularity of the DPJ government, however, was quickly lost due to the difficulty in raising fiscal resources to finance its distributive and redistributive programs as well as by its inept handling of foreign policy matters such as the U.S. military base relocation in Okinawa and the crash of a Chinese fishing boat with a Japan Coast Guard ship near the Senkaku/Diaoyu islands.

The coalition government led by the DPJ lost its majority in the House of Councilors in the election of July 2010, again making the passage of laws extremely difficult. In response, the DPJ grudgingly scaled down the children's allowance scheme and the free access to public highways; it also shelved its proposed bill revising the Law on Dispatched Workers. As had been true for the LDP, the initially articulated demand-side policies of the DPJ were stymied by the need for political accommodation, although in this case it was the commitment to welfare policies and the effort to establish a new party constituency that gave way to fiscal demands and the resurgent power of the LDP.

Furthermore, the Great East Japan Earthquake of March 2011 forced the DPJ government to expand public work expenditures. On the other hand, Yoshihiko Noda who became the third DPJ prime minister in September 2011 was known for his neoliberal orientation, and as a result he bitterly clashed with Ichiro Ozawa over the party's leadership and policies. Policy inconsistency was further deepened and the DPJ heavily lost the House of Representatives election of December 2012. It won only 57 seats, down from the astonishing 308 seats it had won only three years before. In contrast, the LDP succeeded in increasing its seats from 119 to 294, allowing it to regain government power under Prime Minister Abe (*Asahi Shimbun*, December 18, 2013).

Abe declared that his government would prioritize economic revitalization and take expansionary monetary and fiscal policies as well as measures to help expand private investment-based growth (*Asahi Shimbun*, January 28, 2013). Haruhiko Kuroda, the former Asian Development Bank president who was appointed on March 20, 2013 to be the new Bank of Japan governor by the Abe administration, announced that he was ready to enforce an "easy money policy for an indefinite period" (*Asahi Shimbun*, March 22, 2013). On February 26 the Abe administration also passed a 13.1 trillion yen supplementary budget for the 2012 fiscal year and on May 15, 2013, it passed the 2013 budget amounting to 92.6 trillion yen (2.3 trillion yen greater than the original 2012 budget of the DPJ government). Such fiscal expansion raised the accumulated national debt to a record high 154 percent of GDP (*Asahi Shimbun*, January 16, 2013; MOF 2013c).

These expansionary fiscal measures were congruent with the traditional clientelist and welfare-statist agenda of the LDP. However, Abe's growth strategy also contained neoliberal elements such as corporate tax reduction, business deregulation (including labor-market deregulation), the reduction of livelihood assistance, and participation in Trans Pacific Partnership (TPP) negotiations (*Asahi Shimbun*, January 30, April 13, June 14, 2013). The Abe administration also expressed repeatedly that recovery of fiscal health was its medium and long-term focus. For that purpose, the Abe administration raised the consumption tax rate from 5 percent to 8 percent in April 2014, anticipating another increase (to 10 percent) in October 2015 (*Asahi Shimbun*, April 1, 2014).

However, whether the LDP government can survive for long depends on whether this particular mixture of clientelist, welfare-statist, and neoliberal policies can successfully reenergize the economy. In its first year in office, the Abe cabinet looked quite successful as the contribution of domestic consumption and investment to GDP growth was greater in 2013 than in 2010–12 (figure 8.2). However, the poor trade performance in the face of the cheap national currency has raised concerns about the future prospect of the Japanese economy. Furthermore, figure 8.3 shows that the growth of the gross fixed capital investment in 2013 was accounted for by public investment and private housing investment, but not by private-sector plant and equipment investment. The surge of private housing investment suggests that citizens' purse strings were loosened in spite of the continuing stagnation of labor

wages.[7] Such optimism among consumers was partially supported by the
Koizumi-like decisive and uncompromising leadership style that Abe took
in both domestic and external affairs. However, if the rise of the consumption tax weakens domestic consumption and slows down economic recovery,
the LDP will face an abrupt electoral downfall such as that it experienced in
2009 and the rival DPJ experienced in 2012. In this regard it is important to
underscore the fact that the LDP victory in the 2012 general election did not
result from any long-term recovery of its popularity. The LDP's share of votes
among the registered electorate was actually lower in 2012 than in 2009 when
the party suffered its historic defeat (*Asahi Shimbun*, December 18, 2012).
The LDP won the 2012 election thanks to the majoritarian electoral system
and the emergence of many new opposition parties who split the anti-LDP
votes among themselves.

Continuity and Change in the Mixed Nature of Japan's Postwar State

The analysis in the previous three sections has shown that the neoliberal
challenge that emerged in the 1980s and gained strength after the 1990s
has faced strenuous resistance from the proponents of developmental, clientelist, and welfare policies and institutions. The developmental institutions,
half dissolved, have survived due to the judgment of private firms themselves.
Government expenditures for public works, which were attacked as ineffective and wasteful, have repeatedly recovered lost ground thanks to the
frequent introduction of stimulus packages. Welfare-state benefits were curtailed for specific programs but the overall expenditure for social security
has been growing nonetheless in response to the pressures from the aging
society.

However, the neoliberal encroachment into the developmental, clientelist, and welfarist policies and institutions during the 1980s and 1990s was
deep enough to loosen the ties between the LDP and its traditional supporters (small producers of goods and services) and to prevent the party from
consolidating a new support base among welfare-state beneficiaries. The result was the emergence of a new group of politically conscious nonpartisan
voters. As the strength of the LDP declined sharply, electoral competition became intense. Government popularity also fluctuated with great volatility. As

---

7. According to the monthly survey conducted by Japan's Ministry of Health, Labour, and
Welfare (http://www.mhlw.go.jp/english/database/db-l/monthly-labour.html), the average
monthly wage per worker increased by a mere 0.7 percent from 274,764 yen in March 2013
to 276,740 yen in March 2014. The consumer price went up by 1.6% during the same period
(http://www.stat.go.jp/english/data/cpi/1581.htm).

a result, few governments were able to stay in power for very long. The average length of prime ministers' terms was 1,048 days between December 1954 and June 1989. It declined to 549 days for the 1989–2013 period during which thirteen out of sixteen prime ministers served for less than two years.[8]

Leaders of both government parties and opposition parties inevitably became highly sensitive to the fickle shifts in the public mood. The best strategy to win elections appeared to be to enact catchall measures that could satisfy the demands of as many sectors as possible. Such a practice, however, undermined fiscal balance and overall economic efficiency. The result has been the frequent vacillation or overlapping between expansionary policies and belt-tightening policies, between a clientelist/welfare-statist agenda and a neoliberal agenda, and between demand-side measures and supply-side measures. No policy, even if passed, has had enough time to prove its validity. Since most policies have been terminated before delivering meaningful results, voters continue to look for a seemingly promising alternative. Policy drift and voter vacillation are thus caught in a vicious circle.

Policy fluctuation and inconsistency have in turn heightened market uncertainty. For one thing, because of the weakening of the developmental, clientelist, and welfare-statist institutions, employees and small producers are uncertain of their future employment, income, and expenditure. The uncertainty of future tax and social security burdens, as well as the mounting national debt, impedes both consumers and investors from making optimistic evaluations of the future. They cannot help but be conservative and cautious. The result has been the long-term decline of new fixed capital formation and household consumption as we saw in figure 8.2, all of which resulted in Japan's ongoing deflation spiral at least until the Bank of Japan began its inflation targeting policy in April 2013.

To make the situation worse, the change in the nature of the technological innovation for competitiveness has exacerbated the negative impacts of these market uncertainties. As many Japanese industries had matured by the 1980s, the "decreasing average cost of manufacturing" based on the improvement of imported technologies no longer guaranteed high growth rates. Japanese firms were now required to create new technologies to produce marketable products. Such innovation and market testing are inevitably full of uncertainties and, therefore, make investors cautious, especially when other market conditions are insecure. Figure 8.3 demonstrates that private plant and equipment investment has been highly volatile for the last twenty years. This is in a sharp contrast with the 1981–91 period in which plant and equipment investments significantly and continuously contributed to GDP growth (Japanese Government Cabinet Office 2010a).

---

8. These figures are calculated from data retrieved from the Prime Minister's Office webpage (http://www.kantei.go.jp/jp/rekidai/ichiran.html).

In short, once the effectiveness of the "decreasing average cost of manufacturing" model was exhausted in Japan with a concomitant slowing down of economic growth, the mixed and conflictual nature of the postwar Japanese state made political contests highly competitive and brought policy volatility and inconsistency, which in turn heightened market uncertainties and obstructed both investment and consumption, thus bringing about long economic stagnation.

A Comparison with the Korean Experience

Japan and Korea share the experience of high economic growth under developmental state policies and institutions as well as their gradual dismantling. Yet Korea has achieved a far better economic performance in recent years. Consequently, a comparison between the two cases will help highlight the nature of the difficulties Japan faces today.

Two kinds of doubt, however, may be raised with regard to the comparability of the two countries. First, as Tanaka (2005, 205) argues, the nature of the external sector of Japan and Korea contrasts sharply. Korea needed a large capital account surplus in order to cover its equally large current account deficit during the years preceding the 1997 crisis. Facing sudden capital flight, Korea had no choice but to implement some quick reforms to regain foreign investors' confidence. Japan, in contrast, had a huge current account surplus and, therefore, could postpone such reforms by taking an expansionary fiscal and monetary policy domestically. Furthermore, some may argue that the development stages differ in the two countries. Although Korea is rapidly catching up to Japan and has even surpassed it in some sectors, the Global Competitiveness Index compiled by the World Economic Forum shows that the rankings of the two economies have not narrowed for the last ten years.[9] This suggests that Korea still has an ample room for catching up. Japan, in contrast, is already among the most economically advanced countries and, therefore, cannot realize significant growth without its own technological breakthrough. This is more difficult and uncertain than catching up.

These arguments may have some validity. Still, there was no guarantee that the Korean government would implement the reforms it undertook so quickly. If its domestic situation had been similar to that in Japan, the country could have vacillated in its policy choices and failed to bring about reforms in a timely manner, falling into a long-lasting crisis like that in Japan. Since this did not happen, we need an explanation as to why.

---

9. For Japan, the annual averages of ranking for 2001–4 and for 2010–13 were fifteenth and eighth respectively. The corresponding figures for Korea were twentieth and twenty-second.

Since Park Chung Hee took power in 1961, Korea has experienced three major economic crises in 1969–71, 1979–82, and in 1997–98. All three were caused by excess investment based on externally raised money, the overheating of the economy, a debt crisis, and the consequent bursting of the economic bubble. In all three, the Korean government successfully responded to the crisis and quickly brought the economy back to a path of steady and solid growth. We need to consider at least three factors to explain this phenomenon. All three are closely related to the nature of the developmental state in Korea.

First, unlike the Japanese case, the developmental state in Korea was characterized by a very strong executive. This was born of a military coup and the country was subsequently ruled by a semiauthoritarian presidential regime. Although elections were held more or less regularly and the sitting government was frequently embarrassed by a large voter support for the opposition, activities of opposition parties remained severely restricted; even the government party was not allowed to consolidate itself as an entity autonomous from the president of the republic. The president was also powerful vis-à-vis the private sector, since almost all commercial banks were controlled by the state so that, together with public banks, the state controlled all financial resources (except for illicit "curb market" money) including money taken in from abroad.

The transition to democracy in 1987 did not change the basic nature of the party-government relations. Korea's political parties continued to be weak and such weakness helped the president maintain strong power in two respects. First, as the parties were not well institutionalized, the popularity of the top party leader and his place of birth had paramount importance in winning voters' support. Second, the weakness of party identity and internal cohesion allowed the president to take strong policy initiatives without worrying so much about the popularity of his party, unlike the pressures that bedeviled Japan's prime ministers. To be sure, the presidential tenure is constitutionally limited to one five-year term in Korea, and the president usually becomes a lame duck toward the end of his/her term. However, exactly because he/she does not need to consider the prospect of reelection, the president can take bold policy initiatives.

In contrast, the prime ministers who headed the democratic developmental state in postwar Japan needed to share power with their party colleagues. For example, in contrast to Korean presidents elected directly by people, Japanese prime ministers are chosen by their colleagues in the Diet. Furthermore, Japan had a multimember district system (until the 1994 reforms) in which candidates from within the LDP were forced to compete among themselves within the same electoral districts. As a result, within the LDP individual politicians' status could become quite strong.[10] In contrast,

---

10. The 1994 reforms changed the electoral system to one combining single-member districts and proportional representation. They also imposed strict restrictions on monetary contributions to political parties while establishing a system of public financial assistance to

Korea, upon the transition to democracy, had an electoral system combining single-member districts and proportional representation with a single vote. This system was favorable for regional parties and their top leaders, as they could monopolize the seats in any region where their leaders were popular (Onishi 2005, 174). Unlike Korean presidents, then, every Japanese prime minister had to worry constantly about his reputation among his colleagues and the popularity of his party among the electorate, and each was forced to resign whenever his popularity dropped to dangerously low levels with either. Under such a regime, strong policy initiatives were seldom expected or possible by the top executive.

Second, until recently, distributive and redistributive policies were politically less contentious in Korea than in Japan. In contrast to Japan's developmental state, which needed to integrate both a distributive and a redistributive agenda due to democratic pressures, Korea's semiauthoritarian developmental state, facing a serious security threat from the north, could prioritize economic growth, as such growth was regarded as indispensable for strengthening the military defenses of the country. During the Cold War, class-based demands for redistribution were suppressed (Lee 2004, 248–49; Woo-Cumings 1991, 119, 122–23). Limited financial resources were directed to a limited number of private firms most of the time. In consequence, these firms grew to be huge *chaebol* conglomerates while SMEs and farmers were given little attention except for periods in which the developmental state faced serious economic and political crises: one in the 1969–71 and another in 1979–81.[11] The development of welfare programs in Korea was also delayed. Universal pension and health care insurance began only after the transition to democracy in 1987, three decades later than in Japan (Hwang 2006, 145).

In this circumstance, the governing party's ties with policy beneficiaries were never institutionalized as tightly as they were in Japan. Neither did Korea see parliamentarians who formed such close links to specific interest groups and ministries as occurred in Japan. In consequence, political parties in Korea never became the kind of catchall parties that the LDP (and DPJ) became. Until 1987 the main issue of contention in Korea was democracy versus nondemocracy. Thereafter interregional rivalry became the most

---

parties. Such changes were expected to reduce incentives for political corruption and strengthen party leadership. They certainly helped Koizumi and the DPJ strengthen their electoral positions. However, the electoral base of individual politicians continued to be important because the 1994 electoral law allows double votes (one for single member district and the other for proportional representation) and double candidacy (a candidate can be run simultaneously for a single member district and proportional representation).

11. The Food Control Law was enacted in 1969, and the government purchase price for rice was raised consistently. Policy to improve rural infrastructure was also launched (Cooper 1994, 128; Kuramochi 1994, 156). SMEs also drew attention of the government in the early 1980s when the developmental state faced another crisis and was compelled to limit lending to chaebol while increasing credits for SMEs (Moon 1994, 148). In comparison with Japan, however, clientelist ties between the state and small noncompetitive producers in Korea were limited.

important issue for party competition (Lee 2004, 244). Kim Dae-jung, for example, won the 1997 election largely thanks to this very region-based election orientation (Kim 2000, 190–91).

The weakness of clientelist politics and welfare state policies was one of the reasons why Korea, despite the expansionary investment drives, could until recently maintain a relatively low level of fiscal deficit. According to data published by Korea's Ministry of Strategy and Finance, the outstanding government debt was far lower than that in Japan (MOSF 2011). It was 12.4 percent of GDP in 1970. It expanded to 18.2 percent by 1980 but was reduced to 12.8 percent in 1990 and 9.9 percent in 1996. As shown in table 8.1, the corresponding figures for Japan were 37.0 percent in 1990 and 72.0 percent in 2000.

Third, Korean voters recognized the chaebol problem as a clear-cut subject for political contention, especially during economic crises in which the chaebol were frequently accused as the principal culprits of the crises. As mentioned above, the chaebol grew to be prosperous conglomerates largely thanks to the ample access to government-controlled resources, a privilege not available to other parts of the population. Therefore, every time excess investment by chaebol firms caused high inflation, debt accumulation, and bankruptcies, voters' disgust with them surfaced. Thanks to this clear-cut cleavage, the Korean government was able to dodge private-sector resistance and take policies restricting chaebol's insatiable activities; by doing so, it could cool down an overheated economy, liquidate nonperforming firms, and bring the economy back to the path of growth.[12]

All three factors contributed to Kim Dae-jung's quick and decisive response to the 1997 crisis. The chaebol were regarded by broad sectors of the population as responsible for the debt-based excess investment and the consequent crisis. Therefore, it was natural for the government to take policies pressing chaebol companies to correct improper business practices such as extremely high debt financing and intragroup cross lending. The Kim Dae-jung administration forced the closure, merger, or nationalization of numerous insolvent financial institutions (including chaebol-sponsored or chaebol-related ones) by injecting huge amounts of public money into these entities.[13] It further forced the chaebol to close or dismantle superfluous businesses as well as to reduce the debt-equity ratio of their affiliated firms.

---

12. Anti-chaebol policies did not last long, though. Once the economy passed the worst situation, the government again began to be permissive to the chaebol for economic and political reasons. As for the cycle between pro- and anti-chaebol policies, refer to Onishi (2005).

13. Public spending amounted to 26 percent of GDP. It is reported that fifteen commercial banks, twenty-nine merchant banks, fifteen securities houses, seventeen insurance companies, and eleven investment trusts disappeared between January 1998 and June 2006 (Ha and Lee 2007, 899).

Kim Dae-jung was a leader especially suitable for this job because he had been an opposition leader for three decades and, therefore, was ready to take anti-chaebol policies more decisively than Park Chung Hee in 1969–71 or Chun Doo Hwan in 1979–81. Furthermore, since particularistic interests were not well institutionalized in the party structure and the political parties were machines still dependent on the popularity of top leaders, President Kim could stick to his policy preferences without worrying about short-term electoral or party repercussions.[14]

The quick fix of the turmoil in the financial and industrial sectors by the Kim administration contributed to a swift recovery of foreign and domestic investors' confidence in the Korean market. Foreign-controlled banks came to account for between one-third and one-half of bank assets in Korea (Mo 2008, 261), and foreigners' share of the stock market surpassed 40 percent in 2004 (Ha and Lee 2007, 906). The general recovery of the economy was demonstrated by the V-shaped trajectory of the GDP growth rate as shown in figure 8.4. What is notable is that the growth in 1999–2007 was brought about by household consumption and capital formation just as had been occurring during the precrisis period. This is in a sharp contrast with the Japanese situation in which the recovery in 2001–7 was minimal and was led by a rising trade surplus as shown in figure 8.2.

Some authors argue that it was not the neoliberal reforms but the adoption of an expansionary Keynesian policy package in the middle of 1998 that provides the more important explanatory factor for the quick economic recovery of Korea (Shin and Chang 2003, 61–65; Ha and Lee 2007, 897). It is true that the huge injection of public funds made the swift recapitalization of financial institutions possible and alleviated the social costs of the reforms by increasing social benefits and public works. However, one of the reasons why the IMF allowed such expansionary measures was the IMF's appreciation of the government's quick and decisive response to the crisis. Similarly important is the traditionally low government deficit in Korea (Watanabe 2007, 197). The IMF would not have accepted Korea's expansionary policy if the country's public finances had been as bad as those in Japan.

Nor did the Korean economy slow down as badly as Japan did during the GFC. As figure 8.4 shows, capital formation declined but the other three, especially the external balance, compensated for that loss.

---

14. A more troublesome factor for Kim was labor. Labor unions were mostly outside of party politics and some were quite radical. Financial and corporate reforms were expected to produce a large number of unemployed and invite fierce resistance from labor unions. In exchange for the government's acceptance of labor unions' long-term demand for political rights and the unionization of school teachers, however, labor unions accepted redundancy dismissal and the increase of dispatched workers. In the financial sector alone, the number of regular employees was cut from 114,000 to 67,000 between 1997 and 2001 (Kalinowski and Cho 2009, 232).

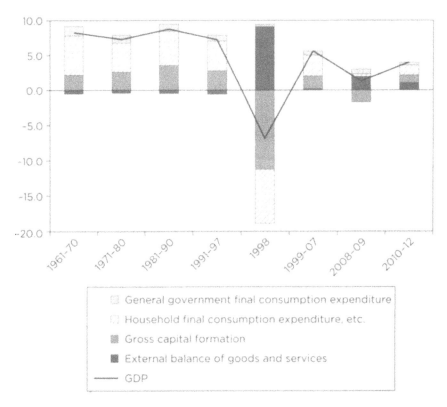

Figure 8.4 Korea's GDP growth rate and its components (% increase, annual average).

Source: Calculated from World Bank database available at http://databank.worldbank.org/data/home.aspx.

The strong executive, weak clientelist networks, the slow development of the welfare state, and the existence of clear-cut issue cleavages, all of which originated from the specific nature of the authoritarian developmental state and its transformation, helped Korea move quickly and decisively to tackle the AFC. In contrast, as we saw in the previous sections, postwar Japan, where the developmental state was formed and transformed under parliamentarian democracy, evolved around a very weak executive, entrenched clientelist networks, expanding welfare-state expenditures, and blurred policy cleavages. These factors impeded any timely and decisive Japanese response to the post-bubble crisis.

As the Korean economy and democracy matured, however, its political economy seems increasingly to resemble Japan's. During the 2002 electoral campaign, regional politics took a less central role (Kimiya 2003, 135–36). Policy contents, rather than leaders' native places, became more important for winning popular support. However, the chaebol issue lost some of its previous electoral appeal because the chaebol, under pressure from the government, had gotten rid of marginal businesses and strengthened their capacity for self-financing,[15] and consequently no longer needed privileged access to government-controlled resources. As a result, distributive and redistributive policies gained importance as electorally appealing issues. One sign of this change was the rapid increase in Korea's government deficit. The national debt outstanding, which almost doubled from 9.9 percent (1996) to 18.4 percent (2000) of GDP due to the economic crisis, went up further to 30.7 percent under the liberal Roh administration (2003–7) and to 33.7 percent under the conservative Lee Myung-bak administration (2008–12) (MOSF 2011; IMF 2013).

This expansion is partially explained by the increase of welfare-state expenditures. Total public social spending as a percentage of GDP has expanded from 5.1 percent in 1998 to 9.6 percent in 2009. This figure, however, is still low in comparison with Japan's 22.2 percent.[16] In Korea, only in 1999 did the national pension programs cover all the population and, therefore, actual pension payments remain limited. However, Korea now has one of the lowest birth rates in the world, while its old-age population is rapidly increasing. Therefore the problem of how to maintain existing welfare programs is already a contentious issue.

The spending for public works has also been expanding. Public works in Korea are mainly carried out by public corporations in charge of railways, housing, electricity, gas, regional development, and other things. The outstanding debt of these public corporations reportedly reached more than 350 trillion won by 2012 (*Joong Ang Ilbo*, Japanese ed., May 29, 2013). In the same year, the deficit of the central government was 438.4 trillion won (IMF 2013). This public corporation debt is a huge hidden national debt which future Korean governments will be forced to tackle.

In short, Korea today looks like Japan around 1980 in terms of the intensifying political contention over distributive and redistributive policies. Korea, however, has two advantages over Japan. The Korean government is not constrained by its agricultural and fishery sectors to the same extent as its Japanese counterpart. It has been able to successfully pursue a dynamic free trade agreement strategy, thus helping Korean manufacturing firms gain enhanced competitiveness in the world market. Second, as discussed in the previous section, the catch-up phase ended in Japan in the 1980s, but the Korean economy still has some additional room for technological catch-up. Simultaneously, firms like Samsung Electronics are already competitive in the most advanced technological sectors. Helped by ample opportunities for technological improvement and innovation, the Korean economy may continue to grow at a much higher rate than the advanced industrial economies,

---

15. The debt equity ratio of the top 30 chaebol went down from 512.8 percent (in 1997) to 218.7 percent (in 1999) and 171.2 percent (in 2000) (Shin and Chang 2003, 85).

16. Data retrieved from http://stats.oecd.org/BrandedView.aspx?oecd_bv_id=socx-data-en&doi=data-00166-en#.

and consequently overcome the inherent contradictions stemming from the expansion of clientelist and welfare-statist policies as they confront neoliberal pressures. If growth slows down, however, the heightening political competition over distributive and redistributive policies may blur policy cleavages and aggravate policy drift and voter float as happened in Japan in the last quarter century.

It is inaccurate to argue that the long-term economic stagnation of Japan has been caused by the inadequacy of neoliberal reforms such as trade liberalization and deregulation. The neoliberal encroachment on the developmental, clientelist, and welfare-statist policies and institutions has indeed been serious over the last three decades. Still, the Japanese economy continued to stagnate. The real cause of Japan's trouble is the lack of any consistent policy orientation. Both voters' preference and government policies have switched too easily between neoliberal reforms and expansionary demand-side measures, thereby obstructing any quick and decisive government response to the postbubble NPL problem aggravated by the AFC. The resultant uncertainty for future market conditions has deterred both investment and consumption, thus prolonging the recession.

This phenomenon can be traced to the historical context in which the developmental state was formed and transformed in postwar Japan. To secure a stable investment climate by winning consecutive democratic elections, the LDP tried to integrate small producers first and welfare-state beneficiaries later into its support base and consequently it became a catchall party. This gave LDP politicians a strong incentive to press their own government to extend benefits to particular clients, thus making it difficult for the executive to take autonomous policy initiatives. To compete with the LDP, opposition parties similarly needed to take on a catchall quality. As the economy matured and liberalized, neoliberal reformers strengthened their influence among politicians, bureaucrats, business people, and academics. However, since neoliberal policies weakened the ties between the LDP and policy beneficiaries and pushed them to become less committed voters, political competition became even more intense, making implementation of consistent neoliberal policies impossible. Koizumi's premiership was the one exception in this respect. The dominant pattern, however, has been a vicious circle of policy drift and vacillating voter demands.

The politically created market uncertainty has aggravated difficulties for Japan in adjusting to the changing nature of technological innovation. Since catch-up development was exhausted by the 1980s, Japanese firms needed technological innovations to design and produce new products whose marketability had not yet been tested. It is difficult to expect a long-term commitment of investment money under such technological uncertainty, especially when insecurity is high within the fiscal, monetary, tax, labor, and social security policy arenas. This combination of difficulties in technological innovation, policy contradictions, and a loss of political certainty has been conspicuously observed in Japan for more than twenty years, but the Japanese case may share some common features with other advanced industrial countries in North America and Europe, many of which are similarly suffering from the lack of political consensus under low-growth economies. In that sense, it may be called a "high income trap."

A comparison with the Korean case helps highlight the nature and the cause of the weakness of the Japanese political economy. Thanks to the specific historical conditions under which the developmental state evolved in Korea, a strong presidential executive was easily able to fend off demands from weak interest groups and political parties. Furthermore, whenever economic crises hit the country, the reform of allegedly defective structures and behaviors of the chaebol emerged as a clear-cut policy alternative. Although such anti-chaebol policies rarely last long, they were usually decisive and timely enough to crush resistance, thus allowing the Korean economy to return to renewed growth.

However, as the Korean economy and democracy matured, some signs are emerging that Korea is getting more similar to Japan with regard to party-executive relations and the significance of distributive and redistributive issues. Most other East Asian countries are less developed than Korea and, as Doner argues in his chapter, their main concern in the short run is avoiding the "middle income trap." However, since they share a semiauthoritarian past with Korea and many of them are experiencing rapid economic maturity and political democratization, they may also face the danger of falling into the same kind of catchall politics and policy immobilism which have bedeviled Japan and are bedeviling Korea.[17]

If Japan can exit from the current stagnation and enhance its role as provider of capital, market, and technology for other East Asian countries, it will help these countries to obtain larger economic resources and successfully tackle the problems associated with economic and political maturity. To do so, Japan needs to overcome its vicious circle of policy drift and voter float and enable the government to stick to a consistent policy—whether neoliberal, statist, or any combination of these two—for a period long enough to test the validity of that policy. Such stability will greatly facilitate private investment aimed at technological breakthroughs. To see this realized, Japan must have a fundamental realignment of political parties so that they can be internally more coherent and ideologically and politically more firm and consistent in their policy commitments.

---

17. Wu (2007, 978) describes Taiwan after 2000 as such an example.

Conclusion

Toward a Second East Asia Miracle?
T. J. Pempel and Keiichi Tsunekawa

This conclusion makes no effort to summarize the material in the pre-ceding chapters. Rather we mobilize aspects of their findings to reflect on the future of East Asia and its place in the global economic pecking order. Drawing on themes and findings from the individual chapters, we specifically address the second major question raised in the Introduction: To what extent does East Asia's successful navigation of the global financial crisis portend that East Asia is on the brink of a second miracle of growth or at least well positioned to enjoy high levels of economic performance, implicitly at the expense of the United States and Western Europe? The answer to this ques-tion depends heavily on one's assessment of the resilience of East Asia's re-spective economies and their abilities to respond to the long-term challenges of global competition.

The evidence throughout the book makes clear that both the Asian Finan-cial Crisis (AFC) of 1997–98 and the Global Financial Crisis (GFC) of 2008–9 sprang from the power of global capital with its ever-more-sophisticated and chancy financial instruments. But the two crises were characterized by two distinct kinds of interaction with domestic regimes. These different patterns help to explain why so many East Asian economies were devastated by the first crisis (AFC) while in general the region weathered the second financial storm (GFC) much better than the United States and Western Europe.

The countries most severely affected during the AFC were hurt primar-ily because of their unregulated exposure to the huge amounts of high-risk capital flooding into their markets. And even though the capital came from outside the region, a number of regionally endogenous causes contributed to how the crisis played out. Most important, the major negative effects of the crisis were concentrated in several East Asian economies that proved espe-cially vulnerable to such fast moving global capital flows. From an East Asian perspective, the causes of the AFC were exogenous while the consequences were endogenous. As a result, major steps were taken across much of East Asia to bolster economic resilience to exogenous capital flows.

In contrast, the epicenter of the second crisis lay in the United States. The crisis stemmed from extensive borrowing by an overspending and undersaving United States combined with the oversaving, and underconsuming "rest of the world," particularly but not exclusively countries in East Asia (Rajan 2010, 6; Chinn and Frieden 2011). Several interlaced factors concentrated within the United States triggered the crisis, most predominantly the moves toward financial deregulation, the prevalence of high-risk financial instruments, the increasing institutionalization of national fiscal policies based on higher levels of debt, and the outsized housing bubble of the 2000s (Lewis 2010; Rajan 2010; Sheng 2009, inter alia). While the epicenter of the crisis lay in the United States, the devastating consequences it unleashed ripped though not only the United States but also most of Europe and much of the rest of the world. But as noted throughout the book, East Asia proved highly resilient to the worst of those effects. Thus in contrast to the AFC, from an East Asian perspective, the GFC was exogenous in both its causes and its consequences. Just as several East Asian economies, including most notably Taiwan, Singapore, and China, proved resilient to the AFC, the region as a whole demonstrated substantial collective resilience to the far more sweeping GFC.

East Asian Resilience

External and internal shocks and challenges are inevitable and complex economies are periodically challenged and knocked off course. As noted in the Introduction, economic resilience of a country lies in its ability to take such shocks and "bounce back" rather deftly.

A number of chapters in this book have laid out a number of positive moves taken by East Asian economies in the wake of the AFC that contributed to their resilience in 2008–9. Most adopted new and more flexible exchange rate policies as well as rejuvenated financial regulations requiring greater prudence by individual institutions; almost all governments across the region also took steps to "self-insure" against future currency attacks by building up what subsequently became gargantuan foreign reserves. This move involved not only the big holders of foreign reserves such as China, Taiwan, Japan, and South Korea but also smaller countries like Singapore, Thailand, and Malaysia. Subsequent actions showed that, across most of East Asia, the collective lesson delivered by the AFC was the value of strict regulatory regimes, financial prudence, and enhanced resilience against external financial jolts. To the extent that postcrisis reforms involved "opening up" financial institutions, it was only the most advanced financial sectors such as those of Japan, Singapore, and Korea that moved in that direction, and such openings involved only minimal exposure to the subprime products and se-curitized instruments that were at the core of the GFC. Few Asian financial institutions saw exposure levels of more than 2 percent; cumulative national exposure was typically far lower (for data on special institutions, see Fitch Ratings 2007). In Taiwan, officials long fearful of external vulnerability were especially vigilant in ensuring that the highest policy priority be given to fi-nancial prudence. As noted by Chu, even ten years of DPP rule was unable to dismantle many financial regulations; instead, the central bank retained its preeminent and prudent role in buffering the country from significant chal-lenges from either foreign penetration or overseas borrowing.

The remaining East Asian countries, with less sophisticated financial sys-tems, continued to concentrate their business primarily on lending to the domestic manufacturing and tertiary sectors while simultaneously accommo-dating enhanced government oversight and insulation from future currency attacks. In Malaysia, in the aftermath of the crisis, one saw perhaps the most explicit rejection of laissez-faire economics as Prime Minister Mahathir and his government pursued rigid capital control policies designed to retain, not jettison, the existing collusive business-government ties examined by Pepin-sky. Similarly, in Indonesia, as Basri notes, policies changed but largely in the direction of stricter and more prudent, rather than looser, controls in finance.

Thus in contrast to the monumental deregulatory moves led by the United States and Britain in the 1980s and 1990s, across most of East Asia, the pat-tern was toward maintaining or enhancing close surveillance over financial transactions and ensuring prudent restrictions over the use of leverage by financial institutions. As Vogel (1996) has noted more generally, during this period many countries both in East Asia and elsewhere added more rules and closer monitoring of systems undergoing nominal deregulation.

As such, when the GFC struck, in contrast to the AFC, East Asia's macro-economic fundamentals were sounder, its credit ratings were healthier, its corporate balance sheets were better, and its banks were stronger. The re-sult was enhanced East Asian resilience against the unchecked movement of high-risk financial behaviors that engulfed the United States and much of Europe, and the region appears well-positioned to avoid falling prey to such vulnerabilities in the near future. The negative consequences of the GFC were limited to slowdowns for a year or two as the result of the contrac-tion in global trade. By 2011 most countries of East Asia were again enjoying substantial gains in their overall economies, even as Europe and the United States continued to suffer slow-to-negative growth rates (see table 1.1).

The Future of East Asia's Political Economies

Despite East Asia's demonstrated resilience in the face of the global financial challenges that began in 2008, its future is by no means without hurdles. The fundamental question is whether the recently demonstrated resilience of East Asian countries portends continued levels of economic growth that will propel them to top positions in the global economic hierarchy. The broad economic picture of the world in the middle of the 2010s easily provides many shards from which to construct a mosaic portraying such a positive East Asian future. But there are many potential impediments to unbridled success, three of which we highlight as worthy of particular attention in the *short run*, and three more of which may present *longer-term* difficulties.

In the short run, the first two looming sets of problems concern domestic economic and political difficulties. The overproduction capacities and the public and private debts accumulated during the pre-GFC boom and/or during the GFC downturn must be dealt with on the economic front. And while these present explicit economic problems, they also trigger political problems involving potential strategies to deal with them. Debates on economic strategies are sure to elicit sharp differences among political actors. As a third concern, East Asia faces pressing regional security challenges. The countries of the region have taken a number of collective steps to bolster their institutional firewalls against any possible repeat of the AFC and the specter of IMF assistance with its concomitant strictures on national sovereignty over policy formation. Institutionally, this resulted in a broadening and deepening of regional institutions from the ASEAN Plus Three (APT) to the East Asia Summit (EAS) (see Dent 2008; Grimes 2006; Pempel 2005; Ravenhill 2011). Institutional building has also fostered a measure of cross-national political cooperation and boosted mutual trust, particularly in the economic and financial arenas. Such achievements, however, are still precarious and can be greatly jeopardized by security-related competition among the East Asian countries. The deterioration of such conflicts can even obstruct smooth functioning of the regional production chains that have supported rapid growth of many East Asian economies.

How these three factors evolve will deeply affect the *short-term* future of the East Asian political economy. Even if these are adequately dealt with, the region still faces other longer-term problems. First, there is the challenge of dealing with the aging of societies and the population shrinkages that are looming for much of the region. In addition, most governments are facing or soon will face greater popular demands for enhanced political and economic participation as well as greater welfare distributions precipitated by past economic growth; these could well jeopardize the political stability which has undergirded East Asian economic development for many years. Finally, the current patterns of development need to be reformulated for many countries if they are to successfully overcome the limitations stemming from the aging of their population and the difficulties associated with continual technological upgrading.

On the basis of these six factors, we present what we believe are three feasible future scenarios: "Best Case Scenario," "Collapse Around the Corner," and "Lost Decade Ahead?" Each of these three scenarios is designed to draw attention to the kinds of problems that the East Asian countries will face when they attempt to achieve a higher economic development. Reality is unlikely to unfold in complete accord with any one of these three but we believe they alert both readers and decision makers to most powerful possibilities and probable problems on the horizon.

Three Scenarios

East Asia's "Best Case Scenario"

A best case scenario for East Asia's near-to-middle term future emerges as the consequence of a straight line continuation of the political and economic conditions prevalent in the early 2010s. These imply that countries manage their political and security problems at both the domestic and regional levels while enjoying continued economic development. The result would be a broadly optimistic future in which the region will continue to beef up economically, gaining enhanced shares of global production at the expense of previously dominant producers in Europe and the United States. Indeed, the individual chapters in this book offer considerable evidence to bolster such upbeat economic projections.

China, of course, with its breathtaking thirty-plus years of double-digit growth rates and its huge population, is usually the country pointed to as the iron core of any such East Asia juggernaut, often as the prelude to more sweeping conclusions about more extensive shifts in global economic and political power (e.g. Eichengreen, Wyplosz, and Park 2008; Jacques 2009; Mearsheimer 2001, inter alia). And indeed, Naughton's analysis of the country highlights its economic resilience as an ongoing theme, particularly since the AFC. As he also notes, in the aftermath of the GFC, Chinese leaders themselves were particularly self-congratulatory about their country's relative and absolute economic future, particularly in light of the apparent sapping of U.S. economic vigor and global prestige as a consequence of the subprime crisis and the subsequent global financial debacle.

If the current Chinese leadership successfully proceeds with its remarketization policies and solves the accumulated debt problems stemming from its widespread "shadow banking"; if it can avoid further deterioration of relations with its neighbors; and if it can persuade or suppress any domestic resistance against such policies, China will certainly continue to be the engine of economic growth, not only of East Asia, but also of the entire world. The hurdles may be many, but China's leaders have in the past demonstrated considerable coping facility.

China's neighbor Taiwan benefits from economic growth on the mainland as it has become ever more deeply woven into China's expanding production networks, particularly since the return to power of the KMT and the presidency of Ma Ying-jeou. Taiwan, as Yun-han Chu emphasizes, has seen a massive amount of private investment capital flocking back to the island that has stimulated local stock and property markets. Perhaps equally important, foreign multinational firms based in the United States and Europe have suddenly found new possibilities by which to incorporate the island into their Greater China strategies.

Basri's analysis of Indonesia's future is also positive, particularly for the next ten to fifteen years, despite a number of obvious impediments. Meaningful reforms were made in the economic technocracy following the AFC while demography and natural resources promise substantial future advantages for a decade or more. Politically, Indonesia succeeded in shifting from an autocracy to a democracy without jeopardizing a close business-government relationship, although, as Pepinsky notes, the nature of that relationship has changed from predatory to rent seeking. Doner, meanwhile, despite raising longer-term doubts about their economic futures, demonstrates how both Malaysia and Thailand have benefited from a combination of macroeconomic measures and financial sector reforms allowing them to shift from lower to higher value-added manufacturing products, though with limited local inputs.

Having weathered the dangerous first months of the GFC, South Korea's economy also seems poised for sustained growth as both Okabe and Tsunekawa's analyses indicate. And as of this writing, even long-dormant Japan was showing signs of a perky economic turnabout as fiscal and monetary stimulus programs kicked in; the stock market delivered a nominal 57 percent increase in 2013; and promises of domestic structural reform, including participation in the Trans-Pacific Partnership negotiations, held out the prospect that twenty years of sluggish economic growth was beginning to reverse.

In addition to the effort made by individual countries, intraregional cooperative mechanisms such as Chiang Mai Initiative and regional bond markets fused with the national steps noted above to bolster the region's collective resilience against the potentially depredatious challenges of global finance. Bilateral or minilateral free trade agreements (FTA), a large number of them with intra-Asian partners, have helped many East Asian countries to continue their reliance on exports, decrease unit production costs, and reinforce the competitiveness of regional production chains. Additionally, they allow economies to become more open to foreign investors and foreign products and less protective of domestic firms while still ensuring a powerful governmental role in selectively structuring the particulars of FTA openings. In such ways, government-business cooperation is less likely to be fractured than it might have been by more comprehensive trade, finance, and intellectual property liberalization. Intraregional trade has thus deepened and most East Asian economies now have other East Asian economies as their most important export destinations, a shift that has reduced short-term national and regional reliance on the U.S. market while strengthening the economic and institutional interdependence of countries throughout the region.

Contributing to the positive evaluations for East Asia is the fact that even as late as 2014, the GFC continued to dampen economic performances across much of Europe and the United States, despite the fact that the recession it triggered officially ended in 2009 and despite stock market bursts in the United States, Germany, Ireland, Iceland, and even Greece. Yet glittering stock market performances remained overshadowed by staggering levels of bad debt, combined with well below normal economic growth rates and unemployment and income inequality rates that remained substantially above historical levels in at least a dozen countries. Europe staggered also under massive toxic debt levels in the range of US$1–2 trillion combined with the threat of sovereign debt crises in Greece, Spain, Portugal, and even Italy. Furthermore, the Eurozone was struggling to maneuver toward collective economic policies aimed at accommodating widely disparate levels of productivity between its northern and southern segments even as it remained collectively cosseted by the straightjacket on monetary flexibility imposed by the commitment to protect the single currency. The consequence has been widespread austerity and slow growth for much of Europe (Blyth 2013, 223). Finally, both the United States and Europe were fraught politically with battles over whether to create banking and financial oversight mechanisms that would prevent a recurrence of the runaway irresponsibility of institutions "too big to fail" or too critical to the maintenance of the Euro not to require taxpayer rescue packages.

The United States and much of Europe were therefore still struggling, both politically and economically, to pull themselves out of the morass created by their financial institutions five years earlier. In the face of such troubles elsewhere, East Asia, if only by comparison, seemed redolent with economic resilience and broad political stability (except perhaps Thailand). It is thus easy to envision a scenario based on simple projections and to conclude that the problems in Europe and the United States combined with sustained growth in East Asia leave the latter region with excellent prospects to continue garnering ever larger shares of global GDP at the expense of the United States and the European Union, and as a consequence of such economic successes to enjoy enhanced legitimacy for its current political systems.

Any such ceteris paribus projections must, however, quickly confront the reality that these linear projections rarely continue for very long, as can be recalled from the triumphal projections about Japan's economic future in the late 1980s, or those of America's "dot.com" bubble in the early 2000s. Moreover, they are predicated on the assumption that any serious problems faced by East Asia will be successfully managed, an assumption that is at best exceedingly optimistic. As numerous chapters throughout the book have made clear, despite its present luster, East Asia faces a bevy of domestic political and economic hurdles while new and challenging problems are equally likely to arise. Nor are international conditions likely to remain static and favorable either. The underlying political and economic strengths of the United States and Europe, for example, should not be glibly dismissed in the face of post-GFC problems. Neither is the stability and resilience based on regionwide East Asian cooperation guaranteed. With this in mind it is possible to suggest at least two alternative and less upbeat scenarios that also hold a measure of plausibility.

Collapse around the Corner

Prior to the AFC, East Asian politics and economics were entwined in a positive spiral. Close business-government ties fused with rising production levels and an expanding global market to generate the "East Asian miracle." Rapid economic growth in turn became a legitimating mantra regularly intoned by political leaders to enhance their popular support. And with V-shaped recoveries after the AFC, that positive political-economic cycle largely resumed and remains pervasive today. It forms an underlying premise behind the previously sketched "best case scenario."

Yet a number of economic and political landmines appear to be "just around the corner" and short of astute near-term political and economic management, they could quickly unravel the positive relationship between politics and economics, thus toppling the region from its current perch. Three linked but analytically separable types of vulnerabilities demand attention—domestic economic problems, domestic political difficulties, and regional security challenges. Potential short-term hazards in all three loom large; individually or in combination they could quickly derail continued East Asian success.

Consider first the economic challenges. Given its importance as a regional production hub, as the major trading partner of virtually all other East Asian economies, and as the long-churning engine of the region's economic dynamism, China is the likely place where economic challenges begin.

As Naughton notes, the basic policy directions taken by the Chinese leadership were diametrically opposite during the AFC and the GFC. In the former, despite suffering only minimal direct effects from the crisis, except for efforts to buffer the Hong Kong stock market from speculative attacks, Chinese leaders concluded that externally driven financial crises could still pose problems that necessitated internal changes. As a result, the national financial system was subjected to massive overhaul. Trillions of RMB in bad loans were written off and the government pumped as much as 28 percent of GDP into the financial sector, eventually inviting partnerships with overseas institutions and moving to list the now more solid institutions on the Shanghai and Hong Kong stock exchanges. In contrast, in response to the GFC, Chinese leaders strengthened their policy of reversing earlier market reforms adopted by the middle of the 2000s. As part of the 2008 G-20 effort to stimulate the global economy following the financial freeze-up, China put forward the largest stimulus package in its history, disbursing it mainly through the channels of the central and local governments. The economy soared but so did debt as local governments competed to push forward a variety of costly infrastructure projects (Pettis 2013). Moreover, China's expanding investment levels have generated overcapacity in multiple industries, including steelmaking, shipbuilding, and solar panel manufacturing. Government efforts to rein in its post-GFC stimulus slowed GDP growth from its thirty years of double digit gains to a still respectable 7.6 percent in 2013 (table I.1), but the country's high debt levels remained a worrisome specter. Mann et al. (2013, 8–9) found China's credit to GDP ratio to be 217 percent and even more ominous, its total credit has been expanding much faster than its GDP to the highest levels in East Asia, in effect indicating that ever greater levels of debt are needed to create a single unit of economic growth.

If China, as the spark plug of East Asia's economic dynamism, confronts slower growth, particularly as the result of its high and rising debt levels, the number-two economy in the region, Japan, is not terribly well poised to take up the slack. Again, debt is a major problem. At 200 percent at the end of 2013, Japan has the developed world's highest ratio of central and local government debt to GDP (MOF 2013c, 5). This debt has been the result of decades of slow growth, depressed government tax revenues, and a stream of fiscal stimulus packages.

To some extent, Japan's debt reality is less worrisome than the absolute number might suggest. The net government debt is "only" 130 percent; total debt remains largely denominated in yen, limiting the threat of a sovereign debt crisis, and the current account has generally been positive. Moreover, as was noted earlier, following a landslide victory in December 2012, Prime Minister Abe's widely touted "Abenomics," with its promise to revive the economy by weakening the yen, increasing spending, ending deflation, and promoting reforms, did indeed spur a jump in corporate profits, a slight but continuous increase in prices, and a stark rise in the stock market.

However, the trade balance, which supported the Japanese economy for many years when domestic consumption and investment stagnated, turned red in 2011 due first to the triple disaster in Fukushima (Mann et al. 2013, 69–71) and then to the surge of import bills caused by the decline in the value of the yen. By the end of 2013, Japanese GDP growth had slowed; energy costs were soaring as the result of widespread shutdowns in the nation's nuclear plants; government policies showed little real evidence of major structural reforms, the key third arrow of Abenomics; and the country faced an impending drag on its growth as the consumption tax was raised in April 2014. Moreover, high debt levels continued to absorb nearly one-quarter of the country's annual budget, diverting government resources from more productive and risking, in the words of *Der Spiegel,* turning Japan into "the next Greece" (Seith 2013).

China and Japan are by no means the only countries in the region facing substantial debt and leveraging problems. Korea, Hong Kong, and Singapore also flash red for their high debt levels, while Hong Kong, Indonesia, and Thailand are rife with extremely high growth rates in their debt to GDP levels (Mann et al. 2013, 8–10). The specific culprits in these diverse debt bubbles differ from country to country. In Vietnam and China, the heaviest debt burden arises from state-owned enterprises (including local development corporations in China). Banks in Malaysia and Thailand meanwhile are particularly vulnerable to the buildup in household borrowing due to rapid growth in debt, relatively low incomes, and banks' significant exposure to auto, personal, and unsecured loans, which tend to have a higher risk of default. Household debt levels are also high in Singapore and South Korea (Brereton-Fukui 2013). Despite such differences in the sources of debt, however, the commonality across the region is rising debt and, more worryingly, the escalating amount of debt needed to generate additional GDP. In combination, these suggest that the underlying economies of many of these countries are less solid and resilient than would be implied by rapid rises in GDP.

Some of the rising debt across the region, particularly in the household sector, is logical enough; as households become wealthier they tend to take on more debt. Moreover, global capital markets are awash in cheap liquidity, driven most forcefully by the US$85 billion monthly being pumped into financial markets by the U.S. Federal Reserve. In addition, most economies across the region continue to have positive current account balances, and Asian debt levels remain below those in Europe. Still, such high and rising levels of debt and overcapacity will necessitate delicate political steering, particularly as the U.S. Federal Reserve moves to reduce the levels of its quantitative easing and "easy money" across the world begins to dry up. Certainly a slowing of growth across most of the region is almost inevitable and East Asian governments face the bigger risk that tightening liquidity too sharply will completely slam the brakes on overall growth. The avoidance of upward interest rate adjustment will weaken their currencies and consequently strengthen inflationary pressures. Equally important, reducing overcapacity in manufacturing will jeopardize employment levels. The result is likely to be a decline in popular support for governments that have long depended for their legitimacy on delivering high rates of economic growth, more jobs, and improved lifestyles. In brief, a host of economic problems, circling around, but not limited to, high and rising debt levels, present immediate and serious challenges to continued East Asian economic success.

The politics of negotiating these and other imposing economic hurdles will be difficult. And the region is not devoid of additional domestic political problems not explicitly linked to economics. Although most political regimes in the region appear secure, China confronts some 180,000 popular protests annually and a steady game of internet censorship and surveillance-avoidance; both pose ongoing challenges to the tightness of CCP control

(O'Brien 2008). Social diversification and political awakening, as the result of high economic growth, are the background conditions under which the top-down management of social and political issues can no longer work. Thus many East Asian countries including Thailand, Malaysia, Indonesia, and Korea also face a surge of new sociopolitical forces challenging the primacy of the traditional probusiness coalitions and the implicit guarantees they provided of a close cooperation between governments and businesses. For instance, since the mid-2000s, Thailand has been undergoing a recurring set of street battles between red shirt supporters of Thaksin largely from the rural areas, and yellow shirt backers of the political establishment.

Furthermore, Pepinsky notes the numerous problems that continue to fester across island Southeast Asia, not least of which is corruption, a problem hardly absent in Thailand or Vietnam as well. And Naughton warns of the numerous challenges facing China, where corruption is supersized to the point that the families of top communist leaders enjoy billion-dollar bank accounts, their children thrive on criminal immunity while being competitively recruited by high flying investment firms, and local officials engage in confiscatory land grabs. In short, a host of political trap doors could swallow up continued growth and political stability.

Still a third short-term set of obstacles to a "best case scenario" for East Asia lies in the arena of regional security. With few exceptions, state-to-state diplomatic and political relations across the entire region improved rather steadily from the 1980s until roughly 2010. For the most part, improved ties continued to be the case in Southeast Asia where Acharya (2009) goes so far as to suggest that ASEAN has become sufficiently adept at conflict management to allow the region to be classified as a genuine security community, one in which state-to-state use of force has become highly unlikely (see also Ba 2009). Yet Southeast Asia's reduction in state-to-state tensions is by no means paralleled by state behaviors of neighbors to the North.

Until roughly 2010, Northeast Asia also appeared to be moving toward greater security cooperation (Pempel and Lee 2012). Despite unresolved territorial contests and other geopolitical tensions, China, Japan and South Korea found a basis for cooperation in their increased economic interdependence; the Six Party Talks to address the North Korean nuclear challenge; an annual trilateral summit meeting that became institutionalized with an office in Seoul; the forging of a common investment treaty; and work on a trilateral free trade pact that was active into 2012. Behind a regionwide charm offensive (Kurlantzick 2007), Chinese leaders were pursuing a "peaceful rise," while Japan took pride in its "Gross National Cool" (McCray 2002), and Korea extolled the cultural benefits of its K-pop and dramas. For all three countries, "soft power" was more frequently utilized than "hard power."

That harmony was shattered over the next several years as North Korea carried out a sequence of missile and nuclear tests, sank a South Korean corvette, and shelled the South Korean island of Yeonpyeong, leading to the first civilian victims in North-South conflicts since the 1953 Korean armistice. While condemning the DPRK's 2009 and 2011 nuclear tests, the Chinese government refused to assign any guilt to its North Korean ally on the latter two provocations. Jettisoning its prior charm offensive, China continued to boost its military budget by roughly 10 percent per year; it dramatically expanded its maritime claims, including its presentation of a risible "nine dash line" that claimed virtually all of the East China and South China Seas as Chinese; and it took strong quasi-military actions to advance its claims over disputed territories in both of those waters. Further, its ships cut Vietnamese oil exploration cables; it introduced a contentious Air Defense Identification Zone (ADIZ) that overlapped with zones claimed by South Korea and Japan; and according to the US Navy, Chinese military vessels engaged in provocative actions toward US ships operating in international waters.

Further adding to the deterioration in relations, Japan, for its part, triggered a territorial dispute with China by purchasing three islands previously in private hands, thus triggering a cut-off in rare earth exports from China, the arrest of four Japanese businessmen, a series of well-coordinated anti-Japanese protests in dozens of Chinese cities, as well as a steady infusion of Chinese vessels into waters claimed by Japan. And with the return to office of a conservative government headed by Abe Shinzo, Japan escalated its own nationalism and xenophobia by producing a steady diet of denials of Japanese responsibility for aggression or official promotion of sexual slavery during World War II, making ongoing claims to islands under South Korean administration, revising history textbooks, promising to revise Japan's "peace constitution," and making official governmental visits to the controversial Yasukuni Shrine. South Korea did its part to fuel the fires in the run-up to the 2012 elections as outgoing President Lee Myung-bak made an official visit to islands contested by Japan and Korea (Dokdo/Takeshima), and his successor Park Geun-hye joined Chinese premier Xi Jin-ping in refusing to meet Abe in any official or semiofficial forum.

This rise in tensions was at least partly the consequence of each leader playing to his or her domestic base, castigating neighboring countries as threats to national security. But artificial theater or not, the escalating tensions resulted in a freezing of numerous top level meetings among the three countries, including the halting of the Trilateral Summits; the halting of negotiations on the trilateral trade pact; and to a cessation of security cooperation and intelligence sharing by purported allies Japan and South Korea. Although China and South Korea continued to explore a bilateral FTA, China-Japan trade which had dropped 26 percent between July 2012 and February 2013 (Katz 2013b) further contracted by 5.1 percent in 2013 (*Asahi Shimbun*, evening edition, January 10, 2014). The rapid deterioration in geopolitical relations in Northeast Asia could not only weaken bilateral economic relations but could also challenge the regional linkages so critical to sustained regional growth as well as the mechanisms specifically instituted to defend against a new global crisis.

Lost Decade Ahead?

Even if East Asian governments and their economies manage to clear such short term hurdles on issues like debt, overcapacity, political instability, and geopolitical tensions, they face at least three longer-term problems that could haunt them over the next decade or longer. These involve demographic challenges, increased demands for social spending, and the challenges of transitioning from models of political economy that previously worked but whose future potential is limited.

Dangerous demographic challenges lie ahead for a number of countries in East Asia. In the early years of their economic growth spurt, most East Asian countries benefited from a demographic boom—a large working population and high birth rates combined with a limited elderly population. But economic gains led to reductions in childhood births and increased life spans, meaning that family sizes tended to shrink and population pyramids that once were bulky in the below forty to forty-five years age range thinned out.

Japan, which in 1990 saw only 12 percent of its population over sixty-five, saw that percentage jump to 23 percent in 2010, and that is projected to rise to 28 percent in 2020 (this is compared to 16 percent in the US, 20 percent in both France and the UK, and 23 percent in Germany) (World Bank 2014; Japanese Ministry of Internal Affairs and Communications 2010). Alternatively viewed, in 2013, a baby was born every 31 seconds in Japan while someone died every 25. This meant a yearly drop of 244,000 in Japan's population. The result is a shrinking as well as an aging population (Warnock 2013).

South Korea and China are poised to follow in Japan's demographic footsteps. In China's case, this would mean a population that became old before it had become rich. Vietnam, Thailand, and Singapore, among other countries in Southeast Asia, confront similar demographic time bombs. Even in youngish Indonesia, the aging population will rise quickly after 2020–30. Overall, in Northeast Asia, the fertility rate dropped from 4.7 to 1.7 between 1970 and 2008. Southeast Asia is now only slightly behind the north; the region's total fertility rate has fallen from 6.0 to 2.3 in the same period. Meanwhile, life expectancy has risen from fifty-eight to seventy-two for Northeast Asian males and from forty-six to sixty-eight for males in Southeast Asia (Hugo 2008, Appendix 1).

Beneficial as such changes may be for individuals and families no longer confronting multiple childhood deaths and short life spans, the situation poses a daunting problem for national political economies since fewer and fewer workers are contributing to production and paying taxes to support ever larger numbers of the elderly and their costly retirement pensions and health care. The cumulative consequence for much of the region is that unless the demographic time bomb is addressed—through migration, higher retirement ages, jobs retraining, and the like—the greater the difficulties in sustaining moderate to high levels of economic growth.

A second potential medium-term impediment to sustained growth and political quietude arises with increased demands for popular (and costly) public social programs. The economic successes achieved by most of East Asia prior to the AFC was often initiated and led by authoritarian governments that were able to insist on short-term sacrifices by their citizens by promising longer-term benefits. Governments could also count on traditional family and village solidarity to assist the elderly, unemployed, or ill. Democratization in Taiwan, South Korea, Indonesia, and Thailand and enhanced citizen pressures in Malaysia have created a broader need for governments to legitimate their rule by delivering popular benefits. This has made it more difficult to rely on past promises of future benefits or traditional social models to deflect the rising demand for increased government social programs. In the wake of the AFC, even longstanding conservative governments confronted enhanced popular pressures to expand their support base by creating or bolstering policies for social spending. The AFC pushed these countries as well as others to further enhance redistributive policies in efforts to recoup some of the popularity their governments had lost due to crisis-driven austerity measures.

With its much longer history of postwar democracy, Japan again proved to be the precursor of popular social programs and their impacts on public finance. As Tsunekawa notes, postwar Japan, in contrast to most countries that were under more authoritarian regimes as they grew, advanced its industrialization under a full and functioning democracy. This led it to develop a range of welfare programs that started as early as around 1960 and expanded in the 1970s, all under the same conservative government. Although Japanese policymakers sought on numerous occasions to roll back increasingly costly programs, most remain intact, and in the 2009 and 2012 campaigns both parties outdid themselves in their efforts to secure voter majorities by outbidding one another with lavish promises of government largesse.

Welfare programs typically focused on health care, unemployment insurances, and aid to the poor. These were introduced or expanded in Korea, Taiwan, and Thailand as these countries began to experience democratization in the late 1980s or early 1990s (Haggard 2008). In 2008, the Philippines put in place a conditional cash transfer (CCT) program designed to identify and target poor households, and as of July 2011, 5.2 million poor households were identified, of which 2.3 million were enrolled in the CCT. In 2014, Indonesia introduced the world's largest single-payer health care system, which is to cover the whole nation by 2019. Few of East Asia's economic success stories have been able to shunt aside citizen demands for increased benefits and a more comprehensive social safety net (relatively rich Singapore is perhaps the most conspicuous exception).

The central point here is simply that political demands for greater distribution are being expressed across virtually all countries in East Asia. It will thus become ever more difficult for governments across the region to rely simply on annual increases in GDP as their claim to legitimacy. All will be under pressure to reduce the resources they devote to investment and infrastructure and to increase the amounts given over to social spending.

Still a third type of medium-term problem looms on the horizon, namely the difficulties associated with letting go of past economic development strategies that once worked but are unlikely to achieve still higher economic levels. East Asian countries will all face the continual challenge of bringing about ongoing technological upgrading and enhanced efficiencies in the labor and capital markets; failure to do so will surely slow down their growth rates.

Institutional change is clearly difficult and path dependency and policy stickiness tend to persist. Thus, although the Korean *chaebol* came under harsh attack by the Kim Dae-jung government, most rode out the economic and political storms by disinvesting from unprofitable businesses and drastically reducing their debt-equity ratios, leaving them to continue as the leading actors of economic development of Korea. Their positions were bolstered further by the return of the conservative pro-chaebol governments of Lee Myong-bak and subsequently Park Guen-hye Meanwhile, with the financial reform process left largely to the private sector in Thailand, big banks successfully circumvented extensive foreign intrusion and maintained their influence on the economy and the government. In Malaysia, pro-*bumiputera* institutions were only slightly weakened by the AFC and subsequent reforms, and even following Indonesia's political democratization, the business-politician nexus continued to be influential, although, as Pepinsky points out, it was much more diffused and decentralized. Despite some rising voices for more market-oriented reforms, state-owned enterprises and banks survived in China and Vietnam as strong market players even though they suffered short term challenges in the immediate aftermath of the AFC.

Japan is a particularly nettlesome reminder of the difficulties associated with bringing about sweeping institutional change from patterns that no longer work. By the 1990s, Japan had entered the phase where technological breakthroughs were needed if firms were to continue producing profitable and marketable products (Yamamura and Streeck 2002). Borrowing the distinction made by Hall and Soskice (2001, 38–41) on the nature of technological development, Japan's and East Asia's other highly developed companies are finding it collectively more difficult to make the transition to breakthrough innovations and away from the incremental improvements using imported technologies that for so long sufficed to ensure constant growth.

It is not as though reforms are impossible. For instance, the mutual or long-term stockholdings among companies and banks in the same business group, SMEs working as subcontractors for big manufacturers, and the share of regular (long-term) employment, which were all the backbone of the developmental state, declined significantly by the end of the 1990s (see also Pempel 1999b). The broad aim was to transform a highly regulated, but often opaque, bank-oriented financial system into one that was more transparent and market based. Yet the Japanese case is far more demonstrative of the ability of the powerfully placed to resist change. As Tsunekawa's analysis also shows, the country's politics has rarely made a clear break from the past in favor of new directions, but rather it reflects an ongoing layering of new approaches and programs on top of old patterns, the result of which has been a stymieing of Japan's economic transformation. And as noted above, as of early 2014, Abenomics showed few indications of successfully initiating structural reforms.

Such political resilience can of course be an economic positive as was shown in Taiwan. There, when the opposition Democratic People's Party (DPP) took office under President Chen Shui-bian in 2000, it set out on a politically motivated course of reforms designed to inject DPP loyalists into power positions while also advocating looser financial regulation to soften existing tight financial oversight. Yet such efforts ran into considerable bureaucratic, business, and financial counterpressures limiting Chen's capacity to effect the neoliberal changes he sought. Especially important, the authority of the central bank remained intact. And with the return of the KMT government in spring 2008 large portions of the prior tight regulatory regime were strengthened to the benefit of the economy.

The case of Taiwan demonstrates that neoliberal measures *a la Anglo-Saxon* may not be the optimal solution for East Asian countries. Still, fundamental rebalancing among various market players and the government, with concomitant changes from past approaches and institutions, are likely to be needed if Japan and other industrially advanced countries in the region are to further advance and if certain Southeast Asian countries like Thailand, Malaysia, and Vietnam are to escape "the middle income trap" by upgrading the nature of their technological innovations.

The East Asian countries are likely to be further pushed to deepen market reforms directly or indirectly by the United States and the European Union with which they maintain highly interdependent relations. First, although the rejection of extensive protectionist measures in North America and Europe helped the swift recovery of East Asian economies during the GFC, the weakening competitiveness of the economies of the United States and EU countries may push them to be more sensitive to the exchange-rate policy, competition policy, and trade impediments in East Asia. Their governments are likely to demand broader market opening in their FTA negotiation with the East Asian countries. Such direct political pressure aside, the continuation of the current development pattern of the East Asian countries based on a large export market in the United States and Europe could be counterproductive in the long run. As demonstrated by the GFC, the world economy is now so interdependent that the excessive trade surplus of the East Asian countries could result in huge capital-account surplus in the form of accumulated debts on the American and European sides. These debts can lead to the recurrence of devastating financial crises and the precarious response based on their own debt accumulation in the East Asian countries.

In short, to deal with the aging of their societies, to cope with enhancing popular demands for better social welfare, and to explore new approaches for sustained growth, East Asian countries may face the challenge to undergo deep institutional reformulations of their political economies. However, countries rarely, if ever, assess the present as if it were a blank slate. They go through a continual process of evolution, as demonstrated so convincingly by Sven Steinmo (2010), as well as by America's political inability or unwillingness to scrap its inefficient system of health care in favor of the proven effectiveness of some version of a single-payer system. Specific policies are enmeshed in and interdependent with other cognate policies as well as on entrenched institutions (Pierson 2002; Steinmo, Thelen, and Longstreth 1992; Thelen 2004, inter alia). Changing, say, monetary policy cannot be easily decoupled from policies concerning taxes, budgets, or employment. Nor can such changes be easily decoupled from the existing banking and financial structures. The implications of this for the future, of course, remain ambiguous. But in the effort to move from what worked in the past to what is likely to work in the future, we can by no means count on a set of governing philosopher-kings to quickly move those countries in new and more suitable directions.

While recent data provide strong evidence that East Asia is an economically vibrant region, several reasons remain to caution against excessive optimism about the short- and medium-term prospects of its economies. Unbridled optimism or pessimism in the face of any country or region's economic fortunes should be tempered by the realization of how quickly these fortunes can change. Thus the AFC hit the region only four years after the publication of the first *East Asian Miracle*. And despite predictions of doom and gloom for the United States in the face of Japan's seemingly unstoppable success in the 1980s, as well as that following the "dot-com" collapse, the U.S. economy again soared to new heights, even to the extent of the "irrational exuberance" that preceded the Global Financial Crisis. Between 2003 and 2007, tiny Iceland went through "the most rapid expansion of a banking system in the history of mankind," making it "Wall Street on the Tundra" in Michael Lewis' apt term (2011, 2); in less than a year its financial system was a total shambles. To the extent that we may collectively wish for a second East Asia miracle or a "best case scenario" for the region, we have pointed out the significant medium- and longer-term impediments that could prevent successful crisis management, structural changes, and adjustments in strategy needed to bring about its actualization.

Additionally, we need to acknowledge that while they may prove resilient to global capital flows, the economies of East Asia may eventually succumb to other underlying vulnerabilities to economic globalization, not the least challenging of which is their continued dependence on a vigorous global market for their exports. Should the United States and Western Europe continue to struggle economically or should global demand plummet, East Asian governments are likely to face different challenges to their previously demonstrated economic resilience levels.

East Asia is today so much better off than it was twenty years ago—more rich, more technologically sophisticated, more globally competitive, and more democratic. Even if problems do slow down absolute growth, the lifestyles of East Asians are now vastly superior to what they once were. Numerous OECD countries have shown that it is possible to grow at less than blistering rates and still deliver comfortable and rewarding lifestyles for their citizens. That could well be a lesson to growth-obsessed East Asian policymakers. However, even slower growth at high levels of individual productivity requires astute political management domestically, regionally, and globally. Higher levels of growth and transformation in the face of the short-term and long-term hurdles on the horizon for East Asia will surely pose even more daunting challenges.

Works Cited

Abrami, Regina, and Richard F. Doner. 2008. "Southeast Asia and the Political Economy of Development." In *Southeast Asia in Political Science: Theory, Region, and Qualitative Analysis*, ed. E. M. Kuhonta, D. Slater, and T. Vu, 227–51. Stanford: Stanford University Press.

Acharya, Amitav. 2009. *Constructing a Security Community in Southeast Asia*. 2nd ed. London: Routledge.

Aggarwal, Vinod K., and Min Gyo Koo. 2008. *Asia's New Institutional Architecture: Evolving Structures for Managing Trade, Financial, and Security Relations*. Berlin: Springer.

Agosin, Manuel. 2007. "Export Diversification and Growth in Emerging Economies." Department of Economics, University of Chile, SDT #233, 2007. Available at http://www.econ.uchile.cl/SDT.

Ahn, Choong Yong. 2010. "Weathering the Storm: The Impact of the Global Financial Crisis on Asia." *Global Asia* 5 (1): 59–68.

——. 2012 "Can Asia Save the Sinking World Economy?" *East Asia Forum*, February 2. Available at http://www.eastasiaforum.org/2012/02/02/can-asia-save-the-sinking-world-economy.

Ammar, Siamwalla. 2005. "Anatomy of the Crisis." In *Thailand: Beyond the Crisis*, ed. Peter C. Warr, 66–104. London: Routledge Curzon.

Amornivat, Sutapa. 2013. "Firms Struggle for Staff in a Mismatched Society." *Bangkok Post*, November 20.

Andrews, Edmund L. 2008. "Greenspan Concedes Error on Regulation." *New York Times*, October 23.

Aoki, Masahiko, and Hugh T. Patrick, eds. 1995. *The Japanese Main Bank System: Its Relevance for Developing and Transforming Economies*. Oxford: Oxford University Press.

Archanun, Kohpaiboon, et al. 2010. "Global Recession, Labor Market Adjustment, and International Production Networks: Evidence from the Thai Automotive Industry." *ASEAN Economic Bulletin* 27 (1): 98–120.

Asako, Kazumi, et al. 2011. *Nyumon nihon keizai* [Introduction to the Japanese Economy]. 4th ed. Tokyo: Yuhikaku.

Asian Development Bank (ADB). 2000. *Key Indicators of Developing Asian and Pacific Countries 2000*, Vol. 31. Hong Kong: Oxford University Press.

——. 2008. "The US Financial Crisis, Global Financial Turmoil, and Developing Asia: Is the Era of High Growth at an End?" *ADB Economic Working Papers Series* (139).

——. 2010. "The Rise of Asia's Middle Class." In part 1 of *Key Indicators for Asia and the Pacific 2010*, 1–57. Manila: ADB.

——. 2011. *Development Effectiveness Review 2011*. Manila: ADB.

——. Various years. "Economic Indicators." Available at http://sdbs.adb.org/sdbs/jsp/index.jsp.

Aswicahyono, H., and Hal Hill. 2002. "'Perspiration' versus 'inspiration' in Asian Industrialisation: Indonesia before the Crisis." *The Journal of Development Studies* 38 (3): 138–63.

Ba, Alice. 2009. *(Re)Negotiating East and Southeast Asia*. Stanford: Stanford University Press.

Baird, Mark, and Maria Monica Wihardja. 2010. "Survey of Recent Developments." *Bulletin of Indonesian Economic Studies* 46: 143–70.

Bank of Korea. 2000. *Financial Statement Analysis for 2000*. Seoul: Bank of Korea.

——. 2006. *Financial System in Korea*. Seoul: Bank of Korea.

Bank of Thailand. 1992. *50 Years of the Bank of Thailand: 1942–1992*. Bangkok: The Bank of Thailand.

——. 2008. "Thailand's Banking System Performance in the Third Quarter of 2008 and Impact of the Global Financial Crisis on Thai Banks." *Bank of Thailand News* (42).

Basri, M. Chatib, and Hal Hill. 2011. "Indonesian Growth Dynamics." *Asian Economic Policy Review* 6 (1): 90–107.

Basri, M. Chatib, and Arianto A. Patunru. 2006. "Survey of Recent Developments." *Bulletin of Indonesian Economic Studies* 42 (3): 295–319.

——. 2008. "Indonesia's Supply Constraints." Background paper prepared for OECD.

Basri, M. Chatib, and Sjamsu Rahardja. 2009. "Indonesia Navigating Beyond Recovery: Growth Strategy in an Archipelagic Country." Paper presented at the Conference on Growth Performance and Sustainability in the Enhanced Engagement Countries, OECD Economics Department, Paris, September 24.

——. 2010. "The Indonesian Economy amidst the Global Crisis: Good Policy and Good Luck." *ASEAN Economic Bulletin* 27 (1): 77–97.

——. 2011. "Should Indonesia Say Goodbye to Strategy Facilitating Export?" In *Managing Openness: Trade and Outward-Oriented Growth after the Crisis*, ed. Mona Haddad and Ben Shepherd. Washington, DC: World Bank.

Basri, M. Chatib, and Reza Y. Siregar. 2009. "Navigating Policy Responses at the National Level in the Midst of the Global Financial Crisis: The Experience of Indonesia." *Asian Economic Papers* 8 (3): 1–35.

Bates, Robert. 1995. "Social Dilemmas and Rational Individuals: An Assessment of the New Institutionalism." In *The New Institutional Economics and Third World Development*, ed. John Harris, Janet Hunter, and Colin Lewis, 27–48. New York: Routledge.

Bell, Martin, et al. 2003. *Knowledge Resources, Innovation Capabilities, and Sustained Competitiveness in Thailand: Transforming the Policy Process*. Final report prepared for the National Science and Technology Development Board with support from the World Bank, Bangkok.

Beresford, Melanie. 2008. "*Doi Moi* in Review: The Challenges of Building Market Socialism in Vietnam." *Journal of Contemporary Asia* 38 (2): 221–43.

Bhaskaran, Manu, and Ritwick Ghosh. 2010. "Global Economic and Financial Crisis: Impact on Developing Asia and Policy Responses." In *A Resilient Asia amidst Global Financial Crisis: From Crisis Management to Global Leadership*, ed. Harinder S. Kohli and Ashok Sharma, 19–75. London: Sage Publications.

Blyth, Mark. 2013. "This Time It Really is Different: Europe, the Financial Crisis, and 'Staying on Top' in the Twenty-first Century." In *The Third Globalization: Can Wealthy Nations Stay Rich in the Twenty-First Century?* ed. Dan Breznitz and John Zysman, 207–31. Oxford: Oxford University Press.

Bordo, Michael D., and John S. Landon-Lane. 2010. "The Global Financial Crisis of 2007–2008. Is it Unprecedented?" World Paper No. 16589, National Bureau of Economic Research, Cambridge, MA. Available at http://www.nber.org/papers/w16589.

Bosworth, Barry. 1998. "The Asian Financial Crisis: What Happened and What Can We Learn?" *Brookings Review* 16 (3): 6–9.

Brandt, Loren, and Xiaodong Zhu. 2007. "China's Banking Sector and Economic Growth." In *China's Financial Transition at a Crossroads*, ed. Charles W. Calomiris, 86–36. New York: Columbia University Press.

Brereton-Fukui, Natasha. 2013. "Asia's Rising Debt Levels Bring Back Memories of 2007." *Wall Street Journal*, October 31.

Breslin, Shawn, et al. 2002. *New Regionalism in the Global Political Economy*. New York: Routledge.

Bresnan, John. 2005. *Indonesia: The Great Transition*. New York: Rowman and Littlefield.

Briguglio, Lino, et al. 2008. "Economic Vulnerability and Resilience: Concepts and Measurements." *Wider Research Paper* 55. Available at http://hdl.handle.net/10419/45146.

Brown, Andrew. 2004. *Labour, Politics, and the State in Industrializing Thailand*. London: Routledge.

Butt, Simon. 2009. "'Unlawfulness' and Corruption under Indonesian Law." *Bulletin of Indonesian Economic Studies* 45 (2): 179–98.

Buzan, Barry, and Ole Weaver. 2003. *Regions and Powers: The Structure of International Security*. Cambridge: Cambridge University Press.

Cargill, Thomas, and N. Yoshino. 2003. *Postal Savings and Fiscal Investment in Japan: The PSS and the FILP*. Oxford: Oxford University Press.

Cariolle, Joel. 2010. "The Economic Vulnerability Index: 2010 Update." FERDI Working Paper 9. Available at http://www.ferdi.fr/en/publication/i09-economic-vulnerability-index-2010-update.

Cerny, Philip. 1994. "The Dynamics of Financial Globalization: Technology, Market Structure and Policy Response." *Policy Sciences* 27: 319–42.

Chalongphob, Sussangkarn, and Somchai Jitsuchon. 2009. "The Sub-Prime Crisis and Thailand's Growth Rebalancing." *TDRI Quarterly Review* 24 (2): 3–9.

Chambers, Paul. 2008. "Factions, Parties and the Durability of Parliaments, Coalitions, and Cabinets: The Case of Thailand (1979–2001)." *Party Politics* 14 (3): 299–323.

Chang, Ha-joon. 1994. *The Political Economy of Industrial Policy*. London: MacMillan.

——. 1999. "The Political Theory of the Developmental State." In *The Developmental State*, ed. Meredith Woo-Cumings, 182–99. Ithaca: Cornell University Press.

———. 2000. "The Hazard of Moral Hazard: Untangling the Asian Crisis." *World Development* 28 (4): 775–88.

———. 2003. "Kicking Away the Ladder: Infant Industry Promotion in Historical Perspective." *Oxford Development Studies* 31 (1): 21–32.

Chen, Shang-mao. 1998. "The Political Economy of Taiwan's Banking Policy." [In Chinese.] MA thesis, National Chengchi University.

Chen, Tun-jen, and Stephan Haggard. 1987. *Newly Industrializing Asia in Transition.* Berkeley: University of California Press.

Chen, Yan-chien. 2007. "The Country's Fiscal Condition." [In Chinese.] National Policy Research Backgrounder, Finance and Banking Research Paper 091.001. March. Taipei: National Policy Research Foundation. Available at http://www.npf.org.tw/post/3/1457.

China Banking Regulatory Commission (CBRC). 2009. *China Banking Regulatory Commission 2008 Annual Report.* Available at http://www.cbrc.gov.cn/chinese/home/docView/200906016A540A030280DDDCFF4762FBD0BA4F00.html.

Chinese Communist Party Central Committee (CCP). 2013. "Decision of the Central Committee of the Communist Party of China on Some Major Issues Concerning Comprehensively Deepening the Reform." Available at http://www.china.org.cn/china/third_plenary_session/2014-01/16/content_31212602.htm.

Chinese National Audit Office (NAO). 2013. *Results of the National Audit of Government Debt.* [In Chinese.] Report No. 32. Available at http://www.audit.gov.cn/n1992130/n1992150/n1992500/n3432077.files/n3432112.pdf.

Chinese National Development and Reform Commission (NDRC). 2008. "Mingque renwu zhua luoshi, kuoda neixu cucengzheng" [Clarify Responsibility and Grasp Implementation; Expand Domestic Demand and Foster Growth]. November 10. Available at http://xwzx.ndrc.gov.cn/xwfb/200811/t20081110_245191.html.

Chinn, Menzie D. 2000. "Before the Fall: Were East Asian Currencies Overvalued?" *Emerging Markets Review* 1:101–26.

Chinn, Menzie D., and Jeffrey A. Frieden. 2011. *Lost Decades: The Making of America's Debt Crisis and the Long Recovery.* New York: W. W. Norton.

Cho, Yoon Je, and Joon Kyung Kim. 1997. *Credit Policies and the Industrialization of Korea.* Seoul: Korea Development Institute.

Choi, Byung-Sun. 1993. "Financial Policy and Big Business in Korea: The Perils of Financial Regulation." In *The Politics of Finance in Developing Countries*, ed. Stephan Haggard, Chung H. Lee, and Sylvia Maxfield, 23–54. Ithaca: Cornell University Press.

Chongvilaivan, Aekapol. 2013. "Taking the Income Gap in Southeast Asia Seriously." *ISEAS Perspective* 19: 1–11.

Chu, Yun-han. 1999. "Surviving the East Asian Financial Storm: The Political Foundation of Taiwan's Economic Resilience." In *The Politics of the Asian Economic Crisis*, ed. T. J. Pempel, 184–202. Ithaca: Cornell University Press.

———. 2005. "Taiwan's Democracy at a Turning Point." *American Journal of Chinese Studies* 11: 901–924.

———. 2007a. "Re-engineering the Developmental State in an Age of Globalization: Taiwan in Defiance of Neoliberalism." In *Neoliberalism and Institutional Reform in East Asia: A Comparative Studies*, ed. Meredith Woo-Cumings, 91–121. Basingstoke, UK: Palgrave MacMillan.

———. 2007b. "Taiwan in 2006: A Year of Political Turmoil." *Asian Survey* 47 (1): 44–51.

——. 2009. "The Road to Sustainable Growth: An East Asian Perspective." Annual Conference of Club de Madrid, Madrid, October.

Chung, Un Chan. 1994. "Is Financial Deregulation a Panacea?" In *The Korean Economy at a Crossroad: Development Prospects, Liberalization, and South-North Economic Integration*, ed. Sung Yeung Kwack, 105–22. Westport: Praeger.

Claessens, Stijn, Daniela Klingebiel, and Lue Leaven. 2001. "Financial Restructuring in Banking and Corporate Sector Crises: What Policies to Pursue?" NBER Working Paper No. 8386. National Bureau of Economic Research, Cambridge, MA.

Cohen, Benjamin J. 1998. *The Geography of Money*. Ithaca: Cornell University Press.

Cohen, Wesley, and Daniel Levinthal. 1990. "Absorptive Capacity: A New Perspective on Learning and Innovation." *Administrative Science Quarterly* 35 (1): 128–52.

Cole, Robert. 1979. *Work Mobility and Participation: A Comparative Study of American and Japanese Industry*. Berkeley: University of California Press.

Cooper, Richard. 1994. "Fiscal Policy in Korea." In *Macroeconomic Policy and Adjustment in Korea 1970–1990*, ed. S. Haggard et al., 111–44. Cambridge, MA: Harvard Institute for International Development.

Corrales, Javier. 1997. "Do Economic Crises Contribute to Economic Reform? Argentina and Venezuela in the 1990s." *Political Science Quarterly* 112 (4): 617–44.

Coulibaly, Brahima, and Jonathan N. Millar. 2008. "The Asian Financial Crisis, Uphill Flow of Capital, and Global Imbalances: Evidence from a Micro Study." Board of Governors of the Federal Reserve System, International Finance Discussion Paper No. 942. Washington, DC: Federal Reserve, August. Available at http://www.federalreserve.gov/pubs/ifdp/2008/942/ifdp942.pdf.

Crotty, James, and Kank-Kook Lee. 2005. "From East Asian 'Miracle' to Neo-liberal 'Mediocrity': The Effects of Liberalization and Financial Opening on the Post-crisis Korean Economy." *Global Economic Review* 34 (4): 415–34.

Cumings, Bruce. 1984. "The Origins and Development of the Northeast Asian Political Economy." *International Organization* 38 (1): 1–40.

Dapice, David, et al. 2008. "Choosing Success: The Lessons of East and Southeast Asia and Vietnam's Future." Cambridge, MA: Harvard Kennedy School.

Democratic Party of Japan (DPJ). 2009. *Minshuto no manifesuto 2009* [Manifesto 2009 of the Democratic Party of Japan]. Available at http://www.dpj.or.jp/policies/manifesto2009.

Dent, C. M. 2008. *East Asian Regionalism*. London: Routledge.

Department of Statistics, Malaysia. 2013. "Informal Sector Work Force Survey Report."

Deyo, Fredrick. 1989. *Beneath the Miracle: Labor Subordination in the New Asian Industrialism*. Berkeley: University of California Press.

Directorate General of Budget, Accounting and Statistics, Republic of China (Taiwan). 2014. "National Accounts Statistical Tables." Available at http://eng.stat.gov.tw/ct.asp?xItem=25763&CtNode=5347&mp=5.

Dixon, Chris. 2010. "The 1997 Economic Crisis, Reform, and Southeast Asian Growth." In *The New Political Economy of Southeast Asia*, ed. Rajah Rasiah and Johannes Drabsbaek Schmidt, 103–38. Cheltenham, UK: Edward Elgar.

Doner, Richard F. 2009. *The Politics of Uneven Development: Thailand's Economic Growth in Comparative Perspective*. New York: Cambridge University Press.

Doner, Richard F., Bryan Ritchie, and Dan Slater. 2005. "Systemic Vulnerability and the Origins of Developmental States: Northeast and Southeast Asia in Comparative Perspective." *International Organization* 59 (2): 327–61.

Doner, Richard F., and Daniel Unger. 1993. "The Politics of Finance in Thai Economic Development." In *The Politics of Finance in Developing Countries*, ed. Stephan Haggard, Chung H. Lee, and Sylvia Maxfield, 93–122. Ithaca: Cornell University Press.

Doner, Richard F., and Peter Wad. Forthcoming. "Financial Crises and Automotive Industry Development in Southeast Asia." *Journal of Contemporary Asia.*

Dooley, Michael, and Inseok Shin. 2000. "Private Inflows When Crises Are Anticipated: A Case Study of Korea." In *The Korean Crisis: Before and After*, ed. Inseok Shin, 145–82. Seoul: Korea Development Institute.

Dore, Ronald. 2000. *Stock Market Capitalism: Welfare Capitalism: Japan and Germany versus the Anglo-Saxons.* Oxford: Oxford University Press.

Dowling, John Malcolm, and Pradumna Bickram Rana. 2010. *Asia and the Global Economic Crisis: Challenges in a Financially Integrated World.* Basingstoke, UK: Palgrave Macmillan.

Drucker, Peter F. 1975. "Economic Realities and Enterprise Strategies." In *Modern Japanese Organization and Decision-Making*, ed. Ezra Vogel, 228–44. Berkeley: University of California Press.

Eichengreen, Barry, and Torben Iversen. 1999. "Institutions and Economic Performance: Evidence from the Labour Market." *Oxford Review of Economic Policy* 15 (4): 121–38.

Eichengreen, Barry, Charles Wyplosz, and Yung Chul Park. 2008. *China, Asia, and the New World Economy.* Oxford: Oxford University Press.

Elman, Colin. 2005. "Explanatory Typologies in Qualitative Studies of International Politics." *International Organization* 59: 293–326.

Estevez-Abe, Margarita. 2008. *Welfare and Capitalism in Postwar Japan.* Cambridge: Cambridge University Press.

Etemad, Hamid, and Yender Lee. 2001. "Technological Capabilities and Industrial Concentration in NICs and Industrialised Countries: Taiwanese SMEs versus South Korean Chaebols." *International Journal of Entrepreneurship and Innovation Management* 1 (3–4): 329–55.

Fane, George, and Ross Macleod. 2004. "Banking Collapse and Restructuring in Indonesia, 1997–2001." Economics Division RSPAS, Australian National University.

Fast Market Research. 2010. "Taiwan Commercial Banking Report Q3 2010." *Business Monitor International.* Available at http://www.prlog.org/10788857-taiwan-commercial-banking-report-q3-2010-is-now-available-at-fast-market-research.html.

Felker, Greg. 2001. "The Politics of Industrial Investment Policy Reform in Malaysia and Thailand." In *Southeast Asia's Industrialization: Industrial Policy, Capabilities and Sustainability*, ed. Jomo K.S. 129–82. New York: Palgrave.

——. 2003. "Technology Policies and Innovation Systems in Southeast Asia." In *Southeast Asian Paper Tigers? From Miracle to Debacle and Beyond*, ed. Jomo K.S., 136–72. New York: Routledge.

Financial Sector Restructuring Authority (FRA). 2002. *Financial Crisis and Resolutions in Thailand 1997–2002: Roles of the Financial Sector Restructuring Authority.* Bangkok: Research and Information Office FRA.

Financial Supervisory Commission. 2011. *Basic Financial Statistics.* [In Chinese.] Taipei: Banking Bureau of Taiwan Financial Supervisory Commission, Executive Yuan of the Republic of China (Taiwan).

Fisher, Stanley. 1998. "The Asian Crisis: A View from the IMF." Address at the Midwinter Conference of the Bankers' Association for Foreign Trade, Washington, DC. January 22.

Fitch Ratings. 2007. "Limited Direct Impact on Asia-Pacific Banks from Subprime Exposure." Securitization.Net. Available at http://www.securitization.net/news/article.asp?id=463&aid=7551.

Francks, Penelope, J. Boestel, and C. H. Kim. 1999. *Agriculture and Economic Development in East Asia: From Growth to Protectionism in Japan, Korea and Taiwan.* London: Routledge.

Freeman, Richard. 1993. "Does Suppression of Labor Contribute to Economic Success? Labor Relations and Markets in East Asia." World Bank Policy Research Department, Working Paper on the East Asian Miracle. Washington, DC: World Bank.

Frizen, Scott. 2002. "Growth, Inequality and the Future of Poverty Reduction in Vietnam." *Journal of Asian Economics* 13: 635–57.

Fulbright Economics Teaching Program (FETP). 2008. "Surviving a Crisis, Returning to Reform." Policy Discussion Paper no. 2.

Gallagher, Mary, and Jonathan K. Hanson. 2009. "Coalitions, Carrots, and Sticks: Economic Inequality and Authoritarian States." *Political Science and Politics* 42 (4): 667–72.

Gerschenkron, Alexander. 1962. *Economic Backwardness in Historical Perspective.* Cambridge: Harvard University Press.

Ghosh, Swati R. 2006. *East Asian Finance: The Road to Robust Markets.* Washington, DC: World Bank.

Gill, Indermit, and Homi Kharas. 2007. *An East Asian Renaissance: Ideas for Economic Growth.* Washington, DC: World Bank.

Goldstein, Judith, and Robert O. Keohane. 1993. "Ideas and Foreign Policy: An Analytical Framework." In *Ideas and Foreign Policy: Beliefs, Institutions, and Political Change,* eds. Judith Goldstein and Robert O. Keohane, 3–30. Ithaca: Cornell University Press.

Gomez, Edmund Terence, and Jomo K. S. 1999. *Malaysia's Political Economy: Politics, Patronage and Profits.* 2nd ed. Cambridge: Cambridge University Press.

Gourevitch, Peter. 1986. *Politics in Hard Times: Comparative Responses to International Economic Crises.* Ithaca: Cornell University Press.

———. 2013. "Afterward: Yet More Hard Times? Reflections on the Great Recession in the Frame of Earlier Hard Times." In *Politics in the New Hard Times: The Great Recession in Comparative Perspective,* ed. Miles Kahler and David A. Lake, 253–74. Ithaca: Cornell University Press.

Greenspan, Alan. 2013. "Never Saw It Coming: Why the Financial Crisis Took Economists by Surprise." *Foreign Affairs* 92 (6): 88–96.

Greenville, Stephen. 2000. "Capital Flows and Crises." In *The Asian Financial Crisis and the Architecture of Global Finance,* ed. Gregory W. Noble and John Ravenhill, 36–56. Cambridge: Cambridge University Press.

Grimes, William W. 2006. "East Asian Financial Regionalism in Support of the Global Financial Architecture? The Political Economy of Regional Nesting." *Journal of East Asian Studies* 6: 353–80.

———. 2009. *Currency and Contest in East Asia: The Great Power Politics of Financial Regionalism.* Ithaca: Cornell University Press.

Guillaumont, Patrick. 2008. "An Economic Vulnerability Index: Its Design and Use for International Development Policy." Research Paper No. 2008/99, UNU WIDER.

———. 2009. *Caught in a Trap: Identifying the Least Developed Countries.* Clermont-Ferrand, France: Economica.

Gunawan, Anton H., Helmi Arman, and Anton Hendranata. 2009. "Indonesia 2009 Economic Outlook: Slowing, Not Falling." PT Bank Danamon Indonesia, Tbk., Jakarta, January 7.

Ha, Yong-Chool, and Wang Hwi Lee. 2007. "The Politics of Economic Reform in South Korea." *Asian Survey* 47 (6): 894–914.

Haggard, Stephan. 1986. "The Newly Industrializing Countries in the International System." *World Politics* 89 (2): 343–70.

———. 1990. *Pathways from the Periphery: The Politics of Growth in the Newly Industrializing Countries.* Ithaca: Cornell University Press.

———. 2000. *The Political Economy of the Asian Financial Crisis.* Washington, DC: Institute for International Economics.

———. 2008. "Democratization, Crisis and the Changing Social Contract in East Asia." In *Crisis as Catalyst: Asia's Dynamic Political Economy*, ed. A. MacIntyre, T.J. Pempel, and J. Ravenhill, 93–116. Ithaca: Cornell University Press.

Haggard, Stephan, and Robert Kaufman. 2008. *Development, Democracy, and Welfare States.* Princeton: Princeton University Press.

Hahn, Chin Hee. 2000. "Implicit Loss-Protection and the Investment Behavior of Korean *Chaebols*." In *The Korean Crisis: Before and After*, ed. Inseok Shin, 215–51. Seoul: Korea Development Institute.

Hall, Peter A., and David W. Soskice, eds. 2001. *Varieties of Capitalism: The Institutional Foundations of Comparative Advantage.* Oxford: Oxford University Press.

Hamilton-Hart, Natasha. 2000. "The Singapore State Revisited." *Pacific Review* 13: 195–216.

———. 2008. "Banking Systems a Decade after the Crisis." In *Crisis as Catalyst: Asia's Dynamic Political Economy*, ed. Andrew MacIntyre, T. J. Pempel, and John Ravenhill, 45–69. Ithaca: Cornell University Press.

Haris, Sjamsudin. 2010. "Ketika Koalisi di Kontrol Golkar" [When the Coalition Is under the Control of Golkar]. *Kompas* (newspaper), May 10.

Hashimoto, Hisao et al. 2011. *Gendai Nippon keizai* [The Economy of Contemporary Japan]. Tokyo: Yuhikaku.

Hatch, Walter, and Kozo Yamamura. 1996. *Asia in Japan's Embrace: Building a Regional Production Alliance.* Cambridge: Cambridge University Press.

Hausman, Ricardo, and D. Rodrik. 2003. "Economic Development as Self-Discovery." *Journal of Development Economics* 72(2): 603–33.

Helleiner, Eric. 1994. *Regionalization in the International Political Economy: A Comparative Perspective.* East Asian Policy Papers Series. University of Toronto.

Henderson, Jeffrey, and Richard Phillips. 2007. "Unintended Consequences: Social Policy, State Institutions, and the 'Stalling' of the Malaysian Industrialization Project." *Economy and Society* 36 (1): 78–102.

Hewison, Kevin. 2005. "Neo-liberalism and Domestic Capital: The Political Outcomes of the Economic Crisis in Thailand." *Journal of Development Studies* 41 (2): 310–30.

Hicken, Allen. 2008. "Politics of Economic Recovery in Thailand and the Philippines." In *Crisis as Catalyst: Asia's Dynamic Political Economy*, ed. A. MacIntyre, T.J. Pempel and J. Ravenhill, 206–30. Ithaca: Cornell University Press.

Hill, Hal. 1999. *The Indonesian Economy in Crisis: Causes, Consequences, and Lessons.* Singapore: Institute of Southeast Asian Studies.

——. 2000a. "Export Success Against the Odds: A Vietnamese Case Study." *World Development* 28 (2): 283–300.

——. 2000b. "Indonesia: The Strange and Sudden Death of a Tiger Economy." *Oxford Development Studies* 28: 117–39.

——. 2010. "Where the Power Lies in Indonesia." *The Wall Street Journal,* May 17.

Hishikawa, Isao. 2003. "Financial Sector FDI in Asia: Brief Overview." An internal memo for the meeting of the CGFS Working Group on FDI in the Financial Sector, the Bank of Japan, March.

Honohan, Patrick, and Daniela Klingebiel. 2000. "Controlling Fiscal Costs of Banking Crises." Policy Research Working Paper No. 2441, Washington, DC: World Bank.

Huang, Mengfu. 2009. "Some Sectors Have Already Experienced the State Advancing at the Expense of the Private Sector; We Will Pay a Heavy Price." [In Chinese.] *Diyi caijingbao*, September 22. Available at http://www.umetal.com/html/cnyjsh/newsDetail.jsp?id=1836068.

Hugo, Graeme. 2008. *Emerging Demographic Trends in Asia and the Pacific: The Implications for International Migration.* Washington, DC: Migration Policy Institute.

Huguet, Jerrold, and Sureeporn Punpuing. 2005. "International Migration in Thailand." Bangkok: International Organization for Migration.

Huo, Kan, Wang Changyong, and Wang Jing. 2009. "Can Stimulus Light China's Consumer Fire?" *Caijing*, March 6. Available at http://english.caijing.com.cn/2009-03-06/110114349.html.

Hutchcroft, Paul D. 1999. "Neither Dynamo nor Domino: Reforms and Crises in the Philippine Political Economy." In *The Politics of the Asian Economic Crisis*, ed. T.J. Pempel, 163–83. Ithaca: Cornell University Press.

Hwang, Gyu-Jin. 2006. *Pathways to State Welfare in Korea: Interests, Ideas, and Institutions.* Aldershot: Ashgate.

Imbs, Jean, and Romain Wacziarg. 2003. "Stages of Diversification." *American Economic Review* 93 (1): 63–86.

Institute of Governmental Studies. 2013. "Building Resilient Regions." University of California, Berkeley. Available at http://brr.berkeley.edu/economic-resilience.

Intarakumnerd, Patarapong, Pun-arj Chairatana, and Tipawan Tangchitpiboon. 2002. "National Innovation System in Less Successful Developing Countries: The Case of Thailand." *Research Policy* 31 (8): 1445–57.

International Labor Organization (ILO). 2007. "The Contribution of Migrant Workers to Thailand: Towards Policy Development." December 13.

International Monetary Fund (IMF). 2007. *Global Financial Stability Report.* Washington, DC: IMF.

——. 2010a. *Global Financial Stability Report.* Washington, DC: IMF.

——. 2010b. "How Did Emerging Markets Cope in the Crisis?" IMF Policy Paper, June 15, Washington, DC: IMF.

——. 2010c. "International Financial Statistics." Available at http://www.imfstatistics.org/imf/.

——. 2013. *World Economic Outlook Database*, October. Available at http://www.imf. org/external/pubs/ft/weo/2013/02/weodata/index.aspx.

Jacques, Martin. 2009. *When China Rules the World: The Rise of the Middle Kingdom and the End of the Western World.* London: Allen Lane.

Jao, Y. C. 2001. *The Asian Financial Crisis and the Ordeal of Hong Kong.* Westport, CT: Quorom Books.

Japan Statistics Bureau. 2013a. "Historical Data: Employed Persons by Status in Employment." Available at http://www.stat.go.jp/data/roudou/longtime/zuhyou/lt51.xls.

——. 2013b. *Historical Statistics of Japan.* Available at http://www.stat.go.jp/english/data/chouki/19.htm.

——. 2013c. *Labour Force Survey Historical Data.* Available at http://www.stat.go.jp/data/roudou/longtime/zuhyou/lt51.xls.

——. Various years. *Japan Statistical Yearbook.* Available at http://www.stat.go.jp/english/data/nenkan/back62/1431–03.htm.

Japanese Government Cabinet Office. 2010a. "2009 nendo kokumin keizai keisan" [National Account 2009]. Available at http://www.esri.cao.go.jp/jp/sna/data/data_list/kakuhou/files/h21/tables/21a1_jp.xls.

——. 2010b. "Shin seicho senryaku: genki na Nippon fukkatsu no shinario" [New Growth Strategy: A Scenario for Revival of a Vibrant Japan]. Available at http://www.cao.go.jp/.

——. 2014. "Shihankibetsu GDP sokuho" [Quarterly Estimates of GDP]. Available at http://www.esri.cao.go.jp/jp/sna/data/data_list/sokuhou/files/2013/qe134_2/pdf/jikei_1.pdf.

Jeong, Dae Yong, and John Lawler. 2007. "A New Framework of Enterprise Unionism: A Comparative Study of Nine Asian Countries." *Advances in Industrial and Labor Relations* 15: 155–211.

Jiminez, Emmanuel, Vy Nguyen, and Harry Patrinos. 2012. "Stuck in the Middle? Human Capital Development and Economic Growth in Malaysia and Thailand." World Bank Policy Research Working Paper 6283. World Bank: Washington, DC.

Johnson, Chalmers. 1982. *MITI and the Japanese Miracle.* Stanford: Stanford University Press.

Johnson, Simon. 2009. "The Quiet Coup." *The Atlantic*, May. Available at http://www.theatlantic.com/magazine/archive/2009/05/the-quiet-coup/7364/.

Jones, Randall. 2007. "Income Inequality, Poverty, and Social Spending in Japan." OECD Economics Department Working Papers No. 556. Paris: OECD.

Jung, Yong-duck. 2001. "Institutions, Interests, and the Post-IMF Structural Adjustments in Korea." *The Korean Journal of Policy Studies* 16 (1): 11–22.

Kabashima, Ikuo. 2004. *Sengo seiji no kiseki: Jiminto sisutemu no keisei to henyo* [Trajectory of Postwar Japan: Formation and Transformation of the LDP System]. Tokyo: Iwanami Shoten.

Kalinowski, Thomas, and Hyekyung Cho. 2009. "The Political Economy of Financial Liberalization in South Korea." *Asian Survey* 49 (2): 221–42.

Kanbur, Ravi. 2009. "The Crisis, Economic Development Thinking, and Protecting the Poor." Presentation to the World Bank Executive Board. July 7. Available at http://www.kanbur.aem.cornell.edu/papers/WorldBankBoardPresentation 7July09.pdf.

Kang, David C. 2002. *Crony Capitalism: Corruption and Development in South Korea and the Philippines.* New York: Cambridge University Press.

Kato, Takatoshi. 2009. "Why Has Asia Been Hit So Hard by The Global Economic and Financial Crisis." Presentation to the 18th General Meeting of the Pacific Economic Cooperation Council, Washington DC, May 12.

Katz, Richard. 2003a. *Japanese Phoenix: The Long Road to Economic Revival*. Armonk: M. E. Sharpe.

———. 2013b. "Why Chinese-Japanese Economic Relations Are Improving: Delinking Trade from Politics." *Foreign Affairs*, December 30. Available at http://www.foreignaffairs.com/articles/140615/richard-katz/why-chinese-japanese-economic-relations-are-improving.

Katzenstein, Peter J. 1985. *Small States in World Markets: Industrial Policy in Europe*. Ithaca: Cornell University Press.

———. 2005. *A World of Regions: Asia and Europe in the American Imperium*. Ithaca: Cornell University Press.

Katzenstein, Peter J., and Stephen C. Nelson. 2013a. "Reading the Right Signals and Reading the Signals Right: IPE and the Financial Crisis of 2008." *Review of International Political Economy* 20 (5): 1101–31. Available at http://dx.doi.org/10.1080/09692290.2013.804854.

———. 2013b. "Worlds in Collision: Uncertainty and Risk in Hard Times." In *Politics in the New Hard Times: The Great Recession in Comparative Perspective*, ed. Miles Kahler and David Lake, 233–52. Ithaca: Cornell University Press.

Katzenstein, Peter J., and Takashi Shiraishi, eds. 1997. *Network Power: Japan in Asia*. Ithaca: Cornell University Press.

———, eds. 2006. *Beyond Japan: The Dynamics of East Asian Regionalism*. Ithaca: Cornell University Press.

Keefer, Philip. 2009. "Inequality, Collective Action, and Democratization." *PS: Political Science and Politics* 42 (4): 661–66.

Kerkvliet, Ben. 2005. *The Power of Everyday Politics: How Vietnamese Peasants Transformed National Policy*. Ithaca: Cornell University Press.

Keynes, John Maynard. 1936. *The General Theory of Employment, Interest, and Money*. London: Macmillan.

Kim, Byung-Kook. 2000. "Electoral Politics and Economic Crisis, 1997–1998." In *Consolidating Democracy in South Korea*, ed. L. Diamond and Byung-Kook Kim, 173–201. Boulder: Lynne Rienner.

———. 2002. "The Politics of Financial Reform in Korea, Malaysia, and Thailand: When, Why, and How Democracy Matters?" *Journal of East Asian Studies* 2 (1): 185–240.

Kim, Dong-hwan, and Soon-ho Lee. 2008. "Caution Urged in Easing Bank Ownership Rules." In *Financial Industry at a Crossroads*, Insight into Korea Series, vol. 7, eds. The Korea Herald and The Korea Institute of Finance, 173–80. Korea: Jimoondang.

Kim, Hong-Bum, and Chung H. Lee. 2006. "Financial Reform, Institutional Interdependency, and Supervisory Failure in Postcrisis Korea." *Journal of East Asian Studies* 3 (6): 409–31.

Kimiya, Tadashi. 2003. *Kankoku: minshuka to keizai hatten no dainamizumu* [Korea: Dynamism of Democratization and Economic Development]. Tokyo: Chikuma Shobo.

Kimura, Fukunari. 2005. "International Production/Distribution Networks and Indonesia." *Developing Economies* 43 (1): 17–38.

Kindleberger, Charles. 1985. "The Functioning of Financial Centers: Britain in the Nineteenth Century, the United States since 1945." *International Financial Markets and Capital Movements: A Symposium in Honor of Arthur Bloomfeld, Essays in International Finance no. 157.* Princeton University, Department of Economics.

———. 1986. "International Public Goods without International Government." *American Economic Review* 76: 1–11.

Kingston, Jeff. 2004. *Japan's Quiet Transformation: Social Change and Civil Society in the Twenty-first Century.* London: Routledge Curzon.

Kirschner, Jonathan. 1995. *Currency and Coercion: The Political Economy of International Monetary Power.* Princeton: Princeton University Press.

Kojima, Kiyoshi. 2000. "The Flying Geese Model of Asian Economic Development: Origin, Theoretical Extensions, and Regional Policy Implication." *Journal of Asian Economics* 11 (4): 375–401.

Kolodko, Grzedgorz. 2000. "Globalization and Catching-up: From Recession to Growth in Transition Economies." IMF Working Paper WP/00/100, June, Washington, DC: IMF. Available at http://www.imf.org/external/pubs/ft/wp/2000/wp00100.pdf.

Komine, Takao. 2011a. *Nippon keizai no kiroku: Dainiji sekiyu kiki heno taio kara baburu hokai made 1970 Nendai ~ 1996 Nen* [A Record of Japanese Economy: From the Second Oil Crisis to the Bursting of the Bubble Economy, 1970s–1996]. Tokyo: Cabinet Office Economic and Social Research Institute.

———. 2011b. *Nippon keizai no kiroku: kinyu kiki defure to kaifuku katei 1997 Nen–2006 Nen* [A Record of Japanese Economy: Financial Crisis, Deflation, and Recovery Process, 1997–2006]. Tokyo: Cabinet Office Economic and Social Research Institute.

Krasner, Stephen D. 1984. "Approaches to the State: Alternative Conceptions and Historical Dynamics." *Comparative Politics* 2 (16): 223–46.

Kroeber, Arthur. 2010. "Mother of All Stimuli." *China Economic Quarterly* 14 (2): 27.

Krugman, Paul. 2009. "How Did Economists Get It So Wrong?" *New York Times Magazine,* September 2.

Kuo, Yi-ling. 2009. "Governor Perng, We Were Wrong." *Business Weekly* no. 1145, November 12.

Kuramochi, Kazuo. 1994. *Gendai kankoku nogyo kozo no hendo* [Transformation of Agricultural Structure in Contemporary Korea]. Tokyo: Ochanomizu Shobo.

Kurlantzick, Joshua. 2007. *Charm Offensive: How China's Soft Power Is Transforming the World.* New Haven: Yale University Press.

Kusano, Atsushi. 1992. *Daitenho keizai kisei no kozo: gyosei shido no kozai wo tou* [Structure of Regulation by the Law on Large-scale Stores: Merits and Demerits of Administrative Guidance]. Tokyo: Nihon Kezai Shimbunsha.

Lake, David A., and Patrick M. Morgan, eds. 1997. *Regional Orders: Building Security in a New World.* University Park: Pennsylvania University Press.

Lall, Sanjaya. 1992. "Technological Capabilities and Industrialization" *World Development* 20 (2): 165–86.

———. 1998. "Thailand's Manufacturing Sector: The Current Crisis and Export Competitiveness." Paper presented at the conference on Thailand's Dynamic Economic Recovery and Competitiveness, Bangkok, May 20–21.

Lardy, Nicholas. 1998. *China's Unfinished Economic Revolution.* Washington, DC: Brookings Institution.

———. 2012. *Sustaining China's Economic Growth after the Global Financial Crisis.* Washington, DC: Peterson Institute.

Lauridsen, Laurids. 2002. "Struggling with Globalization in Thailand: Accumulation, Learning, or Market Competition." *South East Asia Research* 10 (2): 155–83.

Lee, Johee. 1998. "Micro-Corporatism in South Korea: A Comparative Analysis of Enterprise-Level Industrial Relations." *Economic and Industrial Democracy* 19 (3): 443–74.

Lee, Kap Yun. 2004. "Kankoku seitousei henka no tokusei to youin, 1987–97" [Characteristics and Factors of the Transformation of the Korean Party System]. In *Hendoki no nikkan seiji hikaku* [Comparing Japan and Korea in the Era of Change], ed. Y. Sone and J. Choi, 229–61. Tokyo: Keio University Press.

Lee, Kyu-sung. 2011. *The Korean Financial Crisis of 1997: Onset, Turnaround, and Thereafter.* Washington, DC: World Bank and the Korea Development Institute.

Lee, Pei-shan, and Yun-han Chu. 2008. "The New Political Economy after Regime Turnover in Taiwan." In *Presidential Politics in Taiwan*, ed. Steven Goldstein and Julian Chang, 143–69. Norwalk: EastBridge.

Lee, Sook-Jong. 2002. "Financial Restructuring in Korea and Japan: Resolution of Non-performing Loans and Reorganization of Financial Institutions." *Journal of East Asian Studies* 2 (2): 143–85.

Lee, Wang Hwi. 2004. "The Political Power of Economic Ideas: Comparative Policy Responses to the East Asian Financial Crisis in South Korea and Malaysia." Ph.D. diss., London School of Economics and Political Science, University of London.

Leung, Suiwah, and James Riedel. 2001. "The Role of the State in Vietnam's Economic Transition." Australian National University, Asia Pacific School of Economics and Government, Working Papers 01–1. Available at https://crawford.anu.edu.au/degrees/idec/working_papers/IDEC01-1.pdf#search='Leung+Riedel'.

Lewis, Michael. 2010. *The Big Short: Inside the Doomsday Machine.* New York: Norton.

——. 2011. *Boomerang: Travels In the New Third World.* New York: Norton.

Lim, Wonhyuk. 2003. "The Emergence of the *Chaebol* and the Origins of the *Chaebol* Problem." In *Economic Crisis and Corporate Restructuring in Korea: Reforming the Chaebol*, eds. Stephan Haggard, Wonhyuk Lim, and Euysung Kim, 35–52. Cambridge: Cambridge University Press.

Lim, Wonhyuk, and Joon-Ho Hahm. 2004. "Financial Globalization and Korea's Post-Crisis Reform: A Political Economy Perspective." Working Paper 2004–01. Seoul: Korea Development Institute.

LPEM-FEUI. 2005. "Inefficiency in the Logistics of Export Industries: The Case of Indonesia." Report in Collaboration with Japan Bank for International Cooperation, Jakarta.

——. 2006. "Monitoring Investment Climate in Indonesia: A Report from the End of 2005 Survey." Report in Collaboration with the World Bank, Jakarta.

Ma, Guonan. 2006. "Sharing China's Bank Restructuring Bill." *China and World Economy* 14 (3): 19–36. Available at http://www.bis.org/repofficepubl/apresearch0605ma.pdf.

MacIntyre, Andrew. 2001. "Institutions and Investors: The Politics of the Economic Crisis in Southeast Asia." *International Organization* 55 (1): 81–122.

MacIntyre, Andrew, and Barry Naughton. 2005. "The Decline of a Japan-Led Model of the East Asian Economy." In *Remapping East Asia*, ed. T. J. Pempel, 77–100. Ithaca: Cornell University Press.

MacIntrye, Andrew, T. J. Pempel, and John Ravenhill, eds. 2008. *Crisis as Catalyst: Asia's Dynamic Political Economy.* Ithaca: Cornell University Press.

Malesky, Edmund, Regina Abrami, and Yu Zheng. 2009. "Institutions and Inequality in Single-Party Regimes: A Comparative Analysis of Vietnam and China." Unpublished draft, July 9.

Mann, David, et al. 2013. "Asian Leverage Uncovered." Standard Chartered, Global Research. Available at https://www.sc.com/jp/_documents/jp/reports/economist-reports/Scout-Asia-leverage-uncovered-01072013.pdf.

Mason, A., S. Lee, and G. Russo. 2000. "Population Momentum and Population Aging in Asia and Near-East Countries." Report produced by East West Centre, Hawaii.

McCauley, Robert, and Jens Zukunft. 2008. "Asian Banks and the International Interbank Market." *BIS Quarterly Review* 72 (June): 67–79.

McGray, Douglas. 2002. "Japan's Gross National Cool." *Foreign Policy* 130:44–54. Available at http://www.foreignpolicy.com/articles/2002/05/01/japans_gross_national_cool#sthash.XcifxpTn.dpbs.

McKendrick, David, Richard F. Doner, and Stephan Haggard. 2000. *From Silicon Valley to Singapore: The Competitive Advantage of Location in the Hard Disk Drive Industry.* Stanford: Stanford University Press.

McKinnon, Ronald I. 1993. *The Order of Economic Liberalization: Financial Control in the Transition to a Market Economy.* Baltimore: The Johns Hopkins University Press.

McLeod, Ross H., and Ross Garnaut, eds. 1998. *East Asia in Crisis: From Being a Miracle to Needing One?* London: Routledge.

Mearsheimer, John J. 2001. *The Tragedy of Great Power Politics.* New York: Norton.

Ministry of Agriculture, Forestry, and Fisheries (MAFF), Japan. 2004. *Annual Report on Food, Agriculture and Rural Areas in Japan 2003.* Tokyo: MAFF.

———. 2007. *Kako ni okonawareta yunyu jiyukatou no eikyo hyouka* [Impact Evaluation of Import Liberalizations]. Tokyo: MAFF.

Ministry of Economy, Trade, and Industry (METI), Japan. 2003. *White Paper on International Trade 2003.* Tokyo: METI.

Ministry of Finance (MOF), Japan. 2011. "Wagakuni no zaisei jijo (Heisei 24 nendo yosan seifuan)" [Fiscal Situation of Japan (2012 Budget Plan of the Government)]. Available at http://www.mof.go.jp/budget/budger_workflow/budget/fy2012/seifuan24/yosan004.pdf.

———. 2012 "Zaiseitouyushi shikinunyou houkokusho (heisei 24 nendo)" [Report on FILP Management 2012]. Available at https://www.mof.go.jp/filp/reference/management_report/unyo24b.pdf.

———. 2013a. "Heisei 24 nendo kessan no setsumei" [Statement of Account for the 2012 Fiscal Year]. Available at http://www.mof.go.jp/budget/budger_workflow/account/fy2012/ke_setsumei24.htm.

———. 2013b. "Japan's Fiscal Condition (December 24, 2013)." Available at http://www.mof.go.jp/english/budget/budget/fy2014/02.pdf.

———. 2013c. "Wagakuni no zaisei jijo (Heisei 25 nendo yosan seifuan)" [Fiscal Situation of Japan (2013 Budget Plan of the Government)]. Available at http://www.mof.go.jp/budget/budger_workflow/budget/fy2013/seifuan25/04zaisei.pdf.

Ministry of Strategy and Finance (MOSF), Korea. 2011. *National Debt Management Plan 2010–2014.* Seoul: MOSF.

Miyamoto, Taro. 2008. *Fukushi seiji* [Welfare Politics]. Tokyo: Yuhikaku.

Mo, Jongryn. 2008. "The Korean Economic System Ten Years after the Crisis." In *Crisis as Catalyst: Asia's Dynamic Political Economy,* ed. A. MacIntyre, T.J. Pempel, and John Ravenhill, 251–70. Ithaca: Cornell Univ. Press.

Mo, Jongryn, and Chung-in Moon. 2003. "Business-Government Relations under Kim Dae-Jung." In *Economic Crisis and Corporate Restructuring in Korea: Reforming the Chaebol*, eds. Stephan Haggard, Wonhyuk Lim, and Euysung Kim, 127–49. Cambridge: Cambridge University Press.

Moon, Chung In. 1994. "Changing Patterns of Business-Government Relations in South Korea." In *Business and Government in Industrializing Asia*, ed. Andrew MacIntyre, 142–66. Ithaca: Cornell University Press.

Mortgenson, Gretchen. 2011. "A Bank Crisis Whodunit: With Laughs and Tears." *New York Times*, January 30.

Murakami, Yasusuke. 1996. *An Anticlassical Political-Economic Analysis: A Vision for the Next Century*. Stanford: Stanford University Press.

Murakami, Yasusuke, and Hugh T. Patrick, eds. 1987–92. *The Political Economy of Japan*. 3 vols. Stanford: Stanford University Press.

Muramatsu, Michio. 2005. "Furyo saiken shori sakiokuri no seijigakuteki bunseki" [Political Analysis on the Delay in the Treatment of the NPL Problem]. In *Heisei baburu sakiokuri no kenkyu* [The Collapse of the 1990s Bubble: A Study of the Non-performing Loan Problem], ed. M. Muramatsu, 2–44. Tokyo: Toyo Keizai Shinposha.

Muscat, Robert. 1994. *The Fifth Tiger: A Study of Thai Development Policy*. New York: M. E. Sharpe.

Naim, Moises. 1994. "Latin America: The Second Stage of Reform." *Journal of Democracy* 5 (4): 32–48.

National Bureau of Statistics of China. 2013. *China Statistical Yearbook 2013*. Beijing: National Bureau of Statistics of China.

National Economic Advisory Council (NEAC). 2010. *New Economic Model for Malaysia*. Kuala Lumpur: NEAC.

Naughton, Barry. 2007. *The Chinese Economy: Transitions and Growth*. Cambridge, MA: MIT Press.

——. 2009. "Understanding the Chinese Stimulus Package." *China Leadership Monitor* 28. Available at http://www.hoover.org/publications/china-leadership-monitor/3571.

——. 2011. "China's Economic Policy Today: The New State Activism." *Eurasian Geography and Economics* 52 (3): 313–29.

Nelson, Joan. 1999. *Reforming Health and Education: The World Bank, The IDB, and Complex Institutional Change*. Washington, DC: Overseas Development Council.

Ngiam, Kee-Jin. 2001. "Coping with the Asian Financial Crisis: The Singapore Experience." In *From Crisis to Recovery: East Asia Rising Again?* ed. Xu Dianqing, Yu Tzong-Shian, and Yu Zongxian, 141–72. Singapore: World Scientific Publishing.

NHK Hoso Bunka Kenkyujo. 2004. *Gendai nihonjin no ishiki kouzo* [Opinion Distribution of the Contemporary Japanese]. Tokyo: NHK Books.

Noble, Gregory W., and John Ravenhill. 2000. "The Good, the Bad, and the Ugly? Korea, Taiwan and the Asian Financial Crisis." In *The Asian Financial Crisis and the Architecture of Global Finance*, ed. Gregory W. Noble and John Ravenhill, 80–107. Cambridge: Cambridge University Press.

Noland, Marcus. 2000. "The Philippines in the Asian Financial Crisis." *Asian Survey* 40 (3): 401–12.

O'Brien, Kevin J., ed. 2008. *Popular Protest in China*. Cambridge, MA: Harvard University Press.

Okazaki, Tetsuji. 1994. "The Japanese Firm under the Wartime Planned Economy." In *The Japanese Firm: The Sources of Competitive Strength*, ed. M. Aoki and R. Dore, 350–78. New York: Oxford University Press.

Onishi, Yutaka. 2005. *Kankoku keizai no seiji bunseki* [The Politics of Finance in South Korea]. Tokyo: Yuhikaku.

Osawa, Mari. 2011. *Social Security in Contemporary Japan*. London: Routledge.

Ozawa, Terutomo. 2009. *The Rise of Asia: The "Flying Geese" Theory of Tandem Growth and Regional Agglomeration*. Northampton, MA: Edward Elgar.

Pack, Howard. 2000. "Research and Development in the Industrial Development Process." In *Technology, Learning, and Innovation: Experiences of the Newly Industrializing Economies*, ed. Linsu Kim and Richard R. Nelson, 69–94. New York: Cambridge University Press.

Packard, Truman, and Thang Van Nguyen. 2013. "Work in East Asia and the Pacific." In *East Asia and Pacific Update: Rebuilding Policy Buffers, Reinvigorating Growth*, 52–67. Washington, DC: World Bank.

Painter, Martin. 2003. "The Politics of Economic Restructuring in Vietnam: The Case of State-owned Enterprise 'Reform.'" *Contemporary Southeast Asia* 25 (1): 20–41.

Papanek, Gustav, M. Chatib Basri, and Daniel Schydlowsky. 2009. "The Impact of World Recession on Indonesia and Appropriate Policy Response: Some Lessons for Asia." Paper prepared for Asian Development Bank Report.

Park, Chang-Gyun. 2010. "Political Economy of Macro-prudential Regulation in Korea." In *Post-crisis Regulatory Reforms to Secure Financial Stability*, eds. Seok-Kyun Hur and Taehoon Youn, 41–70. Seoul: Korea Development Institute.

Park, Donghyun, Kwanho Shin, and Juthathip Jongwanich. 2009. "The Decline of Investment in East Asia since the Asian Financial Crisis: An Overview and Empirical Examination." ADB Economics Working Paper Series No. 187. Manila: Asian Development Bank, December. Available at http://www.adb.org/sites/de fault/files/pub/2009/Economics-WP187.pdf.

Park, Yung Chul. 1998. *Financial Liberalization and Opening in East Asia: Issues and Policy Challenges*. Seoul: Korea Institute of Finance.

Park, Yung Chul, and Dong Won Kim. 1994. "Korea: Development and Structural Change of the Banking System." In *The Financial Development of Japan, Korea, and Taiwan: Growth, Repression, and Liberalization*, eds. Hugh T. Patrick and Yung Chul Park, 188–221. Oxford: Oxford University Press.

Pasuk, Phongpaichit, and Chris Baker. 2002. *Thailand: Economy and Politics*. 2nd ed. Oxford: Oxford University Press.

——. 2008. "Thaksin's Populism." *Journal of Contemporary Asia* 38 (1): 62–83.

Patrick, Hugh, and Henry Rosovsky, eds. 1976. *Asia's New Giant*. Washington, DC: Brookings Institution.

Patunru, A. A., N. Nurridzki, and Rivayani. 2007. "Port Competition in Indonesia." Paper prepared for the Asian Development Bank Institute, 2007. Also as "Port Competitiveness: A Case Study of Semarang and Surabaya, Indonesia." Forthcoming. In *Infrastructure's Role in Lowering Asia's Trade Costs: Building for Trade*, ed. D. Brooks and D. Hummels. Cheltenham, UK: Edward Elgar.

Pelofsky, Jeremy, and David Lawder. 2008. "White House Sees Record Budget Gap in 2009." *Reuters*, July 28. Available at http://mobile.reuters.com/article/politicsNews/idUSN2847371220080728?p=1.

Pempel, T. J. 1978. "Japanese Foreign Economic Policy: The Domestic Bases for International Behavior." In *Between Power and Plenty*, ed. Peter J. Katzenstein, 139–90. Madison: University of Wisconsin Press.

——. 1997. "Trans-Pacific Torii: Japan and the Emerging Asian Regionalism." In *Network Power: Japan in Asia*, ed. Peter J. Katzenstein and Takashi Shiraishi, 47–82. Ithaca: Cornell University Press.

——. 1998. *Regime Shift: Comparative Dynamics of the Japanese Political Economy*. Ithaca: Cornell University Press.

——, ed. 1999a. *The Politics of the Asian Economic Crisis*. Ithaca: Cornell University Press.

——. 1999b. "The Developing Regime in a Changing World Economy." In *The Developmental State*, ed. Meredith Woo-Cumings, 137–81. Ithaca: Cornell University Press.

——. 2005. *Remapping East Asia: The Construction of a Region*. Ithaca: Cornell University Press.

——. 2006. "The Race to Connect East Asia: An Unending Steeplechase." *Asian Economic Policy Review* 1: 239–54.

——. 2008. "Restructuring Regional Ties." In *Crisis as Catalyst: East Asia's Dynamic Political Economy*, ed. Andrew MacIntyre, T. J. Pempel, and John Ravenhill, 164–82. Ithaca: Cornell University Press.

——. 2010a. "Between Pork and Productivity: The Collapse of the Liberal Democratic Party." *Journal of Japanese Studies* 36 (2): 227–54.

——. 2010b. "Soft Balancing, Hedging, and Institutional Darwinism: The Economic-Security Nexus and East Asian Regionalism." *Journal of East Asian Studies* 10: 209–38.

Pempel, T. J., and Chung-Min Lee, eds. 2012. *Security Cooperation in Northeast Asia: Architecture and Beyond*. London: Routledge.

Pempel, T. J., and Keiichi Tsunekawa. 1979. "Corporatism without Labor: The Japanese Anomaly." In *Trends toward Corporatist Intermediation*, ed. Philippe Schmitter and Gerhard Lembruch, 231–70. Beverly Hills, CA: Sage, 1979.

Pepinsky, Thomas B. 2008a. "Capital Mobility and Coalitional Politics: Authoritarian Regimes and Economic Adjustment in Southeast Asia." *World Politics* 60 (3): 438–74.

——. 2008b. "Institutions, Economic Recovery, and Macroeconomic Vulnerability in Indonesia and Malaysia." In *Crisis as Catalyst: Asia's Dynamic Political Economy*, ed. A. MacIntyre, T. J. Pempel, and J. Ravenhill, 231–50. Ithaca: Cornell University Press.

——. 2009. *Economic Crises and the Breakdown of Authoritarian Regimes: Indonesia and Malaysia in Comparative Perspective*. New York: Cambridge University Press.

——. 2012. "The Global Economic Crisis and the Politics of Non-Transitions." *Government and Opposition* 47 (2): 135–61.

Perng, Fai-nan. 2010. "Fai-nan Perng." *The Banker*, August 30. Available at http://www.thebanker.com/World/Asia-Pacific/Taiwan/Fai-nan-Perng?ct=true.

Pettis, Michael. 2013. *Avoiding the Fall: China's Economic Restructuring*. Washington, DC: Carnegie Endowment for International Peace.

Pierson, Paul. 2004. *Politics in Time: History, Institutions, and Social Analysis*. Princeton: Princeton University Press.

Pietrobelli, Carlo, and Rajah Rasiah. 2012. *Evidence-based Development Economics: Essays in Honor of Sanjaya Lall.* Kuala Lumpur: University of Malaya Press.

Pritchett, Lant. 2003. "A Toy Collection, a Socialist Star, and a Democratic Dud? Growth, Theory, Vietnam, and the Philippines." In *Search of Prosperity: Analytic Narratives on Economic Growth*, ed. Dani Rodrik, 123–51. Princeton: Princeton University Press.

PRS Group. 2013. "International Country Risk Guide (ICRG)." Available at http://www.prsgroup.com/ICRG.aspx.

Qiang, Daming. 2008. "Speed Up the Construction of Projects that Affect Shandong's Long-term Development." [In Chinese.] *Dazhong Daily*, November 12. Available at http://www.gov.cn/gzdt/2008-11/12/content_1146573.htm.

Qureshi, Mahvash S., et al. 2011. "Managing Capital Inflows: The Role of Capital Controls and Prudential Policies." NBER Working Paper No. 17363, Cambridge, MA, National Bureau of Economic Research. Available at http://www.nber.org/papers/w17363.

Radelet, Steven, and Jeffrey Sachs. 1998. "The East Asian Financial Crisis: Diagnosis, Remedies, Prospects." *Brookings Papers on Economic Activities* 1: 1–90.

Rajan, Raghuram G. 2010. *Fault Lines: How Hidden Fractures Still Threaten the World Economy.* Princeton: Princeton University Press.

Rasiah, Rajah. 2001. "Southeast Asia's Ersatz Miracle: The Dubious Sustainability of its Growth and Industrialization." In *Southeast Asia's Industrialization: Industrial Policy, Capabilities, and Sustainability*, ed. Jomo K.S., 86–112. New York: Palgrave.

——. 2003. "Manufacturing export growth in Indonesia, Malaysia and Thailand." In *Southeast Asian Paper Tigers: From Miracle to Debacle and Beyond*, ed. Jomo K.S., 19–80. New York: Routledge Curzon.

Ravenhill, John. 2011. "Understanding the 'New Asian Regionalism.'" *Review of International Political Economy* 17 (2): 173–77.

Reinhart, Carmen M., and Kenneth S. Rogoff. 2009. *This Time Is Different: Eight Centuries of Financial Folly.* Princeton: Princeton University Press.

Riedel, James, and William S. Turley. 1999. "The Politics and Economics of Transition to an Open Economy in Viet Nam." OECD Working Paper No. 152. Paris: OECD.

Ritchie, Bryan. 2010. *Systemic Vulnerability and Sustainable Economic Growth: Skills and Upgrading in Southeast Asia.* Northampton, MA: Edward Elgar.

Robison, Richard, and Vedi R. Hadiz. 2004. *Reorganizing Power in Indonesia: The Politics of Oligarchy in the Age of Markets.* London: Routledge Curzon.

Robison, Richard, and Andrew Rosser. 1998. "Contesting Reform: Indonesia's New Order and the IMF." *World Development* 26 (8): 1593–609.

Rodan, Garry, Kevin Hewison, and Richard Robison, eds. 2005. *The Political Economy of South-East Asia: Markets, Power, and Contestation.* Melbourne: Oxford University Press.

Rodrik, Dani. 2004. "Industrial Policy for the Twenty-First Century." Harvard University, Kennedy School of Government, Cambridge, MA.

——. 2007. *One Economics, Many Recipes: Globalization, Institutions, and Economic Growth.* Princeton: Princeton University Press.

Rosenbluth, Frances, and Michael F. Thies. 2010. *Japan Transformed: Political Change and Economic Restructuring.* Princeton: Princeton University Press.

Ruiz-Arranz, Marta, and Milan Zavadjil. 2008. *Are Emerging Asia's Reserves Really Too High?* Paper No. 2008–2192. International Monetary Fund, Washington, DC.

Sachs, Jeffrey. 1997. "IMF Orthodoxy Isn't What Southeast Asia Needs." *International Herald Tribune,* November 6.

Saw, Swee-Hock, and John Wong, eds. 2010. *Managing Economic Crisis in East Asia.* Singapore: ISEAS.

Schneider, Ben Ross, and David Soskice. 2009. "Inequality in Developed Countries and Latin America: Coordinated, Liberal, and Hierarchical Systems." *Economy and Society* 38 (1): 17–52.

Schoppa, Leonard. 1997. *Bargaining with Japan: What American Pressure Can and Cannot Do.* New York: Columbia University Press.

——. 2006. *Race for the Exits: The Unraveling of Japan's System of Social Protection.* Ithaca: Cornell University Press.

Schwartz, Herman M. 2009. *Subprime Nation: American Power, Global Capital, and the Housing Bubble.* Ithaca: Cornell University Press.

Schwarz, Adam. 1999. *A Nation in Waiting.* Sydney: Allen and Unwin.

Seith, Anne. 2013. "The Greece of Asia: Japan's Growing Sovereign Debt Time Bomb." *Spiegel Online International,* January 3. Available at http://www.spiegel.de/international/world/massive-japanese-sovereign-debt-could-become-global-problem-a-875641.html.

Sethaput, Suthiwartnarapeut. 2010. "GDP Growth Not Indicative of Better Living." *Bangkok Post,* August 8.

Shambaugh, David. 2013. *China Goes Global: The Partial Power.* Oxford: Oxford University Press.

Sharma, Shalendra D. 2003. *The Asian Financial Crisis: Crisis, Reform, and Recovery.* Manchester, UK: Manchester University Press.

Sheng, Andrew. 2009. *From Asian to Global Financial Crisis: An Asian Regulator's View of Unfettered Finance in the 1990s and 2000s.* Cambridge: Cambridge University Press.

Sheng, Lijun. 2003. "China-ASEAN Free Trade Area: Origins, Developments and Strategic Motivations." ISEAS Working Paper: International Politics & Security Issues Series No. 1. Available at http://www.iseas.edu.sg/documents/publication/ipsi12003.pdf.

Shin, Jang-Sup. 2010. "Foreign Exchange Crisis in Korea." In *Managing Economic Crisis in East Asia,* eds. Saw Swee-Hock and John Wong, 162–89. Singapore: ISEAS Publishing.

Shin, Jang-Sup, and Ha-Joon Chang. 2003. *Restructuring Korea Inc.* London: RoutledgeCurzon.

Shinkawa, Toshimitsu. 2005. *Nihongata fukushi rejiimu no hatten to henyo* [Development and Transformation of the Japanese-style Welfare State]. Kyoto: Minerva Shoten.

Shirai, Sayuri. 2009. "The Impact of the US Subprime Mortgage Crisis on the World and East Asia." Munich Personal RePEc Archive (MPRA) Paper No. 14722. Munich, Germany.

Shirk, Susan L. 2007. *China: Fragile Superpower.* Oxford: Oxford University Press.

Simmons, Beth. 1999. "The Internationalization of Capital." In *Continuity and Change in Contemporary Capitalism,* ed. Herbert Kitschelt et al., 36–69. Cambrige: Cambridge University Press.

Singh, Bilveer. 2010. "Malaysia in 2009: Confronting Old Challenges through a New Leadership." *Asian Survey* 50 (1): 173–84.

Singh, Kavaljit. 2000. *Taming Global Financial Flows: Challenges and Alternatives in the Era of Financial Globalisation.* London: Zed Books.

——. 2010. "Emerging Markets Consider Capital Controls to Regulate Speculative Capital Flows." *Occasional Papers.* Public Interest Research Centre, New Delhi, July 5.

Small and Medium Enterprise Agency, Japan. 2000. *White Paper on Small and Medium Enterprises in Japan 2000.* Tokyo: SMEA.

Soesastro, M. Hadi. 1989. "The Political Economy of Deregulation in Indonesia." *Asian Survey* 29 (9): 853–69.

Soesastro, M. Hadi, and M. C. Basri. 1998. "Survey of Recent Developments." *Bulletin of Indonesian Economic Studies* 34 (1): 3–54.

——. 2005. "The Political Economy of Trade Policy in Indonesia." *ASEAN Economic Bulletin* 22 (1): 3–18.

Solingen, Etel. 1998. *Regional Orders at Century's Dawn: Global and Domestic Influences on Grand Strategy.* Princeton: Princeton University Press.

Somchai, Jitsuchon. 2010. "Thailand in a Middle-Income Trap." *TDRI Quarterly Review* (June): 13–20.

State Council, People's Republic of China. 2006. "Medium and Long-Term Plan for Science and Technology Development (2006–2020)." [In Chinese.] Available at http://www.gov.cn/zhengce/content/2008-03/28/content_5296.htm.

Steinfeld, Edward. 2008. "The Capitalist Embrace: China Ten Years after the Asian Financial Crisis." In *Crisis as Catalyst: Asia's Dynamic Political Economy,* ed. Andrew MacIntyre, T. J. Pempel, and John Ravenhill, 183–205. Ithaca: Cornell University Press.

Steinmo, Sven. 2010. *The Evolution of Modern States: Sweden, Japan and the United States.* Cambridge: Cambridge Univesity Press.

Steinmo, Sven, Kathleen Thelen, and Frank Longstreth, eds. 1992. *Structuring Politics: Historical Institutionalism in Comparative Analysis.* Cambridge: Cambridge University Press.

Stiglitz, Joseph E. 2002. *Globalization and its Discontents.* London: Penguin.

Stiglitz, J., and Bruce Greenwald. 2003. *Towards New Paradigm in Monetary Economics.* Cambridge: Cambridge University Press.

Stolz, Stéphanie Marie, and Michael Wedow. 2010. "Extraordinary Measures in Extraordinary Times: Public Measures in Support of the Financial Sector in the EU and the United States." *Discussion Paper Series 1: Economic Studies.* Deutsche Bundesbank, Research Centre. Available at http://ideas.repec.org/p/zbw/bub dp1/201013.html.

Strange, Susan. 1986. *Casino Capitalism.* New York: St. Martin's.

Streeck, Wolfgang. 2011. "The Crisis of Democratic Capitalism." *New Left Review* 71 (September/October): 5–29.

Suehiro, Akira. 2005. "Who Manages and Who Damages the Thai Economy? The Technocracy, the Four Core Agencies System, and Dr. Puey's Networks." In *After the Crisis: Hegemony, Technocracy, and Governance in Southeast Asia,* eds. Takashi Shiraishi and Patricio N. Abinales, 15–68. Kyoto: Kyoto University Press.

——. 2008. *Catch-Up Industrialization: The Trajectory and Prospects of East Asian Economies.* Singapore: Kyoto University Press.

Suehiro, Akira, and Nateneapha Wailerdsak. 2004. "Family Business in Thailand." *ASEAN Economic Bulletin* 21: 81–93.

Sugita, Shigeyuki. 2005. "Baburu hokai kyokumen ni okeru seisakuragu to sono has-sei kouzou" [Policy Lag at the Early Phase of the Bubble Bursting]. In *Heisei baburu sakiokuri no kenkyu* [The Collapse of the 1990s Bubble: A Study of the Nonperform-ing Loan Problem], ed. M. Muramatsu, 45–91. Tokyo: Toyo Keizai Shinposha.

Sumarto, Sudarno, Asep Suryahadi, and Wenefrida Widyanti. 2002. "Designs and Implementation of Indonesian Social Safety Net Programs." *The Developing Econo-mies* 40 (1): 3–31.

Sumitomo Mitsui Banking Cooperation (SMBC), Seoul Branch. 2009. "Kankoku no gaikaryudosei oyobi kongo no keizai nitaisuru kenkai" [Outlook on Foreign Currency Liquidity and Future Economy of South Korea].

Takayasu, Yuichi. 2010. "Kankoku niokeru shihon ido to keizai kozo no henka: 1997 nen tsuuka kinnyu kiki wo chushin ni" [Change of Capital Flows and Economic Structure in Korea after the Asian Crisis]. In *Kokusai shikin ido to Higashi Ajia shinko koku no keizai-kozo-henka* [International Capital Flows and Changing Eco-nomic Structures in Emerging Asian Countries], ed. Kozo Kunimune, 177–215. Tokyo: IDE-JETRO.

Tanaka, Takayuki. 2005. "Nihon ni okeru furyo saiken mondai no sakiokuri" [Delay in the Treatment of the NPL Problem in Japan]. In *Heisei baburu sakiokuri no kenkyu* [The Collapse of the 1990s Bubble: A Study of the Nonperforming Loan Problem], ed. M. Muramatsu, 159–213. Tokyo: Toyo Keizai Shinposha.

Taniguchi, Masaki. 2012. *Seito shiji no riron* [Theories of Party Support]. Tokyo: Iwa-nami Shoten.

Taylor, John B. 2009. *Getting Off Track: How Government Actions and Interventions Caused, Prolonged, and Worsened the Financial Crisis.* Palo Alto: Hoover Institution Press.

Teorell, Jan, Marcus Samanni, Nicholas Charron, Sören Holmberg, and Bo Roth-stein. 2013. "The Quality of Government Dataset, version 15May13." University of Gothenburg: The Quality of Government Institute. Available at http://www.qog.pol.gu.se.

Thai Asset Management Corporation (TAMC). 2002. *Annul Report.* Bangkok: TAMC.

Tham, Siew-Yean, and Chei-Siang Liew. 2004. "Foreign Labour in Malaysian Manu-facturing: Enhancing Malaysian Competitiveness." In *Globalisation, Culture, and Inequalities: In Honour of the Late Ishak Shari*, ed. Abdul Rahman Embong, 253–74. Malaysia: Penerbit Universiti Kebangsaan Malaysia.

Thelen, Kathleen. 2004. *How Institutions Evolve: The Political Economy of Skills in Ger-many, Britain, the United States, and Japan.* Cambridge: Cambridge University Press.

Thitinan, Pongsudhirak. 2001. "Crisis from Within: The Politics of Macroeconomic Management in Thailand, 1947–1997." Ph.D. diss., London School of Economics.

Todoh, Yasuyuki. 2010. *Tojokokuka suru Nippon* [Japan Becoming a Developing Country]. Tokyo: Nihon Keizai Shimbunsha.

Tourres, Marie-Aimée. 2003. *The Tragedy that Didn't Happen: Malaysia's Crisis Manage-ment Strategy and Capital Controls.* Kuala Lumpur: ISIS Malaysia.

Tsunekawa, Keiichi. 2010. "Kiseikanwa no seijikatei: nani ga kawattaka" [Politi-cal Process of Deregulation: What Has Changed?]. In *Kozo mondai to kiseikanwa* [Structural Problems and Deregulations], ed. J. Teranishi, 77–147. Tokyo: Eco-nomic and Social Research Institute.

Turner, Donna. 2005. "Malaysia's Regime of Labour Control and the Attempted Transition to a Knowledge Based Economy: The Problematic Role of Migrant Labour." *Review of Indonesian and Malaysian Affairs* 39 (2): 45–68.

Uchiyama, Yu. 2007. *Koizumi seiken: patosu no shusho ha nani wo kaeta noka* [The Koizumi Administration: What Did the Prime Minister with Pathos Change?]. Tokyo: Chuo Koron Shinsha.

United Nations Conference on Trade and Development (UNCTAD). 1998. *World Investment Report 1998.* New York: United Nations.

United Nations Development Programme (UNDP). 2007. *Thailand Human Development Report 2007: Sufficiency Economy and Human Development.* Bangkok: UNDP.

United States Agency for International Development (USAID). 2004. "Impact of Transport and Logistics on Indonesia's Trade Competitiveness." Arlington, VA: Carana Corporation.

Van der Hoeven, Rolph, and Catherine Saget. 2004. "Labour Market Institutions and Income Inequality: What Are the New Insights After the Washington Consensus?" In *Inequality, Growth, and Poverty in an Era of Liberalization and Globalization,* ed. Giovannia Andrea Cornea, 196–220. New York: Oxford University Press.

Veerathai, Santiprabhob. 2003. *Lessons Learned from Thailand's Experience with Financial-Sector Restructuring.* Bangkok: Thai Development Research Institute (TDRI).

Vogel, Steven K. 1996. *Freer Markets, More Rules: Regulatory Reform in Advanced Countries.* Ithaca: Cornell University Press.

Wad, Peter. 2009. "Automotive Industry in Malaysia: Evolution and Impact of Global Crisis." Geneva: International Labour Office.

Waldner, David. 1999. *State Building and Late Development.* Ithaca: Cornell University Press.

Walter, Carl, and Fraser Howie. 2012. *Red Capitalism: The Fragile Financial Foundation of China's Extraordinary Rise.* New York: Wiley.

Wan, Ming. 2010. "The Great Recession and China's Policy toward Asian Regionalism." *Asian Survey* 50 (3): 520–38.

Wang, Changyong. 2013. "Closer Look: Rise in Total Government Debt—to 30.3 Trillion Yuan—Means Change Is Needed." *Caixin English,* December 12. Available at http://english.caixin.com/2013-12-31/100624015.html.

Warnock, Eleanor. 2013. "Japan's Aging Reflects Asia's Future." *Wall Street Journal,* January 6. Available at http://blogs.wsj.com/japanrealtime/2014/01/06/japans-aging-reflects-asias-future.

Watanabe, Yuichi. 2007. "Kankoku zaisei no saihen to kadai" [Restructuring and Issues in the Government Finance]. In *Keizai kikigo no kankoku* [Korea after the Economic Crisis], ed. S. Okuda, 193–228. Chiba: IDE-JETRO.

Weiss, Linda. 1999."State Power and the Asian Crisis." *New Political Economy* 4 (3): 317–42.

Wen, Jiabao. 2010. "Report on the Work of the Government." Third Session of the 11th National People's Congress, March 5. Available at http://www.npc.gov.cn/englishnpc/Speeches/2010-03/19/content_1564308.htm.

Whittaker, D. Hugh, Tianbiao Zhu, Timothy Sturgeon, Mon Han Tsai, and Toshie Okita. 2010. "Compressed Development in East Asia." *Studies in Comparative International Development* 45 (4): 439–67. Earlier version as MIT IPC Working Paper 08–005.

Wilensky, H. L. 2012. *American Political Economy in Global Perspective.* Cambridge: Cambridge University Press.

Winters, Jeffrey A. 1999. "The Determinants of Financial Crisis in Asia." In *The Politics of the Asian Economic Crisis,* ed. T. J. Pempel, 79–97. Ithaca: Cornell University Press.

Woo, W. T., and C. Hong. 2010. "Indonesia's Economic Performance in Comparative Perspective and a New Policy Framework 2049." *Bulletin of Indonesian Economic Studies* 46 (1): 33–64.

Woo, Jung-en, 1991. *Race to the Swift: State and Finance in Korean Industrialization.* New York: Columbia University Press.

Woo-Cumings, Meredith, ed. 1999. *The Developmental State.* Ithaca: Cornell University Press.

World Bank. 1993. *The East Asian Miracle: Economic Growth and Public Policy.* Oxford: Oxford University Press.

———. 2007a. *Regulation and Supervision Survey.* Washington, DC: World Bank.

———. 2007b. "Tracking Informal Sector Remittances in Malaysia-Indonesia Remittance Corridor." Washington, DC: World Bank.

———. 2008. *Thailand Economic Monitor.* Bangkok: World Bank, April.

———. 2010. *Thailand Economic Monitor.* Bangkok: World Bank, June.

———. 2011a. *Indonesian Economic Quarterly.* Jakarta: World Bank.

———. 2011b. "Thailand Now an Upper Middle Income Economy." August 2. Available at http://www.worldbank.org/en/news/press-release/2011/08/02/thailand-now-upper-middle-income-economy.

———. 2012. *World Development Report 2012.* Washington, DC: World Bank.

———. 2014. "Population Ages 65 and Above." Available at http://data.worldbank.org/indicator/SP.POP.65UP.TO.ZS.

———. Various years. "World Development Indicators." Available at http://www.worldbank.org/data.

Wu, Yu-Shan. 2007. "Taiwan's Developmental State: After the Economic and Political Turmoil." *Asian Survey* 47 (6): 977–1001.

Wyss, D. 2007. "The Subprime Market: Housing and Debt." *Standard and Poors Research*, March 15.

Xiao, Liang. 2009. "The 130 Billion Central Investment Plan Has Begun to Be Allocated; 95 Billion Will Be Allocated to Localities." *21 Shiji Jingi Baodao* [21st Century Economic Herald], February 3. Available at http://finance.sina.com.cn/roll/20090203/01305807294.shtml.

Yamamura, Kozo. 2003. "Germany and Japan in a New Phase of Capitalism: Confronting the Past and the Future." In *The End of Diversity? Prospects for German and Japanese Capitalism*, ed. K. Yamamura and W. Streeck, 115–46. Ithaca: Cornell University Press.

Yamamura, Kozo, and Wolfgang Streeck, eds. 2002. *Embedded Capitalism: Japan and Germany in the Postwar Period.* Ithaca: Cornell University Press.

Yano, Tsuneta Kinenkai. 2006. *Suji de miru Nippon no hyakunen* [Hundred Years of Japan in Figures]. Tokyo: Yano Tsuneta Kinenkai.

Yen, Ching-chang. 1998. *Taiwan's Fiscal Policy: Its Role in the Asian Financial Turmoil.* Ministry of Finance, 1998.

Yomiuri Shimbunsha. 2002. *Nippon no Yoron* [Public Opinion in Japan]. Tokyo: Yomiuri Shimbunsha.

Yoshitomi, Masaru, and Kenichi Ohno. 1999. "Capital-Account Crisis and Credit Contraction: The New Nature of Crisis Requires New Policy Responses." ADB Institute Working Paper Series 2. Tokyo: Asian Development Bank Institute.

Youngyuth, Chalmwong, and Raphaella Prugsamatz. 2009. "The Economic Role of Migration: Recent Trends and Implications for Development." *TDRI Quarterly Review* 24 (3): 3–9.

Yu, Yongding. 2007. "Global Imbalances and China." *Australian Economic Review* 40 (1): 3–23.

Yuen, Chi Ching, and Lim Ghee Soon. 2000. "Globalization, Labour Market Deregulation, and Trade Unions in Singapore." In *Globalization and Labour in the Asia Pacific Region*, ed. Chris Rowley and John Benson, 154–83. London: Frank Cass.

Yusuf, Shahid, and Kaoru Nabeshima. 2009. *Tiger Economies under Threat: A Comparative Analysis of Malaysia's Industrial Prospects and Policy Options*. New York: Cambridge University Press.

Zhang, Xiaoke. 2003. *The Changing Politics of Finance in Korea and Thailand: From Deregulation to Debacle*. London: Routledge.

Zolli, Andrew, and Ann Marie Healy. 2012. *Resilience: Why Things Bounce Back?* New York: Free Press.

Index

9 780801 453403